The Promise of
India's Secular
Democracy

The Promise of India's Secular Democracy

Rajeev Bhargava

OXFORD
UNIVERSITY PRESS

OXFORD
UNIVERSITY PRESS

YMCA Library Building, Jai Singh Road, New Delhi 110 001

Oxford University Press is a department of the University of Oxford. It furthers the
University's objective of excellence in research, scholarship, and education
by publishing worldwide in

Oxford New York
Auckland Cape Town Dar es Salaam Hong Kong Karachi Kuala Lumpur
Madrid Melbourne Mexico City Nairobi New Delhi Shanghai Taipei Toronto

With offices in
Argentina Austria Brazil Chile Czech Republic France Greece Guatemala
Hungary Italy Japan Poland Portugal Singapore South Korea Switzerland
Thailand Turkey Ukraine Vietnam

Oxford is a registered trademark of Oxford University Press
in the UK and in certain other countries

Published in India
by Oxford University Press, New Delhi

ISBN-13: 978-019-806044-4
ISBN-10: 019-806044-0

Typeset in 10.5/12.4 Dante MT Std
by Excellent Laser Typesetters, Pitampura, Delhi 110 034
Published by Oxford University Press
YMCA Library Building, Jai Singh Road, New Delhi 110 001

For Tani

Contents

List of Tables and Figure   ix
Preface   xi
Publisher's Acknowledgements   xv
Introduction   xvii

I ENVISIONING INDIA

1. Democratic Vision of a New Republic: India, 1950   3
2. The Evolution and Distinctiveness of India's
   Linguistic Federalism   34
3. Indian Secularism: An Alternative, Trans-cultural Ideal   63

II A FAILING VISION

4. History, Nation, and Community: Reflections on
   Nationalist Historiography of India and Pakistan   109
5. Between Revenge and Reconciliation: Gandhi and
   Truth Commissions   131
6. Muslim Personal Law in India and the
   Majority–Minority Syndrome   152
7. On the Persistent Political Under-representation of
   Muslims in India   182
8. Inclusion and Exclusion in India, Pakistan, and
   Bangladesh: The Role of Religion   217

III SPECULATIVE AND CONCEPTUAL EXPLANATIONS

9. Liberal, Secular Democracy, and Explanations of
   Hindu Nationalism   251

viii   Contents

10. The Ethical Insufficiency of Egoism and Altruism:
    India in Transition   272

IV FEAR AND HOPE

11. The Right to Culture   291
12. Secular States and Religious Education:
    The Indian Debate   301
13. Indian Democracy and Well-being:
    Employment as a Right   315
14. Academic Freedom in India   322

Appendix: Multiple Incarnations of Secularism   327
Index   333

Tables and Figure

TABLES

2.1	Population by Religion	40
2.2	Population by Major Language Groups	40
2.3	States and Union Territories by Population Size	41
3.1	Comparative Moral Evaluation of Secular and Religion-centred States	82
7.1	Lok Sabha, 1952	190
7.2	Lok Sabha, 1957	190
7.3	Lok Sabha, 1962	190
7.4	Lok Sabha, 1967	190
7.5	Lok Sabha, 1971	191
7.6	Lok Sabha, 1977	191
7.7	Lok Sabha, 1980	191
7.8	Lok Sabha, 1984	191
7.9	Lok Sabha, 1989	192
7.10	Lok Sabha, 1991	192
7.11	Lok Sabha, 1996	192
9.1	Main Features of Indian Secularism	268

FIGURE

8.1	Religion-related Exclusion	222

Preface

These essays, written over the last two decades, would probably never have seen the light of day had it not been for my—sometimes close, at other times distant—involvement in the tumultuous events of the period. Between 1989 and 2002, marches, demonstrations, and meetings were part of daily routine. People with different political ideologies came together and then fell apart. Novel, unexpected solidarities were forged and new friendships or enmities were born. For much of the time, many of us were in fire-fighting, activist mode. Intensive research and extensive reading on an issue or a privileged view from afar was simply not available, particularly to some of us who seemed to carry more weight on their shoulders than their frail bodies could manage. These academic essays bear an imprint of that period and exude an activist flavour. In some, the academic overwhelms the activist; in others, the activist gets the better of the scholar. But both coexist in virtually every piece.

This nearly real politics was quite a new experience for a decidedly old-fashioned teacher who thrived in only one habitat, that of the classroom, and who, therein and daily, found an entire public in a small group of students. I have not been a political being by habit, temperament, or training. I was born in a typical middle-class, Hindu home that kept aloof from active politics. Gandhi was revered and Nehru adored by my family, but probably not for their political vision. My grandfather identified with Gandhi's moral values, my father with Nehru's modern outlook. But above all, Gandhi and Nehru were loved as personalized, familial, semi-religious icons in line with Rama, Krishna, and Ramakrishna. An intensely private, sombre, and religious person, my grandfather was easily disturbed by anything mildly devious or manipulative. The outside world was a source of continuing perturbation. But politics rarely angered him. I saw him really incensed just once—when he lashed out at a maternal grand uncle, a genial and loving enough man in private, with strong affiliations to the Hindu right wing. For my grandfather, politics was what the Rashtriya Swayamsevak Sangh (RSS) did.

I cannot remember when the term 'left' appeared in my apolitical life. Probably not until I met Tani and came into contact with her parents, Hardev and Sheila. Together, in our first year of college, Tani and I read Ernst Fischer's *Marx in His Own Words* and attended the Party school where I discovered the stolid, Moscow editions of Marx's *Selected Works*, larger and more crimson than the *Little Red Book*. So, politics was not as slimy and sneaky as my grandfather believed. It was exhilarating, resplendent with poetry and lofty political ideas. But it all happened only in books, not in the real world.

Forty years on, I doubt if I have really learnt to think politically. A series of fortuitous events flung me into the discipline of political science and then at the Centre for Political Studies, Jawaharlal Nehru University (JNU), where I began teaching in 1980. Slowly, I learnt to think about politics and, in 1990, to write about it. I have hundreds of people to thank for my political education. In the early 1990s, my association with Sahmat and the People's Movement for Secularism was an invaluable resource. More influential have been my friends. All these years, I have sat with and silently learnt about day-to-day politics and long-term political trends from Anu and Kamal Chenoy, Achin Vanaik, Pamela Phillipose, Praful Bidwai, Tanika and Sumit Sarkar, the late S.P. Singh, Ritu and Pogey Menon, Rohini and Deepak Nayyar, and Romila Thapar. We were joined frequently by Zoya and Mushirul Hasan, and occasionally by Shabana Azmi, Javed Akhtar, Prabhat Patnaik, and P.K. Datta. Aarti Jairath, Andrew Graham, Peggotty Graham, Ajoy Bose, Shalini Advani, Neeladri Bhattacharya, Alok Rai, Chitra Joshi, Pankaj Butalia, and Nilufer Kaul have been warm interlocutors on political and not-so-political matters.

With Valerian Rodrigues, Christophe Jaffrelot, Peter deSouza, Gopal Guru, Shalini Randeria, and V.B. Singh, conversations have always been rewarding. I have consistently benefited from the learning and insights of Dhirubhai Sheth, T.N. Madan, Ashis Nandy, Javeed Alam, Partha Chatterjee, Akeel Bilgrami, Shahid Amin, Alfred Stepan, Jose Casanova, Tariq Modood, Gerald Cohen, Sudipta Kaviraj, and Charles Taylor. The intellectual warmth of Dhirubhai, Loki, Bhikhubhai, and Jose is always comforting. Jerry Cohen's analytical mind has been inspirational. He was infatuated by India and tickled by Indian politicians whose names he repeatedly intoned with characteristic gusto. His sudden absence is sad and numbing. My longest, continuing conversation is with Sudipta Kaviraj. We have struck a rare intellectual friendship that shows no signs of aging. Chuck Taylor's catholicity melded effortlessly with my own coalitional temperament. His profound influence on my work was destined. His generosity and affection are deeply treasured.

My daughters, Aranyani and Vanya, continue to offer the same enchantment as they did when they were born; my brothers, Sanjeev and Tarun, have stood by me through hell and high water; my mother binds us all together to just the right extent and degree. In her own inimitable, mysteriously intuitive ways, Tani has done all this and much more. Her munificence is matched only by the big-heartedness of Tata, Sunita, Mohan, Kesar, Ajaib, and Stephen. With all my gratitude, this book is dedicated to them.

Publisher's Acknowledgements

The publisher acknowledges the following for permission to include articles/extracts in this volume.

James Curry for 'The Evolution and Distinctiveness of India's Linguistic Federalism', in David Turton (ed.), *Ethnic Federalism*, Oxford, 2006, pp. 93–118.

Economic and Political Weekly for 'History, Nation, and Community: Reflections on Nationalist Historiography of India and Pakistan', vol. XXXV, no. 4, 22–8 January 2000, pp. 2161–9.

Sage Publications for 'Between Revenge and Reconciliation: Gandhi and Truth Commissions', in Ranabir Samaddar (ed.), *Peace: A Reader*, New Delhi, 2005, pp. 390–412.

McGill-Queen's University Press for 'Muslim Personal Law in India and the Majority–Minority Syndrome', in Michel Seymour (ed.), *The Fate of the Nation-State*, Montreal, 2004, pp. 327–56.

Journal of Law and Ethics of Human Rights for 'On the Persistent Political Under-representation of Muslims in India', vol. 1, Ramat Gan Law School, Tel Aviv, 2007, pp. 77–133.

Indian Journal of Human Development for 'Inclusion and Exclusion in India, Pakistan, and Bangladesh: The Role of Religion', Inaugural issue, vol. I, no. 1, January 2007, pp. 67–98.

Taylor and Francis for 'Liberal, Secular Democracy and Explanations of Hindu Nationalism', *Commonwealth and Comparative Politics*, vol. 40, no. 3, November 2002, pp. 72–96.

Sage Publications for 'The Ethical Insufficiency of Egoism and Altruism: India in Transition', in R. Vora and S. Palshikar (eds), *Indian Democracy: Meanings and Practices*, New Delhi, 2003, pp. 215–31.

Manohar Publishers for 'The Right to Culture', in K.N. Panikkar (ed.), *Communalism in India*, Delhi, 1989.

Duke University Press for 'Indian Democracy and Well-being: Employment as a Right', *Public Culture*, vol. 18, no. 3, 2006, pp. 445–51.

Academe for 'Academic Freedom in India', July–August 1999.

Frontline for 'Strands of Secularism', 27 April–10 May 1991, pp. 49–51.

Introduction

Even small men can have big tales to tell about themselves, so I hope the reader will forgive me for beginning the book on an autobiographical note. As a young teacher in the late 1970s, I did not distinguish between social and political theory. For me social or political theory meant a general, comprehensive understanding of anything large—structures, processes, events—that occurred in society. Machiavelli, Hobbes, Locke, Rousseau, Montesquieu, and, more importantly, Hegel were key figures in my intellectual life. But the tradition of Western Marxism kept me more occupied. I was consumed by an obsessive need to possess everything written by Gramsci, Lukacs, Adorno, Korsch, Althusser, Colletti, Timpanaro, Della Volpe, to name a few Marxists. I not only read all these thinkers but also taught them to my students. It was an exhilarating world of stimulating thoughts, dreams, passions, and startling discoveries.

But, it was also a world far removed from the dominant ethos of the university where I completed my postgraduate studies. Oxford was dominated by liberalism and analytical philosophy. I unabashedly shunned both. At that time I found, and pronounced, analytical philosophy hopelessly dull, excruciatingly microscopic in content, and self-consciously dry and anti-literary in form. It seemed the kind of writing from which every drop of emotion had been squeezed out. Liberalism, my intellectual comrades had told me, was a political theory of the status quo, a somewhat devious, shameless justification of the capitalist order. Sociologically naïve, it failed to provide any insight into how and why any social and political universe holds or changes. I tried my best to evade liberal political philosophy. Rawls's *A Theory of Justice*, published in 1971—though it had not yet become a classic—was part of every discussion among political theorists. Dworkin's essays on rights had appeared in *The New York Review of Books* and were taken very seriously indeed by teachers and co-students. Nozick's *Anarchy, State, and Utopia* was already considered a masterpiece by his friends and foes alike. I tried my best not to read any of these. Sheer waste of time, I thought.

I continued in the same vein when I returned to Oxford to do my doctoral thesis several years later. My concerns were still dominated by social theory which, by now, had become even more abstract. Meanwhile, I realized that despite all its limitations, analytical philosophy had its virtues: clarity of thought, analytical precision, conceptual sensitivity, a flair for consistency, and an abiding passion too—for arguments. The objective of my thesis was to defend, and argue for, a Hegelian–Marxist conception of the social reality and to challenge methodological individualism, a perspective in the social sciences that was gaining currency, thanks to analytical Marxists such as Jon Elster.

I have described this intellectual phase in my life only to emphasize how far removed it was from normative ideals, from liberalism, and from the real world of Indian society and politics. I inhabited the loftiest ever ivory tower—a world aloof, insulated, and totally abstracted from India and its abiding problems. It was an imaginary homeland of a miniscule subculture, but one shaped entirely by western academia. This is amply evident in the book that followed the thesis in which no reference is to be found either of India or of an Indian author, not even Amartya Sen!

On my return to India, predictably the first crack in the walls of this unassailable tower appeared. Safdar Hashmi, a theatre person and a political activist of the Communist Party of India (Marxist) [CPI (M)], was killed brutally, in broad daylight, by a goon of the Congress party. It was a murderous assault not only on the workers' movement but also on middle-class sensibility and the most basic rights of the liberal democratic order: the right to freedom of expression and the right to dissent. Two other interrelated processes, in motion for some time, had also accelerated during this period. First, with the emergence of a number of anti-upper caste movements, the north was fast catching up with the south. Demands for a more effective equality had become increasingly strident. But, the equality at issue was strikingly at variance with the more familiar clarion calls of the past. This assertion for equality in its initial stage was grounded in an identity-based social and political recognition of the not-so-upper and 'lower' castes. The door for such politics had creaked open in the late 1960s and, more particularly, after the Emergency with the electoral defeat of the Congress party. This period saw an assertion not only of caste but of Muslims qua Muslims. I believe this gave fresh impetus to political Hinduism, with which Congress flirted slyly, and the newly formed Bharatiya Janata Party (BJP) militantly and with open arms by the late 1980s. Assertive political Hinduism with its new name Hindutva had emerged from the shadows. Varied members of the Hindutva family agreed on two related issues: one that any right to the minorities is automatically a privilege denied to the majority and an unbearable burden; two, falsely, that secularism in India is deeply flawed because it permits the state to intervene in the affairs of the majority and abstain from every issue related to the minorities, particularly Muslims. In unison, they clamoured to banish from Indian politics, indeed from the Indian constitution itself, this allegedly biased, minority-appeasing secularism perpetuated by the Congress and the Left. The less concessive among Hindutva forces asserted that virtually everything since Independence, in Indian constitutional and legislative practices, was a disaster. They exhorted Indians to abandon their constitution and return to India's primarily Hindu, civilizational roots.

Clearly, Indian social and political atmosphere in the 1980s was suffused with a robust discourse on values. Freedom, rights (both individual and collective), secularism, rule of law, democracy, and social justice—these values and principles were upheld by many who defended them and plenty who opposed them. Worse, the frequency of the use of these terms was inversely related to clarity and precision. To me, none appeared to know what the other was really talking about. This confusion left me itching to use analytical skills that I had picked up at Oxford. Besides, were not terms such as liberty, rights, equality, and justice anchored firmly in the liberal tradition, one that I had failed to warm up to as a postgraduate student?

Gradually, much to the bewilderment of students and all but a couple of teachers, in an optional course at Jawaharlal Nehru University (JNU) on Texts in Political Philosophy, I included John Rawls's *A Theory of Justice*. (I had introduced this course in 1983 and at that time, it was launched by a collective, detailed reading of Marx's *Economic and Philosophical Manuscripts* over an entire semester.) It was not long before some of us felt a pressing need to defend political freedoms and minority rights, equality, justice, and secularism. Within a year or so, I wrote three short pieces. The first piece, 'The Many Incarnations of Secularism', was written when N. Ram, the editor of *Frontline*, phoned to ask if I would write a regular column for the newly launched fortnightly magazine. Neither prolific nor a quick writer, I hesitated initially. But Ram did not budge, so it was published in April 1991 as 'The Strands of Secularism', in which I examined the multiple uses of the term secularism in everyday Indian politics. I claimed that secularism as a doctrine about the relation between the state and religion is used in at least five different senses in India: anti-religious, non-religious, multi-religious, multi-communal, and uni-communal, as benefiting the communal agenda of just one religious group.

A piece called 'The Right to Culture' followed, entirely based on a presentation at Nehru Memorial Library Seminar, organized sometime in 1989 by the historian, K.N. Panniker. In this paper, I claimed that a demand for a right to anything presupposes a shared culture without which rights can neither be exercised nor indeed be properly articulated in the public domain. Per force I had to return to Ronald Dworkin's article on rights that, unfortunately, I had so neglected in the past.

In January 1991, *Seminar* carried my paper called 'What is Democracy?'. Here, I drew a distinction between a political and an ethnic majority. I argued that while a political majority in a democracy is temporary, ethnic majorities are relatively permanent and the rule of a permanent majority is antithetical to the basic values of democracy. In a proper democracy, no place exists for a permanent majority.

In a matter of a year, I had unwittingly returned to a tradition and its texts that I had treated with some disdain and much carelessness. All around me, my intellectual companions were amused and puzzled by this move. No one appeared to accompany me on this journey, but there was something in the context that bred such deep anxiety that no one objected to what I had begun to slowly embrace. Over a period of time, some began to feel that though the normative world view implicit in liberal democratic practices was not ideal, it filled the vacuum created by the collapse of socialism and was a much needed bulwark against communalism, ultra-nationalism, and fascism. Others were willing to partake in this language but for purely instrumental reasons. The discourse that underpinned our common political practices was not one they wanted to own but certainly what they desperately needed in order to survive, to live to fight the battle for another day.

I have never been fond of labels, neat and compact pigeon holes into which the entire thoughts of a person are stacked away. I hesitate to call myself a Marxist, a liberal, or, for that matter, a secularist. This is particularly true if the label is directly linked to a set of ideas that have been turned into an 'ism'. It is one thing to be called a liberal because of your commitment to certain values and quite another to be called so as a representative of a bounded, well-demarcated tradition which has some strengths but also severe limitations. So, being a liberal is just about *okay* as long as the entire baggage of liberalism does not come with it. I guess the same is true of the label 'Marxist'. Our world has so many different and valuable intellectual traditions that it is extremely impoverishing to belong wholly to any one. Why would anyone want to do that? Yet there are certain contexts, crucial historical junctures when the need is felt to temporarily claim a label for oneself. In the late 1980s and 1990s, in the face of all kinds of threats to the normative, partly liberal–democratic vocabulary of the Indian constitution, and because the intellectual circles in which I moved were reluctant, or at least hesitant, to openly defend this normative vocabulary, I felt compelled to say that I was a liberal. (No such compulsion existed to explicitly say that one was a democrat because everybody around me had no qualms about using that label for self-description.) I felt called upon to defend liberal values in a more explicit, systematic, and coherent manner. And, in addition, to bring some conceptual clarity in an increasingly cacophonous world. Three short articles would not suffice, I told myself. There had to be more depth and complexity in the defence of many values. Hence, the move from social to political theory, from understanding and explanation to normative arguments, and from Marxism to liberalism. It also helped me to turn away from at least a partially disengaged, partly self-invented western intellectual world towards a little more engaged, ethico-political world inhabited by the people of India.

I believe this movement away from a Marx-inspired socio-historical explanation of structures and processes to a normative political theory of collective practices, institutions, and policies, liberal and democratic in content, possessing a formal imprint of Anglo-Saxon philosophy and focused on India is both the strength and self-imposed limitation of this book. A reader who expects large historical–sociological explanations, detailed ethnographic accounts, thick descriptions of cultural background, or social imaginary is bound to be disappointed. On the other hand, someone looking for conceptual clarification and political argument for different positions in contemporary Indian politics will, I hope, find something useful here, if only to contend with it, to challenge and argue against it.

Before I end this introduction, I would like to make a few remarks on the meaning of normative theory and on the role of argument in political discourse. I also respond in anticipation to the possible charge that many essays are excessively focused on the state. I suppose one way to set up a contrast between an explanatory/interpretative and a normative perspective is that the former deals with actions already accomplished. The latter, however, is about actions to be performed in the future. Understanding or explanation is always post-facto. In contrast, the structure of a normative question is: given a set of constraints and opportunities, what *should* I/we do? Answers to this question vary. Some claim that they should do what is in their best or, more specifically, whatever maximizes their interest. Others may say that they should do what their heart tells them to. Still others that one ought to do what is morally right or is in the common good. Finally, there exists the view that none of these must be discounted and all factored into a deliberative process before an answer is reached. Normative theories offer a detailed justification for any or all of these proposed answers.

In this book, however, I use the term 'normative theory' in a restricted sense to mean a theory that justifies why a certain action should be undertaken in terms of a range of factors that *must* include values related to the good, the right, or both. Most essays in this book possess a normative content in this more restricted sense, in that they refer to moral and ethical values such as freedom, equality, justice, sanctity of life, solidarity, and so on. In virtually every class where I taught normative social and political theory, my students repeatedly asked me: But aren't values subjective? Isn't it the case that what is good for one is bad for another, what is right for one is wrong for another? Aren't values merely opinions espoused by a person? A slightly more sophisticated version dismisses value-talk by saying that the very distinction between value and interest or value and the will to power, is incoherent. Such views, we might note, do not dismiss the idea of normative theory. After all, which human agent does not wrestle with how to act in the future? However, it is strongly implied by these views that the term 'normative' in all normative theories is exhausted by reference to interests, feelings, instincts, drives, and so on, and that values are nothing but one or all of these.

I do not have the space in this introduction to argue against such views. I merely wish to emphasize my opposition to them. I do not hold that our ethical and moral values are reducible to preferences, feelings, and instincts. Moreover, I strongly believe that reason plays an important contributory role in helping us arrive at inter-subjective value judgements about good and bad or right and wrong. To give a very simple example: consider a situation where three friends, X, Y, and Z, of roughly the same appetite and who have not eaten for a whole day find a clump of six bananas. X is quick but Y is quicker and grabs three. X is able to get two, leaving just one for the less enterprising Z. Given the general though rough equality of condition (being hungry, all three friends have identical needs), no one would challenge the claim that justice requires that Y give one banana away to Z. Nor would one object if Y was told by Z that he was greedy. A fairly clear distinction, as reasonably objective as can be in a given human context, between what is just and unjust (in this case, greedy) can be drawn. I doubt if it will wash if Y were to tell Z that Z's judgement about his character is just his opinion and that he himself did not think he was being greedy. Inescapably and rightly, we make such normative value judgements all the time. We do not all live by the same values and often act against them, but it is difficult to find people who do not have or have never had a sense of some values before acting.

Allow me to move to the next issue. It would not be a wrong judgement on the book if someone, halfway through it, mutters to himself: this is all too reason-centred and exaggerates the role of argument in politics. Politics is not about arguments and deliberation alone. The stuff of politics consists of rhetoric, passion, the play on prejudice, marketing of ideas, and, therefore, the power of advertising. It is about strategic thinking, negotiation, bargaining, and the ability to outwit rivals. It is about patience, a waiting game, the sense of timing, a knack of knowing when to attack opponents, of selecting which interests to pursue and when. Above all, it is about the power of numbers: mustering enough people on your side. It is foolish to deny the role of these in politics. But the acceptance of such a claim need not lead to the conclusion that arguments are irrelevant to politics. There are always people in a polity who can only be won over by argument. For such people, everything else matters far less. Notice that I said that such people can *only* be won over by argument, not that *they can be won over* only by argument. So, my claim is that arguments are necessary though not sufficient in politics for some. Only a fool believes that arguments are necessary *and* sufficient in politics. Nothing is won by arguments alone, but arguments do matter. Indeed, those who know how to argue must be ready with arguments so that precisely when needed most, these can be supplied immediately and with ease. Bad arguments do not work for those persuaded by good ones, and good arguments take time to make and cannot be offered in a sound byte. It is better to begin constructing them even when there is no apparent or immediate need for them, to iron out their deficiencies, and to keep them ready.

Finally, why this focus on the state? My first defence is that this is a self-imposed limitation. My normative work relating to the state is meant not to substitute but to complement work on other institutions and practices. Second, I have nowhere made the claim that only states can perform the role that they sometimes do perform. I concede that institutions outside the state can better achieve several results that are also secured by it. Third, whatever the judgement on the institutions and practices of the state, the fact remains that the state cannot be wished away. Once states exist, we can either make them comply with what is good, that is, of value, or allow them to generate undesirable, even morally reprehensible, outcomes. This is particularly true of democratic states where public pressure makes a difference. Finally, democratic institutions and practices are not automatically reproduced but require multiple collective agents. In order to reproduce conditions of democracy, states are vital. Under conditions of modernity, it is hard not to conclude that a society with even an authoritarian state is better than a stateless society. As a rule, arbitrary violence is worse than institutionalized violence, if only because there is a much better chance to collectively fight and defeat it. The arbitrary violence of multiple political agents is difficult to counter. So, we have and need states, and should muster enough strength, including moral strength required to ensure that state power is put to good rather than bad ends. It is an important task of political theory to contribute towards ensuring that states behave!

Most of these essays were written between 1990 and 2003 and reflect the dominant flavour of this period. In no way do they cover the entire ground of secular democracy. Although some of them were published a little later, many of them appear in this volume in the form they appear elsewhere, while others have been modified. Much of the change has been done to avoid repetition and overlap. Some of them were written in specific political contexts in response to a request from a journal or for an academic conference. As already stated, most papers share a common philosophical, political, and normative orientation, though not to the same degree or in the same manner. I am neither a political scientist nor a sociologist. I have no training as a historian. When I read the work of historians and social scientists, I do so with the angular vision of a political theorist who absorbed analytical philosophy simply by being in a university where it was pervasive. If I were to write the same papers today, I would bring into them much more Indian history and sociology.

In the same vein, there are some views, arguments, and positions in these papers with which I no longer identify, at least I did not formulate them in the manner I would do now. For example, although I generally continue to accept the thesis that the discourse of rights presupposes a culture that makes that discourse possible and that those who use the language of rights must partake of it, I do not think I would now put my argument in the excessively rationalist tone so blatantly manifest in the article. Yet, I have not made any changes in the article and have kept it as it was written twenty years ago. Likewise, the essay on Indian federalism was written for a volume largely for an Ethiopian readership and has detailed footnotes containing information that would be widely known to the Indian audience. I have left these footnotes unchanged. Similarly, the essay on the political under-representation of Muslims was written before the publication of the Sachar Committee Report. Its tone and substance might have been different if written after the publication of this report.

This book is about our collective ideals. I know that they are not shared by all Indians. But I hope that some of them might be persuaded that they are not all that hollow. It is in the nature of regulative ideals that they are never fully realized. Indeed, one of their constitutive features is that they seem most attractive and needed when least present. We realize the value of liberty when we are imprisoned. We understand the importance of the freedom of expression when we are gagged. We fight for peace in times of war. It gives me a quaint satisfaction to see how dependent on liberal, secular, and democratic values those who most furiously denounce them really are. This is as true of some people on the left as it is for most people on the right, as true of those who denounce it in bad faith as it is of those who really wish to dismantle them.

Secular democracy is not perfect. It will never be perfectly realized in India or elsewhere. I hope that in future other better ideals will replace secular democratic values. But for now, especially when they seem most fragile, it is better to believe in the promise of secular democracy than to prematurely abandon it.

I
Envisioning India

1

Democratic Vision of a New Republic

India, 1950★

We live in a world of radical plurality: differences abound, contestation is rampant, every perspective appears to have a unique taker, and a deep-rooted scepticism exists about unified narratives. In this context, it is almost blasphemous to speak of *the* democratic vision of a new republic, but I venture to speak of a single vision on the assumption that despite the absence of a unified collective subject, a loose, disjointed, even partly incoherent vision of India, potentially the object of an overlapping consensus among its most active members, did emerge briefly in 1950.

Here, I try to rearticulate that vision. I argue that:

1. Democracy came to India *as* nationalism and therefore, arguments for nationalism were coterminous with arguments for democracy.
2. The character of this democracy, in one significant sense, just *had* to be liberal not only because of its commitment to civil liberties but also because of its vision of equality and social justice.
3. The predominantly cultural character of nationalism in India and its traditional proclivity for recognizing the importance of collectivities forced the makers of the constitution to move beyond individualist

★ This paper was presented at a conference on 'Democracy and Transformation: India Fifty Years after Independence', held in Delhi in November 1997. It was subsequently published as 'Democratic Vision of a New Republic: India, 1950', in Francine R. Frankel, Zoya Hasan, Rajeev Bhargava, and Balveer Arora (eds), *Transforming India: Social and Political Dynamics of Democracy*, New Delhi: Oxford University Press, 2000, pp. 26–59.

liberalism, in order to wrestle with the tension between constitutive attachments and personal liberty, between group disadvantage and personal merits, and all these factors shaped the character of the emergent secular–democratic state of India.

In presenting this view, I believe I challenge the accepted wisdom of much current history and social science.[1] In particular, I question the view that has considerable currency in intellectual circles today, that is, that the crisis of liberal institutions stems directly from the opposition it faced at its birth.[2] This view claims that liberalism came to India alongwith the British ruling elite, rubbed off on to the skin of Indian imitators who came into contact with it, but was shed soon after because it remained only skin deep. This version of the story of liberalism in India is stunningly simplistic. The constitution did not emerge miraculously out of calm deliberations around a table but from the political struggles of an elite eager to give India a new social order. My rather simple objection then is that this view fails to see the link between the constitution and the continuous intellectual and political labour for over a century. I begin the essay by providing an argument sustaining this objection. After that, I more fully delineate the vision of a democratic India that animated the framers of the constitution. This was a vision marked by a commitment to universal franchise, to rights of linguistic and religious minorities, and to a variant of secularism shaped by sensitivity to such group-specific rights.

WAS THE VISION LIBERAL–DEMOCRATIC?
There is an undeniable crisis of liberal democracy in India today. It appears that the institutions associated with liberal democracy are worn out and frayed at the edges. Given the western origins of liberal democracy and its unmistakable distance from traditional Indian culture, and because liberal–democratic institutions appear so totally to lack legitimacy in contemporary India, it is tempting to believe that whatever else it might be, Indian democracy never was and never can be liberal. However, this view is not convincing. On the contrary, the current crisis of liberal democracy is due in large part to its own success. The introduction of civil liberties gave voice to the mute, and the stage

[1] By not taking into account or drawing upon the world of subalterns, I plead guilty, of course, to the charge of elitism.

[2] Though I explicitly have in mind Sunil Khilnani's *The Idea of India*, London: Hamish Hamilton, 1997, this is also the predominant impression I have gained from several scholars, most notably from Sudipta Kaviraj.

for action was set by the democratic process for those hitherto debarred from the public domain. They entered it with new modes of speech and action to which the initiators of liberal democracy were unaccustomed, and in numbers that greatly exceeded the tiny upper crust that led the national movement. It is no doubt true that those empowered by institutions of liberal democracy do not come from a cultural background with an obviously liberal or democratic character. However, it would be a mistake to conclude from this that this newly empowered class is wholly maladjusted to these institutions. Considerable evidence exists of its successful adaptation to these western institutions (and of these institutions to these groups!). More importantly, tempting as it is, one should not succumb to the implausible idea that liberal democracy was forced out very quickly from the minds of the major political actors of the movement for Indian independence.

Yet, something approaching this view has been elegantly advocated by Sunil Khilnani in his book, *The Idea of India*. For him, Indian liberalism was crippled from its beginning: stamped by utilitarianism, and squeezed into a culture that had little room for the individual.[3] Khilnani claims that 'The idea of natural right, essential to modern liberalisms, was only faintly articulated and failed to find a niche in nationalist thought.'[4] In India, 'Liberty was understood not as an individual right but as a nation's collective right to self-determination.'[5] The discourse of rights was disengaged from its individual moorings and attached quite naturally to groups, particularly to religious communities in a society fashioned for centuries by a collectivist mentality. With its emphasis on separate individuals moved by internal requirements of personal autonomy and tied to others by choice rather than circumstance, liberalism was bound to fail in this culture. And it did. The final nail in the coffin was hammered in by the very political agent that liberalism had nurtured in its initial encounter with India, the Indian National Congress (INC). Gandhi's strategy of turning the Congress into a mass movement made a commitment to liberal and democratic institutions look shallow and irrelevant. 'By the 1930s and 40s, Congress nationalism was divided between opinions that had little interest in liberal democracy.'[6] Not surprisingly, political representation was granted only to ascriptively defined groups, that is, those with immutable interests.

[3] Khilnani, *The Idea of India*, p. 26.
[4] Ibid., p. 24.
[5] Ibid., p. 26.
[6] Ibid., p. 27.

Khilnani's is an attractive portrayal of the intellectual and political history of modern India, not least because it brings order to a criss-crossing, mind-boggling, often mutually incompatible ideas of diverse origin and value. It does this by an explanation of charming simplicity and economy, by nicely reinforcing the view that the current crisis of liberal institutions can be traced all the way back to their origins. But is this not the cultural inadaptability thesis all over again? Does it not bolster the view that western ideas cannot really take root in a cultural environment seemingly hostile to them? Khilnani reconfirms the idea of India as a country whose individuality was throttled at the top by a small group of upwardly mobile men, lacking in self-confidence from years of powerlessness, and swept off their feet by the first great tide of modernity and who, without the effort required to change the course of history but with a great deal of good fortune, used the power which they found in their hands to impose on an unwilling populace a set of ideas from which the souls of the poor people naturally turned away.

This argument appeases our hunger for coherent narratives and fulfils the need for collective individuality instilled in us by romanticism. It also falls in line with a cultivated sympathy for the marginalized. Yet, it presents a very skewed picture. It is nourished by a lopsided view of liberalism, a biased view of the history of liberal democracy in India. Above all, it is guilty of reverse anachronism. It extrapolates features of contemporary India into the past, sees continuity in the wrong places, and projects our own concerns on to remote relatives whose world was markedly different from ours. Views that appear constrictive to us were liberating for our forefathers; they were not exactly the same views, anyway. Besides, this perspective fails to properly account for much that is crying out for explanation. Why did India adopt the constitution that it did? Why were fundamental rights accorded a central place within the constitution? Why adopt a constitution in the first place? Why the scramble to protect the rights of individuals and only a grudging acceptance for group rights? And, in a deeply hierarchical society, why such scant opposition to universal franchise, to the ban on untouchability, and to formal gender equality?

Proponents of the argument that liberal democracy is alien to cultural and social norms in India can respond by claiming that they do possess a meaningful account of the birth of constitutional democracy in India. The constitution, which was 'squarely in the best western tradition', this view believes, was given to the people of India by the political choice of an intellectual elite within a remarkably unrepresentative body.[7] Moreover, it was established in 'a fit of absentmindedness'; the elite had no idea of the political implications of their actions or of the consequences that lay in store once they had extended the franchise to the poor and the uneducated.[8]

I find this an extraordinary perspective on the making of the Indian constitution: chosen, but unwittingly, by a body that claimed to represent the real interests of everyone but was, in fact, wholly unrepresentative, in the best traditions of the West because it turned its back sharply on the homegrown traditions of the national movement. By what magic was this miracle performed? How could the *very* people who allegedly rejected liberal–democratic values adopt at the same time a constitution in the best traditions of western liberal democracy? How could some of the most outstanding figures of the century choose a basic structure for their society without a clue about its impact on that society or on its inherited traditions? This is not an easy question to answer and certainly not one to be dealt with in a few pages. But it is worthwhile to ask whether a response that appears attractive at first sight retains plausibility on closer examination.

THE LIBERAL STRAND IN INDIAN POLITICS

I believe that on careful inspection the argument is neither credible nor appealing. I believe it more plausible to argue that at least since Ram Mohan Roy, and well before the radical politicization of INC, a distinct liberal stream existed, which merged with and inherited a diffuse but persistent strain of something akin to a liberal view within local Indian traditions; and that western modernity could make a considerable impact on an aspiring middle strata of Indian society because it genuinely articulated and responded to their needs. There is more to utilitarianism than its strong collectivist trappings and therefore, even if liberalism came to India through utilitarianism, it washed up ideas that were neutral, to say the least, between the individual and the collective. Moreover, by installing the machinery of a modern state, British imperialism simultaneously opened up opportunities for resistance to it. Therefore, a classical political libertarianism with its emphasis on individual rights came to India as a structural feature of modern political life. Above all, democracy grew in India, as it did in many other places, under the guise of nationalism, and its commitment to political

[7] Ibid., p. 34.
[8] Ibid.

equality fitted in neatly with the egalitarian strands of liberalism as well as of utilitarianism. In the last instance, this meant that even outside the polity, liberal demands for equality of opportunity and for treating individual persons as equal were considerably strengthened. If all this is true, then it is a gross exaggeration to assert that constitutional democracy in India was established in a fit of absent-mindedness, that the discourse of rights was detached entirely from its classical individualist and political moorings, and that Indian nationalism had little interest in liberal democracy. These points need elaboration.

I begin with the claim that the transformation of nationalist demand into a mass movement ended the short phase of liberal politics in India. I do not wish to contest that the politics of mass movement is deeply at odds with the politics of institutionalized opposition. Undeniably, a great distance exists between a politics of resistance to the state—one that tries with popular mandate, if not direct pressure from below, to force rulers out of power—and a politics conducted within parameters of institutionalized opposition permitted by the state. Rather, my point is that the first kind of politics is as much a part of the liberal tradition as the second. Any plausible form of liberalism incorporates within it a right to actively resist illegitimate state power, a right that can hardly be exercised within normal political process. The form taken by this politics of resistance varies in different contexts. People guided by a strong liberal vision, keen to set up a liberal state may have to adopt even violent methods to do so. How else does one explain the American War of Independence or even, perhaps, the French Revolution? The fact that in periods of transition, the American and the French adopted 'revolutionary', non-institutional politics doesn't mean they rejected liberalism. Similarly, Gandhi's adoption of mass politics, a politics of 'coercion and seduction', does not indicate that a liberal agenda had been abandoned, just as the revolutionary phase in France or America does not prove that liberalism had been jettisoned. The plain fact is that liberalism, while admitting the right to resistance to an illegitimate state, is not clear on the methods to be adopted for such resistance. These can vary from violent overthrow to passive resistance, and quite easily accommodate Gandhi's eclectic politics of satyagraha. At any rate, a distinction needs to be made between Gandhian methods of revolt against an oppressive regime and the substantive vision that impelled these methods. Gandhi's programme for the abolition of untouchability, of equality for women, of the extension of franchise to every person, and his deeply individualistic vision of faith and spirituality have much in common with any reasonable interpretation of a number of liberalisms.

My second point about the commitment to civil liberties flows directly from acceptable norms of dissent and the availability of political liberty within the confines of a liberal state. As early as the beginning of the nineteenth century, Ram Mohan Roy protested against a regulation curtailing the freedom of the press. He argued that a state that is responsive to the needs of individuals and ready for intervention on their behalf, makes available to them the means by which such needs are communicated and therefore, must permit unrestricted liberty of publication. The demand for a free press and opposition to its gagging persisted throughout British rule, particularly when the press was the principal instrument for the propagation and consolidation of India's nationalist ideology. Consider the fierce opposition to the infamous Rowlatt Act which gave the colonial state enormous emergency powers, similar to war-time controls. It is true that opposition to this act was not expressed in ways that were obviously liberal, but in its substantive content it was fundamentally liberal. An opposition to arbitrary detention is as classically liberal as you can get and yet, there is simply no one particular, liberal method of opposing it, anytime, anywhere in the world.

Similarly, the claim that liberalism arrived in India already gravely compromised because it was introduced by utilitarianism, in its rampantly collectivist and paternalist mood, is severely overstated. For a start, liberalism did not come to India only as a well-articulated philosophy through standard processes of ideological transmission such as education and the press. On the contrary, many of its core values originated simply as a consequence of practices and institutions set up by the rulers to directly serve British interests, rather than by deliberate design. Consider, for example, the introduction of the postal system or the railways and their dramatic impact on social mobility, or the system of education introduced for the convenience of the rulers, but of immense advantage to the ruled. Many local upper caste men may indeed have been transformed into efficient servants of the empire, but education also unwittingly created Indian nationals who eventually challenged both the empire as well as some oppressive tendencies within their own social order. Similarly, by introducing the Indian penal code, the imperial legal system established the doctrine of equality of all before law. By a curious dialectic, every practice which began as a functional requirement of the Raj contributed, at least partly, to its own undoing over time. Liberalism did not come to India only through the spoken or printed word, it was directly embedded in practices as a structural feature of institutions and technologies. Unsurprisingly, British rulers were unaware, or at least appear to have miscalculated the potential implications of their actions. Whether or not they had *created* the empire in a fit of absent-mindedness, it appears that they had certainly *consolidated* it in that mood!

Let me come to the real point. It is no particular flaw of the Indian elite that constitutional democracy was established in a fit of absent-mindedness. Human agents anywhere in the world are unlikely to be clairvoyant about *all* the potential implications of their actions. It was to counter the myth of this Cartesian translucency, the presumption that agents always have a clear idea of what they are doing, that philosophers such as Hegel introduced the concept of 'the cunning of reason'. Much safer, I believe, is to presume that agents never grasp the *full* implications of their actions or fully know what they are doing. The Indian elite was unaware to the same degree as any set of reasonable agents would be. Indeed, they knew what they were doing to the extent possible; perhaps they had more than average grasp of what they were up to, even though they could not have been fully aware of all the potential implications of their actions.

My next point pertains to the characterization of utilitarianism and liberalism. An emphasis on the collectivist ingredient within utilitarianism should not ignore other components compatible with a rights-based version of liberalism. Likewise, the centrality of rights or autonomy within liberalism should not be interpreted in such a way that other key values within liberalism are overlooked. To be sure, the point about the strong collectivism of utilitarianism is not entirely mistaken; one of its glaring flaws is its failure to appreciate the true significance of the separateness of persons. Utilitarian calculation allows some individuals to subsidize, even at their own expense, the projects of other individuals; from the point of view of an impartial, benevolent observer, some individuals may count for nothing. This is deeply disturbing from an alternative standpoint of moral equality and fairness. Insofar as utilitarianism possesses this collectivist ingredient, it can only have strengthened the unjust anti-individualist biases of Indian tradition.

However, utilitarianism also contains strands neutral towards the individual and the collective, and may strengthen individualist tendencies against traditional, inegalitarian collectivism. Here, I wish to draw attention to three such features. First, its stress on happiness and well-being, and its repugnance for suffering. Second, its idea that in the utilitarian calculus every unit of happiness carries *equal* weight and therefore, a desire cannot be ignored merely on account of the current social rank of its holder or some obscure metaphysics. Finally, the right answer to a moral question is determined by measuring human happiness rather than by relying on a ramshackle tradition or a dubious spiritual leader.[9] Utilitarianism may have generated its own brand of authoritarian collectivism but it was also destined to upset the inegalitarian collectivism of several Indian customs. Indeed, by its emphasis on desire and happiness, on the avoidance of suffering, and by its implicit attack on social hierarchy, it was more than likely to nourish individualist ideas. To cut a long story short, if it is important to point out the link between utilitarianism and collectivism, it is equally necessary to register the precise form of collectivism encouraged by it. The 'happiness of the greatest number' is galaxies apart from 'the happiness of the smallest number', which was the hallmark of traditional collectivism. Indeed, the individualist implications of utilitarianism could hardly have failed to contribute to the development of ideas which eventually coalesced into a set of fundamental rights in the Indian constitution.

THE TENSION BETWEEN INDIVIDUAL AND COMMUNITY RIGHTS

Against the view that a rights-based liberalism was crippled in India from its beginnings, I have argued that for the Indian political elite, civil liberties mattered a great deal, and that these had to be construed individualistically, that is, essentially as features of individuals rather than of groups. True, little interest in the philosophical justification of these rights was evident, but in their practical engagement with an alien, oppressive state, political actors in India fully realized their importance. A practical knowledge that these rights belong to them, qua individuals could not have escaped them even though they did not articulate this knowledge in terms of an indigenous, grand theory. Perhaps, the language and culture of individual rights was not pervasive and did not go very deep. But it went as far and as deep as it possibly could at that time and for the fifty years or so before the adoption of

[9] For utilitarianism's attractive qualities, see Will Kymlicka, *Contemporary Political Philosophy: An Introduction*, Oxford: Clarendon Press, 1990, pp. 10–12.

the constitution, every single resolution, scheme, bill, national demand, or report mentioned it, not just in passing, but as a *non-negotiable value*. The section on fundamental rights in the Indian constitution, with a core of civil liberties, did not fall from the sky fully formed. It grew out of struggles with an oppressive, humiliating political regime. Despite attacks and instrumentalist attitudes towards it, the idea of fundamental rights remains potent even today. After all, the discourse of civil rights hasn't exactly disappeared from India! The fact that it has not gone deeper requires explanation but recognition of this is a far cry from accepting the idea that it was knocked out in India before it even took its first faltering steps.

More importantly, liberalism must not be viewed only as a doctrine of individual rights; nor was it believed to be so by more articulate members of the constituent assembly. For example, take the views of Sardar K.M. Pannikar, who in the Sarojini Naidu Memorial Lecture (1961) argued that Indian liberalism was made up of two streams, each with 'a fairly long history'.[10] For Pannikar, the founder of the first stream was Ram Mohan Roy, who 'by emphasizing the right of women to freedom and the establishment of casteless society put the Hindu people on the road to liberal transformation and contributed to the growth of liberal thought in India.'[11] The second stream comprised of figures like K.C. Sen and M.G. Ranade, but more importantly, Swami Vivekananda, who 'introduced into orthodox Hinduism the spirit of social justice.'[12] By disassociating institutions such as caste and prohibitions like widow remarriage from the Hindu religion and by espousing the view that the reform of such practices is a matter essentially of social justice, Vivekananda spurred a movement of reordering Hindu society infused with liberal principles. Pannikar also argues that Gandhiji's ascendancy within the Congress initiated a programme of political action based on the same ideas for which liberalism stood. The Congress not only advocated political liberalism but emphasized the 'rights of the individuals and the value of essential freedoms, the rule of law, secularism in politics and faith in social justice.'[13] Two features stand out in this account as constitutive of liberalism: equality and social justice. Pannikar's vision of liberalism in

---

[10] K.M. Pannikar, *In Defence of Liberalism*, Bombay: Asia Publishing House, 1962.

[11] Ibid.

[12] Ibid., p. 3.

[13] Ibid., p. 6.

general, and of Indian liberalism in particular, is far more in consonance with the core values of liberalism than the identification of it exclusively with individualistically construed rights.

A concern for liberal justice is nowhere more evident than in constitutional provisions for affirmative action programmes.[14] To tackle the basic inequalities already existing in the Indian social structure, and to make the formal political empowerment of severely disadvantaged groups more effective, the introduction of constitutionally protected preferential treatment of these groups was thought necessary. A mere right to vote and to equality of opportunity, it was widely recognized, is insufficient to ensure meaningful, effective social and political equality. Thus, apart from several general provisions to the right of equality, special constitutional measures were taken to protect and advance the interests of the scheduled castes and scheduled tribes. For example, Article 334 provides for reservations for seats in legislatures for these groups; similarly, under Article 335, the claims of scheduled castes and tribes are taken into consideration while making appointments to public services. Here, the makers of the constitution appealed not only to backward-looking principles justifying compensation to victims of past harm, but also to a forward-looking liberal principle that aims at future equality of opportunity. Indeed, it was precisely because past injustice continued to be a source of current injustice that programmes of affirmative action were believed to be necessary.

The claim that in India, 'liberty was understood not as an individual right but as a nation's collective right to self-determination' is deeply problematic.[15] To begin with, the two are not mutually exclusive. Some rights are irreducibly collective, such as the right to self-determination and the right to preserve a culture against potential threat from other cultural communities. Other rights are irreducibly individual: the right not to be subject to bodily harm, not to be detained arbitrarily, not to be prosecuted for expressing dissent against the state, or the more positive right to, say, gainful employment. Both kinds of rights can be granted, and though they may occasionally conflict, they coexist as well. Proponents of the view that individual rights had no place within Indian discourses may accept this but still argue that the ineffective presence

[14] In all fairness, this is recognized by Khilnani (1997). He acknowledges that 'Reservations had been intended to be a temporary expedient to a less just society' (p. 37). But my point is that he fails to see it as reflecting liberal principles.

[15] Khilnani, *The Idea of India*, p. 26.

of individual rights is explained by the fact that in Indian culture 'the only place for the individual is in the form of a renouncer.'[16] But I doubt if this account is plausible, even for traditional Indian society, and it is certainly less so for urban, middle-class India in the post-Ram Mohan Roy world in which Indians tried somehow to combine or reconcile traditional collectivist and modern individualist strands. To assert that the issue was settled from the beginning in favour of one is to fail to understand the complex world of these persons.

Indeed, the world view of intellectuals in the late nineteenth century was markedly different from the intellectual landscape of left–liberals after the Second World War. Attempts to reconcile individual and collective identities were not uncommon within liberal writing at the turn of the century and for roughly three decades thereafter. T.H. Green, Hobhouse, and John Dewey, to name three prominent liberals, recognized the importance of belonging to a cultural community with its memories, traditions, customs, and a shared way of thinking and feeling, a common language.[17] Without devaluing individual liberty, such liberals recognized community rights with great philosophical ease. The intellectual environment that informed Indian thinking is imbued with liberalism of this hue, rather than the classical libertarianism of the eighteenth century, or by deontological liberalism of the second half of the twentieth century.

The question of group rights needs further scrutiny. The prospect of the break down of hierarchical communities, that is, emotional solidarities that are shot through with asymmetrical relations, provoked many responses. One such view point, known in India as 'communalism', legitimizes a full-blooded conflictual relationship between communities that may view each other as equals, but are obsessively self-focussed and intent upon maximizing their own interests at the expense of the other. Distinct from hierarchical communitarianism and a communalism infused with a Hobbesian view of equality, is *individualist egalitarianism*, a view committed to equality among individuals and marked by a drive towards abstract universalism, and *communitarian egalitarianism* that forges a relationship of equal *respect* among communities. Two features distinguish the aforementioned views: one has to do with their attitude to difference; and the other, with their understanding of the source of this difference. In individualist egalitarianism, differences are

[16] Ibid., p. 26.

[17] On this, see, for example, Will Kymlicka, *Liberalism, Community and Culture*, Oxford: Clarendon Press, 1989, chapter 10.

due to individual choice or to a culturally neutral, socially generated circumstance that must be ignored or eliminated in order to achieve an egalitarian order. In communitarian egalitarianism, differences are a result of irreducibly diverse cultural backgrounds and need to be properly recognized and affirmed rather than be jettisoned from the egalitarian framework.

The strategy of the individualist response is at best to treat difference as a disadvantage suffered by a group; the removal of disadvantages by working through and eventually dissolving groups into individuals is, therefore, a natural objective of state policy. From the perspective of the collectivist view point, this strategy fails to understand how groups sustain culture and why every cultural difference is not a disadvantage that must be shed; the eradication of every difference is impossible and undesirable. Instead, a reasonable parity between irreducibly different cultural communities is required. This does not mean that particular cultural communities never disappear or assimilate into other communities; however, it does mean that a culture-neutral, homogeneous society consisting only of radically self-directing individuals is an impossibility. Though both the individualist and the collectivist responses were in the making in the early twentieth century, post-war liberalism articulated and theorized the former at the expense of the latter.

It is important not to read the mind of the political elite in India with the interpretive grid of post-war liberalism which, to ward off hierarchical communitarianism and communalism, relies exclusively upon the resources of individualist egalitarianism. The Indian political elite may not have made a distinction between hierarchical and egalitarian communities; it frequently failed to keep the idea of communalism distinct from egalitarian communitarianism. But it is difficult to deny that the discourse of mutual respect between cultural communities was always within their reach.[18] To counter the challenge of hierarchical communitarianism and communalism, they relied on and frequently wavered between individualist and non-individualist egalitarianism. The constituent assembly debates reflect this tension. The political elite in India, working with the resources of a ragbag liberalism, was sensitive to both individual and group rights, and wrestled with the tension between them within the context of a forever threatening anti-liberal conception embedded in the then existing political practice. The

[18] On this, see, for example, *The Constituent Assembly Debates*, Vol. 8, 16 May–16 June 1949, p. 326.

constitution, too, reflects, perhaps was even born out of, this turmoil, and uneasily tries to reconcile individual with group rights.

THE MAJORITY–MINORITY FRAMEWORK

Articles 29 and 30 of the constitution granted special rights to groups in order to protect their interests and, in particular, to enable them to establish and administer their own educational institutions. These group-specific rights were frequently viewed as the rights of minorities. By the time the constitution came to be written, the language of majority–minority had taken a firm hold on the dominant political discourse. A special sub-committee on minorities was constituted and most of its members accepted the idea that permanent minorities needed special safeguards. So, by incorporating group rights, the framers of the Indian constitution accepted what might be called the *majority–minority framework*. Was this move on their part defensible? In this section, I argue that it was.[19]

There are two alternative ways of understanding the notions of majority and minority. One is from within the problematic point of communitarianism and nationalism, and the other from the vantage point of a certain conception of democracy. The democratic notion of majority–minority rests on the rule of preference aggregation. No matter what its content or who its holder, every preference must be taken into account and placed on the same scale. Social status and economic position attached to preferences, the intensity of their expression, judgements about their worth, their impact, and on whom are irrelevant. A majority and a minority emerges when such preferences are aggregated

[19] For my reading of the constitution as embodying a majority–minority framework, and for a substantiation of my view that it is justified and that this justification can be found in the debates of the constituent assembly, see B. Shiva Rao (ed.), *The Framing of the India's Constitution*, New Delhi: IIPA, 1967, volume II, part III, pp. 309–86. See, particularly, the reply to a questionnaire prepared by K.M. Munshi on the nature and scope of the safeguards for minorities by M. Ruthnaswamy, who explicitly makes a distinction between political and national/religious minorities and a good case, at least as a temporary measure, for minority rights, and by Jagjivan Ram who argued that while political safeguards for minorities may be eliminated after these minorities are convinced that their rights shall be protected even after they remain unrepresented in the legislature or the administration, some of the other safeguards such as those guaranteeing religious and cultural freedom shall have to remain for all times in the constitution. See, pp. 312–18 and 330–6. Also, see B. Shiva Rao, *The Framing of India's Constitution: A Study*, New Delhi: IIPA, 1968, pp. 741–80.

and counted. Notions of majority and minority within this framework are predicated on preference.[20] I shall call them *preference-based* majority and minority. The idea of preference appears to but does *not* depend on the notion of a self defined independently of fundamental commitments, constitutive attachments, and communities. All it requires is that the self be treated as if, upon entering a common public space, it can leave behind commitments and attachments. This implies that the only feature relevant in public contexts is the capacity of the self to choose among desires it happens to have. Because the preferences of people are never taken as immutable within this conception, the idea of a permanent majority or minority makes little sense.

It is in the nature of preference-based democratic institutions that the minority of today becomes the majority tomorrow. Popular elections constantly reconfigure majorities and minorities, yet, constitutional safeguards may still be required because the basic interests of an individual must not be impaired, even temporarily. At any rate, even in this preference-based model, majorities and minorities may become practically permanent if the outcome of democratic procedures repeatedly favours one kind of preference expressed by a set of individuals. Constitutional safeguards are necessitated by the need to check the injustice of such outcomes, to prevent pitfalls of an intolerable and congealed stability. Therefore, certain preferences are excluded from the arena of aggregation and decision making so that were they to congeal, they would not affect the position or value of other preferences. (For example, if majority preferences persistently express that meat eating be banned, and a minority equally persistently expresses preference in favour of eating meat, then any preference one way or another is excluded from decision making.) On the whole, all constitutions are attempts to prevent democracy from sliding into despotism by controlling the tyrannical elements of political majoritarianism.

The move from an aggregative to a constitutional model of democracy involves granting some guarantees to individuals. This diminishes insecurity among individuals who reason thus: suppose that it turns out that a set of given preferences held persistently by a small

[20] By preference, I mean a desire that we have because we have chosen it. Preferences may be short term or long term. For the purposes of this essay, a long-term preference is an aggregation of short-term preferences. A long-term preference for something is a chain of short-term preferences for the same thing.

number of people is always opposed to or incompatible with those held by larger numbers. Given further that in a democratic system governed entirely by preferences, policy making is unlikely to be shaped by minority preferences, it is reasonable and in the interest of all to inhibit this untrammelled majoritarianism by assuring all relevant individuals that policies exclusively meant for them be formulated by their own internal preferences and not by external ones.[21] Hence, the necessity of individual rights.

To understand the second conception of majority–minority, imagine a set of individuals who define themselves and others not in terms of preference, that is, the desires people choose to have, but rather by the more or less permanent attributes that they happen to possess. These attributes are widely believed to constitute the very identity of individuals.[22] Such individuals also see themselves as constituting a group around this feature. Assume two such groups with differing numerical strengths. A minority and majority exists then on the basis of such identity-constituting features. Let me call these *identity-dependent* majority and minority. In a large society where people do not share the same identity-constituting features, majorities and minorities exist more or less on a permanent basis. (For example, Tamils in Sri Lanka, the Quebecois in Canada, the many linguistic groups within India, and Muslims in Britain.) Here, we can even speak of permanent majorities or minorities.

When such permanent identity-dependent majorities and minorities enter the democratic arena, they bring along desires, possessed simply by virtue of the kind of people they are. I am not, of course, claiming that these desires are natural or immutable, only that because they are culturally inherited and collectively reinforced, they are relatively stable. In such contexts, the outcome of democratic procedures is likely to repeatedly favour not only the preferences of a set of individuals but the more or less permanent desires of a group. Moreover, these desires of the majority may be about the basic structure and organization of society, so that minorities within that society may live as permanent

[21] External preferences are preferences held by people on what others may desire to do. This is roughly the same as the distinction between personal and external preferences drawn by Ronald Dworkin. See his *Taking Rights Seriously*, London: Duckworth, 1977, p. 234.

[22] It may be noted that majority and minority cannot be defined independently of each other and presuppose, in turn, a common framework, some commitment, however tenuous, of living together.

aliens, in perpetual insecurity. When this occurs in reality, a society may be wracked by what I call the *majority–minority syndrome*.[23] It follows that constitutional guarantees are needed for permanent (religious or linguistic) minorities and therefore, more imperatively, a majority–minority framework is necessary to prevent a society from swirling into the vortex of a majority–minority syndrome.[24]

I started off with a majority–minority framework and later referred to the majority–minority syndrome. The two terms are not interchangeable. Syndrome suggested something stronger and pejorative. When a deep malaise sets into the framework causing, for one or other intrinsic reason, a spiralling estrangement between the minority and the majority, we are saddled with a majority–minority syndrome. On the other hand, a majority–minority framework rests on different self-identifications and a modicum of distance between the two groups but implies no galloping alienation or the chronic malaise typical of syndromes. It is important here to note that the majority–minority framework operates with strictly egalitarian premises. A demand for minority rights is occasionally made under conditions where the group

[23] Since when have majorities and minorities existed? At least since the formation of states. For example, numerically small religious groups existed in Empire states, such as the Jews in the Holy Roman Empire. However, enumeration, though necessary, is not sufficient for the constitution of minority and majority. Three other features enter into its current understanding. First, groups must view themselves as a minority or a majority. Self-identification or the persistent identification by others in these terms, simultaneously or subsequently recognized by the group in question, is central to majority–minority formations. Second, the group must believe that its own identity-constituting features have the power to shape the structure of some social and political order, usually the one they happen to live in. In large democracies, this is likely to happen through representative institutions. It is only when this belief is accompanied or followed by the inability to exercise power, that the resulting sense of impotence breeds a perception of disadvantage. Indeed, a majority–minority syndrome has set in when this sense of disadvantage slides into an enduring feeling of insecurity.

[24] The syndrome need not always be well justified. A group may wish to shape the structure exclusively but not be allowed, or try participating with others in determining it but not be permitted to do so. In the first example, there is no effective discrimination against the group. But a majority–minority syndrome is well grounded when the majority really discriminates against minorities. In such instances, minorities do not merely see themselves in terms of constitutive features that differentiate them from a larger group but are seen so, and this difference forms the basis of persistent disfavour.

claiming such rights has the resources as well as the inclination to dominate and oppress other groups in society. (The system of Apartheid in
South Africa is an obvious example.) However, the entire point of
introducing minority rights, on the view outlined here, is to eliminate
hidden inequalities and possible injustice. The idea is to give minorities
some power to shape the social and political structure so that they too
are able to do or get what the majority group routinely procures by
virtue of the structural conditions in that society. A society that needs
to deploy a majority–minority framework is not the best of all possible
worlds, but in my use of the term it is not at all obvious that it connotes
a terrible, avoidable state of affairs.[25]

But can the syndrome be sidestepped in some way other than by the
use of the majority–minority framework? Given the distance it creates
between groups, is this framework necessary? Why have notions of
the majority or minority at all? Why not rid ourselves of the syndrome
by jettisoning the framework itself? There are two issues here. One is
the question of feasibility: are other alternative ways of dissolving the
syndrome available? Which of these is really feasible? Second, of those
which are feasible, which, in the given context, is ethically sustainable?

Several alternatives are indeed available. By delving deep into the
resources of our distinctive traditions, particularly of religion, we may
rediscover ways of living together woven into the fabric of lived experience and embedded in traditional practices. This alternative is developed on the more or less correct assumption that the majority–minority
framework is linked to modern democratic politics and to the formation of modern nation-states. Modernity is the bête noire here; it begets
the minority–majority framework and carries all its ills. In this view,
then, the only way to get rid of the syndrome (and the framework) is to
eject the framework, which, in turn, is done by a rejection of modernity
itself. There is a second alternative. This involves the homogenization
of individuals or their treatment, as if differences amongst them do not
matter. This is believed possible by transforming ascriptive, identity-
constituting features into preferences. This involves a conceptual and
practical move from a communitarian identity-constituting to an individualist, preference-based understanding of the categories of majority

[25] The majority–minority syndrome can also set off when a minority
resists the attempt by the majority to exclusively shape the social and political
institutions in accordance with its own cultural predilections. Equally, a well-
grounded syndrome may be caused by discrimination of the majority, as the
case of blacks in South Africa testifies.

and minority. Usually, this entails a refusal to bestow special rights or a withdrawal of privileges from minority groups and a replacement with a uniform charter of rights.

A third alternative is the homogenization of individuals, not by the process mentioned in the preceding paragraph, but by assimilating the minorities within an overweening majority, by a stipulation that only the identity-constituting features of the majority count in society. Special rights are wrested away from the minority; for example, a watchdog minorities commission may be disbanded. It is not uncommon to find that when enforced, uniformity is resisted and it results in the withdrawal of general rights as well. Finally, a fourth way in which syndrome / framework can be done away with is by the politics of 'overlapping good'. This would entail that different groups and individuals, from their respective standpoints, gather to deliberate over the good life, each contributing distinctively from its original perspective but converging ultimately on a conception shared to some extent by all.

Which of the above are desirable and can be met? The first alternative, delving into tradition to discover ways of living together, is partially desirable. Why only partially? Modernity is a contradictory phenomenon; it contains two blended ribbons of the good and the bad. By exploring resources of tradition, it provides an alternative to the evils of modernity but by exaggerating its importance, it remains wholly blind to its inescapability or its good, and fails to harvest its enormous benefits. Really, it is too caught up in the simple-minded binary opposition of a pristine tradition contrasted with the unrelieved evil of modernity. Therefore, it is not a wholly desirable option, and in any case, it is not even a real possibility. The second alternative, treating individuals as if group-based differences do not matter, requires a certain pattern of modernization that is sociologically naïve in its underestimation of the importance and desirability of constitutive social attachments in the life of people. I rule it out because of its insensitivity to cultural identities. People in India are hardly likely to shed their religious identity; indeed, religion continues to be rather more like the colour of the skin than a consumable item to be chosen from an array on offer in the marketplace. The third alternative, the assimilation of minorities, is undesirable because it can be realized, if at all, only by outright manipulation or force. However, modern politics is not a zero-sum game and has, at best, only temporary winners and losers. Besides, equalization, an integral and irreversible feature of modern societies, has meant that strategies of enforced assimilation have lost even the minimal legitimacy they once possessed. Any asymmetry between groups is resisted sooner, rather than later. As a result, it is extremely difficult to forcibly assimilate or coerce any group into the mainstream. The final alternative, the politics of 'overlapping good' is wonderful, if realizable. However, conditions for its realization do not always exist and even when they do, the need for a fall-back strategy remains.

Though a political condition of 'overlapping good' is a valuable regulative ideal, the makers of the constitution retained the major-ity–minority framework as the only realistic option by which to realize a society free of the majority–minority syndrome. They sought its abandonment by specific constitutional safeguards, that is, by trans-forming a simple majoritarian democracy to one with a constitution, by granting groups a degree of control over their affairs by different rights of self-government, including the right to express cultural par-ticularity. They believed that this strategy would contain discrimination and rectify perceptions of disadvantage among minorities.

It might be argued that their position severely underestimates problems generated by the majority–minority framework. Why must we put up with a permanent state of radically distinct groups, which see themselves in numerical terms and remain potentially divided, distanced, somewhat alienated from one another? Why not aspire to a political society that recognizes the equal standing of all viable groups and simply jettison talk of minorities and majorities?[26] Indeed, why at all take refuge in a divisive discourse of rights? My straightforward response to this objection on behalf of the framers of the constitution is that the best available option is not *always* realizable. Conditions that enable its exercise may be present in a society, but once the opportunity thrown up by the historical process is missed, it may altogether lose even the chance of securing other morally defensible but second-best options.

Let me explain this point. A pervasive myth within modernist self-understanding is that modern conditions destroy every collective formation and unleash different forms of individualism. In this view, collective identities and commitments cannot survive the modernist onslaught. Even a cursory glance at the processes of modernity, how-ever, reveals that while they undermine some *kinds* of groups, they simultaneously generate and bolster others. The most obvious example

[26] Joseph Raz, *Ethics in the Public Domain*, Oxford: Clarendon Press, 1992, p. 159.

of a group made possible and supported by modern processes is the nation (and other sub-national groups).[27] Now, the same processes that generate national identity also produce a sense of equality and intense competitiveness, ingredients that contribute substantially to the formation of what I called the majority–minority syndrome. It is of course true that a syndrome is not inevitable. A mechanism ensuring equality and mutual respect may well be introduced before competitiveness among groups goes too far. If a society succeeds in doing so, then it secures dignified and peaceful coexistence of groups without even resorting to a framework of rights. However, in most instances, the very formation of groups is dependent upon, and accompanied by, a sense of equality and radical competitiveness. Indeed, groups are formed within a process of rivalry that threatens to spiral out of control. One possible solution to contain it, to foster institutionalized toleration is to have a system of group rights. Collective self-government rights, special rights for representation within legislatures, or rights to express distinctive cultural particularities enable viable groups in society to live with dignity. At this stage, a society possesses a system of group rights without talk of minority and majority, without what I have called the majority–minority framework. However, if such rights are not granted at the appropriate time, complex feelings of disadvantage and marginalization grow and a majority–minority syndrome sets in, and once entrenched—precisely this is my argument—the only way to eliminate it is to introduce a majority–minority framework.

This point can be formulated differently. Group rights need not always be perceived as minority rights. They are viewed as rights of minorities if introduced after an irreversible condition of radical alienation between groups has come into existence. A majority–minority framework is then needed to get rid of the syndrome; no need for it exists if the syndrome did not exist in the first place. In short, the framework *follows* the syndrome. To insist upon the futility or irrelevance of the framework when, in fact, the syndrome is already entrenched, is to belie, at best, a shallow utopianism, and at worst, to shamelessly disguise inequalities between groups. The point I am hammering home is that societies which grant equal recognition to groups at an opportune moment avoid the majority–minority syndrome and therefore,

[27] It would likewise be a mistake to believe that pre-modern social processes undermine every version of individualism and uphold all forms of collectivism. These processes also support some individualist tendencies while disrupting others.

have no need for a majority–minority framework. However, once they miss this opportunity and a syndrome bedevils them, the only ethically defensible option then is to live with a majority–minority framework. Other ways of ridding the syndrome are, quite simply, morally unsustainable. On constructive interpretation of the intentions of the framers of the constitution, this was the logic behind their acceptance of the majority–minority framework.

A MODERN, INDIAN SECULARISM

The acceptance of group rights and the majority–minority framework had a profound impact on the conception of secularism implicit in the constitution. A variant of secularism was developed, which is at once Indian and modern.[28]

There is a tendency in the literature on secularism in India to first posit a highly idealized version of secularism derived partly from, say, the American experience and then judge the practice of the secular state in India by standards evolved from these models. (Secularists have often done this and then lamented the failure of Indian secularism. Likewise, opponents of secularism have used the ploy to first highlight the inconsistencies of Indian secularism and then conclude that the collapse of secularism in India is imminent.) To illustrate this point, let me take the example of Donald Smith's *India as a Secular State*, still the locus classicus on the subject.[29] Smith's conception of the secular state involves three distinct but interrelated relations concerning the state, religion, and the individual. The first relation concerns individuals and their religion, from which the state is excluded. Individuals are thereby free to decide the merits of the respective claims of different religions without any coercive interference by the state. They are free to revise or reject the religion they were born into or have chosen. (This is the liberal ingredient within secularism.) The second concerns the relation between individuals and the state, from which religion is excluded. Here, the state views individuals without taking into account their religious affiliation. The rights and duties of citizens are not affected by the religious beliefs held by individuals; for example, no discrimination exists in the holding of public office or taxation. (This is the egalitarian

---

[28] For a detailed defence of this view, see Chapter 3 of this book. Also, see my article, 'What is Secularism For?', in Rajeev Bhargava (ed.), *Secularism and Its Critics*, New Delhi: Oxford University Press, 1998, pp. 486–542.

[29] D.E. Smith, *India as a Secular State*, Princeton: Princeton University Press, 1963.

component within secularism.) Finally, for Smith, the integrity of both these relations is dependent on the third relation, between the state and different religions. Here, he argues that secularism entails separation of powers, that is, the mutual exclusion of state and religion in order that they may operate effectively and equally in their own respective domains. Just as it is not the function of the state to promote, regulate, direct, or interfere in religion, just so is political power outside the scope of religion's legitimate objectives. So, for Smith, secularism means the strict separation of religion and the state for the sake of the religious liberty and equal citizenship of individuals.

Clearly, on this account of secularism, any intervention in Hinduism—for example, the legal ban on the prohibition of dalit entry into temples—is illegitimate interference in religious affairs and therefore compromises secularism. Similarly, the protection of socio-religious groups (minorities) is inconsistent with an individualistically grounded secularism. For example, the right to maintain one's educational institutions entails a departure from secularism simply on the ground that it depends on a communally suspect classification. Together, these policies violate the ideal of neutrality or equidistance which plays a pivotal role in Smith's view of secularism. Smith believed that despite these flaws, the Indian state, at least in the early 1960s, was secular. However, he also believed that these constituted serious deviations from the model of secularism and unless quickly brought in line, the secular state in India would plunge into crisis. Was he correct?

I do not think so. Smith remained in the grip of a particular model of western secularism and therefore, was unable to get a handle on the basic features of Indian secularism. The distinctiveness of the Indian variant of secularism can be understood only when the cultural background and social context in India is properly grasped. At least four such features of this socio-cultural context call for attention. First, there exists the mind-boggling diversity of religious communities in India. Such diversity may coexist harmoniously but it invariably generates conflicts, the most intractable of which, I believe, are deep conflicts over values. Second, within Hinduism in particular, and in South Asian religions more generally, a greater emphasis is placed on practice rather than belief. A person's religious identity and affiliation are defined more by what she or he does with and in relation to others, than by the content of beliefs individually held by them. Since practices are intrinsically social, any significance placed on them brings about a concomitant valorization of communities. Third, many religiously sanctioned social practices are oppressive by virtue of their illiberal and inegalitarian character, and deny a life of dignity and self-respect. Therefore, from a liberal and egalitarian standpoint, they desperately need to be reformed. Such practices frequently have a life of their own, independent of consciously held beliefs, and possess a causal efficacy that remains unaffected by the presence of conscious beliefs. Furthermore, a tendency to fortify and insulate themselves from reflective critique makes them resistant to easy change and reform. It follows that an institution vested with enormous social power is needed to transform their character. Fourth, in Hinduism, the absence of an organized institution such as the church has meant that the impetus for effective reform cannot come exclusively from within. Reform within Hinduism can hardly be initiated without help from powerful external institutions such as the state.

In such a context, India needed a coherent set of intellectual resources to tackle inter-religious conflict, and to struggle against oppressive communities not by disaggregating them into a collection of individuals or by derecognizing them but by somehow making them more liberal and egalitarian. A political movement for a united, liberal, democratic India had to struggle against hierarchical and communal conceptions of community but without abandoning a reasonable communitarianism. Besides, the state had an important contribution to make in the transformation of these communities; for this reason, a perennial dilemma was imposed on it. The state in India walked a tightrope between the requirement of religious liberty that frequently entails non-interference in the affairs of religious communities, and the demand for equality and justice which necessitates intervention in religiously sanctioned social customs. Secularism in India simply had to be different from the classical liberal model that does not recognize groups, and dictates strict separation between religious and political institutions.

If we abandon the view, such as Donald Smith's, that political secularism entails a unique set of state policies valid under all conditions which provide the yardstick by which the secularity of any state is to be judged, then we can better understand why, despite 'deviation' from the ideal, the state in India continues to embody a model of secularism.[30] This can be shown even if we stick to Smith's working definition

---

[30] For an interesting critique of Smith's interpretation of Indian secularism as derived from the American model with an 'extra dose of separation', see Marc Galanter, 'Secularism, East and West', in Bhargava (ed.), *Secularism and Its Critics*, pp. 234–67.

of secularism as consisting of three relations. Smith's first relation embodies the principle of religious liberty construed individualistically, that is, pertaining to the religious beliefs of individuals. However, it is possible to make a non-individualistic construal of religious liberty by speaking not of the beliefs of individual but rather of the practices of groups. Here, religious liberty would mean distancing the state from the practices of religious groups. The first principle of secularism can then be seen to grant the right to a religious community to its own practices. Smith's second relation embodies the value of equal citizenship. But this entails—and I cannot substantiate my claim—that we tolerate the attempts of radically differing groups to determine the nature and direction of society as they best see it. In this view, then, the public presence of the religious practices of groups is guaranteed and entailed by the recognition of group differentiated citizenship rights. Smith's version of secularism entails a charter of uniform rights. But it is clear that the commitment of secularism to equal citizenship can dictate group-specific rights and therefore, differentiated citizenship. Smith's third principle pertains to non-establishment and therefore, to a strict separation of religion from state, under which religion and the state both have the freedom to develop without interfering with each other. Separation, however, need not mean strict non-interference, mutual exclusion, or equidistance, as in Smith's view. Instead, it could be a policy of principled distance, which entails a flexible approach on the question of intervention or abstention, combining both, dependent on the context, nature or current state of relevant religions.

It is important to understand that principled distance is not mere equidistance. In the strategy of principled distance, whether or not the state intervenes or refrains from action depends on what really strengthens religious liberty and equality of citizenship for all. If this is so, the state may not relate to every religion in exactly the same way, intervene to the same degree, or in the same manner. All it must ensure is that the relation between religious and political institutions be guided by non-sectarian principles that remain consistent with a set of values constitutive of a life of equal dignity for all.

It was largely this group-sensitive conception of secularism of the principled distance variety that legitimized the practices of the state wherein religion was alternatingly excluded and included as an object of state policy. By its refusal to allow: (i) separate electorates; (ii) reserved constituencies for religious communities; (iii) reservations for jobs on the basis of religious classification; and (iv) the organization of states on religious basis, the Indian state excluded religion from its purview on the ground that its inclusion would inflame religious and communal conflict and produce another partition-like scenario. However, the very motive that excluded religion from state–institutions also influenced its inclusion in policy matters of cultural import. For example, a uniform charter of rights was not considered absolutely essential for national integration. Separate rights were granted to minority religious communities to enable them to live with dignity. Integration was not seen as identical to complete assimilation. Similar liberal and egalitarian motives compelled the state to undertake reforms within Hinduism. By making polygamy illegal, introducing the right to divorce, abolishing child marriage, legally recognizing inter-caste marriages, regulating the activities of criminals masquerading as holy men, introducing temple entry rights for dalits, and reforming temple administration, the state intervened in religious matters to protect the ordinary but dignified life of its citizens.

To sum up: (i) modern secularism is fully compatible with, indeed even dictates, a defence of differentiated citizenship and of rights of religious groups; and (ii) the secularity of the state does not necessitate intervention, non-interference, or equidistance but rather any or all of these, as the case may be. If this is so, the criticism that the constitution envisages a state that cannot be secular because it explicitly abandons equidistance is mistaken. A secular state need not be equidistant from all religious communities and may interfere in one religion more than another. A critique of constitutional secularism on the ground that it acknowledges group rights or that it gives up on neutrality, simply does not wash.

WHY UNIVERSAL FRANCHISE? OR DEMOCRACY AS NATIONALISM

Franchise in India was restricted before the adoption of the constitution. Citizenship was based on what Dahl calls, 'the contingent principle of inclusion', that is, restricted to only those qualified to rule and who could claim citizenship.[31] Citizenship in the constitution was based instead on the categorical principle of inclusion: to be an adult member in the society is sufficient qualification for full citizenship of the state. Rights of citizenship, including the right to vote, were justified by

[31] Robert Dahl, *Democracy and its Critics*, New Haven and London: Yale University Press, 1989, chapter 9.

exclusive reference to this principle. In a society ravaged by persistent social inequalities and marked by a subordinate role for women within the patriarchal system, how could this come about? I offer three possible reasons: first, the influence of liberal individualist ideas in which the self is constituted not by a place within the group arena, but in abstraction from it. Such ideas are unlikely to have influenced those who played a key role in public deliberations.[32] A second reason may well have to do with the less explicit, unselfconscious motivations of political actors. In a country dominated by poor peasants belonging either to backward castes or falling altogether outside the caste structure, a restricted franchise would certainly have meant their exclusion from the political process. In a numbers-dominated democratic system, this could have significantly weakened the bargaining power of Hindus. I remain unpersuaded by this strongly communitarian, almost communal argument. A third reason might have to do with the growth of the idea of the nation. It is more or less integral to the concept of the nation that members who comprise it are equal. If so, and if the idea of democracy has been accepted, then no member of the said nation can be excluded from the exercise of franchise. This response needs further examination.

In 1916, nineteen members of the Imperial Legislative Council that included Madan Mohan Malaviya, Tej Bahadur Sapru, and Mohammad Ali Jinnah sent a signed memorandum to the viceroy, outlining a scheme of self-government for India which claimed that without self-government, Indians in India feel that 'though theoretically they are equal subjects of the king, they hold a very inferior position in the British empire'.[33] 'Humiliating as this position of inferiority is to the Indian mind', the memorandum continued, 'it is almost unbearable

[32] It is not implausible to claim, however, that for the leaders of the national movement a part of the self could be abstracted from the substantive commitment flowing from one's tradition and custom, from family and community. In short, a domain existed where a person could be legitimately viewed simply as an individual rather than a member of this or that particular community. Significantly, in this domain, a person's unequal status within a particular community also had no relevance. The process of individualization went hand in hand with the process of equalization. Once this idea of political equality—equality in the public domain—grew in importance, universal adult franchise was only a small step away.

[33] B. Shiva Rao, *The Framing of the Constitution: Select Documents*, Vol. 1, Delhi: Universal Law Publishing Co., 1967 (reprint 2004), p. 21.

to the youth of India whose outlook is broadened by education and travel in foreign parts where they come in contact with other free races. In the face of these grievances and disabilities, what has sustained the people is the hope and the faith inspired by promises and assurances of fair and equal treatment by the sovereign'.[34] The signatories argued that to regain self-respect, the Indian people needed not merely good government or efficient administration but a government 'that is acceptable to the people because it is responsible to them'.

The memorandum to the viceroy reflects how western modernity was lived from the inside by the elites of a conquered culture. A traditionalist refusal of western modernity would have entailed a turning away from popular rule, but Indian elites embraced the idea and complained, in the name of that very idea, that to be denied self-rule is to be demeaned, to be diminished in one's own eyes. Moreover, this loss of self-esteem was a shared experience—the experience of humiliation was irreducibly collective. The emotional power of nationalism is derived from this register of collective pride and humiliation.[35] Therefore, self-respect could only be restored and felt collectively. Self-government had to be a collective matter too.

But, how large must this collectivity be? Should it be restricted to the aspiring elite, denied full access, but already on the margins of power? It is of course true that a link exists between nationalism and self-governance and the nationalist demand is indistinguishable from the demand for self-governance, but why should the nation include the entire people? Why could it not have been restricted to a small elite? Why should everyone govern or why should some govern in the name of everyone? Why have universal franchise? Why must nationalism be almost identical to democracy?

One possible answer to these questions may be that the particular form of community known as a nation is a functional requirement of a distinctively modern society where social ranks, no longer fixed and immutable, are up for grabs, and the smooth operation of which requires flexible, context-free agents who not only move freely across physical and social space but communicate easily with each other. This freedom from social rank and content brings with it ideas of symmetrical (equal) relations as well as a degree of individualization. It

---

[34] Ibid.
[35] On this aspect of nationalism, see Charles Taylor, 'Nationalism and Modernity', unpublished.

follows that ideas of equality and individualism go hand in hand with the idea of a nation. The making of a nation, therefore, is the process of binding together a particular kind of people, those who have begun more or less to see themselves as individuals and relate to each other as equals. The functional tie envisaged by this account assures that no particular temporal sequence need be followed; a nation-state may precede or succeed a modern society of individualized and equalized human beings.

If the abovementioned is true, then we have at least some explanation for why no one within the social order can really be left out of the nation. If social hierarchy and strongly particularized identities cease to matter, then no reason exists to exclude anyone. (Or so it appears, because nationalism brings with it its own forms of strong exclusions.) Liah Greenfeld has helpfully drawn our attention to a change in the semantics of the term 'nation'.[36] In the late thirteenth century, the term 'nation' meant a community of opinion where the constituents of the said community were representatives of cultural and political authority. In short, a nation was a group of social elites. In the sixteenth century, however, the reference of 'nation' changed; it began to be applied to the entire population of a country and became synonymous with the word 'people'. This change in meaning signalled the symbolic elevation of the rabble into an elite, its movement from the wings onto centre stage, from irrelevance to relevance. Henceforth, every member of the population could partake of this superior, elite quality. The transformation of a rabble into a people and of the people into an elite, presupposes a profound change in the way societies are imagined, that is, from hierarchical communities to networks consisting of free and equal individuals.

This effected yet another change; in their self-understanding, the nation exists prior to and independent of the political organization of society, which has the power to give itself a constitution. I have already touched upon the background which makes this possible and which includes, among other things, complex constituents such as a particular frame of time and of common action, and I shall not spend much time on it. The important point I want registered is that the idea of the basic rules of society as stemming from the common action of a people, of a nation, is identical with the democratic idea for which sovereignty

[36] Liah Greenfeld, *Nationalism: Five Roads to Modernity*, Cambridge and London: Harvard University Press, 1992, Introduction.

is located within a people fundamentally equal to one another. As Greenfeld puts it, 'nationalism was the form in which democracy appeared in the world, contained in the idea of the nation as a butterfly in a cocoon'.[37]

This is precisely what appears to have happened in India. Once the idea of a nation took root among the elite, a conception of a political order growing out of the will of every single member of society and eventually, the idea of democratic self-government could not but have followed. The idea of universal franchise lay securely within the heart of nationalism. In the Constitution of India Bill (1895), the first non-official attempt at drafting a constitution for India, the author, probably Tilak, did not contest that the 'sovereign power of India is vested in the sovereign of Great Britain and Ireland, the supreme head of the Indian nation' or challenge the authority of the viceroy as representative of the sovereign. He did, though, declare at the same time that every citizen, that is, anyone born in India, had a right to take part in the affairs of his or her country and be admitted to public office, and therefore, hoped that 'under the benign government of the British', Indian citizens would 'in future enjoy and use the rights proposed to the greatest advantage of their country and the British government'.[38] The Motilal Nehru Report (1928) reaffirms this conception of citizenship. Section 9 of the report reiterates that every person of either sex who has attained the age of twenty-one is entitled to vote for the House of Representatives or Parliament. It defines the word citizen as any person who is born or whose father is either born or naturalized within the territorial limits of the commonwealth and has not been nationalized as a citizen of any other country.[39] The Motilal Nehru Report is unequivocal about the powers of government as derived from the people. In his presidential address to the National Convention of Congress Legislators (1937), Jawaharlal Nehru opposed the Government of India Act (1935) for not representing the will of the nation. He declared that the convention stands for a genuine democratic state in India where political power has been transferred to the people as a whole. Such a state, he said, can only be created by the Indian people themselves, through the medium of the constituent assembly elected on the basis of adult suffrage, and having the power to determine finally the constitution of

[37] Ibid., p. 10.
[38] Rao, *The Framing of the Constitution*, pp. 5–14.
[39] Ibid., p. 59.

the country.[40] Not much more evidence is required to substantiate my claim that democracy came to India in the guise of nationalism, with universal franchise as the most important and legitimate instrument by which the will of the nation was to be properly expressed.

[40] Ibid., pp. 86–92.

2

The Evolution and Distinctiveness of India's Linguistic Federalism*

An agile reader might have noticed that the first chapter does not say anything about Indian federalism. The omission was deliberate. The dominant vision embedded in the constitution did not find a place for multi-cultural federalism. However, it was not long before it was forced to do so. This chapter is an account of how this vision was broadened and made more democratic. In what follows, I trace the evolution of Indian federalism from a purely functional arrangement with a unitary bias, to a genuine language-based federalism and identify the distinctiveness of Indian federalism. The essay is divided into four sections. First, I provide a brief outline of the origins of Indian federalism. I claim that the modern Indian polity was torn between a unitary and a federal state because of the struggle between colonial and anti-colonial forces. On the one hand, its unitary character is a legacy of the centralizing policy of the British colonial government. On the other hand, a democratic, anti-colonial struggle gave impetus to the federalization of the emerging nation-state along linguistic lines. Yet, the deep religious division that resulted in partition prevented the organization of new states, even along linguistic lines, and saw the birth of a largely unitary

* This paper was presented at a seminar on 'Ethnic Federalism: The Challenges for Ethiopia' held at the Addis Ababa University, Ethiopia, in April 2004. Three scholars were brought into the discussion to place the Ethiopian experience in comparative perspective. It was subsequently published as 'The Evolution and Distinctiveness of India's Linguistic Federalism', in David Turton (ed.), *Ethnic Federalism*, Oxford: James Curry, 2006, pp. 93–118.

state. In the second section, I give a brief account of how linguistic federalism was resurrected soon after independence and the acute problems it faces, particularly in Punjab, the North-East, and Kashmir. I claim that, on balance, the democratic and linguistic federalism of India has managed to combine legitimate claims of national unity with equally legitimate claims of the political recognition of relatively distinct cultural groups. In the third section, I argue that the federal structure of India has, over time, developed characteristics that are distinct from the standard western models of federalism. I discuss five features that give a distinct character to Indian federalism. Finally, in the last section, I draw some tentative conclusions from the Indian experience that may be relevant to the future of federalism in other parts of the world which need a federal structure but are still uncomfortable with it.

THE ORIGINS OF INDIAN FEDERALISM

At the time of the Mughal Emperor Aurangzeb, who ruled between 1665 and 1707, pre-British India was divided into twenty-one administrative units or *subas*, some of which coincided with a single, distinct socio-cultural region, while others incorporated several. This is not surprising, because every large political entity must divide itself into its constituent units. Even ancient Indian empires were divided into *janapadas*, or territorially bounded communities, based on an admixture of culture, dialect, geographical location, social mores, and political status. Ancient Indian literature refers to six 'natural' regions, with 165 janapadas.

But, although it is true that the federal idea has some resonance in non-modern traditions, the current federal arrangement has its origins in colonial modernity. Under British colonialism, provinces were the result of an ad hoc and completely arbitrary process of annexation, accomplished by outright conquest, by treaties that lapsed due to a mixture of manoeuvre and neglect or that were framed under conditions of unequal bargaining strength. All these large provinces were multi-lingual and multi-ethnic. They were not the result of a policy of divide-and-rule, a key instrument of colonial power, but, once formed, they were certainly sustained by such a policy. In many cases, people speaking the same language were broken up to form parts of different provinces. This happened, for example, to the Oriyas, the Kannadigan, and the Marathas. The vastness of the empire—the sheer size of its territory—compelled the British to devolve power to these provinces. Yet, no matter how substantive the devolution of authority to the provinces under the 1919 Government of India Act, nor how apparently federal the provisions of the 1935[1] Act, power was centralized and always in British hands. This was to shape the political structure of independent India in the initial period of its formation.

Early resistance to colonialism did little to unsettle the multi-linguistic and multi-ethnic character of provinces. Later, the necessity of broadening the base of resistance, turning it into a mass anti-colonial struggle, made it very tempting for political movements to mobilize on the basis of linguistic or even religious identities. The Indian National Congress (INC),[2] the main protagonist of the freedom struggle, recognized the potential of relatively stable ethno-linguistic territorial identities. To channelize this potential and ensure that it was tapped exclusively for an anti-colonial struggle aimed at building an inclusive civic nationalism, it evolved an organizational framework for their integration into a newly imagined political community. The *pradesh*, a democratic, ethnically sensitive alternative to the colonial province, was projected as the

[1] The British government attempted a series of reforms to address the problems of their empire in India. The first of these reforms resulted in the Government of India Act of 1919. This Act introduced substantial changes in provincial administration, for example, the transference of subjects such as local self-government, education, and law and order becoming the preserve of provinces. Legislative and executive power in the provinces increased on an unprecedented scale, though a small franchise and limited availability of finances continued to present serious limitations. Similarly, in the early 1930s, the imperial government invited prominent Indians to three Round Table Conferences in London, in which, along with British politicians, they discussed the making of a new constitution with which to govern India. These discussions finally took shape in the 1935 Government of India Act. The Act was a recognition by the government that the continuation of the empire in India posed a massive political problem for which an immediate political solution had to be found. Its main aim was to 'buttress the empire not to liquidate it'. However, for all its limitations, it was a major experiment in the devolution of power in a non-white part of British Empire. For details, see Judith Brown, *Modern India: The Origin of an Asian Democracy*, Oxford: Oxford University Press, 1994, chapter 4, pp. 205–9; chapter 5, pp. 251–316.

[2] The INC was formed in 1885 by Indians educated in Britain. It was inspired by Dadabhai Nauroji who lived in the imperial capital and attempted not only to foster a sense of Indian identity but to pressurize British rulers to make public policies more sensitive to Indian needs. Until the First World War, it remained a pressure group, composed of elites who wanted more recognition from the British Empire and greater participation in its activities. Later, largely due to efforts of Gandhi, it became a mass organization and demanded, at first, a greater degree of autonomy and later, complete independence from the British Empire.

basic territorial unit of a new federation. Language was to be the organizational basis of each pradesh. Thus, sub-national linguistic identities
were recognized and given their legitimate due, but in a manner that
contributed to the larger civic national identity. By 1920, the Congress
decided to reorganize all its units along linguistic lines. From then on,
national politics began systematically to draw deeper sustenance from
various aspects of these language-based regional cultures. The Congress
recognized not only that the struggle for Indian nationalism had to be
pursued along federal lines but also that a responsible, representative
government of the future needed a linguistically organized federal state.
In the policy adopted at the Karachi session of the Congress (1929), the
approach was to give substantial powers to the provinces. Gandhi, in particular, realized the significance of ethnic identities and sought to forge a
unity without glossing over the country's diversities. The Cabinet Mission Plan,[3] in 1946, envisaged a very weak centre in a confederation-like
arrangement. The jurisdiction of the union was to be limited to foreign
affairs, defence, communications, and the power to raise finances for
the discharge of these functions. All other subjects were to be within
the jurisdiction of provinces. They were also to be vested with residu-
ary powers. Thus, till as late as the 1940s, there was little disagreement
about the need for a federal constitution.

Along with the idea of language-based federal units, however, came
the notion of religion-based segments and constituencies. Just as the
partition of Bengal in 1905 propelled movements of linguistic solidarity
everywhere, just so its annulment[4] consolidated a trend towards the

[3] The Cabinet Mission put forward a plan for a three-tiered constitution of
a federation, groups of provinces which chose to act together for agreed topics,
and provinces at the base. This plan was at the centre of a fierce controversy
between the INC and the Muslim League. The Congress President, Jawaharlal
Nehru, made it clear that once an Indian Constituent Assembly came into
being it would not be bound by the Cabinet Mission Plan, particularly on the
issue of voluntary grouping by provinces. The Muslim League then rejected
this plan on the ground that the new constituent assembly might not safeguard
the interests of Muslim majority areas. See Brown, *Modern India*, p. 334.

[4] Partition came about because Bengalis, with a strong linguistic identity,
felt that the imperial government had sought illegitimately to divide them.
This led to a burst of solidarity. Once Bengal was divided, however, it also
created a Muslim majority in East Bengal and a Hindu majority in West Bengal.
This helped foster the politicization of religious identities and the birth of the
idea that a religious community can be the sole bearer of all economic, social,
and political interests. The annulment of partition destroyed the 'communal'
hopes of Muslim elites in East Bengal.

potential organization of political units based on religion. The idea of separate electorates for Muslims had always found favour with Muslim elites. Had Muslims been dispersed more evenly in the territory of the sub-continent, and had they not been in a majority in some provinces, both religion and language could have been given political recognition without practical contradiction. Self-governing units could have been drawn along linguistic lines and special representation rights could have been given to religious minorities. But a large concentration of Muslims in the North-West and in East Bengal ensured that potentially either religion or language could become the basis of self-governing political units and they, therefore, began to compete for the same political space. This conflict between two competing forms of ethnicity suited the designs of imperial power. To contain the growing popularity of the national movement, it exploited divisions along religious lines and proposed a power-sharing arrangement that included representation along ethno-religious lines. A parallel mobilization process was then set in motion on the basis of religious differences. From then on, the Muslim elites felt that provinces grounded purely on language reflected a Hindu bias. Now, one ethnic principle of self-government was to be in continuous conflict with another ethnic principle of self-government.

As is well known, the independence of India was accompanied by its partition along religious lines. This had a traumatic impact on the psyche of members of the Congress party. Most of them began to be obsessively concerned with the dangers of further fragmentation and disintegration and began to view with suspicion the political expression, even of linguistic identities. No one was more uneasy with these identities than Nehru himself. During the course of his work in the committee which enquired into the demand for the linguistic organization of states, Nehru wrote:

[This inquiry] has been in some ways an eye-opener for us. The work of 60 years of the Indian National Congress was standing before us, face to face with centuries-old India of narrow loyalties, petty jealousies and ignorant prejudices engaged in mortal conflict and we were simply horrified to see how thin was the ice upon which we were skating. Some of the ablest men in the country came before us and confidently and emphatically stated that language in this country stood for and represented culture, race, history, individuality, and finally a sub-nation.[5]

[5] See Ashis Banerjee, 'Federalism and Nationalism', in Nirmal Mukarji and Balveer Arora (eds), *Federalism in India: Origins and Development*, New Delhi: Vikas Publishing House, 1992, p. 56.

The unitary mindset shaped by the experience of a centralized colonial state was now resurrected and, for a while, it appeared that the idea of a multi-cultural Indian federation was lost forever. Though committed to the maintenance of pluralism and to granting powers to provinces, the Congress reversed its stand after independence, giving the security and unity of India as its primary reasons. It is true that Nehru believed that some kind of reorganization was inevitable, but he was convinced that language must be supplemented by cultural, geographic, and economic factors. The question of linguistic provinces was examined by a special committee appointed by the constituent assembly. After an exhaustive enquiry, this committee, known as the Dar commission, concluded that 'the formation of provinces on exclusively or even mainly linguistic considerations is not in the larger interests of the Indian nation and should not be taken in hand.'[6] Another three-member committee that included Nehru was appointed by the Congress to examine the report of the Dar commission and to make final recommendations. This committee also felt that 'the present is not an opportune moment for the formation of new provinces.'[7] Yet, they conceded that 'if public sentiment is insistent and overwhelming, we, as democrats, have to submit to it, but subject to certain limitations in regard to the good of India as a whole ...'. They all agreed that the assembly must not attempt to solve the problem 'when passions are roused', but 'at a suitable moment when the time is ripe for it.'

Given the vast size and diversity of the country, however, federalism in India was less a matter of choice than of necessity. India has eight major religious systems, at least fifteen major language groups, and about sixty socio-cultural sub-regions with distinct sub-national identities. Besides, India also has one of the largest tribal populations in the world. This, along with its huge population, made it impossible for India to be anything but 'a continental federal polity constituted into a single territory'.[8] (See Tables 2.1, 2.2, and 2.3 on the multi-cultural base of India).

But, although its federal character had an air of inevitability about it, the form it assumed, and the justifications for it, did not. India was formed as a federation, but the second tier of government was justified primarily

[6] Granville Austin, *The Indian Constitution: Cornerstone of a Nation*, Oxford: Oxford University Press, 1966 (reprint 1999), p. 242.

[7] Ibid. All the quotes in the paragraph are from the same reference.

[8] Rashiduddin Khan, *Federal India: A Design for Change*, New Delhi: Vikas Publishing House, 1992, p. 2.

TABLE 2.1: Population by Religion

Religious Groups	1961 Number (Million)	1961 % to Total	1971 Number (Million)	1971 % to Total	1981 Number (Million)	1981 % to Total	1991 Number (Million)	1991 % to Total
Hindus	366.5	83.5	453.3	82.7	549.7	82.6	672.6	82.41
Muslims	46.9	10.7	61.4	11.2	75.6	11.4	95.2	11.67
Christians	10.7	2.4	14.2	2.6	16.2	2.4	18.9	2.32
Sikhs	7.8	1.8	10.4	1.9	13.1	2.0	16.3	1.99
Buddhists	3.2	0.7	3.8	0.7	4.7	0.7	6.3	0.77
Jains	2.0	0.5	2.6	0.5	3.2	0.5	3.4	0.41
Others[1]	1.6	0.4	2.2	0.4	2.8	0.4	3.5	0.43
Total	439.2	100.0	548.2	100.0	665.3	100.0	816.2[2]	100.0

Notes: 1981 data do not include Assam.
1. Including unclassified persons.
2. Excludes Assam and Jammu & Kashmir.
Source: Census of India, 1981, Series I, Paper 1 of 1995 (Religion), Paper 1 of 1991 (Religion).

TABLE 2.2: Population by Major Language Groups

Languages	Number (Million) 1971	Number (Million) 1981	Percentage 1971	Percentage 1981
Hindi	208.5	264.5	38.0	42.9
Bengali	44.8	51.3	8.2	8.3
Telugu	44.8	50.6	8.2	8.2
Marathi	41.8	49.5	7.6	8.0
Tamil	37.7	3.8	6.9	0.6
Urdu	28.6	34.9	5.2	5.7
Gujarati	25.9	33.1	4.7	5.4
Malayalam	21.9	25.7	4.0	4.2
Kannada	21.7	25.7	4.0	4.2
Oriya	19.9	23.0	3.6	3.7
Punjabi	14.1	19.16	2.6	3.2
Assamese	9.0	0.1	1.6	0.01
Sindhi	1.7	2.0	0.3	0.3
Kashmiri	2.5	3.2	0.5	0.5

Source: Census of India, 1981, Part IV-B (ii), Series-I, India.

TABLE 2.3: States and Union Territories by Population Size

Rank in 1991	State/ Union Territory	Population 1991	Percentage of Total Population of India 1991	1981	Rank in 1981
1	Uttar Pradesh	139,112,287	16.44	16.18	1
2	Bihar	86,374,465	10.21	10.20	2
3	Maharashtra	78,937,187	9.33	9.16	3
4	West Bengal	68,077,965	8.04	7.97	4
5	Andhra Pradesh	66,508,008	7.86	7.82	5
6	Madhya Pradesh	66,181,170	7.82	7.52	6
7	Tamil Nadu	55,858,946	6.60	7.06	7
8	Karnataka	44,977,201	5.31	5.42	8
9	Rajasthan	44,005,990	5.20	5.00	9
10	Gujarat	41,309,582	4.88	4.97	10
11	Orissa	31,659,736	3.74	3.85	11
12	Kerala	29,098,518	3.44	3.71	12
13	Assam	22,414,322	2.65	2.90	13
14	Punjab	20,281,969	2.40	2.45	14
15	Haryana	16,463,648	1.95	1.89	15
16	Delhi	9,420,644	1.11	0.91	16
17	Jammu & Kashmir (J&K)	7,718,700	0.91	0.87	17
18	Himachal Pradesh	5,170,877	0.61	0.62	18
19	Tripura	2,757,205	0.33	0.30	19
20	Manipur	1,837,149	0.22	0.21	20
21	Meghalaya	1,774,778	0.21	0.19	21
22	Nagaland	1,209,546	0.14	0.11	22
23	Goa	1,169,793	0.14	0.15	23
24	Arunachal Pradesh	864,558	0.10	0.09	24
25	Pondicherry	807,785	0.10	0.09	25
26	Mizoram	689,756	0.08	0.07	26
27	Chandigarh	642,015	0.08	0.07	27
28	Sikkim	406,457	0.05	0.05	28
29	Andaman & Nicobar	280,661	0.03	0.03	29
30	Dadra & Nagar Haveli	138,477	0.02	0.02	30
31	Daman & Diu	101,586	0.01	0.01	31
32	Lakshadweep	51,707	0.01	0.01	32

Note: The 1991 Census was not held in J&K. The population projections of J&K as on 1 March 1991 made by the Standing Committee of Experts on Population Projections (October 1989) is given.
Source: Census of India, 1991, final population totals (1) PCA Part-II-B (i), 1991 (2) PCA-Part-IIB (i), 1981 (PPXX).

in functional terms. Thus, despite a strong social base for federalism, its institutional expression, at least in the initial period, was weak. Arguably, this was due to the anxieties of a newly empowered political elite, which showed a lack of faith in the power of the democratic process to appropriately articulate and channelize ethno-regional aspirations in such a way that they led neither to violent conflicts nor towards separation. Nehru's reasons for being reluctant to endorse a linguistic organization of states, however, had some plausibility. First, he believed that a federation structured along ethno-linguistic lines would give some politicians an opportunity to mobilize permanently on the basis of language and give rise to regional chauvinism. This, he feared, might divert attention from issues of welfare and material well-being. Second, such a federation would 'freeze' ethno-linguistic identities, or certain forms thereof. The fluidity, flexibility, and multiplicity of identities would then give way to a valorization of one single identity. It would also prevent the formation of other more inclusive collective identities. But most of all, he feared that these frozen collective identities would increase the likelihood of intra-ethnic violence, encourage separatism and eventually lead to the balkanization of the country.

This third reason was decisive and gave Indian federalism a strong centralizing and unitary bias. Article 1 of the constitution speaks of a dual polity.[9] But, due to the provision of single citizenship, single integrated judiciary, uniform criminal law for all the states, and a unified all-India Civil Service (see Articles 5, 11, 14, 15, 44, 131–41, and 312 of the constitution), India remains a unified polity. The constitution gives general supremacy to the Union Parliament and Executive in all matters vis-à-vis the states (Article 365), especially in the making of laws on items included in the state list, in the appointment and dismissal of governors, in the dismissal of state ministry officials, and in the appointment of judges to the states' High Courts. It not only gives the residual powers to the union (Articles 245–6, 249–54, and 356)—a clear index of centralization—but also envisages easy and flexible procedures

[9] The reference to dual polity clearly suggests a commitment to a form of federalism. However, several other features of the constitution suggest that this federalism was hugely attenuated. The reference to dual polity was made initially by B.R. Ambedkar, the main architect of the constitution. Introducing the draft constitution, he said, 'The proposed Indian Constitution is a dual polity with a single citizenship. There is only one citizenship for the whole of India.... There is no State citizenship.' See, *The Constituent Assembly Debates, Vol. 7*, Official Report, New Delhi: Lok Sabha Secretariat, 1999, p. 34.

of constitutional amendment (Article 368), and assigns a larger share of the revenue and a greater fiscal authority to the centre (Part XII). But even more than this, it has provided a legitimate means, in the form of emergency powers (Articles 352–60), to enable the centre to transform the federal system into a virtually unitary system under three conditions: external aggression or internal disturbance; breakdown of the machinery of law and order; and threat of financial breakdown. There is no right of secession for the states, on the principle that, in Ambekar's words, 'the union is indestructible'. The union also has the authority to create new states, adjust boundaries between states, and generally restructure the Indian union (Articles 2–3). The President's rule in the states, which was declared ninety-five times between 1951 and 1995 (that is, on average, more than twice a year during the last forty years), and the dramatic imposition of a state of national emergency between June 1975 and March 1977, underlined the capacity of the centre to dominate the federal polity.[10]

LINGUISTIC FEDERALISM AND ITS PROBLEMS

When the constitution was inaugurated in 1950, the country was divided into four kinds of states. There were, first, the Part A states: former provinces of British India such as Assam, Bihar, Bombay, Madras, Orissa, Punjab, Uttar Pradesh, and West Bengal. Second, there were Part B states, which were products of the integration of the princely states. These included Hyderabad, Jammu and Kashmir, Mysore, Rajasthan, Saurashtra, Madhya Bharat, and Travancore Cochin. Third, Part C states were either the former Chief Commissioner's provinces or smaller units formed by the integration of princely states. These included Ajmer, Bhopal, Delhi, Himachal Pradesh, Kutch, Manipur, and Tripura. Finally, there was a Part D state, that is, the Andaman and

[10] On 26 June 1975, the President of India, at the request of the Indian Prime Minister, Mrs Indira Gandhi, imposed a national emergency on the ground that there was a grave internal threat to the security of the country. In fact, the move was propelled by a massive opposition to her continuation in office. In 1973–4, food shortages and rising prices had produced violent demonstrations in several Congress-ruled states. In 1974, Jayaprakash Narayan, one-time Congress member, a socialist, and a friend of Nehru, took the leadership of the agitation in the Indian state of Bihar and offered a direct personal challenge to the authoritarian rule of Mrs Gandhi. In June 1975, the Allahabad High Court invalidated the election of Mrs Gandhi on grounds of corrupt practices. A mass mobilization campaign was launched against Mrs Gandhi who responded by arresting all her principal opponents and unleashing a short period of terror.

Nicobar Islands. As is evident, this structure was the result of historical accident rather than the realization of a coherent principle for the organization of territories.

This system of states, based on the absorption of ethnic identities into a larger civic identity and, therefore, on the rejection of every trace of ethno-nationalism, proved inadequate. As Rajni Kothari pointed out, it began to fall apart when, thanks to its democratic nature, it was forced to encounter mass politics.[11] Demands were immediately made by regional and ethnic leaders for autonomy and for the sharing of political power. The issue of linguistic states became the focus of popular agitation. After a massive agitation in 1953, the state of Andhra Pradesh, where a large number of Telugu-speaking people live, was created. This, once again, foregrounded the question of whether the entire structure of states in India should be reorganized on a linguistic basis. In 1954, a States Reorganisation Committee was set up. In the committee, the advocates of linguistic reorganization gave the following reasons in its favour. First, the creation of such states would remove the frustration and anxieties of minorities within the existing heterogeneous regions. Second, by alleviating tensions and fostering internal harmony within regions, national unity would be assisted. Third, a unilingual region would involve less administrative complexity, thereby enhancing administrative efficiency. Fourth, political units with a greater degree of homogeneity would encourage the internal cohesiveness in regions and facilitate a more democratic government.[12]

Following the committee's recommendations, states were reorganized in 1956. Instead of the four-tier structure, there were now only states and union territories. Even so, the linguistic principle was given only partial recognition. It took another mass agitation to divide the province of Bombay into Maharashtra and Gujarat. In 1966, Punjab was reorganized into three units: the core Punjabi suba, the new state of Haryana, and Himachal Pradesh. Several new states have since been carved out in response to popular agitation. These include not only the states of the North-East but more recently, the states of Jharkhand, Chattisgarh, and Uttarakhand. Although the constitution did not

---

[11] Rajni Kothari, 'Integration and Exclusion in Indian Politics', *Economic and Political Weekly*, vol. XXIII, no. 43, 22 October 1988, p. 225.

[12] A.S. Narang, 'India: Ethnicity and Federalism', in B.D. Dua and M.P. Singh (eds), *Indian Federalism in the New Millennium*, New Delhi: Manohar, 2003, pp. 74–5.

originally envisage this, India is now a multi-lingual federation. Each major linguistic group is politically recognized and all are treated as equals.

It is of course true that this political recognition does not cover every large linguistic community. Only languages that had already received official recognition under the British rule, undergone some grammatical standardization and literary development, and had become entrenched in the government schools of a particular region could claim to be dominant. Such a claim, required immense political mobilization. Only linguistic groups who were capable of this mobilization could be granted equal political recognition. The current form of linguistic federalism in India depends, as Paul Brass demonstrates, on four formal and informal rules.[13]

The first rule is that no secessionist demand shall be recognized. The Indian constitution does not give any state the right to secede. Therefore, it can suppress such demands by force. The Indian army has ruthlessly suppressed the secessionist demands of tribal groups in the North-East, and of groups in Assam and Punjab, and continues to be militarily engaged in Kashmir. Whenever a linguistic group has dropped its secessionist demands, however, as the Dravida Munnetra Kazhagam (DMK) did in Tamil Nadu in 1960s, the Government of India has made concessions and even granted statehood to placate leaders of groups previously dubbed secessionist. The second rule is that the state shall not accommodate the religious principle of state organization. It took long for the Indian state to reorganize Punjab along linguistic lines because the creation of a Punjabi-speaking state was widely believed to be merely a cover for a Sikh-majority state. A separate Punjabi-speaking state was acceptable only when the sincerity and loyalty of the leader of the Punjabi suba movement was believed to be entirely unquestionable. The third rule was that the mere existence of a distinct language group shall not be sufficient for the formation of a separate political sub-unit of the federation. It had to find political articulation. Even political articulation was not sufficient, however, if it was limited to the cultural or literary elite. It had to have the backing of popular will. Without democratic legitimacy, no language could be the basis of a new state. Finally, the reorganization of a province was unacceptable if such a demand was made by only one of the important language groups in the

[13] Paul R. Brass, *The Politics of India since Independence*, Cambridge: Cambridge Press, 1990, pp. 172–4.

relevant area. Thus, Madras was reorganized because it had the backing of both Tamil-speaking and Telugu-speaking peoples, but Bombay had to wait a long time before it could be reorganized because it had the support only of the Marathi-speaking people and was not backed by the Gujaratis.

The reorganization of states on the basis of language gave equal recognition and dignity to all the dominant language groups. But how have these states fared in the treatment of their own internal linguistic minorities? There is in effect a hierarchy of official statuses in the languages and mother tongues of India.[14] Hindi and English are the official languages of the union. The various regional languages are the official languages in the linguistically reorganized states. These are also listed in the Eighth Schedule of the Constitution.[15] Finally, there is a third level, consisting of those languages listed in the Eighth Schedule without official status in any state. The Indian constitution gives every linguistic minority the right to maintain its own script and language (Article 30). It also gives it the right to establish and administer educational institutions of its choices (Article 26). Finally, it obliges every state to provide adequate facilities for instruction in the mother tongue at the primary stage of education to children belonging to linguistic minority groups (Article 350A). Thus, any language that is mentioned in the Eighth Schedule is recognized as a minority language in states where other languages are dominant. This gives the speakers of a minority language a right to have schools where the medium of instruction is their mother tongue.

In contrast to the accommodating pluralist politics at the centre, many of the states have pursued discriminatory policies towards their internal minorities. Moreover, the centre has been unable to protect such minorities from the opposition of the concerned state governments. Among the languages that have been disadvantaged are Urdu and other 'mother tongues' of Hindi and other larger languages. The struggle of linguistic minorities in various states has therefore had at least two aims: to enforce Article 350A; and to ensure that their language is listed in the Eighth Schedule. Assimilationists in each of the

[14] On official and dominant state languages, see the Table in Brass, *The Politics of India since Independence*, p. 176.
[15] The various Schedules, twelve in all, each of which is attached and relevant to specific Articles of the Constitution, are to be found at the end of the Indian constitution. Eighteen languages are currently listed in the Eighth Schedule of the Constitution.

states have tried to deny linguistic minorities these rights. Urdu has faced discriminatory policies in both Uttar Pradesh (UP) and Bihar which has contributed to a severe decline in its use as a medium of communication in northern India. Only one in four Urdu speakers in UP receives instruction in Urdu. Similarly, there is a proportionate decline in the number of newspapers in Urdu. The central government has been unable to intervene effectively in this matter. In Assam, there has been an alternate domination over time. To begin with, Bengalis tried to deny the separateness of Assamese. Later, when Assamese was recognized as a separate language, and the Assamese took control of the state government, they began to discriminate against Bengali-speaking people. Generally, even languages listed in the Eighth Schedule confront difficulties outside their own homelands. The governments of Punjab and Haryana, for example, do not admit that there are linguistic minorities in their respective regions.

Nonetheless, it would not be unfair to say that the democratic and linguistic federalism of India has managed to combine claims to unity with claims to cultural recognition. No doubt citizen alienation exists, but this is not due to the repression of cultural identities. A fairly robust political arena exists that allows for the play of multiple identities that complement one another. However, I do not claim that the linguistic reorganization of states has been an unqualified success. I have already noted that minority language speakers are discriminated against by the dominant language speakers in several states. A more serious problem, however, is persistently present in parts of India along the border. Many of these such as Punjab, Kashmir, and the North-East have been wrecked by secessionist movements.[16] Here, the crisis of federalism is acute and has resulted in bitter, sustained, and violent confrontations between those who claim that their secessionist movement is legitimate, and the Indian army and national para-military forces. As usual, the heaviest price for this volatile and violent situation has been, and is being, paid by ordinary people, and by the poorest of the poor.

Punjab

Religious differences had always played a crucial role in political mobilization in Punjab, which witnessed partition on religious grounds. Western Punjab, with a Muslim majority, was incorporated into Pakistan. Religion and politics could not be separated here because the formation

---

[16] On the crises of linguistic federalism, see Brass, *The Politics of India since Independence*, pp. 192–227.

of Sikhs as a distinct religious community was itself the product of a political movement. After India's partition, the Sikh demand for a separate Punjabi suba was not immediately met. Punjab was not only denied a special status in India but was not even reorganized along religious lines, as desired by sections of the Sikh elite. Furthermore, even after the demand for a Punjabi suba was finally met in 1966, several outstanding issues between Punjab and its neighbouring states remained unresolved. For example, Chandigarh remained the capital of both Punjab and Haryana. Similarly, there has been a recurrent dispute over river waters between these two states.

On their own, however, these regional and religious factors do not explain the resurgence of a secessionist movement in Punjab. The 'green revolution' of the 1960s had created a new class of rich middle-class peasants. Sections of this group felt that Punjab's contribution to the rest of the country was incommensurate with the costs that it had to pay. In their view, the centre did not reciprocate the benefits bestowed on the rest of the country by Punjab. The privileged sections in Punjab, therefore, began to feel at a disadvantage and their allegiance to the very idea of India weakened. Matters got worse when profits in agriculture began to decline. Unemployed and angry youths then began to turn to militancy, directed against the centre. A new, soured form of religious nationalism began to take shape.

A wiser leadership at the centre might have helped to diffuse the crisis. But by this time, the Congress party had weakened. As often happens when a party starts to lose its hold on power, the Congress party began to use all kinds of unfair methods to enhance its power in states such as Punjab. Under Mrs Indira Gandhi, unlike under Nehru who played the role of mediator and was reluctant to intervene in state politics, the Congress party played a deceitful and manipulative role against strong opposition parties in order to prop up its own local leaders, or politicians who could be made subservient to it.[17] Over time, the Sikh leadership lost trust in the party at the centre. This led to the deterioration of relations between Punjab and the rest of the country. The political situation in Punjab has improved now, but only after a long and violent struggle that took the lives of several thousand innocent people and several politicians, including that of Mrs Gandhi herself.

[17] Ibid., pp. 193–201.

The North-East[18]

Problems in Assam result from the intersection of different kinds of ethnic confrontations. These involve Hindus and Muslims, Assamese and Bengalis, plains people and tribal hill people, plains tribals and non-tribals and the indigenous population, and a large migrant population. Most of these problems centre, however, around the demands of the tribal people who fiercely rejected an Indian identity.

Secessionists movements in the North-Eastern tribal areas were based not only on their cultural distinctiveness—in many cases, both language and religion are different from mainstream Indian languages and religions—but also because of the initial failure to grant self-government rights to these regions. The Nagas rebelled because the Assam government violated an agreement with the Naga National Council to recognize it as the principal political and administrative force in the Naga Hill district. The Mizos were victimized when the Assam government failed to given them adequate relief after a famine in the late 1950s. As noted earlier, the policy of the government in the Nehru period was to suppress forces of secession and to encourage and negotiate with moderate non-secessionist leaders. Thus, it was by adopting a conciliatory attitude to the moderates among the Nagas that the state of Nagaland was formed in 1960 and Mizoram was formed into a union territory in 1971.[19]

These moves were unlikely, however, to put an end to all insurgent activities, and secessionists problems were also faced by Mrs Gandhi. As already indicated, her policies were different from that of her father's. Instead of isolating the extremists, she hobnobbed with them. This was part of a calculated, interventionist strategy of loosening the hold of moderate regional leaders and bolstering the leadership of Mrs Gandhi's own, much weakened, Congress party. The all important

[18] On the North-East, see Sanjib Baruah, *India Against Itself: Assam and the Politics of Nationality*, New Delhi: Oxford University Press, 2001; Hiren Gohain, 'Bodo Stir in Perspective', *Economic and Political Weekly*, vol. XXIV, no. 25, 24 June 1989, pp. 1377–9; and Monirul Hussain, 'Tribal Question in Assam', *Economic and Political Weekly*, vol. XXVII, nos 20 and 21, 16–23 May 1992, pp. 1047–50.

[19] The union territories are centrally administered, unlike states which have substantial autonomy. Initially, only Part D states such as Andaman and Nicobar Islands were deemed a union territory. Later, others were added, such as Delhi and Pondicherry. Many territories such as Manipur and Tripura began as union territories but later became states.

demarcating line between party and state was continuously blurred by Mrs Gandhi. This was always a dangerous policy, because it undermined the relatively impartial and mediatory role of the central government and strengthened militancy in these regions. Though Mizoram was finally granted statehood in 1987, low-intensity confrontation between militants and government forces continues in the North-East and a system of dual loyalty has yet to develop fully in this region.

Kashmir[20]

The Kashmir problem is especially intractable. In British India, Kashmir was a semi-autonomous princely state. The conflict between India and Pakistan over Kashmir arose because, though the population of the state is predominantly Muslim, its ruler was Hindu. While he dilly-dallied on accession to India or Pakistan, the Pakistan forces marched towards the state capital of Srinagar in 1948. This precipitated its formal accession to India. However, Kashmir was informally partitioned, with a small portion of it going to Pakistan, while the larger portion, consisting of three distinct cultural constituents, the Kashmir Valley, Jammu, and Ladakh, remained with India.

Kashmir is important in Indian politics for two reasons. First, Kashmir has remained a litmus test for India's secular nationalism and perhaps even for its linguistic federalism. If India's contestation of the two-nation theory is correct, then Kashmir remains integral to India.[21] On the other hand, if the two-nation theory is valid, then Kashmir belongs to Pakistan. While there is some truth in this argument, it does not fully take into account Kashmir's own understanding of its position, which is based on Article 370 of the Indian constitution. According to this self-understanding, Kashmir remains, in important ways, unique and therefore, deserves a special status within the Indian union. If this

[20] On Kashmir, see Navnita Chadha Behera, *State, Identity and Violence: Jammu, Kashmir and Ladakh*, New Delhi: Manohar, 2000; Sumit Ganguly, *The Crisis in Kashmir: Portents of War, Hopes of Peace*, Cambridge: Cambridge University Press, 1999; and Balraj Puri, *Kashmir Towards Insurgency*, New Delhi: Orient Longman, 1993.

[21] In the early 1940s, the Muslim League launched the theory that Hindus and Muslims were two nations and therefore, according to the nationalist principle, should have a separate state of their own. This was called the two-nation theory. This theory was vehemently opposed by the INC, which argued that religion was irrelevant to nationality and citizenship and that the Indian nation was composed of one people regardless of religious affiliation.

special status is not possible, then it deserves its own separate state. The Kashmiris have always believed that they are a distinct society or nation. Its Muslim-majority character is an important factor here, as long as we remember that Kashmiri Islam is different from that found elsewhere, on the sub-continent. Kashmir has always been a test case, therefore, of India's linguistic federalism and, in particular, of how asymmetrical it can be. This asymmetricity has always been contested by homogenizing forces that are opposed to any kind of autonomy for the people of Kashmir.

Following Paul Brass, I have written earlier on the strength of Nehru's accommodative politics, which had the potential of solving almost any crisis generated within India's linguistic federalism. However, Kashmir remains a blot on Nehru's politics. There are many explanations for Nehru's failure. The one I wish to emphasize is that, in Nehru's world view, while civic nationalism in the Indian context could be made congruent with linguistically grounded ethnic sub-nationalism, it could never fall in line with religiously grounded sub-nationalism. This made people like Nehru suspicious even of those who did not explicitly ground their politics in religion. Nehru was suspicious not only of Sikh politics, within which religion and language overlapped, but also of the politics of Kashmiris like Sheikh Abdullah. When Abdullah imagined a politics of genuine regional autonomy, different from that envisaged by those who wanted it incorporated into either Pakistan or India, he was never entirely able to convince Nehru of his sincerity. This was due partly to the inter-penetration of religion and language in Kashmir, particularly in the case of its Muslim majority. When Muslim Kashmiris acted with an independent spirit, or spoke with an independence of mind, their Muslimness remained a source of suspicion even for secular-minded people such as Nehru. Perhaps this was due to his experience of the Muslim League, which demanded the separate state of Pakistan. Whatever the case, unless Kashmiri Muslims acted with a substantial degree of subservience towards the central government, their loyalty remained questionable. Kashmiri Muslims had to prove their loyalty to India by being anti-Pakistan.

It was this anxiety and insecurity which made even Nehru adopt an overly interventionist *real politik* in Kashmir. Sadly, the more he followed this approach, the more alienated the Kashmiri people became. After Nehru, the government at the centre treated the state government of Kashmir as its own fiefdom. A vast supply of patronage was made personally available to politicians who monotonously asserted the finality of Kashmir's accession to India. Over time, such governments were thoroughly discredited in the eyes of the Kashmiri people, particularly its youth, who responded to the demands of militants partly because they were constantly ridiculed for being timid and feminine. The more people said that Kashmiris were incapable of revolt, the more the youth turn to insurgency. Once an insurgency started, an attempt was made to suppress it violently and with this, the alienation of Kashmiris from India was nearly complete.

Two points emerge from this discussion of the problems of linguistic federalism in India. First, whenever a hitherto dominant political party begins to lose its grip and becomes anxious and insecure about its own future, it gives up the very principles that brought it success in the past. As long as the Congress party enjoyed dominance throughout India, it was able to keep firm the distinction between the party and the state, remain relatively impartial in inter- or intra-state disputes, and adopt a conciliatory stance towards those ethnic communities that used democratic procedures to demand greater autonomy for themselves. But once it lost its dominance, it blurred the distinction between party and state, took a blatantly partisan stance in troubled states, and, if it helped its own self-interest, did not hesitate or demure to bolster even extremists. This unprincipled, manipulative, and interventionist politics of the parties in power has been a major cause of the eruption of violent ethnic conflicts and the crisis of linguistic federalism in India. The failure to abide by basic principles of constitutional democracy remains, in my view, one of the principal reasons of the crisis of Indian federalism.

A second reason has to do with the intransigent nature of any politics in the sub-continent that is grounded in religion. The roots of this intransigence go back to the formation of extremist Muslim and Hindu political parties that eventually led to the partition of the country. Suspicion about religiously grounded nationalism and sub-nationalism made it impossible for the framers of the constitution even to consider the possibility of a deeper asymmetry in constitutional arrangements. Could the country have evolved a constitution with a secular state in a multi-religious society, one that organized some states on the basis of language and others on the basis of religion? A federal state with its constituent sub-units organized wholly along religious lines was unacceptable to the leaders of the national movement. In their political imagination, the furthest one could go was to give political recognition to linguistic communities. My own view is that these leaders were right, and that the intransigent nature of politicized religions made it impossible for democratic federations in the sub-continent to be organized along religious lines. If the fire is extinguished from the belly of these religions, and if religion genuinely becomes a mere marker of the separate but complimentary identities of people, then, I suppose, we could have asymmetric federations in a deeper sense. However, that is not the case for the moment and therefore, the real test of Indian federalism remains dependent on what happens in Punjab, the North-East, and especially, in Kashmir.

The Hindu nationalist party has not undermined the character of Indian federalism, although we might have expected it to do so. However, it has consistently opposed Article 370 in Kashmir, has blamed Christianity for the secessionist demand in the North-East, and has frequently refused to accept that Sikhs are separate from Hindus. And yet, the logic of power continues to take them in a direction more federal than was ever achieved by the Congress party in the post-Nehruvian era. Such is the cunning of Reason in the sub-continent!

THE DISTINCTIVENESS OF INDIAN FEDERALISM

Let me begin with a set of distinctions that help to identify the character of the Indian state and the nature of its federalism. First, there is the obvious distinction between a unitary and a federal state. A federal state is one where 'some matters are exclusively within the competence of certain local units—states or provinces—and are constitutionally beyond the scope of the authority of the national government; and where certain other matters are constitutionally outside the scope of the authority of the smaller units'.[22] If so, a unitary state is one where all matters are within the competence and authority of one, national government. A federal state with a unitary bias is one where some matters are within the competence of local units and others are under the authority of a national government, but with two qualifications. First, matters within the scope of the national government are far greater in quantity or significance than those that fall within the scope of local governments. Second, there may be too many contexts where national governments may intervene in the affairs of local governments. Thus, a federal state with a unitary bias is one where, of the two levels of governments, the national government is stronger than local governments.

[22] Robert A. Dahl, 'Federalism and the Democratic Process', in R.A. Dahl (ed.), *Democracy, Identity and Equality*, Oslo: Norwegian University Press, 1986, p. 114.

Another distinction may be drawn between strongly nested and weakly nested federations. In strongly nested federations, the centre and the state work in close cooperation with one another and the centre, apart from executing tasks assigned exclusively to it, frequently facilitates the functioning of the states. In weakly nested federations, the two governments perform there own separate functions but do not depend on one another for the tasks assigned exclusively to each. The USA is usually thought to be an example of such a federation.

A third distinction may be drawn between purely functional federations, that is, federations evolved purely for the sake of more efficient, or perhaps more democratic, governance, and multi-cultural, multi-ethnic, or multi-national federations that have evolved also to meet the identity-related aspirations of the demos. Purely functional federations presuppose mono-cultural societies. Such mono-culturalism may be of two kinds. The homogeneity in culture may exist because the public culture of these societies has transcended or side-stepped religion, language, or any other ethnic factor. Such a society may be called a civic national society. The US is an example of a functional, mono-cultural federation. It may also exist because these societies are grounded exclusively in one religion, language, or any other ethnic factor. Militant Hindu nationalists in India believe that Indian federalism presupposes, or can work only on the basis of, a religiously grounded idea of a single nation.

On the basis of these distinctions, we can have different kinds of states along a unitary–federal continuum. To begin with, there exist unitary states in mono-cultural societies of the civic or the ethnic variety. Then we have federal states with a unitary bias, which may be strongly or weakly nested, whether purely functional or not, and which may exist in mono-cultural or multi-cultural societies. We may also have genuinely federal states, purely functional or not, and weakly or strongly nested in mono-cultural societies. Finally, we can have genuinely federal states in multi-cultural societies that are not purely functional but which may or may not be strongly nested. According to the theoretical self-understanding of American federalism (but not, of course, to political reality), the USA is a weakly nested, functional federal state, in a mono-cultural civic national society. India began as a federal state with a unitary bias that purported to be functional but was strongly nested. It has increasingly shed its unitary bias, has not been purely functional (at least since 1956), and has remained strongly nested.

Next, I want to make two points about the familiar western/non-western dichotomy, as it applies to the discussion of federalism. First, it is true that modernity originated in the West. It is equally true that it has migrated to non-western societies. Together, these two facts throw up three possibilities. First, modernity may have failed to take root in non-modern cultural systems because these were deeply resilient to change and were, therefore, not easily displaceable. Second, modernity may have quite easily found a safe niche in these societies. Perhaps a powerless people, entirely lacking in self-confidence, quickly lapped up anything new that came their way. They converted to a modern way of life by blind emulation or sheer seduction, or perhaps for purely instrumental reasons. But a third possibility also exists. When western modernity began to interact with local cultural systems, something like a hybrid culture may have begun to emerge, possibly by creative adaptation, for which an analog can be found neither in western modernity nor in indigenous tradition. I believe, any non-western social formation has responded to western modernity in each of these three ways. There is a layer of a largely unaffected, non-modern system of practices, as well as a layer of a thoroughly westernized, modern system. But, in addition, there is a distinct layer of 'local modernity'.

If this argument is correct, it is important for people in non-western societies to avoid a pattern of thinking which is encouraged by the irritatingly dichotomous grid that divides the social world into two halves, the western/modern and the indigenous/traditional. For those who accept this grid, if something is modern, it must be western. Similarly, for something to be part of the culture of a non-western society, it must be entirely homegrown. For example, one may believe that, because it is a modern, democratic idea, federalism must be western. And because it is western, it must be derived from a particular western source. For example, the great exemplar of democratic federalism is the USA and therefore, federalism anywhere must be seen through the prism of the experience of the USA. Such a view is mistaken, for it misses the simple point that something can be at once non-western and modern. Something which started out as western can be transformed in responding to the specific problems of non-western societies and by being nurtured in local context. It can become distinctively different, both from its western counterpart and from anything found within indigenous traditions—a point made already in relation to secularism in this book.

My second point follows from this and has already been made in relation to Indian secularism. It is not uncommon to find the failures of scholars and practitioners to recognize a change in the meaning of terms such as federalism. Federalism in India means something different from what it means elsewhere. This is simply because like secularism, federalism too has evolved differently in societies with a different cultural background.[23] The deep diversity of India and the absence of strong, centralized political structure has made a profound difference to the kind of federalism developed and needed in India.

With this, I come to the five features which I consider distinctive of Indian federalism.[24] First, the distinctive historical pattern of its emergence; second, its cooperative nature; third, its asymmetrical character; fourth, its demos-enabling character; and fifth, its context-sensitivity, particularly its relationship with contextual moral and political reasoning. The framers of the constitution were confident that Indian federalism would be different from others. India had unique problems, they believed, problems that had not confronted other federations in history. Although they drew on existing federations, they did not hesitate to modify them to suit the 'genius' of the nation. Thus, the constituent assembly produced a new kind of federation to meet India's peculiar needs.

First, the historical and political logic of the emergence of federalism in India is vastly different from the manner in which federalism developed in America. In both the USA and Switzerland, polities with strong identities and substantial sovereignty came together to mitigate commonly perceived external threats. On this account of the federal bargain, even the smaller and weaker constituent units of the federation are able to maintain their identity and sovereignty because the bigger and stronger members are willing to pay a price for improving their own security. In India, however, as Mohit Bhattacharya points out, the background conditions for such a bargain had ceased to exist by the time the federation was formed.[25] India was already partitioned and most

[23] On the Indian contribution to the development of secularism, see the next chapter.

[24] A. Stepan's work on federalism has helped me identify two, if not three of these. See Alfred Stepan, *Arguing Comparative Politics*, Oxford: Oxford University Press, 2001, pp. 315–61.

[25] Mohit Bhattacharya, 'The Mind of the Founding Fathers', in Nirmal Mukarji and Balveer Arora (eds), *Federalism in India: Origins and Development*, New Delhi: Vikas Publishing House, 1992, pp. 81–102, esp., pp. 101–2.

of the 568 princely states had already acceded to the Indian union. Most of the units had therefore ceased to possess the strong bargaining power of units typical of the American case. Yet, some kind of a federation was envisaged with the objective of holding the union together. Thus, old provinces of the colonial period, with parts of princely states that merged with them, were reborn as constituent states in a new federal set-up arranged along ethno-linguistic lines. The pattern and sequencing of the emergence of federalism in India is perceptibly different from the one characterizing the USA. This ought to have been expected but has not always been noted.

Second, the framers of the constitution embraced what later came to be called 'cooperative' federation. The general tendency in the self-understanding of the federalism of the USA is to build walls separating the independent jurisdictions of distinct authorities, such as the church and the state or the central and regional governments, so that they are independent of each other and are able to perform their functions without reference to the other within their respective spheres. The assumption is of a zero-sum game: more power for one means less power for the other. The idea of cooperative federation is different. Both governments can have 'more'.[26] Moreover, the constitution could be federal or unitary according to the requirements of the situation.[27]

Third, despite the unitary bias of the Indian constitution, there are important constitutionally embedded differences between the legal status and prerogatives of different sub-units within the same federation. Unlike the constitutional symmetry of American federalism, Indian federalism has been constitutionally asymmetric. In a sense then, just as, in some respects, India is less federal than the USA, in other respects it is more federal. To meet the specific needs and requirements of some sub-units, it was always part of the original design to have a unique relationship with them or to give them special status. For example, the accession of Jammu and Kashmir to the Indian union was based on a commitment to safeguard its autonomy under Article 370 of the constitution. This is the only state that is governed by its own constitution. Similarly, under Article 371A, the privilege of special status was also accorded to the North-Eastern state of Nagaland. This article not only confers validity on pre-existing laws within Nagaland but also protects

[26] This happens because some subjects are on a concurrent list and, therefore, decisions about them are taken both at the state and the federal level.

[27] See Austin, *The Indian Constitution*, pp. 318–19.

local identity through restrictions on immigration. Naga customary law can be modified, and resources and land transferred to non-Nagas, only with the approval of the Naga legislature. The Nagas are also accorded preferential financial treatment. After the accession of Sikkim to the Indian union, such special status was also extended to Sikkim. Special provisions have also been enacted for Mizoram. Goa, Maharashtra, and Gujarat are also beneficiaries of some of the provisions of Article 371.[28] According to the Indian constitution, then, there is nothing invidious about this differential treatment.

Fourth, the Indian constitution treats various states unequally in another respect. The states are unequally represented, on the basis of their populations, in the Lok Sabha and the Rajya Sabha and in the matter of indirect election to the Presidency. As is well known, all federations have a legislative chamber that represents the specific territories of the constituent sub-units (usually the upper house) and one legislative chamber that represents the people as a whole (usually the lower house). The whole point of the upper house is that it is meant to attend to issues of special relevance to the sub-units. In the USA, all states are represented equally in the upper house, which is to say that states with small populations are hugely over-represented. For example, both Wyoming, the state with the smallest population in the USA, and California, the state with the largest population, have the same number of senate seats, that is, two. Thus, one vote in Wyoming is worth sixty-six votes in California. This is not the case with India, where the size of a state's population is a relevant factor in the number of seats it has in the upper and the lower chambers. States with relatively small populations, therefore, cannot totally block the democratic concerns of states with relatively larger populations. This makes Indian federalism one of the most demos-enabling in the world. The demos can be severely constrained if legislators representing say 10 per cent of the electorate were able to thwart the wishes of the majority. This cannot happen in India.

There is another form of asymmetry that the Indian constitution did not recognize, although discussion of the federal structure of the polity did open up its possibility. This is a form of asymmetry which is not just about different legal provisions but about the organizing principle of

[28] Rajeev Dhavan and Geetanjali Goel, 'Indian Federalism and its Discontents: A Review', in Gert W. Kueck, Sudhir Chandra Mathur, and Klaus Schindler (eds), *Federalism and Decentralisation: Centre-State Relations in India and Germany*, New Delhi: Vedam Books, 1998, pp. 43–85.

the federation itself. The form of asymmetry that is currently acceptable does not question that there is just one basis—language—on which the constituent units of the federation are formed. The boundaries of states are determined roughly in accordance with the location of speakers of the dominant language in different parts of the country. Thus, all states are symmetrical in the sense that they are grounded in a single, uniform principle, while asymmetry results from the varying needs of different linguistic units. But another possible form of asymmetry could arise from variation in the grounding principle itself. Here, the bases on which the sub-units of the federation were formed would be different. Some boundaries could be drawn, for example, on the basis of language, while others could be drawn on the basis of religion. Could the partition of India have been avoided if the main political protagonists had accepted such a plural foundation for state organization? The framers of the constitution did not think so. But it remains a question worth asking. Is it possible that in societies with multiple pluralities that go very deep, people may still be able to live together if political recognition is given to different grounding principles of the constituent units of a federation?

This brings me to the fifth distinguishing feature of Indian federalism; indeed, of Indian political culture more generally. Political thinking in India is marked by a high degree of contextual reasoning and therefore shuns rigidity. A remarkable degree of flexibility and pragmatism is built into several institutional designs in the Indian polity. Politics in India has rarely been a field for the implementation of single principles, and this is how it should be. In politics, one should not try to apply a principle. Rather one should act while keeping principles in mind. Very occasionally, our actions may realize them fully. Sometimes they may partially embody them. But, one must recognize that there are occasions when our acts are unable to realize them at all. This way of conceiving the relationship between political thinking and practice differs from a dichotomous way of thinking, according to which one either acts by implementing principles perfectly or by completely disregarding them. It also recognizes that occasionally, in the very process of taking action, our principles are themselves modified or even transformed.

A context-sensitive conception of federalism encourages accommodation—not the giving up of one value for the sake of another but rather their reconciliation and possible harmonization. This accommodation may be accomplished in at least two ways: by placing values at different levels; and by seeing them, not as belonging to water-tight compartments but as sufficiently separate so that an attempt can be made to recognize a value within its own sphere, without frontally conflicting with another value operating in a different sphere.[29] This way of thinking, which is at once ethical and contextual, is at the heart of the development of the idea of federalism anywhere. But, nowhere else is it as clearly manifest as in India. It was certainly at the heart of deliberations of the constituent assembly that resulted in a constitution that appeared both federal and unitary.[30] It was this fruitful ambiguity that paved the way for the deepening of Indian democracy via linguistic federalism.

* * *

I have argued that British India began with a strong legacy of centralization. The requirements of the anti-colonial mass movement were such that the Congress not only had to organize itself as a federal party and mobilize federally but also had to demand a federal polity. Such a polity had to be not just 'a confused mosaic created by a foreign imperial power unmindful of the valid basis for the territorial organization of the sub-continent',[31] but had to be organized on a basis that met the aspirations of a diverse people. The unprecedented mobilization along religious lines, however, particularly by the increasingly separatist Muslim League, which eventually led to the partition of the country, caused acute anxiety amongst the national leaders who had developed, by then, a unitary mindset. But, with democratization, a country of the size of India simply had to divide itself into political units along linguistic lines, which it had eventually done by 1956.

The linguistic reorganization of states, however, could only work if the polity followed certain rules. The most important rule was that regional demands of autonomy were to be sympathetically treated, as long as they were not violent. A non-manipulative negotiation and deliberation was believed to be the most appropriate response to the legitimate demands of regions with a distinct culture and language. With this model of contextual moral reasoning, the politicians sought to accommodate the needs of one region, the aspirations of

[29] Austin, *The Indian Constitution*, pp. 308–25.

[30] The constituent assembly was set up in December 1946, to draft the constitution of independent India. It completed its work in December 1949, and the new constitution was implemented when India was declared a Republic on 26 January 1950. Between 15 August 1947 and 26 January 1950, the constituent assembly became a provisional Parliament.

[31] Khan, *Federal India*, p. 39.

neighbouring regions, and the good of the whole country. Linguistic federalism succeeded as long as this principle was followed. Problems occurred as soon as an insecure government at the centre began to deal with regional aspirations in a ham-fisted, manipulative, and self-seeking manner.

I have also argued that, over time and despite all its problems, India has developed a distinctive form of federalism which should be compared to other federalisms, not with the aim of finding out where it is falling short of a western standard, but rather to identify those features that broaden our very conception of federalism. Indian federalism today is not just of the 'holding together' variety but rather has come to possess features of the 'coming together' form of federalism. This shows that regional parties are becoming stronger not only in the regions but also at the centre. A stable centre has begun to emerge, not by force but by the consent and participation of regional groups that, at another level, are also self-governing. Indian federalism has also attempted to remove its own rigidities by incorporating asymmetries in the distribution of power between the centre and different states. What lessons might there be here for Other parts of the world which need federalism but are uncomfortable with it? This is a difficult question to answer, and one that lies well beyond my own competence. But, I believe that three very general lessons can be drawn from the Indian experience that might be relevant to the future of federalism in Other parts of the world.

First, every country, in responding to its own demands and needs, and nourished by its own traditions, will over time develop its own distinct form of federal structure. Comparisons with other cases are in order, but only to illuminate the specificity of the particular case in question, rather than to judge whether it measures up to a yardstick derived from elsewhere. The federal structure of any polity may have lessons to learn from other federations, but it must ultimately be evaluated by standards which are partly shaped by the tradition and experience of that polity. Second, federalism is part of a larger democratic process. The very raison d'etre of federation is to grant political recognition to a distinct people who, roughly speaking, are culturally similar and, to some extent, wish to govern themselves. Inter-group equality and self-governance are the two values underlying federalism. This means that federalism must be seen as a constitutional and democratic practice with which to check any form of cultural or ethnic domination. Federalism will not survive in a polity where one community is bent upon dominating others. Conversely, when they work well, federal institutions check the majoritarian and hegemonizing potential of any one community within the polity.

However, a federal structure is not just an aggregation of federated political units. The whole is more than the sum of its parts. There is an irreducible federal level and therefore, an urgent need to work out an appropriate working relationship between the federal centre and the states. The Indian experience shows that whenever the centre has been non-manipulative, has treated politicians and people of regional states with respect—indeed, whenever regions identify with the centre and genuinely participate in governance at the federal level—the entire polity works smoothly and peacefully. On the other hand, whenever norms of democratic functioning are abandoned and regions are treated with disrespect, then powerful, even violent, forces have been unleashed, leading to grave instability and causing even greater harm to the general well-being of Indian society. In short, the second lesson to be drawn is that democratic functioning, and an accommodating spirit towards multiple communities and their multiple values, is the only way to make a federal system successful.

Finally, it must be recognized that, even within the same polity, different communities have different, sometimes distinct, needs. If so, the federal government cannot blindly treat them in the same manner. If the value of equality is at the heart of federalism, and if treating each region as an equal is at the heart of federal equality, then in some contexts, different regions may have to be treated differently. In a diverse society with different levels of economic development and variable historical traditions, asymmetrical treatment is the only way of realizing an appropriately interpreted equality. The demand that there be symmetrical treatment of all states, as made by those in India who oppose Article 370, can only lead to injustice and eventually, to resistance against it. Federalism in other parts of the world must also discover its own legitimate asymmetries, because in most societies, it is rare to find symmetrical federalism realizing justice.

3

Indian Secularism

An Alternative, Trans-cultural Ideal*

It is frequently argued that secularism in India is in crisis. However, an ambiguity lying at the very heart of this claim has not altogether been dispelled: is the crisis due, primarily, to external factors as when a good thing is undermined by forces always inimical to it, when it falls into incapable or wrong hands, when it is practised badly? Or, is it rather that the blemished practice is itself an effect of a deeper conceptual flaw, a bad case of a wrong-footed ideal? Madan, Nandy, and Chatterjee have all argued that the external threat to secularism is only a symptom of a deeper internal crisis.[1] Secularism, in their view, has long faced an internal threat in the sense that the conceptual and normative structure of secularism is itself terribly flawed. In different ways, each argues that secularism is linked to a flawed modernization, to a mistaken view of rationality, to an impractical demand that religion be eliminated from public life, to an insufficient appreciation of the importance of

* This paper was first presented at the Political Theory Colloquium, a series of seminars run by Will Kymlicka, John Mcguire, and Margaret Moore at Queens University, Kingston, February 2004. It was subsequently published as 'The Distinctiveness of Indian Secularism', in T.N. Srinivasan (ed.), *The Future of Secularism*, New Delhi: Oxford University Press, 2007, pp. 20–53.

[1] T.N. Madan, 'Secularism in its Place', in Rajeev Bhargava (ed.), *Secularism and Its Critics*, New Delhi: Oxford University Press, 1998, pp. 297–320; Ashis Nandy, 'The Politics of Secularism and the Recovery of Religious Toleration', in Bhargava (ed.), *Secularism and Its Critics*, pp. 321–44; Partha Chatterjee, 'Secularism and Tolerance', in Bhargava (ed.), *Secularism and Its Critics*, pp. 345–79.

communities in the life of people, and a wholly exaggerated sense of the positive character of the modern state. In what follows, I try to argue against this view. I do not wholly dispute their claims about modernity, nation-state, or rationality and the importance of religion and community—in limited but significant ways their critique is valid. But I disagree both with the general implications of their claim as well with their understanding of Indian secularism as necessarily tied to a flawed modernist project. In particular, I contend that these critics fail to see that India developed a distinctively Indian and differently modern variant of secularism.

Ideals are rarely, if ever, and never simply, transplanted from one cultural context to another. They invariably adapt, sometimes so creatively to suit their new habitat that they seem unrecognizable. This is exactly what happened to secularism in India. Indian critics of secularism neither fully grasp the general conceptual structure of secularism nor properly understand its distinctive Indian variant. Indian secularism did not erect a strict wall of separation, but proposed instead a 'principled distance' between religion and state. Moreover, by balancing the claims of individuals and religious communities, it never intended a bludgeoning privatization of religion. It also embodies a model of contextual moral reasoning. All these features that combine to form what I call contextual secularism remain screened off from the understanding of these critics.

Though I do not agree with these critics that the conceptual and normative structure of secularism is flawed, I do agree that it faces an internal threat. However, I have a different understanding of the nature of this threat. Isaiah Berlin has reminded us that the history of ideas is replete with great liberating ideas slowly turning into suffocating straightjackets. One reason for this is that we forget that they need continual interpretation: no idea can flourish without its defenders finding better and better ways of articulating and formulating them. An idea faces an internal threat when its supporters, out of *akrasia*, wilful or unwitting neglect, ignorance, confusion, or delusion cease to care for it, or when its own proponents mistakenly turn against it. I have no reason to doubt secularism is threatened by forces fiercely opposed to it. But, my focus in this essay is on the internal threats to secularism. The principal contention of my essay is that one such internal threat is the failure to realize the distinctive character of Indian secularism.

THREE PRELIMINARY POINTS

I cannot proceed further without making three preliminary points. The first is a clarification. The term 'distinctive' used in the earlier paragraph may lead one to expect that I will unravel something startlingly uncommon about Indian secularism. If I believed so, I would have used the term 'unique'. I have not. This is because of my belief that, by now, the elementary formal constituents of secularism are the same throughout the world. Broadly speaking, secularism, anywhere in the world, means a separation of organized religion from organized political power, inspired by a specific set of values. Just as without separation there is no secularism, just so a value-less separation does not add up to secularism. In this sense, secularism is a universal normative doctrine. But, it does not follow that these elements are interpreted or related to each other in any one particular way, or that there is a single ideal way in which they should be interpreted or related to one another. Many ways exist of interpreting these elements, as do different ways of relating them. Each conception of secularism may unpack the metaphor of separation differently or select different elements from the stock of values that give separation its point. It may also place different weights on the same values. So, when I talk about the distinctiveness of Indian secularism, I do not imply that it has a unique conceptual structure. I only mean that embedded in it is a specific and interestingly different way of interpreting and relating the basic constituents of secularism. Indeed, this is why the distinctive character of Indian secularism does not make it non-universalizable. Indian secularism has trans-cultural potential.

My second point concerns a mistake not uncommon among those who write and think about contemporary secularism. They unwittingly assume that it is a doctrine with a fixed content. Frequently, it is wholly identified with one of its several current interpretations, as if that is the only one available. It is also believed to be timeless, as if it has always existed in the same form. But, it does not take much to realize that secularism has multiple interpretations which change over time. All living systems of beliefs evolve and therefore, have a history. Secularism too has a history made at one time largely by Europeans, then a little later by North Americans, and much later by non-western countries. Non-western societies inherited from their western counterparts specific versions of secularism, but they did not always preserve them in the form in which they were received. They often added something of enduring value to them and, therefore, developed the idea further.

Western theorists of secularism do not always recognize this non-western contribution. It may have been earlier adequate for western scholars to focus exclusively on that part of the history of secularism which was made in and by the West. But, today, it would be a gross mistake to identify western variants of secularism with the entire doctrine, if the part was viewed as the whole. For a rich, complex, and complete understanding of secularism, one must examine how the secular idea has developed over time trans-nationally.

There are other reasons why we must attend to the histories of secularism. The current crisis of secularism must compel one to ask why we need it at all. After all, one rarely mourns the loss of a useless thing. But, it breaks one's heart to see a valuable thing decay. In such transitional moments, when a thing is born, is dying, or in crisis, evaluative judgements become especially urgent and it is crucial to get them right. However, when a thing is in good health, when it is working well and effectively, such judgements appear to be redundant. In these periods of the stability and well-being of an entity, we bother little about its value and purpose. As it is taken for granted, its purpose recedes into the background.[2] Over time, its underlying point may even be forgotten. This may happen with material things as well as with institutions, ideas, and doctrines. Now, something like this appears to also have happened to secularism. As it began to work well, its beneficiaries took it for granted, stopped showing interest in foregrounding its purpose, and eventually lost sight of it. This forgetting was not troublesome or threatening as long as there existed no serious challenge to secularism. But, when a searching, discomforting scrutiny of it commenced, this forgetfulness became a nerve-wrecking handicap. It is bad enough to let a rich and complex idea be reduced to a dead and monotonously repeated formula, but to know that an ideal is valuable and yet be groping in the dark about what precisely makes it worthwhile is deeply frustrating and debilitating. There is a pressing need to remember and retrieve the value-content of secularism.

But why must this be done with the help of a historical account? This necessity arises because at some remote point in the past, say at the time of its birth, the idea had to prove its worth to its potential beneficiaries. To make place for itself in a climate of fierce competition,

[2] I owe the understanding of this issue to my reading of Charles Taylor's 'Philosophy and its History', in R. Rorty, J.B. Schneewind, and Q. Skinner (eds), *Philosophy in History*, Cambridge: Cambridge University Press, 1984, pp. 17–30.

it had to marshal all forms of argumentative resources. It could not have survived without being explicit about its normative structure. In short, it could not be in the state of inarticulacy in which it currently happens to be. This is why its retrieval from the background involves going back in time. We can no longer do without its history.

Secularism in the single-religion societies of the West is beginning to be challenged not only from religious believers within but also from recently emigrated believers of other religions. This new multi-religiosity is threatening to throw western secularism into turmoil. Recall the controversy over the *hijab* in France. Western societies can no longer take for granted their own current interpretation of secularism, but must re-examine what separation means and what it is for. They must do so because reasons for secularism that are acceptable to the dominant religious majority are not automatically endorsed by religious minorities. For example, on the hitherto dominant interpretation of secularism, it means a strict separation of church and state for the sake of religious liberty construed individualistically, or, at best, for individualistically construed citizenship rights. However, neither the idea of strict separation nor an individualist defence of religious liberty and citizenship rights may be acceptable to non-Protestant, South Asian, or Middle Eastern religions. To convince them of its need and importance, one needs to retrieve the complicated structure of values behind it. Thus, to meet this new challenge to western secularism, it may be necessary to reconstruct its history.

The condition of Indian secularism is no different, though some of the causes for its crisis certainly are. It is not a coincidence, however, that the external threat to Indian secularism has intensified precisely at a time of its degeneration into a meaningless formula (perhaps the real crisis of Indian secularism began when the real meaning of secularism was forgotten and ritualistically, the word 'secular' was introduced in the Indian constitution!), or when it is viewed purely as a procedural doctrine that mechanically separates religion from the state and is foolishly innocent of its ties with substantive values. Critics of secularism are quick to point out its links with all kinds of things they dislike: the nation-state, instrumental rationality, the hegemony of science, mindless industrialization, and realist state-craft. But, both its critics and its defenders appear to have forgotten its constitutive relation with substantive values. Undoubtedly, because of a history that it shares with the West, Indian secularism is at least partly western. But this history can also be told as a history of important values. The distancing of religion from the state became necessary, both in India and the West, to protect individual citizens from their own oppressive religiously sanctioned social customs (intra-religious domination). Hence, the connection of secularism with individualistically conceived liberty and equality. Unfortunately, Indian critics of secularism have developed an amnesia about these values. They also seem not to recall that 'separation', in the early constitutional history of India, was never understood to mean the blanket exclusion of religion from the state.

It is important that we go back in time and retrieve the complex purposes underlying it, to examine how Indian secularism was originally conceived. This would be beneficial not only for us, in India, but also for students of western secularism. For once we unearth the complicated conceptual structure of Indian secularism, we may find that it has the potential to shape the future of western secularism. If so, it is not enough for students of western secularism to look backwards, at the history of its own versions of secularism. They may need to look sideways, at the Indian variant, and discover that in it is reflected not only a compressed version of their own history but also a vision of its future.

I have claimed that students of both Indian and western secularism will benefit from identifying the distinctiveness of Indian secularism. However, this is not always easy. To answer why, brings me to my third point. In India, everything has begun to be seen in terms of an irritatingly dichotomous grid that divides the social world into two groups, the western modern and the indigenous traditional. Those who accept this grid are ineluctably inducted into a certain pattern of thinking. If secularism is modern, they believe, then it must be western. The whole of western secularism is then identified with one's preferred variant, usually that which is currently dominant. For example, the currently dominant western stereotype has it that secularism entails a strict separation of religion and the state for the sake of religious liberty and individual autonomy. This stereotype is uncritically also accepted in India by its defenders as well as its opponents. Thus, those who defend secularism in India proclaim unstinting support for this western stereotype. Similarly, secularism is opposed in India because critics have good reason to be unhappy with this western stereotype. Since they also accept the view that to be Indian, a thing or an idea must be rooted wholly in home-grown traditions uncontaminated by the West, they seek to replace secularism by ideas of toleration available within indigenous religious traditions. Much of the debate on secularism in

India has been framed by this interpretative framework. But I wonder how useful it is to hold on to it, for it misses out on the simple point that something can be at once Indian and modern, that something that started out as western can over time be transformed, and in responding to specific Indian problems and by being nurtured in an Indian context, can become distinctively Indian; different from both its western counterpart and from anything found within indigenous traditions. Unless those who defend secularism grasp this point, they will continue to defend a version that has little validity in the Indian context. Since they are seen to support a doctrine that can be legitimately criticized, the popular legitimacy of every version of secularism is bound to be eroded in the long run. Critics of secularism, too, fail to realize that a persistent attack on the very idea of secularism has grave practical consequences. In a context in which secularism is anyhow under threat from Hindu extremists, the mistaken occlusion of the distinctiveness of Indian secularism only ends up granting intellectual legitimacy to the larger political attack on the secular idea.

In these preliminary remarks, I hope to have drawn attention to the importance of grasping the distinctiveness of Indian secularism. In what follows, I must try to show what this distinctiveness consists in. I argue that Indian secularism is distinguished from others versions by five features. First, its explicit multi-value character. Second, the idea of principled distance that is poles apart from one-sided exclusion, mutual exclusion, and strict neutrality. Third, its commitment to a different model of moral reasoning that is highly contextual and opens up the possibility of multiple secularisms, of different societies working out their own secularisms. Fourth, it uniquely combines an active hostility to some aspects of religion with an equally active respect for its other dimensions. Finally, it is the only secularism that I know that attends simultaneously to issues of intra-religious oppression and inter-religious domination. In my view, these are path-breaking features of any model of secularism.

THE CONCEPTUAL STRUCTURE OF SECULARISM

Non-secular Regimes: Theocracy, Establishment, Multiple Establishment

To identify the conceptual structure of secularism, it is best to begin by contrasting it with doctrines to which it is both related and opposed. These anti-secular doctrines favour not separation but a union or alliance between church/religion and state. A state that has union with a particular religious order is a theocratic state. Such a state is governed by what it claims are divine laws, directly administered by a priestly order claiming divine commission. Major historical examples of theocracies are ancient Israel, some Buddhist regimes of Japan and China, the Geneva of John Calvin, and the Papal states.[3] The Islamic Republic of Iran, as run by Ayatullahs or, at least, as Khomeni aspired to run it, is an obvious example. A theocratic state must be distinguished from a state that establishes religion. Here, religion is granted official, legal recognition by the state and while both benefit from a formal alliance with one another, the sacerdotal order does not govern a state where religion is established.

Just as a theocracy is not always distinguished from establishment of religion, just so a distinction is not always drawn between the establishment of religion and the establishment of a church of a religion (a religious institution with its own distinct rules, functions, and social roles; personnel; jurisdiction; power; hierarchy [ecclesiastical levels]; and a distinct and authoritative interpretation of a religion).[4] But clearly, not all religions have churches. Yet, a state may establish such a church-free religion, that is, grant it formal, legal recognition and privilege. Put differently, the establishment of a church is always the establishment of a particular religion, but the converse is not always true. The establishment of a particular religion does not always mean the establishment of a church. A majority of Hindu nationalists in India may wish to establish Hinduism as state religion but they have no church to establish. Such an establishment may be expressed in the symbols of the state as well in the form of state policies that support a particular religion. Early Protestants may have wanted to disestablish the Roman Catholic Church but they could have not wished the state to derecognize Christianity as the favoured religion. Alternatively,

---

[3] *The Catholic Encyclopaedia of Religion* defines theocracy as a form of political government in which the deity directly rules the people or as the rule of priestly caste. The rule of text-obsessed brahmins in India in accordance with the *Dharam Shastras* would be theocratic. See vol. 14, p. 13.

[4] The whole question of church–state separation, I would claim, emerges forcefully in what are predominantly church-based, single-religion societies. The issue of religion–state separation arises, however, in societies without churches, or/and with multiple religions, or when the hold of religion in societies has considerably declined, when religion is considered by the majority to be largely insignificant.

they tried to maintain the establishment of their preferred religion by the establishment of not one but two or even more churches.[5] The establishment of a single religion is consistent, therefore, with the disestablishment or non-establishment of church, with the establishment of a single church, or with the establishment of multiple churches. This issue is obscured because in church-based religions the establishment of religion *is* the establishment of the church, and the establishment of Christianity is so much a part of background understanding that it does not need even to be foregrounded and discussed.

Finally, it is possible that, at least theoretically, there is establishment of multiple religions, with or without church. I know of no historical instance of the multiple establishment of religions. Possibly, Ashoka in India came closest to it. It may also have been an aspiration of the Mughal King Akbar. Perhaps another example is the fourteenth century Vijayanagar kingdom that granted official recognition not only to Shaivites and the Vaishnavites but even the Jains.

We can see then that there are five types of regimes in which a close relationship exists between state and religion.[6] First, a theocracy where no institutional separation exists between church and state, and the sacerdotal order is also the direct political ruler. Second, states with the establishment of single religion. These are of three types: (i) without the establishment of a church; (ii) with the establishment of a single church; and (iii) with the establishment of multiple churches. Third, states with establishment of multiple religions.

Historically, where a single religion was established by the establishment of a single church—the unreformed established Protestant Churches of England, Scotland, and Germany; and the Catholic Churches in Italy and Spain—the state recognized a particular version of the religion enunciated by that church as the official religion, compelled individuals to congregate for only one church, punished them for failing to profess a particular set of religious beliefs, levied taxes in support of one particular favoured church, paid the salaries of its clergy, and made instruction of the favoured interpretation of the religion mandatory in educational institutions or in the media. In such cases, not only was there inequality among religions but also among the churches of the same religion, and while members of the established

[5] Leonard W. Levy, *The Establishment Clause*, Chapel Hill: The University of North Carolina Press, 1994, p. 7.

[6] The reader must be reminded that the three types of state–religion regimes discussed are all ideal–typical.

church may have enjoyed a modicum of religious liberty (an established
Protestant Church would certainly allow it), those belonging to
churches or religions not established did not enjoy any or the same
degree of liberty. When members of the other church or religious
groups possessed strength or number, then such a multi-religious or
multiple-denominational society was invariably wrecked by inter-
religious or inter-denominational wars. If they did not, then religious
minorities not only failed to enjoy full religious liberty but were not
even tolerated. They faced persistent religious persecution (Jews in
several European countries till the nineteenth century). One exception
to this, however, was the Millet system of the Ottoman Empire which
had Islam as the established religion but three other religious
communities—Greek Orthodox, Armenian Orthodox, and Jewish—
were treated as equals and given a respectable degree of autonomy.
States with substantive establishments have not changed their colour
with time. Wherever one religion is not only formally but substantively
established, the persecution of minorities and internal dissenters
continues, even till today. One has to cite the example only of Saudi
Arabia to prove this point.[7]

In instances of multiple establishment of churches, the state officially
respects more than one denomination without preferring one over
the other.[8] In the past, such a state levied a religious tax on everyone
and yet, gave individuals the choice to remit the tax money to their
preferred church. It financially aided schools run by religious institutions but on a non-discriminatory basis. It may have punished people
for disavowing or disrespecting the established religion, but it did
not compel them to profess the beliefs of a particular denomination.
A state that respects multiple establishments treats members of all
churches non-preferentially. It gives liberty to each church to conduct
its religious affairs but is largely indifferent to the freedom of members within the group. The state of New York in the middle of the
seventeenth century, that allowed every church of the Protestant faith
to be established, furnishes perhaps the earliest example of 'multiple
establishment'. The colonies of Massachusetts, Connecticut, and New
Hampshire show a similar pattern.[9]

[7] Malise Ruthven, *A Fury for God*, London/New York: Granta Books, 2002,
pp. 172–8.
[8] Ibid., p. 12.
[9] Ibid., p. 11.

States with establishment of multiple churches are better than states with singular establishment. They are likely to be relatively peaceful. Members of different denominations are likely to tolerate one another. There may be general equality among all members of a religion (though, historically, this has not always been the case, women and blacks have been the usual victims). The state grants each denomination considerable autonomy in its own affairs. But states with multiple establishments have their limitations. For a start, they may continue to persecute members of other religions and atheists. Second, they are indifferent to the liberty of individuals within each denomination or religious group. They may do absolutely nothing to foster a general climate of toleration that prevents the persecution of dissenters within recognized communities or of other religious communities. Closed and oppressive communities can thrive in such contexts. Third, they may not have legal provisions that allow an individual to exit his religious community and embrace another religion or to remain unattached to any religion whatsoever. Fourth, such states give recognition to particular religious identities but fail to recognize what may be called non-particularized identities, that is, identities that simultaneously refer to several particular identities or transcend all of them. Fifth, such states are unconcerned with the non-religious liberties of individuals or groups. Finally, such states are entirely indifferent to citizenship rights. States which establish multiple religions face similar problems but are better than states with multiple church establishment in one important respect. There is peace and toleration and perhaps equality between all religious communities.

An important difference between a theocracy and states with establishment of churches is easily discernable. Because they do not identify or unify church and state but install only an alliance between them, states with an established church are in some ways disconnected from it. They do so in different ways. For a start, these are political orders where there is a sufficient degree of institutional differentiation between the two social entities. Both the church and the state are distinct enough to have separate identities. This difference in identity may partly be due to role differentiation. Each is to perform a role different from the other; the function of one is to maintain peace and order, a primarily temporal matter. The function of the other is to secure salvation, primarily a spiritual concern. In a theocracy, both roles are performed by the same personnel. In states with established churches, there may even be personnel differentiation. State functionaries and church functionaries are largely different from another. Thus, disconnection between church and state can go sufficiently deep. Yet, there is a more significant sense in which the state and the church are connected to one another: they share a common end, defined largely by religion. By virtue of a more primary connection of ends, the two share a special relationship with another. Both benefit from this mutual alliance. This is also true of states that establish multiple churches. There is finally another level of connection between church and state. The policies of the state directly favour the church and its religion. They flow from and are justified in terms of the union or alliance that exists between the state and the church. The institutional disconnection of church and state goes hand in hand with the first- and third-level connection of ends and policies.

To sum up: I have referred to three possible levels of connection. A primary, first-order connection refers to the connection of ends, purposes, or values. A second-order connection may exist at the level of roles, functions, powers, or more generally, institutions. A third-level connection exists at the level of state policy. In theocracies, church and state are connected at all three levels (common end, no institutional separation, common policy). In states with established churches, the two have, first, primary and third-order connection but at the very best, only partial second-order connection. In principle, it is not impossible for states with established churches to be entirely disconnected from them at the second level. So, this is what differentiates a state with established church-based religion from a theocracy: the second-order disconnection of church and state.

Secular States
How are secular states different from theocracies and states with established religions? Because it is also a feature of states with established churches, the mere institutional separation of the two is not and cannot be the distinguishing mark of secular states. This second-level disconnection should not be conflated with the separation embedded in secular states because, though necessary, it is not a sufficient condition for their individuation. This is an important clarification. Because institutional disconnection is a necessary condition for secular states and, especially in states with a long tradition of strong establishments or theocracy, and because much of the struggle for the creation of a secular state is directed at this institutional disconnection. For instance, in virulent anti-clericalism, it is not uncommon to identify secularism

with church–state separation. But, by itself, this separation does not install a secular state and is not the distinguishing feature of political secularism.

To grasp this point at a more general theoretical level, let me distinguish three levels of disconnection to correspond with the three already identified levels of connection. A state may be disconnected from religion at the level of ends (first level), at the level of institutions (second level), and the level of law and public policy (third level).[10] A secular state is distinguished from theocracies and states with established churches by a primary, first-level disconnection. A secular state has free standing ends, either substantially, if not always completely, disconnected from the ends of religion or conceivable without a connection with them. States with established religions have something in common with secular states—at least a partial institutional disconnection. But secular states go further in the direction of disconnection; they break away completely. They withdraw favours or privileges that established churches had earlier taken for granted. Finally, a state may be disconnected from religion even at the level of law and public policy. Such a state maintains a policy of strict or absolute separation. The dominant self-understanding of western secularism is that this third-level disconnection is crucial. When a state is disconnected from religion at all three levels, then we may say that a 'wall of separation' has been erected between the two. On the wall of separation conception of secularism, the state must have nothing to do with religion. Religion must be outside the purview of the state, and in this sense, it must be privatized. But there are two other modes of relating to religion at this third level. The state may either be strictly neutral, a stance that may in some circumstances implicate it with religion or it may even go beyond neutrality, connect with it in yet another way, a point to which I return in detail later.

To sum up: a secular state is to be distinguished not only from theocracy but also from a state where religion is established. A non-theocratic state is not automatically secular because it is entirely consistent for a state not to be run by priests inspired by 'divine laws', but to have a formal alliance with one or more religions. Nor is a state separated from the church necessarily secular, because church–state separation is compatible with the establishment of religion. A secular

---

[10] As we shall see, this would also open up the possibility of distinguishing forms of secular states.

state goes beyond church–state separation. To go beyond it is to refuse to establish religion or if it has been established earlier, to disestablish it. Therefore, a secular state follows what can be called principle of non-establishment. Furthermore, the non-establishment of religion means that the state is separated not merely from one but from all religions. Thus, in a secular state, a formal or legal union or alliance between state and religion is impermissible. Official status is not given to religion. No religious community in such a state can say that the state belongs exclusively to it. Nor can all of them together say that it belongs collectively to them and them alone. This does not mean that a secular state is anti-religious but it does imply that it exists and survives only when religion is no longer hegemonic. No one is compelled to pay tax for religious purposes or to receive religious instruction. No automatic grants to religious institutions are available.

What are the ends of a secular state? I have said that at the most general level, secular states aim to end religious hegemony, oppression, and domination, and to do so by separating them from their structure. But something more needs to be said about why we need to separate state and religion. Broadly there are two reasons on the basis of which two types of secular states can be distinguished. First, states may do so simply for self-aggrandizement, for example, when states (political rulers) wish to maximize their own power and wealth. These states are not motivated by values such as peace, liberty, or equality. They may have moral pretense but at root they have no commitment to any moral values. I shall call them self-aggrandizing amoral secular states. Usually, such states are imperial and autocratic. A good example of such a predominantly secular state, despite the not infrequent allegation of its biased, Christian character, is the British colonial state in India that, motivated almost exclusively by power, wealth, and social order, had a policy of tolerance and neutrality towards different religious communities. This is not surprising, given that empires are interested in the labour or tribute of their subjects, not in their religion. In multi-religious societies, for purely instrumental reasons, they may display characteristics of states that establish multiple religions or have a hands-off approach to all religions.[11]

[11] In his very interesting comments on my essay, Faisal Devji remarks that colonial secularism, which meant the strict neutrality of the colonial state with respect to all religions, was also a project of values, in particular the value of a civilizing mission. There is no doubt some truth in this and it is consistent with my own remark that state neutrality under British rule was always attacked for

Values of a Secular State
But there is another kind of secular state, one guided also by some moral values or principles. I shall call such secular states value-based secular states. This brings me to more explicitly articulate the connection of a non-self-aggrandizing secular state with several important and substantive values. The first of these is peace or rather the prevention of a society from its regression into barbarism, not an uncommon tendency where there exist two or more incompatible visions of the good life. I may here mention an auxiliary point. We must eschew the tendency within western modernist discourse to conceive of civil strife as a result purely of a clash of interests. The development of secularism in the West, and elsewhere, cannot be properly understood without fully comprehending the fear of cruelty and disorder that marks the conflict of ultimate ideals. This is equally true of the American and the French experience as it is of India. Consider the USA. One might say that the first amendment, the pivot of American secularism is a product of the widespread feeling of vulnerability experienced in different religious denomination such as the Anglicans, the Presbyterians, and the Quakers, each dominant in one particular area but vulnerable in others and each viewing the other as fanatical, or at least as extremely odd.[12] Closely related to peace is toleration. The state does not kill or expel anyone on grounds of religion. Second, a secular state is constitutively tied to the value of religious liberty that has three dimensions. The first refers to the liberty of members of any one religious group. It is a brute fact that in most religious communities, one or two interpretations of its core beliefs and practices come to dominate. Given this dominance, it is important that every individual or sect within the group be given the right to criticize, revise, or challenge these dominant interpretations. The second aspect of this important liberty in a secular state is that it is granted non-preferentially to all members of every religious community. It is entirely possible that non-preferential treatment by

a hidden Christian agenda. Yet, to forget the instrumental reasons behind the posture of neutrality would be a mistake. To me the secularity of the colonial state was amoral and self-aggrandizing. The difference, if at all, between Devji and me is one of emphasis rather than substance. See Faisal Devji, 'Comments on Rajeev Bhargava's "The Distinctiveness of Indian Secularism"', in T.N. Srinivasan (ed.), *The Future of Secularism*, pp. 54–9.

[12] On this point see, Michael McConnell, 'Taking Religious Freedom Seriously', in Terry Eastland (ed.), *Religious Liberty in the Supreme Court*, Michigan and Cambridge: William B. Eerdmans Publishing Company, 1993, pp. 497–510.

the state of groups that accord religious liberty to its members is also found in states respecting multiple establishment. But, religious liberty is not part of the core principles of multiple establishment. However, it is a constitutive feature of the secular state. The third dimension of religious liberty, unthinkable in states with multiple establishment, is that individuals are free not only to criticize the religion into which they are born but at the very extreme, to reject it and further, given ideal conditions of deliberation, to freely embrace another religion or to remain without one.

Religious liberty, when understood broadly, is one important value of a secular state. To understand another crucial ingredient, it is necessary to grasp the point that liberty and equality in the religious sphere are all of a piece with liberty and equality in other spheres. It is not a coincidence that the disestablishment clause in the first amendment to the American constitution institutes not only religious freedom but also the more general freedom of speech, of peaceful assembly, and of political dissent. It is entirely possible that a state respecting multiple establishment permits *religious* liberty and equality but forbids other forms of freedom and equality. For instance, a person may challenge the authority of the religious head of his own denomination but not be free to challenge the authority of the state. This is impossible in a secular state which is committed to a more general freedom and equality. Thus, the second value to which a secular state is constitutively linked is the equality of free citizenship.

The value of equal citizenship has two dimensions, one active, the other passive. It is a feature of democratic polities that these two roles of citizens coincide and therefore, a democratic government must be continuously justifiable from both points of views.[13] To be a passive citizen is to be entitled to physical security, a minimum of material well-being, and a sphere of one's own in which others ought not to interfere. Although a part of this idea of passive citizenship goes back to ancient Rome, the radical emphasis on material well-being and on privacy is a result of a profound trans-valuation of values that has taken place under conditions of modernity.[14] This lies at the root of the idea of the right to life, liberty, material welfare, and perhaps, education—crucial elements if ordinary people are to lead their ordinary life with dignity. Any citizen

[13] Charles Beitz, *Political Equality*, Princeton: Princeton University Press, 1989, chapter 5.

[14] See Charles Taylor, *Sources of the Self*, Cambridge: Cambridge University Press, 1989.

of the state must be entitled to these benefits. This is partly an extension of the point implicit in the defence of religious liberty but, in part, it adds something substantial of its own. The benefits of citizenship—resources that enable a dignified ordinary life—must be available to everyone and there is no room here for discrimination on grounds of religion. This equal treatment is entailed by equal (passive) citizenship. State agencies and the entire system of law must not work in favour of one religious group. If the state works to protect the security and well-being of some individuals or groups but fail to secure these meagre but important benefits to others, then the principle of equal (passive) citizenship is violated. Likewise, since citizenship is conditional upon education, no one must be denied admission to educational institutions, solely on grounds of religion.

The active dimension of citizenship involves the recognition of citizens as equal participants in the public domain. Such active citizenship rights can be denied in two ways. Either when they are brutally excluded from the political domain (they are politically dead),[15] or when their recognition in the public domain betrays the social acceptance of a belief in the intrinsic superiority of one group as when there is communally weighed voting or efforts to dilute the votes of religious minorities through the use of gerrymandering techniques.[16] Groups singled out as less worthy are demeaned and insulted, and encouraged to feel that patterns of disrespect existing in society at large enjoy official sanction. In contrast to this, equality of citizenship to which secularism is tied conveys a community-wide acknowledgement of equal respect for everyone in the political domain.

From what has been stated, two further conclusions must be drawn. First, secularism must not be mistakenly identified with other conceptions of state–religion relationships. The core idea of secularism then is this: separation of religion and state for the sake of religious liberty and equality of free citizenship. From what I have said earlier, some alleged conceptions of secularism are ruled out as conceptions of secularism. First, the point about the constitutive links between a secular state and the values of liberty and equality removes a widespread misunderstanding that the only thing required for a state to be secular is its separation from religions. On this, the purely instrumentalist view of secularism, whether or not any substantive value is realized, even

[15] This idea is closely related to the notion of social death to be found in Oscar Patterson's writings. See Beitz, *Political Equality*, p. 109.

[16] Ibid., p. 110.

when some key values are undermined, a state is secular if religious and political institutions of the society are separated, and the neater and stricter the separation, the more secular it is. But, I have argued that mere separation of religion and politics does not create a secular state. Second, a non-instrumental view that overburdens secularism is equally mistaken. This view identifies secularism with rationalism, individualism, disenchantment, scientization; indeed, with a particular extremely partial, prejudiced understanding of the whole process of modernization.[17] Secularism is not a comprehensive doctrine laden with every single substantive value in the empire of modernity, nor is it merely a strategy with instrumental significance. Rather, it seeks separation, for the sake of specific values. Third, secularism is not a single-value doctrine. So, suppose we have a state that prevents religious conflict, then this feature alone does not make it secular. Although every secular state prevents barbarism, not every state that manages to prevent evil is secular. For example, some states bring about religious peace by undermining religious liberty and such states cannot be deemed secular. Moreover, a state that permits, even promotes, religious liberty but violates the principle of equal citizenship, either in its passive or its active dimension, is not secular. Indeed, even a 'tolerant state' is not a secular one. Recall that to tolerate is to refrain from interfering in the affairs of any individual or group, however disagreeable or morally repugnant, despite the fact that one has the power to do so. Given this definition of tolerance, a tolerant attitude, particularly of the state, certainly engenders a truce between warring religious groups. Tolerance is compatible with, though not the same as religious liberty. But, it does not encourage respect and equality between two groups. At any rate, it is fully compatible with inequality. A tolerant state does not necessarily encourage an attitude of *equal* respect. And certainly, a tolerant state need have no truck with political equality and the idea of equal citizenship. However, in the view outlined earlier, a state that does not show equal respect to all religious groups and its members and more particularly, a state that does not grant equal citizenship rights is not a secular state. It follows that tolerance and secularism are two different, quite incompatible ideals.

Second, a simple comparison between different types of state–religion political orders shows that at least in multi-religious society, and relative to theocracies and states with established religion, a secular

---

[17] See Ashis Nandy, 'The Politics of Secularism and the Recovery of Religious Toleration', in Bhargava (ed.), *Secularism and Its Critics*, pp. 321–44.

state gives maximum liberty and equality, conceived individualistically or non-individualistically to all its citizens. This point can be made with reference to a table given next (Table 3.1).

INDIAN SECULARISM

Which of the different religion-related political orders mentioned earlier is found in India? We may answer this by examining the relevant articles of the Indian constitution. The state in the Indian constitution appears to posses all the features of a secular state. The constitution follows the principle of non-establishment illustrated, for instance, in Article 28(1), under which, 'no religious instruction is to be provided in any educational institution wholly maintained out of state funds.'

Articles 25, 27, and 28 guarantee religious liberty. Under Article 25(1), 'all persons are equally entitled to freedom of conscience and the right freely to profess, practice and propagate religion.' The phrase 'freedom of conscience' is meant to cover the liberty of persons without a religion. Under Article 27, 'no person is compelled to pay any taxes, the proceeds of which are specifically appropriated in payment of expenses for the promotion or maintenance of any particular religion or religious denomination.' Finally, under Article 28(3), 'no person attending any educational institution ... shall be required to take part in any religious instruction or to attend any religious worship that may be conducted in such institution.'

Equality of citizenship is guaranteed by Articles 14, 15(1), and 29(2) of the Indian constitution. Article 15(1) states that the state shall not discriminate against any citizen on grounds only of religion, race, caste, sex, place of birth, or any of them. Article 29(2) declares that no citizen shall be denied admission into any educational institution maintained by the state on grounds only of religion, race, etc. Articles 16(1) and 16(2) of Indian constitution affirm an equal opportunity for all citizens in matters relating to employment or appointment in any office under the state. It further affirms that no citizen, on grounds of religion or race will be eligible for or discriminate against in respect of any employment or office under the state. The clause on universal franchise, as well as Article 325 that declares a general electoral roll for all constituencies and states that no one shall be ineligible for inclusion in this roll or claim to be included in it on grounds only of religion, etc., embody the value of equal active citizenship.

The implications of accepting that the state in the Indian constitution is meant to be secular are not always spelt out. First, the constitution

TABLE 3.1: Comparative Moral Evaluation of Secular and Religion-centred States

Values → Form of State ↓	Peace with Justice	Religious Liberty			Citizenship Identification			Passive Citizenship Benefits/Rights			Active Citizenship Rights		
		Dominant Groups		Others	Dominant Groups		Others	Dominant Groups		Others	Dominant Groups		Others
		Elites	Others		Elites	Others		Elites	Others		Elites	Others	
Theocracy	A	P	A	A	P	A	A	P	A	A	A	A	A
States with substantive singular establishment	A	WP	A	A	P	P	A	P	A	A	A	A	A
States with substantive multiple establishment	WP	WP	A	WP	P	P	A	P	WP	A	A	A	A
States with formal singular establishment	P	P	P	P	P	P	A	P	P	P	P	P	P
States with formal multiple establishment	P	P	P	P	P	P	WP	P	P	P	P	P	P
Anti-religious 'secular' state	A	A	A	A	P	A	A	P	P	P	A	A	A
Value-based secular state	P	P	P	P	P	P	P	P	P	P	P	P	P

Notes: A—Absent; WP—Weakly Present; P—Present.

rules out theocracy and the establishment of religion. The term 'secular state' is usually contrasted simply with theocracy. This is misleading, if not false, because the absence of theocracy is compatible with the establishment of religion. The secular credentials of the state cannot be derived from the mere absence of theocracy.[18] Second, the Indian state is not meant to be merely tolerant (in the sense specified earlier). Indian secularism must not be confused with a generally professed Hindu tolerance. It is frequently claimed that Indians have a natural, traditional affinity with secularism. In view of our traditional obsession with subtle and not so subtle hierarchies, this claim must be taken with a pinch of salt, if not pepper. Of course, this should not detract from the important point that tolerance, even within a hierarchical framework, forms an important background condition for the development of modern secularism. Elements of this important background condition can certainly be found within India. Third, the secularism of the Indian constitution is neither a simple-minded, single-value idea nor an over-inflated and hyper-substantive one. Rather, it is a complex, multi-value doctrine.

A further point to note concerns the precise form of secularism to be found in the constitution. Broadly, secularism is taken to be the view that religion must be separated from the state for the sake of extensive religious liberty and equality of citizenship. This view can be differently interpreted. In the first chapter, I have shown that Donald Smith's conception of the secular state involves three clearly identifiable relations between state, religion, and the individual.[19] The first relation is between individuals and their religion from which the state is kept out. By freeing individuals from coercive interference by the state, this relation gives secularism its liberal ingredient. A second relation exists between individuals and the state. Religion plays no role here. It has no bearing on the distribution of rights and duties. All citizens are equal regardless of their religious affiliation. This is the democratic/egalitarian component in secularism. Finally, for Smith, both these

[18] Partha Chatterjee's piece on secularism exemplifies this error. Thus, he mistakenly concludes that since the Hindu Right does not want the laws of the state to be in conformity with the general spirit of the Dharam Shastra, it is at peace with the institutional procedures of modern western secularism. See Chatterjee, 'Secularism and Tolerance', in Bhargava (ed.), *Secularism and Its Critics*, pp. 345–79. Arguably, the Hindu Right may wish the de facto, somewhat disguised establishment of its own variant of Hinduism.

[19] Donald Smith, *India as a Secular State*, Princeton: Princeton University Press, 1963, pp. 3–8.

relations presuppose a third relation, one between the state and religion, their separation. Neither is to interfere in each other's jurisdiction. This is also the dominant understanding of western secularism.

DEPARTURES FROM MAINSTREAM WESTERN SECULARISM

Does Indian secularism erect a similar 'wall of separation' for the sake of individualistically construed values? Is it a western idea on Indian soil? Articles 15, 16, 25, 29(2), and 325 support this interpretation. Though there is no direct reference to disestablishment, Articles 27 and 28(1) imply strict separation. By giving the President of the Republic the option of not taking oath in the name of god, Article 60 confirms the strictly neutral character of the Indian constitution. From the discussion so far, it appears that the state in India is constitutionally bound to follow Smith's model of western secularism. However, a further examination of the constitution reveals this impression to be mistaken. To begin with, Article 30(1) recognizes the rights of religious minorities and therefore, unlike other articles applicable to citizens qua individuals, it is a community-based right. Indeed, another community-specific right granting political representation to religious minorities was almost granted and was removed from the constitution only at the last minute. Second, Article 30(2) commits the state to give aid to educational institutions established and administered by religious communities. Also permitted is religious instruction in educational institutions that are partly funded by the state. These are significant departures from the 'wall of separation' view of the secular state. Even more significant are Articles 17 and 25(2) that require the state to intervene in religious affairs. Article 25(2)(b) states that 'nothing in Article 25(1) prevents the state from making a law providing for social welfare and reform or the throwing open of Hindu religious institutions of a public character to all classes and sections of Hindus.' Article 17 is an uninhibited, robust attack on the caste system, arguably the central feature of Hinduism, by abolishing untouchability and by making the enforcement of any disability arising out of it an offence punishable by law. Both appear to take away the individual freedom of religion granted under Section 1 of Article 25 and to contravene Article 26.

These features of the Indian constitution depart from the stereotypical western model in two ways. First, unlike the strict separation view that renders the state powerless in religious matters, they enjoin the state to interfere in religion. Second, more importantly, by giving powers to the state in the affairs of one religion, they necessitate a departure from strict neutrality or equidistance. This power of interference may be interpreted to undermine or promote Hinduism. Either way, it appears to strike a powerful blow to the idea of non-preferential treatment.

In short, some articles in the Indian constitution support an individualist interpretation and others a non-individualist one. Some conceive separation as exclusion, others as non-preferential treatment, and finally, some depart altogether from separation understood as exclusion or neutrality. At the end of the day, a confusing, somewhat contradictory picture on secularism emerges from a reading of the constitution. Critics could hardly fail to notice this and for many of them, Articles 17, 25(2), and 30(1 and 2) compromise the secularity of the Indian state. For Donald Smith, any intervention in Hinduism—for example, the legal ban on the prohibition of dalit entry into temples or any protection of the rights of communities—seriously compromises secularism. For others, like Chatterjee, the presence of these features in the Indian constitution shows why the Indian state cannot be really secular. The Indian constitution does not give an unambiguous criterion for maintaining the secularity of the state and, quite simply, given Indian conditions, it could never have.

By accepting community-based rights for religious minorities and endorsing state intervention in religion, did the constitution depart from secular principles? I do not think it did. Rather, it developed its own modern variant. This distinctiveness of the Indian secularism can be understood only when the cultural background and social context in India is properly grasped. In Chapter 1, I mentioned four features of India's socio-cultural context. First, the profound religious diversity of India which is a standing condition, both for mutual learning and cooperation as well as bitter conflicts over resources and values. Often, the 'resolution' of such conflicts had led in the past to the domination of one community over others. Second, the general disposition of South Asian religions to emphasize practice rather than belief. Since practices are sustained by communities, a concomitant valorization of communities is inevitable in Indian society. Third, the presence of recalcitrant, oppressive practices within religious communities means that intra-religious domination has been a persistent feature of Indian societies. Movements and institutions with enormous collective power are required, therefore, to reduce such domination. Finally, the absence in Hinduism of an organized institution such as the Church has meant that the responsibility for limiting such domination has had to wrest with a powerful, relatively independent institution such as the state.

In such a context, India needed a coherent set of intellectual resources to tackle inter-religious conflict, and to struggle against oppressive communities not by disaggregating them into a collection of
individuals or by derecognizing them (and therefore, not by privatizing
religion) but by somehow making them more liberal and egalitarian.
A political movement for a united, liberal, democratic India had to
struggle against hierarchical and communal conceptions of community
but without abandoning a reasonable communitarianism. Besides, the
state had an important contribution to make in the transformation of
these communities; for this reason, a perennial dilemma was imposed
on it. The state in India walked a tight rope between the requirement
of religious liberty that frequently entails non-interference in the
affairs of religious communities, and the demand for equality and
justice which necessitates intervention in religiously sanctioned social
customs. Secularism in India simply had to be different from the western liberal model that does not recognize communities, and dictates
strict separation between religious and political institutions.

Does this deviation from the liberal model entail that India abandoned secularism? Was this the reason why the term 'secular' or
'secularism' was not used in the original Constitution of India? I do not
think so. Instead, I believe that we had worked out an alternative, quite
distinctive conception of the secular state. This can be demonstrated
even if we worked with Donald Smith's idea of secularism as consisting
of three relations. Recall that Smith's first relation concerns individuals
and their religion from which the state is excluded. Individuals are free
to choose their religious beliefs with no pressure from state institutions.
However, the formal structure of this relation is left intact even when
religious liberty is construed non-individualistically. Religious liberty
now means the distancing of the state from the practices of religious
groups—in short, the autonomy of religious groups from the state to
maintain or alter their practices as they deem fit. The first principle of
secularism can be seen to grant the right to a religious community to
its own practices. Smith's second relation embodies the value of equal
citizenship for all individuals. Smith's conception entails a charter of
uniform rights for all individuals.[20] But why should this be so? Why cannot some fundamental rights be given only to Indian citizens in their

[20] For an interesting critique of Smith's interpretation of Indian secularism
as derived from the American model with an 'extra dose of separation', see
Marc Galanter, 'Secularism, East and West', in Bhargava (ed.), *Secularism and
Its Critics*, pp. 234–67.

capacity as members of particular religious communities? Why should not only Sikhs be given the right to wear turbans in public institutions such as the army? Why, in order to treat all persons as equals, is it not possible to give only minority religious groups some rights so that they can also realize those objectives which majority religious groups routinely achieve? Equality of citizenship can mean both equality among individual citizens and equality of religious groups to which citizens belong. Smith's third principle requires strict separation or mutual exclusion of religion and state. However, separation need not mean strict non-interference, mutual exclusion, or equidistance, as in Smith's view. Instead, it could be a policy of principled distance, which entails a flexible approach on the question of intervention or abstention, combining both, dependent on the context, nature, or current state of relevant religions. This theoretical interpretation of separation sits much better with its own best practice but perhaps also with the practice of other western secular states, something that is never properly recognized by western theories of secularism.

I have argued that at least three features distinguish the Indian model of secularism from mainstream, western variants. Allow me to elaborate these features.

Principled Distance

Clearly, the demand for separation comes in the wake of some undesirable pre-existing unity, in this case, an intermeshing of religion and state. Against the view that religion and state possess an identical overall agenda, a common, indistinguishable project, the separationists argue for a parting of ways, a primary disconnection. Where there are institutional links, they also argue for what I call second-level disconnection. This much is uncontroversial. But from here, a bifurcation occurs. One avenue leads to total exclusion; separation here means, the meticulous refusal of any contact whatsoever between religion and the state. The two must keep off one another, not connect at any level, even at the level of governmental policy. This stand-offishness may be robust or mild. When robust, it generates mutual hostility. For example, the secular state, in this view, must be anti-religious. This anti-religiosity may be interventionist or non-interventionist. In its interventionist form, the state actively discourages religion. It connects with religion only to destroy it, to remove the very possibility of any future connection. In its non-interventionist incarnation, it typifies a hysterical brahminical attitude: religion is untouchable, so any contact with it contaminates secularist purity. Secularism here becomes a doctrine of political taboo; it prohibits contact with certain kinds of activities. The milder variety of exclusion of religion from politics proposes that religious and political institutions live as strangers to each other. At best, mutual incomprehension leads to a half-hearted, benign respectful indifference. The second view on separation does not demand total exclusion. Some contact is possible but also some distance. But the terms of engagement and disengagement are antecedently fixed. This is central to the notion of strict neutrality. Those who interpret separation as neutrality demand that a secular state be neutral with respect to all religions. It may help or hinder all religions to an equal degree. If it intervenes in one religion, it must also do so in others.

The idea of principled distance unpacks the metaphor of separation differently. It accepts a disconnection between state and religion at the level of ends and institutions but does not make a fetish of it at the third level of policy and law. How else can it be in societies where religion frames some of their deepest interests? Recall that political secularism is a political ethic and its concerns are the same as those theories that oppose unjust restrictions on freedom, morally indefensible inequalities, inter-communal domination, and exploitation. This form of secularism is not committed to the mainstream enlightenment idea of religion. It accepts that humans have an interest in relating to something beyond themselves, way beyond themselves, including god, and this manifests itself as individual belief and feeling as well as social practice in the public domain. It also accepts that it is a resource of valuable cumulative tradition as well as a source of people's identities. But, it rests on the belief and insists that even if turned out that god exists and that one religion is true and others false, then this does not give the 'true' doctrine or religion the right to force it down the throats of others who do not believe it. Nor does it give a ground for discrimination in the distribution of liberties and resources.

Similarly, although no religion has to be given *special* favours, it does not follow that relative to other social institutions, it will be disfavoured! Religion may not have special public significance antecedently written into and defining the very character of the state or the nation but it does not follow that it has no public significance at all. Sometimes, on some versions of it, the absolute, strict, or the wall of separation thesis assumes precisely that. The latter conclusion would follow only if the public importance of religion has really declined for wider social, cognitive, or other reasons. But as long as it is publicly significant, a democratic state simply has to take this into account. Indeed, institutions of religion may influence individuals as long as they do so through the same process, by access to the same resources as anyone, and without undue advantage or unduly exploiting the fears and vulnerabilities that frequently accompany people in their experience of the religious.

Principled distance is premised, therefore, on the idea that a state that has secular ends and that is institutionally separated from the church or some church-like entity must engage with religion at the level of law and social policy. This engagement must be governed by principles undergirding a secular state, that is, principles that flow from a commitment to the values mentioned earlier. The state may engage with religion or disengage from it, engage positively or negatively but it does so depending entirely on whether or not these values are promoted or undermined. A state that intervenes or refrains from interference on this basis keeps a principled distance from all religions. This is one constitutive idea of principled distance.

But how is this idea different from strict neutrality? Because, it rests upon a distinction explicitly drawn by the American philosopher, Ronald Dworkin, between equal treatment and treating everyone as an equal.[21] The principle of equal treatment, in the relevant political sense, requires that the state treat all its citizens equally in the relevant respect, for example, in the distribution of a resource or opportunity. The principle of treating people as equals entails that every person or group is treated with equal concern and respect. This second principle may sometimes require equal treatment, say, equal distribution of resources but it may also occasionally dictate unequal treatment. Treating people or groups as equals is entirely consistent with differential treatment. This idea is the second ingredient in what I have called principled distance. Moreover, it is to admit that a state may interfere in one religion more than in others, depending once again on the historical and social condition of all relevant religions. For the promotion of a particular value constitutive of secularism, some religion, relative to other religions, may require more interference from the state. For example, suppose that the value to be advanced is social equality. This requires in part undermining caste hierarchies. If this is the aim of the state, then it may be required of the state that it interferes in caste-ridden Hinduism much more than say Islam or Christianity. However, if a diversity-driven religious liberty

---

[21] Ronald Dworkin, 'Liberalism', in Stuart Hampshire (ed.), *Public and Private Morality*, Cambridge: Cambridge University Press, 1978, p. 125.

is the value to be advanced by the state, then it may have to intervene in Christianity and Islam more than in Hinduism. If this is so, the state can neither strictly exclude considerations emanating from religion nor keep strict neutrality with respect to religion. It cannot antecedently decide that it will always refrain from interfering in religions or that it will interfere in each equally. Indeed, it may not relate to every religion in society in exactly the same way or intervene in each religion to the same degree or in the same manner. To want to do so would be plainly absurd. All it must ensure is that the relationship between the state and religions is guided by non-sectarian motives consistent with some values and principles.

Consider once again laws that interfere with Hinduism. The relevant consideration in their evaluation is not whether they immediately encompass all groups but whether or not they are just and consistent with the values undergirding secularism. Three reasons exist for why all social groups need not be covered by these laws. First, they may be relevant only to Hindus. Take the abolition of child marriage and *devadasi* dedication, or the introduction of the right to divorce. Here, before deciding whether it was necessary to enact a special provision for Hindus, the legislature took into account their social customs and beliefs. Similar laws for Muslims were simply redundant. Second, laws in liberal democracies require legitimacy; the consent of at least the representatives of communities is vital. If consent has indeed been obtained from the representatives of only one community, it is sometimes prudent to enact community-specific laws. It is wise to apply the general principle in stages, rather than not have it at all. Finally,

it is perfectly within the competence of the legislature to take account of the degree of evil which is prevalent under various circumstances and the legislature is not bound to legislate for all evils at the same time. Therefore, an act passed by the legislature cannot be attacked merely because it tackles only some of the evils in society and does not tackle other evils of the same or worse kind which may be prevalent.[22]

Thus, if the legislature, acting on these considerations, wanted to enact a special provision with regard to, say, bigamous marriages among Hindus, it cannot be said that the legislature was discriminating against Hindus only on the ground of religion. The Indian courts have frequently followed this line of reasoning. They have defended a policy if they found that its purpose is the eradication of a social evil traceable

---

[22] AIR, 1952, Bom.84, *The State of Bombay vs. Narasu Appa.*

to religious practices, even if the policy was targeted at specific communities. It has argued that so long as the state has taken gradual steps towards social welfare and reform, and has not introduced distinctions or classifications that are unreasonable or oppressive, equality before law is not breached. A state interfering in one religion more than in others does not automatically depart from secularism. Indian secularism rejects the assumption that one size fits all.

Does principled distance also entail that religion intervene in the affairs of the state? In some contexts, it may certainly do so. Religion may intervene in the affairs of the state if such intervention promotes freedom, equality, or any other value integral to secularism. For example, citizens may support a coercive law of the state, grounded purely in a religious rationale, if this law is compatible with freedom or equality.[23] Likewise, and as already suggested earlier, the state may grant social, perhaps even political, recognition to religious communities. Religion may get into the affairs of the state either when individual citizens bring religious reasons in support of laws and policies or when the state is compelled to recognize religious communities for social or political purposes. One further implication of our discussion is that unlike mainstream western secularism that appears to impose on us a choice between active hostility or benign indifference, Indian secularism brings to bear on religion an attitude of critical respect. From the perspective of Indian secularism, respect for religions is entirely consistent with the identification of local faults within them. Respecting other religions as equals does not entail their blind acceptance or endorsement. It is also this idea of deeper idea of respect or care for something that allows one to critically intervene in it. Indian secularism does, in a way, respect all religions but by embodying the idea of respectful transformation of religions. In doing so, it inherits a venerable tradition of the great Indian religious reformers who tried to change their religions precisely because they meant so much to them.

---

[23] Principled distance rejects the standard liberal idea that the principle of equal respect is best realized only when people come into the public domain by leaving their religious reasons behind. Principled distance does not discourage public justification. Indeed, it encourages people to pursue public justification. However, if the attempt at public justification fails, it enjoins religiously minded citizens to abandon restraint and support coercive laws that are consistent with freedom and equality based purely on religious reasons. See Christopher J. Eberle, *Religious Conviction in Liberal Politics*, Cambridge: Cambridge University Press, 2002.

Community-specific Rights

It is sometimes argued that the recognition of community-specific rights for religious minorities violates the core principles of secularism. Is that so? A cursory reading of the assembly debates might yield the impression that some members at least found the recognition of *any* community-specific rights morally and politically disturbing. Granting community-specific rights was seen to encourage a spiralling estrangement between social groups, what elsewhere I have called the majority–minority syndrome.[24] For these members of the constituent assembly, the very words 'minority' or 'minority-interest' were anathema. Deshmukh, a member from CP and Berar, found 'no more monstrous word in the history of Indian politics than the word "minority".' He claimed it to be 'a demon that hampered the progress of the country'.[25] Sidhwa, a Parsi from CP and Berar, wanted 'the phrase "minorities" to be wiped out from history'.[26] Closer reading of the debates reveals that this venom is directed not against the idea of minorities per say but specifically against the notion of *religious* minorities. They claimed that to grant religious minorities a *social* right to establish their own educational institutions 'will block the way to national unity, promote communalism and a narrow anti-national outlook'. It was further contended that 'in a secular state, minorities based on religion or community should not be recognized. Recognition of minorities based on religion is the very negation of secularism. Only minorities based on language deserve recognition'.[27] A more detailed examination of the debates shows that even this objection to religious minorities was limited to a few members. Most members justified the grant of social rights not only to linguistic but also to minority religious communities. In other words, they willingly endorsed what might, in contrast to the syndrome, be called a majority–minority framework. Their principal objection was directed at *community-specific political rights*, in particular against the demand for a separate electorate. For them, separate electorates were outside the acceptable framework and could not help generate

[24] Rajeev Bhargava, 'Should We Abandon the Majority-minority Framework?', in D.L. Sheth and Gurpreet Mahajan (eds), *Minority Identities and the Nation-State*, Oxford: Oxford University Press, 1999, pp. 169–205.

[25] *The Constituent Assembly Debates*, 27 August 1947, New Delhi: Lok Sabha Secretariat, p. 201.

[26] Ibid., p. 209.

[27] *The Constituent Assembly Debates*, 8 December 1948, New Delhi: Lok Sabha Secretariat, p. 899. Therefore, it was argued, only minorities based on language should be recognized.

a syndrome. Their quarrel was not with religious minorities per say but with the specific *political* form of their demands. The demand for separate electorates was seen to be inherently anti-secular. Elsewhere, I have examined the reasons for and against separate electorates for Muslims and have argued that community-specific political rights were not granted to Muslims for contextual reasons.[28] The exclusion of religious classification from political representation was necessary in India because religion-based divisions had become too dangerous here, and not because such exclusion is necessarily required by every form of secularism.

Indeed, the rejection of community-specific political rights was entirely consistent with the acceptance of community-specific social rights. The rights granted under Article 30 were as necessary for a democratic state as the rejection of separate electorates under Article 325. The reason for their inclusion is also found in the debates. Members believed that even if the majority–minority framework was subject to the 'historical process of assimilation', 'the minorities must be dissolved into the majority by *justice*'. As one member of the constituent assembly, Hridaya Nath Kunzru put it, 'if this elementary justice is not given to minorities, we may open up the dangerous path of fanatical nationalism'. The principle of elementary justice, and the very same principles of liberty and equality that ruled community-differentiated political rights, necessitated community-differentiated social rights. Ambedkar's riposte to Mahavir Tyagi is very telling on this issue. Tyagi asked him if the grant of cultural and educational rights to minorities in India should not wait till the fate of minorities residing in Pakistan was more clearly known. Ambedkar replied firmly that the rights of minorities are not relative or conditional upon the decision of other states but were absolute:

No matter what others do, he urged, we ought to do what is right in our own judgement and, therefore, every minority, irrespective of any other consideration, is entitled to the right to use their language, script and culture and the right not to be precluded from establishing any educational institution that they wish to establish.

Contextual Secularism

A context-sensitive secularism, one based on the idea of principled distance, is what I have elsewhere called contextual secularism. Contextual secularism is contextual not only because it captures the idea that the precise form and content of secularism will vary from context

[28] See pp. 194–201 of this volume.

to context and from place to place but also that it embodies a certain model of contextual moral reasoning. This it must do because of its character as a multi-value doctrine. Let me explain this point by introducing a distinction between types of situations and types of moral doctrines. Some conflict-ridden human situations are such that their morally defensible resolution is dictated by single-value doctrines, that is, those which give priority to a value held to be supreme. For example, bodily integrity may be viewed as such an important value that nothing can justify its violation. I may be prevented from torturing someone no matter what my reasons for doing so: neither self-interest nor pursuit of truth may justify it. Other human situations are different because they genuinely involve a value conflict and the resolution of this conflict cannot be read off the values themselves. Single-value doctrines do not suffice here because they always dictate a unique outcome antecedently favourable to the protection of one value. In these situations, multi-value doctrines are more appropriate. They take on board these conflicts and admit that no general a priori procedure can antecedently arbitrate between competing value claims. Rather, whether a value will outweigh others or which, if at all, will override others will be decided entirely by the context. Frequently, such situations necessitate a trade-off or compromise, albeit one that is morally defensible.

By explicitly accepting that secularism is a multi-value doctrine, we recognize that its constitutive values do not always sit easily with one another. On the contrary, they are frequently in conflict. Some degree of internal discord and therefore, a fair amount of instability is an integral part of secularism. For this reason, it forever requires fresh interpretations, contextual judgements, and attempts at reconciliation and compromise. No general a priori rule of resolving these conflicts exist; no easy lexical order, no pre-existing hierarchy among values or laws that enables us to decide that, no matter what the context, a particular value must override everything else. Almost everything then is a matter of situational thinking and contextual reasoning. Whether one value overrides or is reconciled with another cannot be decided before hand. Each time the matter presents itself differently and will be differently resolved. If this is true, then the practice of secularism requires a different model of moral reasoning than the one that straightjackets our moral understanding in the form of well delineated, explicitly stated rules.[29] This contextual secularism recognizes that the conflict between

---

[29] See Charles Taylor, 'Justice after Virtue', in John Horton and Susan Mendus (eds), *After MacIntyre*, Oxford: Polity Press, 1994, pp. 16–43.

individual rights and group rights, or between claims of equality and liberty, or between claims of liberty and the satisfaction of basic needs cannot always be adjudicated by a recourse to some general and abstract principle. Rather they can only be settled case by case and may require a fine balancing of competing claims. The eventual outcome may not be wholly satisfactory to either but still be reasonably satisfactory to both. Multi-value doctrines such as secularism encourage accommodation—not the giving up of one value for the sake of another but rather their reconciliation and possible harmonization, that is, to make each work without changing the basic content of apparently incompatible concepts and values.

This accommodation may be accomplished in a number of ways.[30] First, by placing values at different levels. Second, by seeing them as belonging not to water-tight compartments but as sufficiently separate, so that an attempt is made to make a value work within its own sphere, without frontally conflicting with another value operating in a different sphere. This endeavour to make concepts, view points, and values work simultaneously does not amount to a morally objectionable compromise. This is so because nothing of importance is being given up for the sake of a less significant thing, one without value or even with negative value. Rather, what is pursued is a mutually agreed middle way that combines elements from two or more equally valuable entities. The roots of such attempts at reconciliation and accommodation lie in a lack of dogmatism, in a willingness to experiment, to think at different levels and in separate spheres, and in a readiness to take decisions on a provisional basis. It captures a way of thinking characterized by the following dictum: 'why look at things in terms of this or that, why not try to have both this and that'. In this way of thinking, it is recognized that though we may currently be unable to secure the best of both values and therefore be forced to settle for a watered-down version of each, we must continue to have an abiding commitment to search for a transcendence of this second-best condition.

Such contextual reasoning was not atypical of the deliberations of the constituent assembly in which great value was placed on arriving at decisions by consensus. Yet, the procedure of majority vote was not given up altogether. On issues that everyone judged to be less significant,

---

[30] Here I rely on the interesting discussion of these issues in Granville Austin, *The Indian Constitution: Cornerstone of a Nation*, New Delhi: Oxford University Press, 1999, pp. 311–25.

a majoritarian procedure was adopted. It is by virtue of this kind of reasoning that the Indian constitution appears at once federal and unitary, and why it favours both individual and group-specific rights. It is frequently argued against Indian secularism that it is contradictory because it tries to bring together individual and community rights, and that articles in the Indian constitution such as Articles 25 and 26(b) that have a bearing on the secular nature of the Indian state are deeply conflictual and, at best, ambiguous. This is to misrecognize a virtue as a vice. In my view, this attempt to bring together seemingly incompatible values is a great strength of Indian secularism. Secularism in India is not understood to be a mechanical doctrine with a uniform, technical application. Therefore, the demand that the relevant articles in the Indian constitution give us an unambiguous criteria for evaluating separation, or the complaint that the best of Indian secularists have an inconsistent understanding of the relationship between state and religion, remains wide off the target and altogether fails to grasp the conceptual structure of secularism in India. If secularism embodies contextual reasoning, it must be understood that this is not private moral reasoning applied to politics but rather public–political reasoning infused with a moral character.

BACK TO PRELIMINARIES

This is an appropriate point at which to briefly elaborate two points I made at the very beginning. First, that it is inadequate, if not mistaken, to focus on current formulations of western secularism. To grasp the rich and complicated structure of secularism, it is extremely important to examine the history of the secular ideal. An idea begins to have a life much before its clear formulation and before human beings bring it to self-consciousness. Often, what is taken to be the birth of an idea is partly a discovery, a re-articulation of older ideas and only in part an invention. And, as Hegel reminded us, we grasp this point only when that idea achieves a distinct and clear self-consciousness. This is certainly true of secularism. The complex set of values that coalesce around what later came to be called secularism began to live much earlier. For example, in a religiously diverse society, organized political power simply had to maintain some distance from the dominant religious group for the sake of stability and peace. The same motivation lay behind a partial acceptance and therefore, the toleration of the less dominant religious groups and the half-hearted recognition of particular religious identities. States that promoted peace and toleration can certainly not be called secular but there is no doubt that they are historically connected to modern secular states and can be said to constitute the latter's pre-history. At best, they may be seen to embody a local, customary, and a much older conception of the secular.

This time-honoured 'secularism' is found in different societies and cultures. This is why the development of modern secularism cannot be understood as growing only in terms of the relationship between the church and the state. The church–state model is one variant of a time-honoured secularism. The presence in background cultural conditions of other variants such as the religious strife model is equally conducive to the growth of modern secularism. I have elsewhere written in detail about these two models.[31] Suffice here to say that it is sufficient for the church–state model to be operating within a non-pluralist Christian society. However, a religious strife model necessarily operates within a society in which there exist diverse and radically differing religions or religious denominations. The church–state model is operative in societies in which separation is an internal feature of the dominant religion. The religious strife model of secularism, on the other hand, develops even if separation within some religions is not internally permissible but purely out of the contextual necessity in situations where there exist contending religions. In short, in the first model, the state wrenches away from the church of a single religion, whereas in the other model, it must distance itself from all religions at once. And, as I mentioned, this distancing is dictated by the vulnerabilities experienced by every single religious group. Each one fears persecution from the other as well as the disorder resulting from religious conflict.

States moved further towards the ideal of the secular when, apart from securing peace and toleration, they protected the religious liberties of individuals, in particular by providing secure conditions in which individuals could lead a decent life even when they dissented from the orthodoxy or orthopraxy of their own respective religions (of course, political orders have given such a space to some individuals for many millennia. Or else, there would be no Buddha or Mahavira, no Nanak or Kabir. But not as a normal, legitimate part of the social order). Secularism advanced further when many aspects of an individual's well-being began to be regulated not simply by a regime of toleration but rather by a formal and legal regime of rights, so that it became possible for individuals to make formal claims of entitlement against each other or against the state: to the protection of their life, or to a private sphere in which they were free to do what they want and were secure that any interference by the state in the life or private world of the individual could proceed only according to due process of law. Thus, a secular state comes into its own when it does not discriminate on grounds of religion in the distribution of passive citizenship rights.

It would be wrong, however, to identify secularism simply with the view for which the state must be separated from organized religion for the sake of peace, toleration, religious liberty, and equality of passive citizenship rights. For, over time, at least two values have gradually become integral to the secular idea. First, that a state must not discriminate on grounds of religion in the distribution of active citizenship rights. For example, a state must not debar members of minority religious groups from standing for public office. Second, in keeping with the spirit of inter-religious equality as well as equality of citizenship, a fully secular state extends rights to minority religious groups qua groups. In short, it grants community-based rights to religious minorities.

One can now see that over time the secular idea has both transcended already existing values and/or added to them. For example, after the advent of nationalism and democracy, the value of treating everyone as equal and therefore, not discriminating in the distribution of active citizenship rights was added to existing conceptions of secularism. Similarly, there is a sense in which a regime of rights better articulates the point behind toleration. A rights-based secularism supercedes toleration because it incorporates all values served by toleration and adds something more and valuable to it. Yet, it would be wrong to think that a secular state has no need at all for a regime of toleration. The regime of rights to which it is attached cannot reach every social space and in such not-so-easily approachable spaces, the ones not covered by legal rights, there still remains a need for decent relations governed by the value of toleration.

This brings me to the second point. Western theories of secularism have tended to see it as a single-value doctrine. For them, the state is to be separated from organized religion for the sake of the fullest possible liberties of individuals, including their religious liberty. More recently, this separation is seen to serve individual autonomy. Alternatively, as in France, they are guided solely by the value of equal citizenship. However, a history of the secular idea shows secularism to be a multi-value doctrine, as tied to several important values. The Indian variant of secularism more explicitly recognizes it to be a multi-value doctrine. Furthermore, western theories of secularism, quite in contrast to the internally variegated practice of western states, have tended to unpack the metaphor of separation to mean either exclusion or neutrality. To my mind, this has been a very limiting interpretation of what is meant by separation.

Thus, a proper study of Indian secularism shows not only that it shares a past with the West but also that it has its own distinctive past. Indian and western secularisms have their own distinctive pre-histories as well as a common history. But, apart from and beyond these histories, the Indian version has taken forward the idea of secularism because, from the very beginning, by virtue of an integral link with nationalism and democracy, it has had to be explicitly tied to citizenship rights, including to the rights of religious minorities. By doing so, it has never tried to completely annul particular religious identities.

To discover its own rich and complex structure, western secularism can either look backward, to its own past or else look sideways, at Indian secularism that mirrors not only the past of secularism but in a way, also its future. Doing so will certainly benefit the secularisms of many western societies. For example, French secularism needs to look beyond its own conceptions of laicite in order to take into account its own multi-cultural and multi-religious reality. It cannot continue to take refuge in claims of exceptionalism. I feel that a good hard look at Indian secularism could also change the self-understanding of American liberal secularism.

I have argued that a recognition of its multi-value character, in particular its links with community-specific rights and ordinary life with dignity, is one distinctive feature of Indian secularism. Its other distinctive feature is its commitment to the idea of principled distance. I have also argued that the multi-value character of secularism makes it inherently unstable and necessarily ambiguous but that this instability is inescapable and given the context in which it is meant to work, this vagueness is a virtue. I also argued that Indian secularism both encapsulates the history of western secularism and mirrors its future. Therefore, by examining the Indian version, the West can learn about its own history as well as see its own future direction. Interestingly, at an earlier time, Indian secularism was similarly positioned when it could see its own future in the trajectory of western secularism. The situation has now reversed. It is now the mainstream western countries that have much to learn by from attending to the distinctiveness of Indian secularism.

Ironically, this need to attend to the distinctiveness of Indian secularism is as pressing in India as it is in the West. Several critics of Indian secularism have identified it with one or the other western versions and have ignored its special character. This has been a source of gross misinterpretation and several problems. For example, it is frequently argued that secularism is a purely Christian, western doctrine and therefore, cannot adapt itself easily to the cultural conditions of India, infused as they are by religions that grew in the soil of the sub-continent. This necessary link between secularism and Christianity is exaggerated, if not mistaken. It is true that a time-honoured conception of secularism is derived almost wholly from Christianity. The idea that to achieve religious integrity, peace, or toleration, the state must be strictly separated from different denominational churches is part of Christianity and its internal history. It is also true that church–state separation is an integral feature of a legitimate form of secularism but as we have seen, it is a necessary but not a sufficient condition for the development of secularism, even in societies with church-based religions. It is clearly not a necessary condition for the development of all forms of secularisms. This is so, even when the term 'church' is interpreted to mean institutions that are authoritative centres in which power is wielded by a specialized religious personnel and that have been integral, in this sense, to many religions (including, for example, Hinduism, where certain kinds of brahmins enjoyed political privilege and social power). Moreover, as I have argued, the mutual exclusion of religion and the state is not the defining feature of secularism. The idea of separation can be interpreted differently. Nor are religious integrity, peace, and toleration (interpreted broadly to mean 'live and let live') uniquely Christian values. Most non-Christian civilizations have given significant space to each. Therefore, none of them are exclusively Christian. It follows that, even though we find in Christian writings some of the clearest and most systematic articulation of this doctrine, even our time-honoured conception of secularism is not exclusively Christian. More importantly, this older, Christian secularism, must not be confused with its modern counterpart. As I said, this Christian secularism is a sufficient, but not necessary, part of the background condition of modern secularism. Modern secularism may be emboldened by its presence but it can also be nourished by other traditions of peace and toleration. Moreover, it means more than just church–state separation.

All right, one might say, secularism is not just a Christian doctrine, but is it not western? I have argued earlier that the answer to this question is both yes and no. Up to a point, it is certainly western. More specifically, as a clearly articulated doctrine, it has distinct western origins. Although elements that constitute secularism assume different cultural forms and are found in several civilizations, one cannot deny that the idea of the secular first achieved self-consciousness and was properly theorized in the West. This western theorization was linked to the birth of secular states in western as much as in non-western societies. For example, one particular form of secular state was installed in India by the Queen's Proclamation of 1858, which guaranteed the government's non-interference in Indian religions following the Mutiny of 1856–7.[32]

One might then say that the middle history of secularism is almost entirely dominated by western societies. However, the same cannot be said of its later history. Nationalism and democracy arrived in the West after the settlement of religious conflicts, in societies that had been made religiously homogenous, or had almost become so (with the exception of the Jews, of course, who continued to face persistent persecution). The absence of deep religious diversity and conflict meant that issues of citizenship could be addressed almost entirely disregarding religious context; the important issue of community-specific rights to religious groups could be wholly ignored. This could not be done in

---

[32] See the instructive discussion of this issue in Faisal Devji's comments on my essay. Devji wishes to trace the distinctiveness of Indian secularism to the colonial period, of which, he says, the Republic's constitution is in many ways a juridical culmination. This claim is ambiguous. It could mean either that much of work that makes Indian secularism distinctive was generated before India's independence from colonial rule or that the distinctiveness of Indian secularism is a product largely of colonial forces. I have no disagreement with the first claim. However, I disagree strongly with the second. As I have remarked in this essay, the idea of a secular state, that is, a state strictly neutral with respect to all religions, was a feature of colonial modernity and came to India with British rule, specifically with the Queen's Proclamation of 1858. This idea was inserted within a cultural background suffused with the pre-history of secularism and once installed, was transformed into something entirely different by the efforts of those struggling against the filth in their own traditions as well as against colonial rule. The product of these struggles, the model of secular state in the Indian constitution was vastly different from anything that existed in pre-British India or under British colonial rule. Thus, the distinctiveness of Indian secularism is not traceable to colonial sources.

India. Both national and democratic agendas in India had to face issues raised by deep religious differences and diversity. In India, nationalism had to choose between the religious and the secular. Similarly, the distribution of active citizenship rights could not be conceived or accomplished by ignoring religion. It could be done either by actively disregarding religion or by developing a complex attitude to it. It also had to balance claims of individual autonomy with those of community obligations, and claims of the necessity of keeping religion 'private' with their inescapable, and often valuable, presence in the public. In addressing these complex issues, the very idea of the secular was taken further than had been evolved in the West. In the course of doing so, it also began to embody a form of contextual moral reasoning with which the notion of principled distance is associated. This distinguishes it from other variants of modern secularism that are grounded in more abstract, theoreticist, and context-insensitive conceptions of rationality. Mainstream theories or ideologies in modern, western societies have taken little notice of these features. Hence, they are struggling to deal with post-colonial religious diversity of their societies. The later history of secularism is more Indian than western.[33]

It may still be argued that the Indianness of Indian secularism is derived entirely from its strong link with home-grown traditions and that therefore India had worked out its own conception of secularism that is neither Christian nor western. For example, secularism for many means 'sarva dharma sambhava': (i) religious coexistence; or (ii) inter-religious tolerance; or (iii) equal respect for all religions. Each of these interpretations of 'sarva dharma sambhava' point to a crucial ingredient of secularism but not only fails to capture its full richness and complexity but entirely ignores its relationship with extremely significant, internally constitutive values of secularism. I take religious coexistence to be equivalent to peace but to identify the secular state with a state that maintains peace between religions, that allows different religions to coexist, does little justice to the rich history and conceptual structure of secularism as a multi-value doctrine. Much the same is true of the interpretation of Indian secularism as inter-religious toleration. There are many good reasons why these two ideals should not be conflated but I shall mention only one. The mainstream idea of

---

[33] By implication, the history of secularism must include the history of other non-western societies that have sought to install and maintain secular states.

toleration is that it enjoins us to refrain from interfering in the affairs of others, even when one has the power to do so and additionally, even when one finds the beliefs and practices of others morally repugnant. In this sense, toleration is entirely consistent with a total refusal to respect the religion of others. It is also compatible with gross inequality and hierarchy. One may tolerate the religion of another person even as one treats him as inferior. Secularism, on the other hand, is grounded in notions of equality—equal concern and respect—and therefore, goes far beyond the notion of inter-religious tolerance.

It is equally inappropriate to identify secularism with equal respect for all religions. Now, it must be conceded that there is something valuable in this interpretation and something Indian about this idea. The internal plurality of Hinduism has the potential for a space where equal respect can indeed be accorded to all religions. Besides, a respect for other religions is entirely consistent with the development of their critique and the identification of local faults within them. Respecting other religions as equals does not entail their blind acceptance or endorsement. Indeed, it is precisely because respect is consistent with difference and critique that the idea of equal respect for all religions is closely linked with the proposal for an inter-faith dialogue. It is also this idea of deeper idea of respect or care for something that allows one to critically intervene in it. Indian secularism does, in a way, respect all religions but by embodying the idea of respectful transformation of religions. In doing so, it inherits a venerable tradition of religious reform.

Yet, even an important ingredient of secularism cannot become the whole of it. Indeed, to equate the two is to do gross injustice to secularism. This equation implies that one ignores the non-religious part of human existence that all modern states must confront and which are also an integral part of modern secularism. Let me take an example. The idea of equal respect for all religions is entirely consistent with the equal unavailability of active citizenship rights to all members of society. It is also consistent with a total indifference to the freedom of individuals within each religious group. A fruitful dialogue on equal footing is entirely possible between religious groups that sanction gender and caste-related injustices or remain indifferent to them. But, sensitivity to such issues is the hallmark of modern secularism. If so, it would be a terrible mistake to identify secularism with equal respect for all religions or modern Indian secularism with 'sarva dharma sambhava'. As political attitude and practice, 'sarva dharma sambhava' is more in tune with states that establish multiple religions, than with states that are secular.

I have argued that it is wrong to identify Indian secularism with western secularism or with 'sarva dharma sambhava'. No doubt, Indian secularism has some relationship with both but it is not one of identity. At the heart of such identification is a failure to notice that we developed a version of secularism that was at once modern and Indian. Those who identify Indian secularism entirely with home-grown traditional conceptions are able to grasp the pre-history of Indian secularism (even though they do not see it as such, as pre-history), but they entirely bypass its connection with a larger common trans-national history as well as with its later history towards which Indians contributed significantly. On the other hand, those who identify the Indian variant with western conceptions fail to notice both the pre-history and the later history of secularism. As I mentioned earlier, like western theorists, they focus only on the middle history of secularism, one developed almost exclusively by western societies. This limited vision is shared by both advocates and opponents of secularism. For example, Indian critics of Indian secularism claim that it has privatized religion. Nothing could be further than the truth. Indian religion has a public presence that is ratified by the Indian constitution. The constitution gives official recognition to religious communities to maintain their own educational institutions. Such institutions foster particular religious identities and are sometimes even funded by the state. There could not be a more suitable illustration of the point that far from privatizing religion, the Indian constitution continues to support its publicization.

To be sure, there is an important sense in which religion is meant to be depoliticized by the Indian constitution. Indian secularism would not be a version of secularism if it did not support the some forms of depoliticization of religion. But this depoliticization of religion must not be confused with its depublicization. Indeed, the constitution even allows a contextual politicization of religion, for example, if such politicization advances the cause of equality and freedom. If justice ever required the local politicization of religion, then any defensible version of secularism must support it. For example, if the minority community in Gujarat is mobilized against the present government, then, even though it relies, at least implicitly, on distinctions and classifications made on the basis of religion, such mobilization would entirely be consistent with secularism. It is noteworthy that separate electorates for Muslims were rejected in post-independent India not by an appeal to a secularism of a strict separationist variety but on highly contextual grounds. The abandonment of separate electorates was supported because they were believed to have: (i) started the awful habit of treating Hindus and Muslims as distinct and congealed political entities; (ii) bolstered sectarianism and ghettoized minorities; and (iii) strengthened the resolve of every community to care only for their own interests. In short, separate electorates were rejected keeping in mind not some general moral necessity of separating religion and state but, as Sardar Patel put it, because they had 'sharpened communal differences to a dangerous extent and prevented the development of a healthy national life'.[34] The implication is that if they were compatible with or somehow fostered a healthy national life, then they could easily have been endorsed.

I have focused in this essay on internal threats to secularism. I have argued that a continuous failure to recognize the distinctiveness of Indian secularism strengthens this threat. I believe this problem afflicts the self-understanding of secularism in both India and several western countries. Western secular states need to improve the understanding of their own practices and to have a better theoretical self-understanding. Rather than get stuck on a model they developed at a particular time in their history, they would do well to learn from the original Indian variant. Equally, both the self-proclaimed supporters of secularism and some of its misguided opponents could learn from examining the original Indian variant. Indeed, it is my conviction that many critics of Indian secularism will embrace it once they properly understand its nature and point.

No idea lives forever. But no good idea should be lost because its supporters are intellectually too lazy to properly defend it.

---

[34] Sardar Patel, India's first Home Minister, *The Constituent Assembly Debates, Book 1, Vol. 5*, 1999, pp. 197–251.

II
A FAILING VISION

4

History, Nation, and Community

*Reflections on Nationalist Historiography of India and Pakistan**

I was first drawn to the relationship between national identity and history when I accidentally stumbled upon a copy of Wilfred Cantwell Smith's *Modern Islam in India*.[1] Written between 1943 and 1946, the book is a gripping account of communalism and nationalism by a brilliant, but youthful Marxist, who later became one of the greatest scholars of comparative religion. Though naïve and occasionally too up front about the author's political values, it remains one of the most subtle and insightful books on the subject.

I read the book in one sitting. It set me off on a detective trail that yielded an unexpectedly curious result. Familiar with the book's internal rhythm and flow, I was immediately struck by the last chapter entitled, 'Toward Pakistan', which was wholly discontinuous and discordant with the tone and substance of the rest of the book. In the penultimate

* This paper was first presented at a workshop on 'Historiography, Nationalist Passion and End of the Empires', organized by Natalie Davis and Gyan Prakash at the Davis Center, Princeton University, in March 1996. It was subsequently published as 'History, Nation, and Community: Reflections on Nationalist Historiography of India and Pakistan', *Economic and Political Weekly*, vol. XXXV, no. 4, 22–8 January 2000, pp. 2161–9.

[1] Wilfred Cantwell Smith, *Modern Islam in India: A Social Analysis*, Lahore: Minerva, first published, May 1943; second edition, Lahore: Ripon Printing Press, December 1947. Also see, Smith, *Modern Islam in India*, London: V. Gollancz Ltd, 1946; and New York: AMS Press, 1974, reissued from the 1946 London edition.

chapter, Cantwell Smith was unmistakably critical of the Muslim League, which he did not hesitate to compare to the Nazis. In the final chapter, the argument suddenly changed focus and claimed that the Muslims were merely fighting for sheer survival against the Hindu imperialism of the Congress party. All too soon, I discovered that what I had in my hands was an edition of the book printed in December 1947, in Lahore. Had the author changed his views so dramatically and so very drastically? Was this the impact of witnessing the wanton carnage during the partition of India? After all, entire world views collapse overnight under the tumultuous impact of apocalyptic events. Could this have happened to Cantwell Smith? It seemed unlikely. At any rate, this had stirred enough curiosity in me to sleuth for an answer. Patient research eventually solved the mystery: this last chapter, inserted into the book without the knowledge of the author, was written by an unknown hand which having writ moved on. Whether or not it was the handy work of an individual 'scholar', or an unscrupulous government official, I do not know. However, it is not difficult to surmise that behind it lay the ruse of nationalist passion.[2]

Renan famously observed that a nation is dependent both on the possession of rich remembrances and a shared amnesia, a collective forgetfulness. Surely, it is commonly accepted that nations can barely survive without losing some of the memories they inherit from their founding moment. The play of lies and distortions in the birth and growth of nations is less evident. At least some histories of every nation are manipulated, and patriotic fervour plays an astoundingly central role in the production and consumption of such myths. This essay, however, is not concerned merely with these manipulated, over-politicized, and 'abnormal' histories. It focuses rather on the role of emotions in the writing of 'normal' scholarly history. A wrongheaded division of cognitive labour misallocates the study of emotions to literature, leaving social science with the description or explanation of only the rational action of humans. If it is true that emotions must be brought back into social science, then to begin doing so, surely no better site exists than the study of nation building.[3]

---

[2] I leave it to the reader to judge whether the complex motivations guiding the work of this sleuth includes a passionate commitment to the idea of India, second nature to many of us since childhood.

[3] On the importance of emotions (passions and durable feelings), see J. Elster, *Political Pscyhology*, Cambridge: Cambridge University Press, 1993; and

on the other hand, appeared to have haplessly reacted to events not of its own making and over which it had no control. It was virtually impossible not to smell a rat here, and not to observe things that would otherwise pass unnoticed. To begin with, footnotes were missing in this chapter. Though listed in the table of contents, the title of the chapter had disappeared from the sectional contents of Part 2. This edition, published in Lahore in December 1947, had no preface. My suspicions were further aroused when I checked out reprints from Delhi in 1964 and New York in 1974, from both of which the controversial chapter had once again vanished. These were reprints of the second (London) edition of 1946, which also included the preface to the first edition (1943). From this evidence, I concluded that the second was the last published edition of the book in that period. But, what I had in my hands was a December 1947 edition from Lahore. Was this a rogue chapter inserted into the book without the permission of the author? But direct confirmation eluded me. Months later, a small footnote in another book by Cantwell Smith, unravelled the mystery:

It is perhaps legitimate to point out that the work entitled Modern Islam in India (title page: on the jacket, Modern Islam in India and Pakistan), Rippon Press, Lahore, bearing the present writer's name as author, is a pirated edition made without his knowledge and consent, and includes a chapter 'Towards Pakistan' that is by another hand and is entirely spurious. There are a few other interpolations also.[9]

Other publications of this period from the Government of Pakistan displayed remarkable similarity to this notorious chapter. One of them quotes extensively, even from Savarkar, to prove the wide acceptance of the idea of two distinct nations and the inevitability of partition: 'The logic of events and experience justifies the demand for Pakistan ... for it was the only way in which the cultural separateness, religious identity as well as economic well-being of Muslims could be secure'. Its description of inter-communal massacres during the partition was brief:

At the time of partition ... the Hindus embarked on a systematic decimation of Muslim population by mass killing and forcible evacuation or conversion, with connivance if not collaboration of the police, trains carrying Pakistan personnel, records and furniture was attacked by hordes of Hindus and Sikhs ... in the riots that immediately preceded and followed partition, hundreds

[9] Wilfred Cantwell Smith, Islam in Modern History, Princeton: Princeton University Press, 1957, pp. 210–11n5.

of thousands of Muslims were done to death and thousands of women were abducted. Pakistan was deprived of coal ... every effort was made to sabotage the established government of Pakistan.[10]

Such manipulated history is not uncommon in India, too. Distortion, lies, exaggerations, the maligning of other communities, is found extensively in the historical literature of militant Hindu nationalists. But official history in India, an adjunct of state policy, invented a different common memory. In contrast to Pakistan's state-backed propagation of the two-nation theory, the Indian state vigorously tried to underscore that Hindus and Muslims *not only are but always have been a unified nation.* The justification of official ideology, coming from professional historians, had a pronounced flavour of what Nietzsche called monumental history.[11] For example, in his address to the Indian History Congress of 1964, the President announced:

We must get to the spirit of the movement and the soul of India with an approach that will help surmount the danger of communal, regional, linguistic and class hatreds that beset history writing. History has a mission and obligation to lead humanity to a higher ideal and nobler future ... The historian cannot shirk this responsibility by burying his head in the false dogma of objectivity. History must not call to memory ghastly aberrations of human nature, of dastardly crimes, of divisions and conflicts, of degeneration and decay but of the higher values of life, of traditions of culture and the nobler deeds of sacrifice and devotion to the service of humanity. The facts of Indian history and the process of its march have to be judged by the criterion of progress towards liberty, morality and opportunities for self-expression...The reason for omission is that such things bring in unhealthy trends which militate against the course of national solidarity or international peace.[12]

Criticisms of such official history and of the pronouncements accompanying it came from the Right as well as, more cautiously, from the Left. R.C. Majumdar complained that official directives to historians showed utter disregard for standards of objective history writing.

[10] Government of Pakistan, *Pakistan, The Struggle of a Nation*, Pakistan: Director of Foreign Publicity, 1949, p. 26.
[11] F. Nietzche (trans. Hollingdale), *The Uses and Disadvantages of History for Life in Untimely Meditations*, Cambridge: Cambridge University Press, 1983, p. 68.
[12] Quoted in S.P. Sen (ed.), *Historians and Historiography in Modern India*, Calcutta: Institute of Historical Studies, 1973, p. xxii.

This essay attempts just this. The first part, 'Methodological Prelimi-
naries', outlines my general methodological standpoint.[4] My purpose
is to undermine the motivational reductionism that undergirds both
the selection of explananda and explanans (the properties of actions
selected for study and the variables with which they are explained) and
the self-understanding of the enquirers, the false standards of objectivity
that enquirers often aspire (surely under the influence of a blindingly
passionate search for truth). With the help of this schema, I distinguish
four types of history writing on nationalism: manipulated, strongly
relativist, critical, and objectivist.

Next, in 'Manipulated History', I renew my discussion of Cantwell
Smith's book and closely examine manipulated history. In the third part,
'Histories: Relativist, Critical, Objectivist', I discuss the more common
brands of nationalist history writing in India, which often pretend to
be wholly objectivist but, in fact, contain the usual mix of strongly
relativist and critical histories. I hope to give the reader a flavour of the
debates about manipulated history in India, between strongly relativist
(ultra-nationalist) and critical histories, and over the precise content
of Indian nationalism. Finally, the last section discusses in somewhat
greater detail, how the nation, the cultural community, and the relation
between the two were imagined by historical actors in India. My focus
remains on inter-communal estrangement rather than on confessional
violence, to which no doubt it is related. I argue that a failure to achieve
the objective of living within a single, unified state (it is an established
fact that till 1940, political separation was not on the agenda of the
Muslim League) is to be explained not just by economic or religious
causes but by a lack of political imagination—shaped as it was, as
much by distinct conceptions of nation and community, as by differing
emotions. I argue that even social scientists and historians, much like
the protagonists of these events, could not properly see or explain why
we failed to solve 'the problem facing the sub-continent'.

METHODOLOGICAL PRELIMINARIES
It is probably true that much history writing in the middle of the
twentieth century was dominated entirely by politics and economics.

Stephen Holmes, *Passions and Constraint*, Chicago and London: The University
of Chicago Press, 1995.
    [4] I simply lay bare my methodological beliefs without claiming to offer any
argument in their support.

It worked with the following methodological maxim: look for the condition and cause of events. Among the causes, examine the actions of relevant agents (individuals or groups). Assume that these actions are caused by self-interest (short or long term; real or apparent). Let us refresh our collective memory by recalling Marx's famous statement: human beings make history but not always in circumstances of their own making. I believe the dominant interpretation of this claim continues to be the following: human agents work within constraints that shape their interests. Rational human beings then try to realize these modified objectives, if not with the best available set of actions, at least with a satisfactory one. For example, the interest of capitalists is shaped by the structure of production relations. Most of their actions are therefore best explained as ways of realizing such interests. Likewise, the actions of religious groups whose interests qua religious groups are shaped by their world view may be explained by religious interests.

There is a straightforward objection to this view. First, it is insensitive to the difference between an external and internal interpretation of interests. Second, it fails to see that actions are guided by principles and social norms too. The methodological maxim must now be modified: assume first that action is guided by self-interest. When this hypothesis fails, explain it by principles or social norms. Surely, the development of social and cultural history is unthinkable without this change effected by contributions from:

1. hermeneutics and anthropology (the meaning of a particular action is interpreted by relating the action to the conceptual universe of the agent, much as the meaning of a sentence emerges from the entire text);
2. sociology (the explanation of action by social norms); and
3. moral philosophy and plain common sense (action is guided not only by self-interest but also by other regulating principles).

But now another objection can be raised. It is true that historians are less prone than economists to reduce human motivations to self-interest. In the complex set of subjective motivations, historians include principles and social norms. They also realize that an action may have a predominant motive. Their explanatory schema contains behaviour that is largely principle-governed, norm-induced, and interest-driven. However, it must be recognized that actions may also be propelled by emotions. So, in response to this criticism, our modified methodological maxim may now look like this: assume first that action is caused by self-interest, principles, or social norms but, when an explanation in terms of any of these falls flat, treat the action as pathological and look for the irrational, aberrant, or the bizarre. Why did this individual kill? Answer: because of a sudden fit of madness. Why did a riot take place? Answer: because of a sudden outburst of mass hysteria. Here, history is linked to and benefits from social psychology and psychoanalysis. Perhaps, this is where a large portion of the study of nationalism properly belongs.

However, the objection that emotions suffer from a relative neglect in the social science is not fully met. There are two distinct senses in which the role of emotion is still improperly understood. First, in so called normal, non-pathological action, their part is underplayed. Consider the question: why does resistance to land reforms exist? Answer: the landlord protects his interests. But rarely: the landlord has a sentimental and enduring attachment to his land (to understand this, we must see Ray's *Jalsagar*!). Second, the power of emotion in shaping other motives is left unexamined. For instance, my abstract commitment to socialist principles may be bolstered by a strong emotional attachment to a subculture of like-minded friends from roughly the same class background. How often is the following explanation offered for religious strife: in situations of foregrounded differences, people often suppress self-interest in favour of loyalty to a religious group and when in this manner, interests are trumped by identity, people can simultaneously be selfless and vicious towards others.[5] Such explanations are certainly uncommon in social science and if I may put my neck on the block, in history, too. Indian history writing may well be an exception to this rule, however. As we shall see, Indian historians are more comfortable with the language of emotions and somewhat less inhibited in admitting the role of emotion in actions.

MANIPULATED HISTORY
Chapter 5 of Cantwell Smith's book ends ominously with a warning:

Of late, the situation in the country has denigrated menacingly. Communal hatred, one of the lowest, if not the most powerful, of human motivations, has threatened to become the main driving force on both sides. Instead of an India with freedom for all, united in friendly communal partnership, there have been signs pointing to, at best, a stagnant India of intense mutual bickering, within an atmosphere of moral degradation and of riots; and, at worst, an India of civil

[5] I do not make these claims for social and cultural history. My gut feeling is that the role of passions is universally underplayed but I do not insist on this point.

war. If the liberals are strong in each party, it may yet be possible to conciliate the warring groups. Otherwise the future of India is dark...[6]

Smith made these observations at the end of his chapter on the 'Islamic nationalism of the Muslim League'. He condoned neither the political demands of the Muslim League nor its brown shirt methods of agitation. He claimed that in the 1930s, the League initially propagated a fascist ideology with which it caught the aggressive frenzy and religious bigotry of the middle classes. 'The Muslim League throve on attack. It was anti-Hindu, anti-Congress, anti-"one free India". It attacked the Hindu with fervour, fear, contempt and bitter hatred. It would seek out, air and emphasise the differences between the two communities.'[7] Its method of refusal, he claimed, was to postulate an utterly impossible 'condition' and then to adopt an air of offended generosity when this was not accepted. In short, the Muslim League was concocting an enthusiasm for a separate state of Pakistan based on the fear that, if Hindus and Muslims lived together in independent India, the Muslims would be horribly maltreated.

Chapter 6 begins with the causes of the breakdown of the Simla conference. The book claims that its primary cause was the refusal of the Congress to 'face the fact that Muslims formed quite a distinct people and could not be fitted into any scheme conceived on the basis of a common nationhood'.[8] The book pleads that the Congress may have seen this as the intransigence of the League, but for Muslims it was a question of sheer existence. Every attempt at settlement, the chapter says, floundered because the Congress tried to realize its impossible dream of establishing Hindu imperialism. It further adds that Muslims were already seething with discontent at the insulting treatment meted out to them. But after the massacre of Muslims in Bihar, which overshadowed even the carnage of Calcutta, Jinnah was left with no alternative but to boycott the session of the constituent assembly. As partition became reality, the genocide of Muslims began. Millions of Muslims were killed.

It did not require much intelligence to note that by now the style and substance of the chapter was startlingly discontinuous with the rest of the book. The blame for partition and mass massacre was squarely apportioned to the essentially 'Hindu Congress'. The Muslim League,

[6] Smith, *Modern Islam in India*, chapter 5.
[7] Ibid., p. 317.
[8] Ibid., p. 361.

on the other hand, appeared to have haplessly reacted to events not of its own making and over which it had no control. It was virtually impossible not to smell a rat here, and not to observe things that would otherwise pass unnoticed. To begin with, footnotes were missing in this chapter. Though listed in the table of contents, the title of the chapter had disappeared from the sectional contents of Part 2. This edition, published in Lahore in December 1947, had no preface. My suspicions were further aroused when I checked out reprints from Delhi in 1964 and New York in 1974, from both of which the controversial chapter had once again vanished. These were reprints of the second (London) edition of 1946, which also included the preface to the first edition (1943). From this evidence, I concluded that the second was the last published edition of the book in that period. But, what I had in my hands was a December 1947 edition from Lahore. Was this a rogue chapter inserted into the book without the permission of the author? But direct confirmation eluded me. Months later, a small footnote in another book by Cantwell Smith, unravelled the mystery:

It is perhaps legitimate to point out that the work entitled Modern Islam in India (title page: on the jacket, Modern Islam in India and Pakistan), Rippon Press, Lahore, bearing the present writer's name as author, is a pirated edition made without his knowledge and consent, and includes a chapter 'Towards Pakistan' that is by another hand and is entirely spurious. There are a few other interpolations also.[9]

Other publications of this period from the Government of Pakistan displayed remarkable similarity to this notorious chapter. One of them quotes extensively, even from Savarkar, to prove the wide acceptance of the idea of two distinct nations and the inevitability of partition: 'The logic of events and experience justifies the demand for Pakistan ... for it was the only way in which the cultural separateness, religious identity as well as economic well-being of Muslims could be secure'. Its description of inter-communal massacres during the partition was brief:

At the time of partition ... the Hindus embarked on a systematic decimation of Muslim population by mass killing and forcible evacuation or conversion, with connivance if not collaboration of the police, trains carrying Pakistan personnel, records and furniture was attacked by hordes of Hindus and Sikhs ... in the riots that immediately preceded and followed partition, hundreds

[9] Wilfred Cantwell Smith, *Islam in Modern History*, Princeton: Princeton University Press, 1957, pp. 210–11n5.

of thousands of Muslims were done to death and thousands of women were abducted. Pakistan was deprived of coal ... every effort was made to sabotage the established government of Pakistan.[10]

Such manipulated history is not uncommon in India, too. Distortion, lies, exaggerations, the maligning of other communities, is found extensively in the historical literature of militant Hindu nationalists. But official history in India, an adjunct of state policy, invented a different common memory. In contrast to Pakistan's state-backed propagation of the two-nation theory, the Indian state vigorously tried to underscore that Hindus and Muslims *not only are but always have been a unified nation*. The justification of official ideology, coming from professional historians, had a pronounced flavour of what Nietzsche called monumental history.[11] For example, in his address to the Indian History Congress of 1964, the President announced:

We must get to the spirit of the movement and the soul of India with an approach that will help surmount the danger of communal, regional, linguistic and class hatreds that beset history writing. History has a mission and obligation to lead humanity to a higher ideal and nobler future ... The historian cannot shirk this responsibility by burying his head in the false dogma of objectivity. History must not call to memory ghastly aberrations of human nature, of dastardly crimes, of divisions and conflicts, of degeneration and decay but of the higher values of life, of traditions of culture and the nobler deeds of sacrifice and devotion to the service of humanity. The facts of Indian history and the process of its march have to be judged by the criterion of progress towards liberty, morality and opportunities for self-expression...The reason for omission is that such things bring in unhealthy trends which militate against the course of national solidarity or international peace.[12]

Criticisms of such official history and of the pronouncements accompanying it came from the Right as well as, more cautiously, from the Left. R.C. Majumdar complained that official directives to historians showed utter disregard for standards of objective history writing.

[10] Government of Pakistan, *Pakistan, The Struggle of a Nation*, Pakistan: Director of Foreign Publicity, 1949, p. 26.

[11] F. Nietzche (trans. Hollingdale), *The Uses and Disadvantages of History for Life in Untimely Meditations*, Cambridge: Cambridge University Press, 1983, p. 68.

[12] Quoted in S.P. Sen (ed.), *Historians and Historiography in Modern India*, Calcutta: Institute of Historical Studies, 1973, p. xxii.

When the history of the freedom movement was written, a directive was issued to research workers that they collect only such data as proves that the outbreak of 1857 was a war of independence and not a mutiny of soldiers ... Research workers were instructed to record the evidence of only one group of revolutionaries and to restrict the mention of violence deployed in the freedom movement.[13]

The government, he said, seeks to buttress Gandhian philosophy of non-violence by claiming that this ideal was followed throughout the course of Indian history. Historians, he claimed, were asked to repudiate that Muslim rulers ever desecrated temples or to admit that Aurangzeb was intolerant. History became a handmaiden for contemporary politics and resulted in a rigorous politicization of history.[14]

The tacit support provided by historians to official ideology did not go entirely unchallenged. For example, Parthasarthy Gupta wondered why historians shied away from explaining communal riots or from probing why communal passions are so easily whipped up by leaders of communal parties.[15] Romila Thapar, cautious in her criticism of official ideas of national unity, warned that unity could not be enforced from above and will never exist unless it was felt by various groups which constitute the whole. Thapar offered her own view of national integration as, 'tolerance, an attitude that is willing to accommodate diverse and opposing opinions without suppressing them at various levels of social, economic and intellectual life.'[16]

HISTORIES: RELATIVIST, CRITICAL, OBJECTIVIST

Official histories fabricated to undergird the specific policies of nation-states must be distinguished from other nationalist histories. Official history is shaped almost exclusively by collective self-interest. Other forms of nationalist history writing mix cognitive interest with ephemeral nationalist passion or the more enduring national sentiment. The strong tie between emotion and nationalist history has long been noted. Over two thousand years ago, Polybius wrote that 'historians must

[13] R.C. Majumdar, *Historiography in Modern India*, Delhi: Asia Publishing House, 1970, pp. 37–57.

[14] C.H. Philips (ed.), *Historians of India, Pakistan and Ceylon*, London and New York: Oxford University Press, 1961, p. 426.

[15] Parthasarthy Gupta, Indian History Congress, *Proceedings of the Twenty-fourth Session*, Delhi, 1961; Calcutta, 1963, p. 359.

[16] Romila Thapar, Indian History Congress, *Proceedings of the Twenty-fourth Session*, Delhi, 1961; Calcutta, 1963, p. 345.

show some partiality to their own countries'. Morley expressed the same point centuries later: 'the historian has been the hearth at which the soul of the country has been kept alive'.[17] Such sentiments were echoed in India too. Thapar unhesitatingly admitted that historians are subject to the 'same emotions as others in society'. The crucial issue then is not whether history and national identity can be altogether un-coupled but precisely how the bonds between them are forged. Does reflective distance enable people to work out ambivalent historical lega-cies of their own rather than accept more easily available conventional versions? To admit the inevitability of a link with national identity is one thing, to make it the central aim of history writing is quite another. Indian historians fought with each other not only over the assessment of how much distance could be achieved and the degree to which it was desirable but also over the inflection of an Indian past made accessible by history writing.

Nationalist history was made inevitable by three interrelated causes. First, by the advent of modernity that required a new identity to replace traditional ones. Second, by the passionate desire to restore a sense of dignity lost in the seductive embrace of a conquering culture. Finally, by a commitment to set the historical record straight, warped wilfully or unwittingly by English historians.

Commentators noted the presence of each of these motivations. One claimed that:

Modernity requires a new identity and since identity requires a past, one of (our) prime concerns was the discovery of India's heritage ... Moreover with their self-respect at stake, idealisation of the past became a main stay. A passionate evocation of the past, an effort to prove the continuity between an idealised past and the reformer's own image of a reformed future, was unavoidable.[18]

Historically minded writers such as Nirad C. Chaudhuri confessed:

We were swept by the emotional fervour of the nationalist movement. The first element in this emotion was an intense, almost religious hopefulness. We believed in the second advent of our country and nation with a firmness of conviction which nothing could shake. We knew that our present condition was pitiable: we were poor, subjugated and oppressed and even degenerate

[17] Quoted in Dawidowicz, *The Holocaust and the Historians*, Harvard: Harvard University Press, 1981, pp. 142–3.

[18] S.C. Misra, 'Historical Thought and Indian Heritage in 19th Century Social Reform Movements: Some Observations', in John Webster (ed.), *History and Contemporary India*, New York: Asia Publishing House, 1971, p. 9.

in certain respects but we were great once and should be greater in the future. This amazing faith was justified by itself and needed no evidence of validity external to itself.[19]

In such a milieu, it was hard to see any contradiction between a usable knowledge of the past and knowledge of the past for its own sake, between nationalist and objective history. The diplomat and historian, K.M. Panikkar, captured some of these motivations well: 'Brought up on text books which claimed that there was no such thing as India, we each had to discover India for ourselves: It was a spiritual adventure for each of us to understand the historical processes which have made us what we are.'[20]

The prejudice of English historians was frequently cited as both a spur to nationalist history and as a cause of reverse bias. Crane noted that since Indian nationalism during British rule was unwelcome, nationalism was equated with subversion. Colonial writers defended British rule and by implication critiqued Indian nationalism. Further problems were due to misunderstanding across deeply diverse cultures and to asymmetries of power. British historians almost always relied on official records and described political events only where the British dominated. As a result, history by British historians 'was more a history of British involvement in India rather than a history of Indian people.'[21] Majumdar also noted how woefully inadequate the writing of English historians on India was when judged by the constitutive principles of 'objective history'. He called for three constraining standards: (i) refrain from ignoring data that undercuts the political or moral values of the historian; (ii) avoid philosophical or moralistic interpretations of history; and (iii) have a purely objective approach like that of a scientist. 'A historian must divest his mind of sentiments, prejudices and preconceptions and all kinds of emotions that are likely to distort his vision and judgement'.[22] English historians, Majumdar argued, violated all these fundamental principles. For example, James Mill could

[19] Nirad C. Chaudhuri, *The Autobiography of an Unknown Indian*, New York: Macmillan, 1951.

[20] K.M. Panikkar, *A Survey of Indian History*, Bombay: Asia Publishing House, 1963, p. viii.

[21] R.I. Crane, 'Problems of Writing Indian History: The Case Studies in Indian Nationalism', in *Problems of Historical Writing in India*, Proceedings of the seminar held at the IIC, January 1963, pp. 35–49.

[22] Majumdar, *Historiography in Modern India*, pp. 37–57.

not 'absolve himself of the charge of a deep-rooted prejudice against the Hindus.' Statements such as 'the Hindu like the eunuch excels in the qualities of a slave',[23] show, as Majumdar noticed disapprovingly, that for Mill, the people of Europe were greatly superior to the Hindus. Elphinston's book, he stated, contained similar passages such as: 'The prominent vice of the Hindus is want of veracity, in which they outdo most nations even of the east.'[24] Other historians such as Vincent Smith and Chirol were hardly more objective.

Irfan Habib, historian of 'medieval' India, argued that imperialist historians had their own interest in showing how all 'governments previous to the British had been despotic, intolerant and monstrously cruel, and the Indian people, forever divided, were fit only to be conquered. This attitude lent itself to a peculiar interpretation of medieval Indian history. It was assumed that the Muhammadans were the conquerors and rulers of India in the same sense as the British had been.'[25] Seeds of communal historiography that flowered during and soon after the independence were laid, Habib argued, by British historians.

But, a decent quotient of national sentiment crucial for an 'objective history of the nation' must be distinguished from nationalist fervour that falsifies and distorts. 'If British historiography was tainted by the need to sustain the Empire, the chief defect of Indian historians flowed from a patriotic fervour which magnified the virtues and minimised the defects of their own people.'[26] The most absurd example of ultra-nationalism, cited by both Thapar and Majumdar, is Jaiswal's extravagant claim that ancient India had a parliamentary form of government. Romila Thapar ratified the need to meet the challenge of Eurocentric historians who claimed that the Greeks were superior in every respect to ancient Indian civilization but cautioned that this need to delve into the past, linked to the pride in Indian heritage, could cloud the judgement of the historians. She mentions the alleged presence of tolerance in the past stemming from 'a certain extra-spiritual quality which the ancient Indian possessed.'[27] Ashoka's plea for tolerance is evidence, she argued, not of tolerance but of excessive intolerance in his times. She similarly criticized anachronistic claims about a unified nation.

[23] Ibid.

[24] Ibid.

[25] Irfan Habib, Indian History Congress, *Proceedings of the Twenty-fourth Session*, Delhi, 1961; Calcutta, 1963, p. 350.

[26] Majumdar, *Historiography in Modern India*, pp. 37–57.

[27] Thapar, *Proceedings of the Twenty-fourth Session*, p. 346.

Majumdar also pointed out that intense hatred against the British produced spurious histories. For instance, several historians supplied a long list of evil deeds, errors of omissions and commission of the British in both the economic and political spheres. Their scathing comments leave little doubt that their main object was to draw a lurid picture of the British in India. Majumdar addressed Savarkar's book, *Indian War of Independence*, as a typical specimen of the representation of history from an extremely nationalist point of view.[28] As partisan advocates rather than judges, Indian historians, he added, tended to minimize the harsh treatment of the lower castes by upper caste Hindus. Furthermore, Majumdar claimed that the 'political motive of bringing Hindus and Muslims together against a common imperial enemy glossed over the intolerance and bigotry of Muslim rulers.'[29] Since Indian intellectuals felt part of the national movement and were compelled to advance its cause, 'objective scholarship suffered in the ensuing welter of charges and counter charges.'[30] Crane noted that

all nationalisms carry irrational elements and all nationalist writing tend towards polemics. Indian writers were no exception. Foreign domination brings with it inevitable psychological effects such as the deep need to assert the dignity and capacity of one's own culture. Everywhere this leads to a romantic reconstruction of a nation's past in the most favourable light possible. At times the effect of foreign domination is so great as to cause people to find in their past things which were not only not there and had no reason to be there but worse, are found there only because the conquerors highly value them. This most subtle form of colonial domination did not escape India.[31]

In the immediate aftermath of Indian independence, most historians, I believe, accepted the inescapability of durable national sentiment as an incentive for the writing of history, but also felt the need to separate it from the obsessive nationalist fervour that interfered with objective history. No historian is likely to contradict Majumdar's statement:

nationalist historians are guided in their study of India not only by scientific spirit but by the need to examine and re-examine points of national interest or importance, particularly those on which full or accurate information is not available or which have been misrepresented, misunderstood or misconceived.

[28] Majumdar, 'Nationalist Historians', in C.H. Philips (ed.), *Historians of India, Pakistan and Ceylon*, London and New York: Oxford University Press, 1961, p. 425.

[29] Ibid.

[30] Ibid.

[31] Crane, *Problems of Historical Writing in India*, pp. 35–49.

Such objectives are not necessarily in conflict with critical study and therefore a nationalist historian is not necessarily a charlatan or a propagandist.[32]

No one could agree with this more than Irfan Habib. However, for Habib, Majumdar's own history was not nationalist but communal. Habib argued that I.H. Qureshi, who wrote the semi-official history of Pakistan, and Majumdar, who was initially asked by the Government of India to write a history of the freedom movement—the first draft of which was rejected by the board constituted for this purpose—shared a common communal framework. 'Historians of both schools speak the same language and have an identical interpretation of medieval history. The drama is the same, only the characters with whom they most identify are different. It only remains for one side to paint the other community in the blackest colours.'[33]

Both agreed that the Bhakti movement was a Hindu reaction to a proselytizing Islam, that Aurangzeb was the author of Muslim restoration, and that all revolts against him were essentially Hindu. Their whole analysis, Habib argued, rested on the categorization of Mughal rule as Muslim Empire with Hindu subjects. But, the division of the ruler and the ruled did not coincide with the division between Hindus and Muslims, and many revolts against Mughals were lower class, not Hindu in character.

Against Majumdar's demand that 'we should not bow before the exigencies of political complications, for history does not fear wounding the susceptibilities of the sister community',[34] Habib claimed that objective history does not contradict nationalist history. Historians of different persuasions, some with a liberal outlook, others simply in pursuit of facts, still others such as the 'Canadian clergyman, Wilfred Cantwell Smith', and those historians who 'wrote under nationalist inspiration for which none may feel ashamed', converged on the same truth and thereby laid the foundation of objective history writing in India.[35] It is our duty, Habib urged, to cherish the views of those 'who bequeathed the objective view of history and thus serve the cause of

[32] Majumdar, 'Nationalist Historians', in Philips (ed.), *Historians of India, Pakistan and Ceylon*, p. 417. Majumdar often mentioned R.C. Dutt as an example of a nationalist historian who never strayed from the course of objective history.

[33] Habib, *Proceedings of the Twenty-fourth Session*.

[34] Majumdar, 'Nationalist Historians', in Philips (ed.), *Historians of India, Pakistan and Ceylon*.

[35] Habib, *Proceedings of the Twenty-fourth Session*, p. 353.

national unity.'[36] Habib charged that Majumdar's communal history and tales of ancient India were wrong, and when taught in schools and fed to students, sowed dissension and division in the country.

It is clear that at stake in the controversy is not some abstruse argument about objective, value-free social science, but the wider issue of the public use of history. Also, in competition were two different conceptions of nationhood, one that sidelines religious communities and the other that refused to do so. Thapar saw these points well. Historians, she said, are not infallible and superhuman. 'We are influenced by the same emotions as the rest of society in which we live. No historical writing is ever completely objective and objectivity is relative anyway.'[37]

SENTIMENT, NATION, AND COMMUNITY

In the 1920s, when the Muslim League and the Congress cooperated with each other, it was not uncommon for members of the League to simultaneously be members of the Congress party. By the end of the 1930s, however, the two parties were irrevocably opposed to each other. What caused this estrangement? More generally, what explains the deterioration of relations between the Hindu and the Muslim elite? Why was India partitioned? How did historians see these events and how did emotional entanglement with ideas of nationhood and community affect their perception of Hindu–Muslim relations?[38]

Two constrasting answers dominate the literature. According to the first, the official Pakistani view, Muslims and Hindus are two separate nations. The division of British India into Pakistan and Hindustan is legitimate because every nation must have a state. The second view, the official stance of the Indian Congress Party, does not question the assumption that nations must turn into states but denies that Hindus and Muslims are distinct nations. Thus, on this ground alone, it had a principled opposition to the partition of India. However, despite these differences, both display a failure of collective imagination. Neither

[36] Ibid.

[37] Thapar, *Proceedings of the Twenty-fourth Session*, p. 350. But she added, 'historical training should at least be able to caution the historian, prevent him not only from participating in popular prejudices but also leading him to draw attention to what may be historically fallacies. Only then can the historian claim to be representing man in his actuality.'

[38] Henceforth, when I speak of Hindu–Muslim relations, I really mean relations between Hindu and Muslim elites. The relations between ordinary Hindus and Muslims had a different dynamic and complexity.

is able to acknowledge the possibility of an institutional design that accommodates distinct cultural communities. Nationalist history, probably inspired by a sentimental idea of national unity, replicates this failure on both sides of the border.

There were notable exceptions, however. At the end of 1944, Beni Prasad, in one of the few insightful books on the subject, disputed the use of the term nation for a religious group such as Muslims but then added:

in any case it does not follow that nationhood coincides with statehood. The confusion between the two has been one of the chief sources of disquiet and frustration ... The disassociation of statehood from nationhood is one of the supreme needs of the modern age in the East as well as the West; in a word, the depoliticization of the whole concept of nationality, a definite renunciation of the idea that those who feel themselves to be a nation should necessarily constitute an independent state of their own.[39]

Two decades later, I.H. Qureshi, Vice-chancellor of Karachi University, ruminating on partition, first admitted that, till as late as the early 1940s, Muslims (read Muslim elite) had not abandoned the very real possibility of a modus vivendi with Hindus. He then wondered if the two communities possessed the requisite sophistication, rare even in politically developed societies, required for the maintenance of a multi-cultural society. Perhaps he meant that a modern multi-cultural state is yet to develop anywhere in the world.[40] Majumdar, in a severe attack on the official Congress position, wrote:

Hindu leaders ignored facts that make Hindu and Muslims distinct religious, cultural and political units. The consequence was that no real effort was made by them to tackle the real problem that faced India, namely how to make it possible for two distinct units to live together as members of a single state. Whether this problem could have been solved no one can say with great certainty but the examples of Canada and Switzerland before us would have made the attempt worth making.[41]

[39] Beni Prasad, *India's Hindu-Muslim Question*, Lahore: Book Traders, 1944, p. 82.

[40] I.H. Qureshi, 'A Case Study of the Social Relations between the Muslims and the Hindus, 1935–1947', in C.H. Philips (ed.), *The Partition of India: 1947*, Leeds: Leeds University Press, 1967, pp. 360–8.

[41] R.C. Majumdar, *Freedom Movement in India*, Calcutta: Firma K.L. Mukhopadhyaya, 1962, p. xix. The recognition of this point does not detract from a major shortcoming in accounts such as Majumdar's that appear to conflate relations between Hindu and Muslim elites with relations between

All three historians point to a failure of imagination in the Congress as well as in the Muslim league. Neither could imagine that distinct cultural communities could live together in a single state.[42] What explains this failure? Majumdar provides one answer: 'An impression was created that Hindus and Muslims had shed their differences, that there was a complete transformation in the two and a fusion of two cultures...though every true Indian must devoutly wish for such a consummation, it was unfortunately never a historical fact.'[43]

Majumdar claimed that Syed Ahmed and Jinnah had more realistic views than Gandhi and Nehru. To accept as a fact what is eminently desirable but has not yet been achieved, is not only a great historical error but also a political blunder of the first magnitude which can lead to tragic consequences. Majumdar went on to lambast historians for encouraging an ideology of fanciful fraternity. A solid structure of amity and understanding, he claimed, could not be built on the quicksand of false history and political expediency. Real understanding could only be arrived at by a frank recognition of the facts of history and not by their suppression or distortion. Only such a reorientation would put Hindu–Muslim relations in better perspective and give a rational explanation for the birth of Pakistan.[44]

Majumdar was ambiguous about two claims: (i) the predominantly Hindu leaders of the Congress failed to see the real difference and therefore, the ensuing estrangement between Hindus and Muslims; and (ii) for sheer political expediency, Hindu elites deliberately created the false impression and the fictitious slogan of Hindu–Muslim fraternity. Overall, it would not be incorrect to say that Majumdar interpreted the actions of Hindu leaders in terms of strategic rationality: Congress leaders desired a unified state. They believed that Hindu–Muslim amity is essential for this. Therefore, ignoring the difference and estrangement between the two communities, they invented slogans of Hindu–Muslim

---

all Hindus and Muslims. Such views do not appreciate the deep internal differentiation within each community.

[42] Despite its reflective and illuminating quality, an article that appears to overstate its case is Louis Dumont's somewhat neglected, 'Nationalism and Communalism', *Contributions to Indian Sociology*, no. VII, March 1964, pp. 30–70. On p. 69, he says, 'partition was probably inevitable as a lesser evil in so far as the feeling of the Muslims of being socially distinct was disregarded by the leaders of the Nationalist Congress'.

[43] Majumdar, *Freedom Movement in India*.

[44] Ibid., pp. xix and xx.

fraternity. For Majumdar, this was a calculated act. Indian historians conspired with the Congress party to create and sustain this myth. In so doing, they abandoned standards of good history writing. They are unable to tolerate history that mentions facts incompatible with ideas of national integration. In India, the critique of a usable history came from historians not associated with the Left.

I agree with the assessments of Majumdar, Qureshi, and Beni Prasad that political parties failed the two communities. However, I disagree with the strategic rational explanation offered by Majumdar. I believe that the failure of political imagination was due, first, to the conception of nation and community shared by both groups, one that assumed the necessity of thick commonalty for nationhood. Second, because this conception was influenced by and laden with specific emotions. Finally, because even political expediency was affected by the mechanism of wish fulfilment.

For sub-continental elites, what were the formal features of a community? I propose the following: a community is a dense network of relations binding members into a thick unity of purpose. Fusion rather than the diffusion of identity is critical to this conception. Furthermore, these bonds of solidarity must be experienced emotionally, if they are to exist, or else, at best, they exist very weakly. The language of emotions came naturally to Gandhi and Nehru. Gandhi demanded, 'not a patched up thing but a union of hearts based upon a definite recognition of the indubitable proposition that swaraj for India must be an impossible dream without the indissoluble union between the Hindus and Muslims of India.'[45] He unfailingly insisted that this unity must not be based on fear or merely be a truce (modus vivendi). Hindus and Muslims, he said, 'are one in sorrow'. We must, he often pleaded, help our brethren. Similarly, Nehru reiterated this 'deeper unity of the people of India' and demanded a 'conscious effort on the part of all of us for the emotional integration of all our people.'[46] For the INC, a nation was constituted by a thick common purpose and deep emotional bond.

It might be claimed that this discourse has a familiar ring to it. Does it not, after all, contain the standard romantic conception of community? Is this not the naïve and sometimes dangerous romantic error of grafting features onto a large, impersonal community that are more

[45] M.K. Gandhi, *The Hindu-Muslim Unity*, Bombay: Bhartiya Vidya Bhawan, 1965, p. 9.

[46] S. Gopal (ed.), *Nehru: An Anthology*, New Delhi: Oxford University Press, 1980, pp. 332–3.

appropriate to a smaller face-to-face community, such as the modern family? But, really, this response misses the point. The Gandhi–Nehru discourse, articulated by the Congress party, never strayed from its liberal moorings. Gandhi would say in the same breath that this union of hearts was also a 'partnership between equals, each respecting the religion of the other'. In fact, it is interesting to see how liberal principles of equality were combined in the nationalist discourse with romantic notions of fraternity and how, in particular, Gandhi had his fingers in both pies. Surprisingly, participants in this two-layered discourse rarely saw its internal tension. They did not always realize that by placing *felt* solidarity above the more formal and rational principle of equality of respect to which they also owed allegiance, they undermined their own larger interests.

In my view, this valourization of emotional integration had far reaching consequences for Hindu–Muslim relations. A person distancing himself from fraternal talk was less likely to be seen to prefer a world of formal relations in which self-interest is restrained by a set of moral principles, and more likely to be viewed as having plunged straight into a purely strategic calculation of self-interest. This clearly was a breach of fraternity. To be sure, there was room for strategic calculation but only with outsiders. To insist upon self-interest was to cross the rubicon and align with the outsiders. Such a world leaves little room for conceptions of reasonable disagreement among loosely tied persons. Not surprisingly, often reasonable disagreement was seen as a betrayal tantamount to a declaration of enmity. Qureshi expressed this point well:

It was however difficult to press demands for effective safeguards and substantial autonomy without in any way or another creating in the Hindu mind misgivings of their intentions and what was even more important of their complete identification with Indian nationalism. The average Hindu looked upon such demands as essentially anti-national, narrow-minded, based on prejudice and inevitably resulting in a weak state'.[47]

[47] Qureshi, 'A Case Study of Social Relations between Muslims and the Hindu 1935–1947', in Philips (ed.), *The Partition of India*, p. 361. It is interesting to note how heavily Qureshi's account relies on the language of emotions. 'Muslims are *anxious* to preserve their identity. They are highly *sensitive* to real or imaginary danger to their religion and their culture. Most of the manifestations of *ill-will*, leading sometimes to riots and ugly incidents were basically the result of revivalist *feelings* among Hindus and the anxieties of Muslims. The attitude of Hindu nationalism *filled the Muslim with alarm* and he *resented* all attempts at Hinduizing the language, culture, and education. The congress could not have

An expression of legitimate self-interest was seen as a blatant exhibition of prejudice, brazenly against unity and, therefore, anti-national.

But, does this not show that Hindu–Muslim relations were already pretty bad? The answer is yes and no. Yes, because, at one level, they had always been bad.[48] No, because, at another level, an emotional bond did exist on which relations of mutual respect could have been built.[49] The real question then is not why relations were bad but why they turned sour? My very, very tentative explanation is this: whatever the real nature of its practice, the dominant discourse of the Congress, particularly in relation to Muslims, was driven by *principles and emotions*. The discourse of Muslims, led by Syed Ahmed and others was shaped, on the other hand, by *principles and self-interest*. The foregrounding of emotions by one or self-interest by the other, obscured, even from themselves, the real significance of principles well within their reach and demanded by the very situation in which Hindus and Muslims found themselves. The Hindu elite frequently presented its liberal claim in the romantic language of emotions. The same claim was formulated by the Muslim elite in the language of self-interest. The substantive liberal claim of mutual respect was easily obscured by the formal language in which it was presented.[50] To the Muslim, the emotional talk of Hindus seemed hollow and merely cloaked strong Hindu interest and potential Hindu hegemony. This is not entirely puzzling. I here allude to the underside of benevolence which springs forth amidst hierarchy. Even minimal self-awakening can see through the asymmetry hidden beneath benevolence and recognize how the language of love is frequently intertwined with inequality. The Congress Hindu, on the other hand, saw only hostility in what by his lights appeared cold,

---

resisted this pressure for long and Muslim resistance to this process could have come to the surface before long, because the *injury to deep-rooted Muslim feelings* would have resulted in discontent and frustration' (italics added).

[48] Chaudhuri, *The Autobiography of an Unknown Indian*, p. 225, made this point poignantly. 'When I see the gigantic catastrophe of Hindu-Muslim discord I am not surprised because we as children held the tiny mustard seed in our hands and sowed it diligently.'

[49] Including emotions associated with asymmetric dependence. For example, the love and hate that is so characteristic of master–slave relations.

[50] I am alluding here to the power of language and discourse which had the potential of creating distortions not only in the understanding of others but also in self-understanding. The simple formulation of this point should not be seen as a real causal account of what happened but as a methodological strategy to emphasize what has hitherto been neglected or obscured.

calculating self-interest. Neither could bring himself to trust the other's commitment to impartial principles. Even the wise Mahatma could not break this impasse because he too had no room in his philosophy for the impersonal. His world contained only the near or the distant-personal.

Conceptions of the 'communal' were also affected by emotions. Hindus and Muslims understood the importance of religious/cultural groups, but any deviation from thicker conceptions of commonalty, together with the abrogation of the language of emotions, implied the adoption of the framework of unmitigated self-interest. Mere talk or endorsement of religious community was not therefore 'communal'. This is a much later accretion to the semantics of the term. But any loosening of ties, signalled by the retreat from an informal discourse of emotional integration, was viewed as a willing embrace of the project of self-interest. *This* was 'communal'. Hindu elites, in particular, frequently saw *all* expressions of cultural identity in these terms.[51]

To be sure, no transformation had occurred in the sense of the term 'community', but its reference had shifted from Hindus and Muslims taken collectively to each of them taken singly. Within the parameters set by the Indian national movement, the term 'communal' registers a protest against this shift of the reference of 'community'. A religious group becomes communal when it begins to act with thick purpose, as an emotionally integrated community, as if it were a nation. Is not felt solidarity the natural and exclusive preserve of the nation? And, since it was widely accepted that a nation must have a state, the loosening of ties or a withdrawal from emotional discourse signalled political separation. This is how the terms 'communal' and 'national' became antithetical to each other.

I have tried to show how emotions entered the very conception of community and nationhood, and how the specific nature of estrangement between Hindus and Muslims cannot be understood without a proper grasp of the sentimental component of the Indian conception of community. I do not wish to over-emphasize this point but it is wise not to ignore durable sentiments or deny them some explanatory power. It is surely not my intention to give emotions primacy over other explanatory variables. I merely wish to claim that estrangement and its converse are primarily affective notions and an attempt to reduce them to something else serves no cognitive purpose.

[51] For an interesting account of communalism, see Dumont, 'Nationalism and Communalism', pp. 30–70.

Let me return to Indian historiography. Why did Hindu leaders not see that two cultural communities can live together in a single state? The simple strategic, rational explanation is that they cynically constructed an ideology of Hindu–Muslim brotherhood in the service of their desire for a unified nation-state. The more complex strategic explanation is that their passionate desire for a unified nation prevented them from acknowledging growing estrangement. Passion affected their desire for national unity, and this intense desire induced a false belief of lasting warmth between Hindus and Muslims. In other words, this was a classic case of wish fulfilment. When something is desired strongly, it is seen to exist before it actually does; the very passion that induced the slogan of Hindu–Muslim unity, also obscured the lack of amity in their relations.

Even this does not fully explain the issue. I have argued that a sentimental conception of community affected the perception and evaluation of inter-community conduct. It left no space for relatively impersonal principles that could prevent reasonable disagreements from degenerating into hostility. Majumdar failed to grasp this. To my knowledge, few Indian historians did. To try to explain this failure was part of the task of this essay.

5

Between Revenge and Reconciliation

Gandhi and Truth Commissions*

THE GANDHIAN SCHEMA OF MORAL ACTION IN
THE AFTERMATH OF EVIL

The morning of 16 August 1946 saw the beginning of what came be described as the 'Great Calcutta Killing', in which about 4,000 people were killed and another 11,000 injured. Trouble was already brewing for sometime. 'There was fear about, and fear in India means trouble', Francis Tuker, a colonial army officer, had written in April.[1] But the magnitude of the tragedy caught everyone unawares. The 'intensity of the hatred let loose and the savagery with which both sides killed each other' surprised everyone.[2] Soon people began redescribing the killing as civil war and the foreboding of 'impending terrible disasters' began to grip collective imagination. *Statesman*, the local English daily, in a lament claimed that Calcuttans desperately needed 'psycho-therapy on a mass scale'.[3]

---

* Originally published as 'Between Revenge and Reconciliation: Gandhi and Truth Commissions', in Ranabir Samaddar (ed.), *Peace: A Reader*, New Delhi: Sage Publications, 2005, pp. 390–412.

[1] Dennis Dalton, 'Gandhi during Partition: A Case Study in the Nature of Satyagraha', in C.H. Philips and Mary Wainright (eds), *The Partition of India: Policies and Perspectives, 1935–1947*, Cambridge, MA: MIT Press, 1969, p. 142.

[2] Ibid., p. 146.

[3] Ibid., p. 151.

Gandhi arrived in Calcutta in August 1947, on the very day of the first major sabotage of a train in Punjab and declared that his 'head hung in shame at this continuous recital of man's barbarism.'[4] When, Suhrawardy, the Muslim League Chief Minister of Bengal, pleaded with him to stay on in Calcutta and see it through in times of trouble, Gandhi insisted he would do so only if Suhrawardy agreed to live with him in a local, riot-hit Muslim *bustee*. Gandhi knew that the breakdown of trust between the two communities was the principal cause of the violence and therefore, this 'experiment' by him, a Hindu, would be crucial for winning back the trust of ordinary Muslims. Chastened by the violence he had personally witnessed, Suhrawardy agreed. Hindus, on the other hand, reacted to this proposal with horror. How could Gandhi live with a known Leaguee in the midst of Muslims who had slaughtered Hindus? However, Gandhi's argument and charisma eventually prevailed. Communal violence was halted. Hindus and Muslims flocked to Gandhi with their grievances, pleading innocence and pinning the entire blame for violence on members of the other community or on the *goondas*. Gandhi predictably asked everyone to 'turn the searchlight inwards', and to accept collective responsibility for evil.

For a while the ploy worked. This experiment of rebuilding trust between two estranged communities had effected a remarkable catharsis. Collective ill will was not suppressed but Gandhi had succeeded in transforming it into mutual goodwill. The explosion of communal harmony was intense but short-lived, however, forcing Gandhi to undertake a fast unto death. Now people began to respond with greater resolve: peace demonstrations were held, resistance groups to prevent killings were formed, civil servants joined in the fast, and even goondas offered to submit to any penalty Gandhi wished to impose on them. Peace returned but Gandhi did not stop his fast. His objective was to bring about not merely a temporary truce but a lasting peace dependent, in his view, on a real change of heart. Only when the worst offenders within both communities pledged to forgive one another, reconcile their differences, and vowed to lay down their lives for communal amity did Gandhi break his fast. Hindus who had earlier cried for the blood of Muslims now agreed to protect them. Calcutta began to witness a more stable peace. By all accounts, 'a truly wonderful victory over evil had been achieved'.[5]

[4] Ibid.
[5] Ibid., p. 158.

My objective in recalling this slice of Indian history is to draw attention to something that holds a lesson for all societies. Clearly, any society needs to pull back from barbarism when it has lapsed into it; it must immediately restore peace. After arresting the current round of violence, it must ensure a way out of the cycle of revenge and self-destruction, prevent the recurrence of evil. For Gandhi, this could not be achieved by forgetting or repressing grievances. These must first be allowed full expression and then tamed by 'confronting the goonda we harbour within'.[6] We must own up collective responsibility for the evil that has been generated. This alone helps reconcile differences, and rebuild communal harmony—our final objectives. In Gandhi's view, this then is the structure of moral action in the aftermath of evil: BARBARISM—restoration of peace—expression of grievances—their truthful assessment—the acceptance of collective responsibility for evil—forgiveness—RECONCILIATION (a society where formerly estranged members are morally reconciled may be called a fully decent society).

In what follows, I endorse this broadly Gandhian structure of moral action in the aftermath of evil. Nonetheless, a number of questions remain to be asked. For instance, it is worth asking how a stable peace could have been restored in Calcutta in the absence of Gandhi. Impressed by the 'magician', the Congress leaders urged Gandhi to go to civil war-stricken Punjab. He never managed to go there, but confronted with evil on a much larger scale, would Gandhi have succeeded? How would a society not blessed with a mahatma, without moral saints find a way out of barbarism? What other mechanism can perform roughly the same function? Do societies anyway not require *institutions* for a more stable harmony between two radically differing communities that have been at war with one another? It is one thing to stop violence and quite another to get people to talk to one another, to induct everyone into the process of negotiation. Which institution can perform this function? In Calcutta, the killers were known to the victims but in situations where victims have disappeared without trace, where the basic facts are not known, institutions must do more than become vehicles of collective catharsis. What more will an institution need to do in such situations? I believe that even societies that have had the benefit of moral saints require institutions to perform similar and related functions, particularly when they have faced evil on a large scale. A South African style Truth and Reconciliation Commission is one such institution that

[6] Ibid., p. 151.

could contribute to the realization of the Gandhian structure of basic moral action in the aftermath of evil. However, the principal argument of my essay is that their function is more limited. In one way, truth commissions do more than what is suggested by the Gandhian structure—they help unearth the truth—but overall, they aim to achieve results that are less, and therefore, more modest, than what is suggested therein. This is why, in a way, I also seek to modify the structure. In my view, the structure can be realized only by a complex set of institutions, and in stages, not immediately.

BARBARIC SOCIETIES

In order to amplify this point, I wish to introduce and fully flesh out a distinction implicit in the given account, that is, the distinction between what I call a barbaric and a minimally decent society. A minimally decent society is governed by what I call minimally moral rules. A complete break down of such rules characterizes a barbaric society. In this context, what makes these rules moral is their capacity to prevent evil and not their ability to promote a particular conception of the good life, including a substantive conception of justice. Such rules embody a commitment to abjure violence and include negative injunctions against killing and maiming one another. It follows that a violation of such rules is an act of grave immorality. It is of course true that acts of grave immorality can be committed within minimally decent societies. Consider the case of a serial murderer, say Jack the Ripper, who murdered several persons by slitting their throats and mutilating their bodies with the consummate skill of an expert in human anatomy. Such evil acts can occur in minimally decent societies, within a moral order that is reflected, at least partly, in the law. The offender can be brought within due process of law and punished in proportion to the crime. But, the situation in barbaric societies is qualitatively different, for here the scale of evil is much greater and the potential of the criminal justice system to deal with it far less adequate. Such a situation is beyond legality, and has even crossed a threshold beyond which moral notions are virtually inapplicable. This is a monstrous universe, exemplifying pure and unadulterated evil. Sri Lanka, Afghanistan, Rwanda, and former Yugoslavia provide the most recent examples. But, for Indians, the partition of the sub-continent that left more than half a million dead and many more dispossessed remains a vivid, festering example of that madness. Accounts of partition reveal this collective insanity. Here is a sample:

My earliest memory is of a hot summer day in Delhi in 1948. I remember that as I unlocked the door to our house, I saw, stretched out on the steps below, the body of a man. He was lying face down. The man's limbs were in disarray, his clothes were soaked in blood and the sun had begun to darken his skin. Earlier in the day the man had sought shelter in our house. He was a Muslim trader who had been chased into our locality by violent men seeking revenge for blood spilled in Pakistan. The man had tried to reach our house... but he was killed before he could knock at our door... I have never since forgotten that day. It taught me that a group of people, any people, in their religious passion or tribal pride can always go mad; and that after a time they can relapse into madness again. I became conscious of the fact that the world which most of us had chosen to create, and in which I would have to grow up, was neither safe nor brave. The partition had broken the covenant that men must make with men, castes with castes, religions with other tolerant religions, without which our survival is always precarious and our enslavement to some barbarian is certain. Over the years, I came to realize that my recollections of those days were not private obsessions with the horrific. Similar incidents, known to others, had become a part of their experiential world. My own memories acquired a density and detail from the narratives of a variety of different people. My aunts told me of properties burnt, my grandfather about friends lost; a massacre witnessed, about the public mutilations of women. I grew up trying to understand the problem of evil and to explore the possibilities of magnanimity in such a world as ours.[7]

It is important to recognize the scope and depth of evil, its reach, and what all it destroys. In barbaric societies, it is not public morality alone that is ruined. Evil here has a way of spilling over not only from the public into the private domain but of pervading our intimate realms. Friends, lovers, members of the family can all be complicitous in crime. No one may be presumed innocent. The very distinction between friend and enemy, between those one loves and those one hates intensely is erased. The sociologist, Veena Das, reporting on victims of the massacre of Sikhs in Delhi in 1984, talks of how the traumatic violence of the crowd suddenly revealed to one of its victims the fragility of her kinship universe.[8] Shanti, the victim, disclosed that 'It was my own *mama* (mother's brother) who had advised my husband to hide. He revealed the hiding places of the Siglikar Sikhs to the leaders of the mob. He bartered their lives for his own protection. Go and see his house.

[7] Alok Bhalla, *Stories about Partition in India*, New Delhi: Indus, 1994, pp. x–xi.
[8] Veena Das, 'Our Work to Cry: Your Work to Listen', in Veena Das (ed.), *Mirrors of Violence*, New Delhi: Oxford University Press, 1990, pp. 345–98.

Not even a broken spoon has been looted.'[9] Such personal betrayal is not uncommon in these times. The misfortune of a life without love, of complete friendlessness, surely one of the great evils that can befall human beings, as also rancour and bitterness among siblings was not uncommon, for instance, when India was partitioned.[10]

More importantly, evil eventually ensnares the victim. Typically, in barbaric societies, the very distinction between victims and perpetrators is obliterated. In societies with prolonged phase of barbarism, everyone is trapped in an escalating cycle of revenge. It is true, of course, that even in ordinary situations, it is normal for the victim to experience the impulse to retaliate, to want to punish the perpetrator of crime and get even. However, in barbaric situations, where a downward spiral of violence is firmly set in motion, vengeance invariably leads people to excesses. The retaliatory impulse gets a momentum of its own and forces people to exact more than is necessary. Acting disproportionately, in a manner that is intrinsically hideous, victims, too, become hateful creatures who routinely create new victims.

The association of the concept of evil with the idea of original sin and more generally, with theology is one reason why secular-minded western philosophers are reluctant to give it the attention it deserves. But, its neglect is due also to post-war euphoria—a general sense of well-being through out the industrialized world—and a motivated lack of interest in theorizing the great injustices of colonialism and its destructive consequences in the non-western world. Stuart Hampshire is among a handful of philosophers who has reflected on this issue and not surprisingly, the Second World War, in particular the horror of the Nazi regime compelled him to do so:

I learnt how easy it had been to organize the vast enterprises of torture and of murder, and to enrol willing workers in this field, once all moral barriers had removed by the authorities. Unmitigated evil and nastiness are as natural, it seemed, in educated human beings as generosity and sympathy ... Once notions of fairness and justice are eliminated from public life and from people's minds and a 'bombed and flattened moral landscape' is created, there is nothing that is forbidden or off limits, and the way is fully open to natural violence and domination.[11]

[9] Ibid., p. 347.

[10] Urvashi Butalia, *The Other Side of Silence: Voices from the Partition of India*, New Delhi: Penguin Books India, 1998.

[11] Stuart Hampshire, *Innocence and Experience*, Cambridge: Cambridge University Press, 1989, pp. 8, 69.

One now witnesses evil: 'a force not only contrary to all that is praise-worthy, admirable, and desirable in human lives but which is actively working against all that is praiseworthy and admirable.'[12]

BASIC PROCEDURAL JUSTICE AND MINIMALLY DECENT SOCIETY

For Hampshire, such evil cannot be prevented by substantial concep-tions of justice over which there may be little agreement in society. He argues that in such situations what is required is *basic procedural justice.* This procedural justice is part of 'a bare minimum which is entirely negative and without this bare minimum as a foundation no morality directed towards the greater goods can be applicable and can survive in practice.'[13] Justice, in this view, involves fair procedures of negotiation, a sort of machinery of arbitration that forms the basis for the recognition of untidy and temporary compromises between incompatible visions of a better way of life.[14] It is a means of enabling different conceptions of the good life to coexist and as far as possible, to survive without any substantial reconciliation between them and without a search for the common ground. This coexistence is possible by virtue of a restraint accepted by everyone on unmeasured ambition, on limitless self-assertion, and on the obsessive desire for an ever larger slice of the cake and because people involved in even the fiercest of disputes are prepared to recognize the need to balance argument against argument, concession against concession. Basic procedural justice makes possible a minimally decent life which has a value independent of any wider conception of the good. Its principal objective, in Hampshire's memo-rable phrase, is to prevent 'madness in the soul'.[15]

It follows from what I have said that barbaric societies are character-ized by the breakdown not only of elementary moral injunctions but also of basic procedural justice; indeed, basic procedural justice is part of what I have called minimal morality. Conversely, a minimally decent society is one where basic moral injunctions and procedural justice pre-vail. How do societies recovering from barbarism arrive at a minimally decent order? In my view, they must do so in two distinct stages. In the first stage, violence ceases probably because people have had enough of evil. In the second stage, basic procedural justice is restored and thereby

[12] Ibid., p. 67.
[13] Ibid., p. 72.
[14] Ibid., pp. 72–8.
[15] Ibid., p. 189.

also the process of negotiation between groups previously at war with one another. This then is the first suggested modification to the Gandhian schema: in the immediate aftermath of evil, in the period of brief reprieve from violence, an institution to consolidate basic procedural justice is desperately required. The truth commission is an institution that performs this role. Its primary function is to help societies transit from barbaric to minimally decent societies, particularly by stabilizing a system of basic procedural justice. This it does by publicly establishing that grave wrongs have been committed in the past, and where this is already public knowledge, by showing why this was done. By responding to the needs of victims and by getting perpetrators to acknowledge responsibility for crimes, truth commissions build the trust and confidence crucial for restoring basic procedural justice and thereby reinstate a minimally decent society.

In a minimally decent society, former victims are not reconciled with their former oppressors, nor are groups with inherited hostilities towards one another reunited. The primary objective of a truth commission is not reconciliation but the institution of a minimally decent society. It does not rule out a future cancellation of estrangement, however. Indeed, a truth commission creates conditions for a third stage of future reconciliation. It may do this by: (i) fixing collective responsibility in the appropriate way, and in so doing, changing the ideological climate that facilitates as far as possible, former oppressors to shed prejudice and for victims to regain their self-respect; and (ii) since victims experience retributive emotions, truth commissions may permit their controlled expression and also help victims to eventually overcome them. When this happens, truth commissions may also be seen as *facilitating* mechanisms of forgiveness and reconciliation. So, my suggested modification of the Gandhian schema is this: BARBARISM—truce (*stage 1*)—recall of grave injustice and expression of grievances, and restoration of basic procedural justice, that is, a minimally decent society (*stage 2*)—acceptance of collective responsibility—forgiveness—RECONCILIATION (*stage 3*). (The function of truth commissions is to help societies move from stage 1 to stage 2, that is, they must aim to help realize a minimally decent society; and truth commissions may facilitate conditions favourable to stage 3, to forgiveness and reconciliation.)

As is evident, my intention is not to reject the Gandhian schema. However, I do claim that no simple, linear movement exists from barbarism to a state of moral reconciliation, to full decency. Rather, it is necessary to transit through a complex situation of three stages. In stage 1, a highly frail and temporary truce prevails that may easily collapse generating a fresh burst of violence. With help from appropriate institutions such as the truth commissions, we then move to stage 2, to a minimally decent society. A sufficiently prolonged period of minimal decency may eventually create facilitating conditions for stage 3, for forgiveness and reconciliation, and therefore, to a fully decent society.

JUSTICE IN TRANSITION FROM BARBARIC TO MINIMALLY DECENT SOCIETY

A number of points still need clarification. First, the term 'society' refers to a human collectivity that may be a small configuration within a community; a large community within a society; a large political order such as the nation-state consisting of interacting communities; or indeed the entire world order; or a part thereof. So, as I have used the term 'society', it is possible for there to exist a minimally decent social formation within a larger barbaric society and likewise, for there to be a barbaric social formation within a larger minimally decent society. One of the cases I mention earlier, the massacre of Sikhs in Delhi in 1984, is a barbaric social formation on a relatively small scale. Its existence did not imply that the whole of India had turned barbaric.

Second, the phrase 'minimally decent' implies that the best available ethical standards in a society, even by its own light, remain unrealized. A minimally decent society is not free of exploitation, injustice, or demeaning behaviour. It may not even embody political equality. Yet, it is a social order where almost every voice is heard, some visibility for everyone is ensured in the political domain, and even the most marginalized and exploited are part of negotiation, howsoever unequal the conditions under which it takes place. There remain asymmetries in such a society, but it is not asymmetrically (or symmetrically) barbaric. On the other hand, in a barbaric society, where basic procedural justice is dismembered, the entire mechanism of negotiation and arbitration has vanished. Usually, the violation of norms of procedural justice begins with the politically motivated deployment of excessive force. In the early stages of regression into barbarism, gross violation of basic rights, that is, physical intimidation, torture, murder, even massacres occur on a fairly large scale; active deliberation and opposition is brutally terminated. This initial use of massive force may eventually make physical coercion more or less redundant, as indifference and submissiveness are routinely generated in a depoliticized environment. The noteworthy point here is that in either case, the demise of basic procedural justice is a *political* evil, which creates political victims. If the collapse of basic procedural justice brings about what may be described as political death, then clearly its restoration marks the political rebirth of members of a society. This helps explain why, by making the restoration of basic procedural justice their primary objective, truth commissions focus primarily on the rehabilitation of political victims.

Third, in saying that minimally moral rules are universally endorsable, I deny relativism—the view that the validity of *all* moral rules is culture-relative—but not in the familiar way. The familiar strategy of denial is to abstract from all traditions, cultures, and social roles and reach an archimedean point where universal moral rules wait to be discovered. I follow Michael Walzer in holding the view that every contextually bound, thick morality has an inbuilt set of thin, universalist moral norms because many terms within a moral tradition have both a maximal and a minimal moral content.[16] If so, people do not have to abstract from their moral tradition in order to reach a universal, minimalist morality. Rather, access to it can be had from within. Nor is the idea of minimal morality tied to some version of cold, dry, proceduralist reason commonly in use within many liberal conceptions. On the contrary, as Walzer persuasively argues, thinness and intensity go together. Minimal morality is 'close to the bone', which is why there is universal revulsion at the sight of evil, why evil arouses our passion almost everywhere, in any context.

A final point worth making is this: when transiting from a barbaric to a minimally decent condition, societies are beginning their ascent from hell, are taking the first faltering steps away from a situation of gross injustice on a massive scale brought about probably by people with profoundly deadened moral sensitivities. When it comes to a society standing precariously on the threshold of moral restoration, it is important that we look at it bottom-up rather than top-down. I mean that we must remain firmly anchored in low-level ground realities and begin our search for relevant moral principles from here. We must not first reach out for high, near perfect ethical standards only to subsequently judge ground realities with their help. And, in the ground reality of such societies, the only reasonably certain thing is a diffuse

---

[16] Michael Walzer, *Thick and Thin: Moral Argument at Home and Abroad*, London and Notre Dame: Notre Dame University Press, 1994.

agreement that enough of evil has been wrought and that relief from it is urgently required.

It is important to fully understand the significance of this. It does not mean that enmity or estrangement has ceased between victims and perpetrators or between conflicting groups. Nor that they have begun to view each other with equal respect. However, it does mean that a space has opened up for a new order on terms not entirely unfavourable to all political actors, that a temporary reprieve from civil war or tyranny exists, as also the hope that this can be prevented in future. It also means that force has begun to give way to negotiation, and, although relations of force characteristic of barbaric societies are not totally dismantled, the process has begun to loosen their tenacious grip.

Normally, such transitional moments emerge out of a settlement in which former oppressors refuse to share power unless guaranteed that they will escape the criminal justice system characteristic of a minimally decent society. Alternatively, it typically arises because former victims do not fully control the new order they have set up and lack the power to implement their own conception of justice. However, such transitional moments can also come about by other routes. It is entirely possible that former oppressors are comprehensively vanquished but current victors, victims of the previously existing barbaric society, refuse on moral grounds to avenge themselves, or fully implement the conventional criminal justice system. In short, former victims refuse on moral grounds to don the mantle of victors, something someone like Gandhi might well have done.

What I am trying to get at is this: at issue here are transitional situations of extreme complexity, replete with moral possibilities, including, of course, grave moral danger. The danger is obvious: victims may forever remain victims and their society may never cease to be barbaric. But, what is often missed is that seeds of moral progress are also present herein because former victims are saved the awesome responsibility of wielding absolute power and therefore, may escape the devastating consequences of being corrupted by its use. As a result, the possibility is foreclosed that past wrongs will be annulled only by fresh acts of equally excessive wrongdoing. Instead, we are presented with the possibility of confronting past wrongs by means other than the use of force or the wilful manipulation of the criminal justice system. So, what may begin as mere political constraint opens up moral possibilities and it is these possibilities that lend moral weight to mechanisms like the truth commission.

THE IMPORTANCE OF TRUTH COMMISSIONS

I have claimed that basic procedural justice prevents limitless, negative self-assertion and gives everyone an effective voice in political negotiation. Therefore, in order to break the cycle of revenge, former victims must be inducted into a system of basic procedural justice equipped with a mechanism of arbitration. Persuading them back into the system is not easy, however. Understandably, victims experience deep resentment and hatred towards those responsible for their misery. Besides, a numbing of emotions is at once a symptom and a constituent of their general disengagement from the world. An effective voice in the political process is impossible unless former victims regain self-confidence and renew trust in beneficiaries, perhaps even direct perpetrators of past atrocities, now also part of the negotiations. In short, victims cannot do without confidence- and trust-enhancing mechanisms. Now, without public recognition of wrong done to them in the past, former victims are hardly likely to regain self-confidence in themselves or trust in others. Unless they break their silence, narrate their version of events, and contest public lies, they will not see procedures of negotiation as just. To have an effective political voice, they must recover their voice more generally. Truth commissions, I contend, are precisely such mechanisms by which the submerged voice of victims is retrieved. Given this connection between truth commissions and basic procedural justice, it is not difficult to see why they are necessary for the transition to stage 2.

This claim about the role and significance of truth commissions is not entirely uncontroversial. Even those who abjure revenge disagree on how a transition to a fully decent society must be made. Some, advocating a strategy of silence and forgetting, wish to skip stage 2. Others, disclaiming collective responsibility and forgiveness, reject stage 3. In what follows, I try to meet these objections. In this section, I try to rebut the claim that stage 2 is unnecessary. In the next section, I argue against the view that stage 3 is redundant.

Against the argument that truth commissions are necessary in societies transiting from barbaric to minimally decent societies, one counter-argument frequently levelled is that truth commissions inherently do more than is required in such situations. Those who hold this view inundate the victim with advice to check emotions. Rather than tell publicly and remember past injustice, victims are exhorted to forget. They are asked to contain hatred, overcome resentment; in short, to condone or immediately forgive. Revenge to which resentment may lead them, they are told, is unbecoming of civilized people, anyway full of terrible consequences for society. These critics draw a distinction between the felt needs of the victim and the real needs of the entire community and suggest that the two often run against one another. Instead of focusing on the past, the victim is told to think of the future. In brief, in this view, truth commissions are dangerous or at best, unnecessary. Is this view correct? Is it more appropriate in these circumstances to forget?

Among former perpetrators, a motivated forgetfulness of their own wrongdoing, accompanied with the hope that former victims will quickly forget past suffering is not uncommon at a time when asymmetries of power are in the process of being dissolved. In this context, calls to let bygones be bygones, to wipe the slate clean or start afresh, work unabashedly in favour of perpetrators of crime. In any case, most calls to forget disguise the attempt to prevent victims from publicly remembering in the fear that 'there is a dragon living on the patio and we had better not provoke it'.[17] But, it is doubtful if this is a good strategy for repairing wounds or achieving reconciliation. When a person is wronged, he is made not only to suffer physically but is also mentally scarred, the most injurious of which is the damage to his sense of self-respect, if he is left with any residue of it. As Jeffrie Murphy points out, when a person is wronged he receives a message of his marginality and irrelevance.[18] The wrongdoer conveys that in his scheme of things the victim counts for nothing. Since self-esteem hinges upon critical opinion of the other, the message sent by the wrongdoer significantly lowers the self-esteem of the wronged. In these circumstances, the insult and degradation inflicted constitutes a deeper moral injury. The demand that past injustices be forgotten does not address this loss of self-esteem. Indeed, it inflicts further damage. Asking victims to forget past evils is to treat them as if no great wrong to them has been done, as if they have nothing to feel resentful about. This can only diminish them further.

Forgetting specific instances of past wrongs does not appear to achieve the desired objective anyway, a point to which Jeremy Waldron has drawn our attention:

When we are told to let bygones be bygones, we need to bear in mind also that the forgetfulness being urged on us is seldom the blank slate of historical

[17] Tina Rosenburg, 'Reconciliation and Amnesty: Latin America', in Borain, Levy, and Scheffer (eds), *Dealing with the Past*, Cape Town: Idasa, 1997, p. 66.

[18] Jeffrie G. Murphy and Jean Hampton, *Forgiveness and Mercy*, Cambridge: Cambridge University Press, 1990.

oblivion. Thinking quickly fills up the vacuum with plausible tales of self-satisfaction, on the one side, and self-deprecation on the other.[19]

Beneficiaries of injustice then come to believe that gains accrue to them due to the virtue of their race or culture and victims, too, easily accept that their misfortune is caused by inherent inferiority. Waldron is on to something important here. The call to forget reinforces loss of self-esteem in the victim. Furthermore, moral injuries that are neglected putrefy demoralization in the victim. Under these conditions, past perpetrators feel that they can get away with murder and grow in confidence that such injuries can be inflicted without resistance even in future. Therefore, rather than prevent, forgetting ends up facilitating wrong acts. If so, it is difficult not to conclude that proper remembrance alone restores dignity and self-respect to the victim.

A proper remembrance is critical if wounds of the victim are to be healed. It is also necessary to fulfil the collective need of a badly dam-aged society. This view comes up against a pervasive social condition as well as against a famous argument by Hobbes. It is an uncomfortable fact that while societies remember their heroic deeds, they suppress memories of collective injustice. Recall Ernest Renan's remark that nations are constituted by a great deal of forgetting. In a perceptive essay, Sheldon Wolin wonders if collective memory is an accomplice of injustice and whether by its silence on collective wrongs, it does not signify the very limits of justice.[20] But, he also asks if a society can ever afford to remember events in which members feel tainted by a 'kind of corporate complicity in an act of injustice done in their name'.[21] Can France remember the Saint Bartholomew massacre; America, its civil war; or India, its partition? Can these horrific events be remembered by being represented in civic rituals? One philosopher who thought collective forgetting necessary was Thomas Hobbes. Suppression of memories of past wrongs was essential because if society is treated as a building made of stones then some stones that have an 'irregularity of figure take more room from others' and so must be discarded.[22] Hobbes' covenant was a device to incorporate social amnesia into the

[19] Jeremy Waldron, 'Superseding Historic Injustice', *Ethics*, vol. 103, no. 1, pp. 4–28.

[20] Sheldon Wolin, *The Presence of the Past*, Baltimore and London: Johns Hopkins University Press, 1989, pp. 32–46.

[21] Ibid.

[22] Ibid., p. 37.

foundation of society. Commenting on this, Wolin remarks that for Hobbes a necessary condition of social amnesia is the dehistorization of human beings. Is dehistoricization possible? I think not. 'Muslims' invaded India in the twelfth century but for many Hindus, Muslims continue to be invaders who may kill, destroy, and convert them. The conquest of Quebec by the English happened more than two centuries ago but for Quebec nationalists, their nationalist project 'involves a reconquest of the conquest'. A large part of nationalist agenda all over the world, Ignatieff rightly reminds us, is about settling old scores.[23] In so many countries, people remarkably similar in essential respects appear to go at each other's throat simply because once upon a time one ruled over the other. A simple strategy of forgetting has simply not worked. Only an appropriate engagement with the past makes, then, for a liveable common future. It is true of course that one must guard against cosmetic remembrance. An engagement with the past must take place simultaneously at the level of gut, reason, and emotion. If not properly addressed, grievances and resentments resurface. Oddly, animosity between groups is sustained even when it goes against their current interests. This happens because emotional reactions ingrained in the human mind remain insensitive to altered circumstances and are bequeathed from generation to generation.[24] Like property, animosities are inherited too! Nonetheless, former victims and fragmented societies eventually need to get on with their lives rather than be consumed by their suffering. Perhaps victims need to forget just about as much as they need to remember. People who carry deep resentment and grievance against one another are hardly likely to build a society together. Therefore, to ask people to forget is not entirely unreasonable. I believe timing is the essence of the issue here. Forgetting too quickly or without redressal, by failing to heal adequately, inevitably brings with it a society haunted by its past. One can't forget entirely, too soon, and without a modicum of justice. Clearly, while some forgetting at an appropriate time is necessary, a complete erasure is neither sufficient nor desirable for healing or for the consolidation of a minimally decent society. Moreover, while specific acts of wrongdoing need to be forgotten eventually, a general sense of the wrong and of the horror of evil acts must never be allowed to recede from collective memory. Such remembering is crucial to the prevention of wrongdoing in the future.

[23] Michael Ignatieff, *Blood and Belonging*, London: Vintage, 1994.
[24] David Hume, *Political Writings*, Cambridge / Indianapolis: Hackett, 1991.

I conclude that without a proper engagement with the past and the institutionalization of remembrance, societies are condemned to repeat, re-enact, and relive the horror. Forgetting is not a good strategy for societies recovering from prolonged barbarism. The recognition of this is the raison d'etre of truth commissions and also one of the virtues of the Gandhian schema.

TRUTH COMMISSION FOR RECONCILIATION?

What is the relation of truth commissions to the rest of the Gandhian schema? Can they realize the structure in full? My view is that though they may facilitate the realization of stage 3, that is, reconciliation, they must not aim to do so. However, critics find flaws in the very idea of a passage through stage 3. Two criticisms are fairly common. First, that the notion of collective responsibility is incoherent. Second, that forgiveness is morally inappropriate.

To begin with, my use of the word responsibility is less to do with strict legal or moral liability and linked more with what men and women decide to do. Our decision to perform this or that action is connected by a loose, not always explicit or fully conscious, practical reasoning to our beliefs and desires. I avoid discussing the vexed question of whether or not beliefs and desires are mental states or occurrences. Even if this is so, an important question remains about how their content is to be individuated, their meaning fixed. For me, what these beliefs and desires are about, their meaning is determined by social practice, by collective actions rather than individual mental acts of people.[25] If this is so, and if our decisions to act are constitutively linked to these irreducibly social beliefs and desires, then it follows that, in part, our decisions are social too and so therefore, is responsibility. I share Larry May's view that most of our responsibilities are shared rather than uniquely our own.[26] When such a social view on conceptions of self and agency is taken, the domain of moral responsibility expands beyond what a person directly causes. Moreover, just as social beliefs cause individual action, just so they cause an interlocking set of actions involving several individuals. If that is so, groups, indeed entire collectivities, can be held responsible for various harms. I also agree with May that guilt and blame must be seen to lie on a continuum which also contains shame, remorse, regret,

[25] Rajeev Bhargava, *Individualism in Social Science*, Oxford: Clarendon Press, 1992.

[26] Larry May, *Sharing Responsibility*, Chicago and London: Chicago University Press, 1992.

and the feeling of being tainted.[27] From this brief account it follows that for me, groups can be held morally responsible for wrongs and individuals can partake that responsibility.

It is possible, though not necessary, that when individuals as members of a group publicly acknowledge their crime, they also admit to their role in a collective wrong. This is not something they always know of before matters are brought in the public. An individual may not have a sense of responsibility for wrongdoing when in reality he should. Alternatively, he may feel exclusive responsibility and therefore, excessive guilt for a wrong of which he has only shared responsibility. The act of making something public is not merely to reveal what is known already to each person in private. It is to come to the realization of a fact about ourselves that was not properly known at all. Normally, the recognition of such collective responsibility is accompanied by feelings of shame, regret, or remorse. People qua members of a group may also feel morally tainted. Ignatieff makes the telling Freudian point that something may be confronted in one's head without it being confronted in one's heart or guts. This self-confrontation which takes place at the level of feelings is critical for a deeper change in one's attitudes. Since such encounters with the self are painful, they may be referred to as punishment of the soul, a form of deeper punishment neither noticed by the penal system nor by standard conceptions of retributive justice. Punishment of the soul is critical, affective self-confrontation before radical conversions in identity occur; an acknowledgement not of the wrong one has done but the wicked person one is. It is only when such changes take place on a large scale, and the moral climate of a whole society is altered, that people, particularly former oppressors, shed their prejudices, and former victims begin to regain a deeper, more stable sense of self-respect. Surely, this is necessary for reconciliation.

Under altered circumstances, when evil and suffering is publicly revealed, remembered, and even acknowledged by the perpetrator, should the victim respond with forgiveness? Is forgiveness morally appropriate? If so, what justifies it? Is acknowledgement of responsibility of the crime sufficient for forgiveness? What is it anyway to forgive? It is a fact that victims experience deep, enduring hatred and resentment towards the wrongdoer as well as feelings of revenge towards him. Commonly viewed, forgiveness is the forswearing of these resentments, a determined overcoming of hatred and anger towards a person who

[27] Ibid., p. 35.

has inflicted moral injury.[28] One frequently cited reason in favour of forgiveness points towards the negative qualities that inhere in the very emotions of hatred and resentment. A decent, morally upright person, it is said, simply shouldn't have such emotions, in part because by holding persons rather than being held by them, these emotions inhibit proper judgement and undermine autonomy and, by virtue of their raw motivational power, are likely to drive a person to commit an equally immoral act. For instance, one may be swept, it is argued, by feelings of revenge inconsonant with moral systems in the modern world.

Reasons that require forgiveness because of its productive role in eliminating such emotions are unconvincing, however. For a start, there is nothing wrong inherently in feelings of hatred and resentment. 'Proper self-respect,' observes Murphy, 'is essentially tied to the passion of resentment. A person who does not resent moral injuries done to him is almost necessarily lacking in self-respect.'[29] It follows that resentment is valuable by virtue of its link with something we all value, namely, self-respect. It is terribly odd for a self-respecting person not to resent violation of rights or the seizure of unfair advantage of his labour. Likewise, there is nothing wrong in hatred towards those wholly identified with an immoral cause or responsible for an immoral practice. Distinguishing it from simple hatred—an intense dislike for a strongly unpleasant object, accompanied by an equally strong desire to eliminate it—Hampton calls this moral hatred.[30] Hatred is moral when moved by moral indignation, conjoined with the desire to defeat the ideology of the offending person in the name of a fundamental moral principle. Such moral hatred may be experienced towards neo-Nazis or towards those South African whites who perpetrate or justify violence against blacks. These retributive emotions[31] are essential not only for the preservation of self-respect but also for the stability of the moral order in society. If the only ground for forgiveness is that retributive emotions are intrinsically wrong or harmful, then surely forgiveness is unjustified.

If victims who experience moral hatred and resentment must not feel in the wrong, then why in the first place overcome these emotions and forgive? The answer is that a refusal to forgive often betrays

---

[28] Murphy and Hampton, *Forgiveness and Mercy*, pp. 20–1.

[29] Ibid., p. 16.

[30] Ibid., pp. 79–81.

[31] John Mackie, *Persons and Values*, Oxford: Clarendon Press, 1985, pp. 206–19.

insensitivity to altered circumstances, to a change in the condition or character of the wrongdoer. Murphy lists five grounds for forgiveness, three of which are relevant for our purposes.[32] When the perpetrator repents, undergoes humiliation, or has in turn suffered enough, it may well be appropriate to forgive him, especially since such forgiveness does not diminish the self-esteem of the victim. Indeed, under these circumstances, the act of forgiveness may enhance the self-respect of the victim and contribute towards precisely the kind of healing required in such circumstances. When a person acknowledges the wrongness in his act and the role it played in causing harm to the victim and when, in admitting its immorality he ceases to endorse it, indicating thereby that he is with the victim in condemning all acts of this kind, he initiates the process of restoring parity with the victim. It may become morally appropriate now to forsake hatred for the person and resentment towards his past actions. Likewise, subsequent to punishment and suffering, the perpetrator may be sufficiently humbled to cause the victim to alter his view of the wrongdoer. Much the same is true of someone who admits guilt through an apology. In short, if restoration of moral parity is desireable between self-respecting individuals and if forgiveness contributes to its realization, then it is morally appropriate to forgive.

If forgiveness is to result from the repentance of the perpetrator, to flow from the punishment of his soul, and if this is conditional upon the recognition of collective responsibility, then it follows that a truth commission cannot *aim* to bring about forgiveness. Nor must reconciliation, dependent upon a deeper change in people's identity, be part of its stated objectives. It is of course true that such fundamental changes can eventually occur as a by-product of the activities of a truth commission and therefore, it may certainly be seen to create conditions for future reconciliation. Nonetheless, given the time frame of truth commissions, it is too much to expect them to bear the burden of getting people to forgive or to reconcile with one another.

However, this is not usually the reason why truth commissions are criticized. It is sometimes accepted that a truth commission can get people to forgive but then pointed out that this is morally questionable. Critics frequently attack the very idea of forgiveness. One well-known argument against forgiveness is that it is deeply tied to Christian morality, at any rate that it takes us beyond ordinary morality into

---

[32] Murphy and Hampton, *Forgiveness and Mercy*, p. 24.

the domain of high religion. Victims in South Africa have complained bitterly that the justification of forgiveness derives from a particular moral vision with which they do not identify and therefore, it is not incumbent upon them to heed the plea to forgive. Others object that forgiveness must come from within and only the victim has the proper standing to do so. One can't forgive under compulsion nor can others forgive on behalf of the victim. A third criticism of forgiveness is that it has the effect of erasing wrongdoing, that it is an invitation to reconcile with rather than conquer evil.[33] Finally, it is also argued that the plea for general amnesty with which it is linked can only lead to enraged victims opting for personal acts of vengeance. The demand for forgiveness, in this view, can only exacerbate the settling of scores outside the rule of law.

Within Christianity, it is widely recognized that since the propensity to wrongdoing is pervasive, forgiveness should be generally available too. As original sinners, we seek forgiveness from god. As sinners in our day-to-day existence, we must seek forgiveness from each other. It is therefore undeniable that Christianity provides an important source for the justification of forgiveness. However, from the availability of a virtue in one religious tradition, it hardly follows that it is unavailable in others.[34] More importantly, atheistic humanism must have place for forgiveness too. Even unbelievers can and should admit that in the course of living our lives we wrong others, particularly those about whom we care deeply. If we care about people we have wronged, we would certainly want them to forgive us. Indeed, a humanist must accept that at the heart of the human condition lies a radical fallibility that is futile to try to totally overcome. We need forgiveness from each other, alas, because without god-like features, we often commit wrong and because there may be no god to forgive us. As Murphy notes, 'we do all need and desire forgiveness and would not want to live in a world where forgiveness was not regarded as a healing and restoring virtue.'[35] Furthermore, the domain where this virtue is exercised needn't only be private. We need and expect forgiveness even within the wider public domain. Therefore, I am not entirely convinced with the view

---

[33] Mahmood Mamdani, 'Reconciliation without Justice', *South African Review of Books*, vol. CIV, 1996.

[34] M.K. Gandhi, *Collected Works of Mahatma Gandhi*, vol. CXXXVI, New Delhi: Publications Division, 1982.

[35] Murphy and Hampton, *Forgiveness and Mercy*, pp. 30–1.

that forgiveness is exclusively tied to one religious tradition or that unbelievers have no need for it.

The criticism that forgiveness bypasses the act of wrongdoing is not justified either. To forgive is not to convert a wrong into right. It is not to justify the wrong done. Nor is it identical with excusing the wrong done, as when one excuses a child for causing some harm on the ground that he can't really be held responsible for it. The process of forgiveness begins only after proper recognition of wrongdoing and is conditional upon it. Since the wrong is not simply whitewashed, to forgive is not to compromise with evil. Nor does forgiveness entail amnesty. Forgiveness is not to be confused with mercy.[36] This confusion may well have lain at the heart of the earliest formulation of the objectives of the South African Truth Commission. Reasons for forgiveness are not automatically reasons for mercy. A victim may forgive the perpetrator but not thereby free him of legal accountability. Conversely, he may, out of compassion, reduce punishment for the wrongdoer but not forgive him. Finally, forgiveness is not a virtue in all contexts and is appropriate only when it is consistent with the dignity and self-respect of the victim. The good of the community cannot provide reasons for unconditional forgiveness. A perpetrator cannot be forgiven if he does not repent, for without proper repentance, he may repeat his crime. Nor can the evidence of repentance be a mere expression of regret or remorse. It must also be expressed in deed, by reparative actions directed at victims. This is what Gandhi meant when he insisted that Hindus who only the other day were crying for the blood of Muslims must offer protection to them. Furthermore, the victim may not forgive if he retains the feeling that his suffering is not properly acknowledged. If there is no forgiveness from within, 'then the door is open to private acts of vengeance and retribution.'[37] Given these qualifications, in principle there appears nothing inappropriate or wrong in the Gandhian strategy of reconciliation via acknowledgement of collective responsibility and forgiveness. The basic idea that animates truth commissions is correct, even though, as I have argued, they must modify the schema and aim to achieve much less than what they usually envisage.

[36] Ibid., 1990, p. 34.
[37] Rosenberg, 'Reconciliation and Amnesty', in Borain et al. (eds), Dealing with the Past.

6

Muslim Personal Law in India and the Majority–Minority Syndrome*

The entire gamut of Hindu–Muslim relations after the rise of nationalism in the Indian sub-continent is not the concern of this chapter. Nor is it a theoretical essay on nationalism or community rights. Moving uninhibitedly between normative theory and micro-historical explanation, it deals with one aspect of the contemporary status of Indian Muslims who constitute a little over 11 per cent of India's one billion people. In particular, it focuses on their demand in post-independent India to have the right to live by their own culture; specifically, by their religiously coded personal laws. Successful exercise of this right raises profound worry concerning the violation of individual liberty and gender justice, however. This has led some activists in India to demand its abolition. Many others, including ordinary Hindus, have demanded that the entire discourse of minority rights be jettisoned and replaced by a uniform discourse of individual rights. Predictably, Muslim orthodoxy has reacted obdurately and pressed for not just the retention of minority rights but an even more stringent application of personal laws in exactly the morally objectionable form in which they currently exist.

* A version of this paper was first presented during a study week organized at the Institute of Advanced Studies, Shimla by Dhirubhai Sheth in November 1994. It was subsequently published as 'Muslim Personal Law in India and the Majority–Minority Syndrome', in Michel Seymour (ed.), *The Fate of the Nation-State*, Montreal: McGill-Queen's University Press, 2004, pp. 327–56.

In the second section of this essay, after outlining the relevant history and describing individual and group rights, I offer what I take to be a contextually reasonable position that reconciles the redeemable features in the best interpretation of both. I argue that the discourse of minority rights should be retained, that even personal laws should be accommodated, though not in their present form. Sadly, as we see in the third section, even this reasonable position appears unfeasible in the current context, cast as it is under the shadow of a historically transmitted syndrome that viciously pits the majority against the minority. I begin the first section, however, by delineating the key ideas—the majority–minority syndrome and framework—that frame the discussion that follows.

FRAMEWORK AND SYNDROME

The terms majority and minority are ambiguous and evoke two different conceptions that I have discussed in the first chapter. Here I summarize that account. The first is linked to conceptions of procedural equality and individualist agency wherein every agent, regardless of substantive identity, gender, religion, ethnicity, language, or race, is given one vote per issue that is meant to embody her preference. Majority and minority emerge when such preferences are aggregated. This may be called *preference-based majority/minority*. Such preference-based majorities/minorities are inevitable in democracies so conceived, and because preferences change or vary from issue to issue, are usually temporary.

Preference-based majority/minority must not be conflated with what can be called *identity-dependent majority/minority*—the focus of my essay. To understand this conception, first consider a set of individuals who define themselves and others not in terms of preference, that is, the desires people choose to have, but rather by the more or less permanent attributes they happen to possess—colour, ethnicity, religion, and language—widely believed to constitute the very identity of individuals. Individuals with an identical set of any of these features can be grouped together and be seen as communities. Now consider two such diverse communities with differing numerical strengths. A majority and minority then exists on the basis of identity-constituting features. In a large society where people do not share the same identity-constituting features, majorities and minorities exist more or less on a permanent basis (for example, Tamils in Sri Lanka, the Quebecois in Canada, non-Hindu religious groups within India, and non-Anglican religious groups in Britain). Here we may even speak of (relatively) permanent majorities or minorities.

However, enumeration, though necessary, is not sufficient to constitute a minority and majority. Three other features enter its current understanding. First, groups must view themselves as a minority or a majority. Self-identification or persistent identification by others in these terms, simultaneously or subsequently recognized by the relevant group is central to majority–minority formations. Given this self-awareness, members of such groups are likely to display a fairly high degree of solidarity. Second, the group must believe that it has or should have the power to preserve its attribute-related culture and traditions and, under certain conditions, to shape or alter, in accordance with its traditions and culture, the structure of the social and political order in which it lives. Finally, when this belief is accompanied or followed by the inability to exercise power, the resulting sense of impotence breeds a sense of disadvantage and the group believes itself to be in a non-dominant position. Usually, particularly within systems of representative democracies, the numerically larger group is also the dominant group and numerically smaller groups are non-dominant. However, sometimes the group in a numerical majority feels that its power is thwarted by minorities. Whatever the case, when either one or both groups believe that they are unable to exercise power and blame each other for this real or perceived disadvantage, a *majority–minority syndrome* begins to set in.

The term 'syndrome' suggests something strongly pejorative. When a deep malaise creeps into the system causing, for some reason, a spiralling estrangement between the minority and the majority, then we are burdened with a majority–minority syndrome. Typically, in majority–minority syndromes animosities against each other circulate freely, adding layers upon layers of mutual grievances. Over time, chronic mutual paranoia develops, inter-group relations are perverted, and the majority and the minority begin to play antagonistic games, fighting over nothing at all. It is also a feature of syndromes that, rightly or wrongly, everyone feels continually humiliated. The majority–minority syndrome must be distinguished from a majority–minority 'framework' within which groups have distinct identity, some distance, but no snowballing alienation or chronic malaise that typifies a syndrome. The presence of the syndrome means that the basic trust, mutual confidence, and perhaps, common understanding between the majority and the minority has broken down. On the other hand, a framework suggests that a common understanding between the two has been reached and mutually binding moral rules exist to ensure that all may live with security, self-confidence, and self-respect. The majority–minority framework is entirely compatible with groups making demands on one another in a reasonable form. It allows even for occasional conflict of interests or values between the majority and minority. A polity with a majority–minority framework is not a state of utopian harmony realized on earth!

A majority–minority syndrome is not something that is always 'out there'. It is an agent-dependent process. It is set in motion by a long chain of closely nested, mutually interlocking actions between small sections within the majority and minority but it gradually engulfs almost everyone. It can disappear if certain types of agents stop interacting in particular ways. The primary responsibility for the syndrome may be with the majority, with the minority, or sometimes, even with a third, contextually relevant political actor (as in empire and colonial states). Sometimes it may be set off simply by the will of any one group. For instance, a minority group may wish to shape the structure exclusively or disproportionately but not be allowed to. When this happens, it cannot really complain of injustice. Yet, unflinchingly and unmindful of others, a powerful minority may persist with its own exaggerated demands and precipitate a majority–minority syndrome with disastrous consequences for everyone. Usually, however, it develops when a minority group tries merely to co-determine the social and political structure but is not permitted by the majority to do so. In such instances, partly because the terms of engagement of the two groups are grossly unequal, a syndrome is accompanied by and results in the persistent and very real discrimination, humiliation, marginalization, exclusion, or subordination of minorities. In extreme cases, it threatens the very survival of the minority community.

Such a syndrome may be removed or alleviated by the introduction of the majority–minority framework. Of the two such existing frameworks, one hierarchical, the other egalitarian, the hierarchical framework is irrelevant in this context because it tries to bind the majority and minority in a relation of domination. However, if subordination is itself the primary problem and the cause in the first place of the syndrome, then only an egalitarian majority–minority framework, usually with constitutionally protected minority rights, can be of use here. The entire point of such rights is to eliminate hidden inequalities and injustice, to give minorities some power to shape the social and political structure so that they too are able to do or get what the majority group routinely procures by virtue of the structural conditions in that society. Such rights may be purely political, as when a minority is granted self-government or special representation rights. A framework with such political rights may be called a 'political majority–minority framework'. Alternatively, there may be non-political rights such as the right to a group to maintain its own educational institutions or to protect its language, script, religion, or culture. A framework with such socio-cultural rights may be called a 'social majority–minority framework'. In what follows, when I speak of the majority–minority framework, I refer only to this egalitarian version in both its political and its social forms.

The claim that the majority–minority framework helps remove the syndrome must be read with care and nuance. For a start, the framework and syndrome exist on qualitatively different existential fields, one on the plane of collective psychology and the other on the plane of legality. It is not my contention that law, by itself, can cure a perverted collective psyche. Yet, in the long run, a legally secure discourse of rights can shape preferences and change attitudes. Therefore, though not sufficient, a framework of rights is necessary for the eventual alleviation of the syndrome, particularly in contemporary democracies. Second, care must be taken to work out a framework most suitable in any given socio-cultural and political context. If attention is not paid to the proper form of the framework or if the framework is introduced wrongfully, by the wrong people at the wrong time, it may exacerbate the syndrome.

Anyhow, the majority–minority framework is not the only conceivable solution to the majority–minority syndrome. Sometimes, the syndrome is resolved by the secession of the minority group. Secession is feasible only where the minority group has the will to separate and is concentrated within a particular territory. But, even under these conditions, secession may overshoot its point and be achieved with enormous costs all round. Its feasibility does not entail its moral desirability and it might be better to have a political majority–minority framework instead. Nor is the political majority–minority framework the only conceivable framework to get rid of the syndrome. For example, some people believe that the best way to jettison the syndrome is to install an individualist liberal–democratic framework with a uniform charter of individual rights. Other ways of dissolving the syndrome include the imposition of the majoritarian framework, for example, by the covert assimilation of minorities into an overweening majority. Even more obnoxious methods of eliminating the syndrome exist, such as pushing the minority beyond the borders of the nation-state or even liquidating it. On all such views, the majority–minority framework itself is a problem, the framework *is* the syndrome.

In my view, a perspective that identifies the framework with the syndrome unashamedly ignores morality altogether or at least glosses over the complex strands within it. But, does not insistence on the majority–minority framework underestimate the problems generated by it? Why must we put up with a permanent state of radically distinct groups who see themselves only numerically and remain divided and distanced from one another? Why not aspire to a political society that recognizes the equal standing of all viable groups and simply jettison talk of minorities and majorities?[1] Indeed, why take refuge in a divisive discourse of rights at all? My straightforward response to this objection is that the best available option is not *always* realizable. Conditions that enable its exercise may be present in a society but once the opportunity thrown up by the historical process is missed, a society may altogether lose even the chance of securing other morally defensible but second-best options.

Let me explain this point. A pervasive myth within modernist self-understanding is that modern conditions destroy every collective formation and unleash different forms of individualisms. On this view, collective identities and commitments cannot survive the modernist onslaught. Even a cursory glance at the process of modernity reveals, however, that while it undermines some *kinds* of groups, it simultaneously generates and bolsters others.[2] The most obvious example of a group made possible and supported by modern processes is the nation (and other sub-national groups). Now, the same processes that generate national identity also usher a sense of equality and intense competitiveness, ingredients that contribute substantially to the formation of what I called the majority–minority syndrome. It is of course true that a syndrome is not inevitable. A mechanism ensuring equality and mutual respect may well be introduced before competitiveness among groups goes too far. If a society succeeds in doing so, then it secures

---

[1] See, Joseph Raz, *Liberal Multiculturalism in Ethics in the Public Domain*, Oxford: Clarendon Press, 1994, p. 159.

[2] Likewise, it is mistaken to believe that pre-modern social processes undermine every version of individualism and uphold every form of collectivism. These processes also support individualist tendencies.

dignified and peaceful coexistence of groups, perhaps without resorting even to a framework of rights. However, in most instances, the very formation of groups is dependent upon and accompanied by a sense of equality and radical competitiveness. Indeed, groups are formed within the very same process that produces the conditions of the syndrome. One possible solution to contain it, to foster institutionalized toleration, then is to have a context-sensitive system of group rights. However, if these are not granted at the appropriate time, by the right type of agents, complex feelings of disadvantage and marginalization grow and a majority–minority syndrome sets in, and once entrenched—precisely this is my argument—one time tested though not sufficient feature of the overall solution to curtail it is to introduce a suitable majority–minority framework. To insist then upon the futility or irrelevance of the framework, when in fact the syndrome is already entrenched, is to belie at best a shallow utopianism and at worst, to shamelessly disguise inequalities between groups.

RIGHTS AND REFORM

The partition of the Indian sub-continent left an even smaller (though in absolute terms still very huge) Muslim minority in India, largely composed of the illiterate poor scattered all over the country, a rather beleaguered rump in a state of confusion, guilt, and fear—guilty that they may have had or would be seen to have a hand in partition, confused about their status, fearful and uncertain about their future in a newly born Hindu-dominated nation-state. Clearly, unlike those who successfully made it across the border, Muslims who chose to stay back or were left behind had become extremely vulnerable. The constituent assembly, set up in December 1946, six months before partition but which finished its three-year long deliberations on the new constitution well after it, rejected the political majority–minority framework. This rejection was justified on the ground that special representation rights in India had begun the awful habit of treating Hindus and Muslims as distinct political entities. A system of separate electorates freed majority representatives from the obligation of securing support from the minority, strengthened the resolve of every community to care for only its own interests, bolstered sectarianism, ghettoized minorities, and forced considerations of general welfare out of politics. But most of all, it was seen single-handedly to be responsible for India's partition and 'had sharpened communal difference *to a dangerous extent* and had proved one of the main stumbling blocks to the development of a *healthy and (unified)* national life.'[3]

The rejection of a political majority–minority framework was entirely consistent with the acceptance of a social majority–minority framework, however. Members believed that the majority–minority framework may eventually go but 'the minorities must be dissolved into the majority by *justice*'. As one member put it, 'if this elementary justice is not given to minorities, we may open up the dangerous path of fanatical nationalism'. For Ambedkar, one of the main architects of the constitution, such minority rights had an absolute status:

No matter what others do, he urged, we ought to do what is right in our own judgement and, therefore, every minority, irrespective of any other consideration, is entitled to the right to use their language, script and culture and the right not to be precluded from establishing any educational institution that they wish to establish.

Muslims were recognized as a distinct cultural and religious group and were given a constitutionally guaranteed right to the survival and renewal of their own cultural resources, a right to their languages and its scripts, a right to maintain and administer their own educational institutions, and a right to freedom of worship. Many believe that they also have a right to their own personal laws, that is, laws pertaining to family, marriage, divorce, maintenance, inheritance, child custody, and adoption.

Group Rights and Individual Rights

Of these, the right to their personal laws, though not explicitly guaranteed by the Indian constitution, has become more significant in India. For a number of reasons into which I cannot go in this essay, large sections of Muslims in India have viewed their interests primarily in terms of cultural rights which in turn they have come up to identify

[3] Sardar Patel, India's first Home Minister in *The Constituent Assembly Debates, Book 1, Vol. 5*, Lok Sabha Secretariat, 1999, pp. 197–251. The historian, Beni Prasad, also linked separate electorate to acute civil strife and claimed that if 'separate electorates were introduced for Catholics, Protestants, Presbyterians, and Nonconformists in England, they would take not more than a generation to arouse acute antagonisms. Introduce the system into United States and the greatest of republics would soon resound with the battle cries of all the races and nationalities of Europe'. Beni Prasad, *India's Hindu-Muslim Questions*, Lahore: Book Traders, 1944, p. 54.

with their personal laws. Sadly, Muslim identity is wound up with existing personal laws. Indeed, the entire majority–minority framework has been identified with the right to personal laws.

For my limited purpose, I need refer to only four aspects of these laws. The first has to do with inheritance. Muslim personal law requires that women get a share of the parent's property, albeit roughly half the amount granted to male descendants. The other three relate to marriage, divorce, and maintenance. Of these, polygamy is much talked about and I shall say nothing more on it. The position on *Talaq* is familiar too: if convinced that the marriage has broken down, the man can quietly pronounce divorce which becomes effective only after the period of *iddat* (roughly three months). If the man has not retracted during this period, the marriage is dissolved, though this need not be permanent; provided the woman agrees, the man can revive the marriage. This renewal can occur twice in the life time of the couple, however. With the third pronouncement of Talaq, the marriage is irrevocably dissolved. If divorced, the woman must be paid her *mehar* (her share in matrimonial property). She also gets alimony but only till she is re-eligible for marriage, which, once again is roughly three months.[4]

Should Muslims have a right to these laws?[5] Opinion on this for long has been sharply divided. Modernists in India, Muslims as well as Hindus, Sikhs, and Christians, have firmly demanded the abolition of separate personal laws for religious minorities and the institution of a uniform civil code on liberal grounds of justice for women qua individuals. In the

---

[4] Under the old Criminal Procedure Code (CPC) of 1898, all neglected wives, including Muslim women, were granted rights of maintenance. Confined to the privacy of her home, with little opportunities for employment, the amount for maintenance was surely a woman's only means of survival. This right, therefore, was grounded in her basic material needs. But frequently, when Muslim women sought the help of the court to secure maintenance, the husband divorced her, thus freeing himself from payment of maintenance beyond the required three months. To check this malpractice, the CPC of 1973 amended the relevant Act to include divorced women in this category. Muslim orthodoxy objected to this amendment, complaining that it violated their religious laws. Viewed thus, the conflict between group and individual rights appears irreconcilable, heading for collision between the rival world views of modernity and Islam. I deal with this conflict at greater length later.

[5] A more detailed treatment is to be found in Rajeev Bhargava, 'Should We Abandon the Majority–Minority Framework', in D.L. Sheth and Gurpreet Mahajan (eds), *Minority Identities and the Nation-State*, New Delhi: Oxford University Press, 1999, pp. 169–205.

current context, this amounts to a demand that the majority–minority framework be abandoned. Let this anti-communitarian stance be called the *radical individualist* position or simply position (A). Pitted against it is (B), the *conservative communitarian* position that obdurately seeks the strict preservation of the existing system of separate personal laws on grounds of religious integrity and community identity. Indeed, it desires the further extension of the system of personal laws in order to replace the diverse customary practices that indulge freely in inter-cultural borrowing. This position advocates the retention of the majority–minority framework as it interprets it.

I believe that neither of the two positions is satisfactory. There are many reasons why this is so and I hope to identify them later. For the moment, I wish to emphasize that, despite opposition, (A) and (B) share a number of assumptions. First, an ontological assumption that to treat groups as irreducible is to view them as organisms of which individuals are functional parts and that, therefore, they necessarily subsume individuals within it. Second, the normative assumption that if a group has value then it must always be greater than the value of individuals who make it up, that group interests always override individual interests, including, when necessary, the material interests of individuals. Advocates of (A) associate these assumptions with a defence of group rights and counter it. One objection is that groups cannot have rights, simply because they have no irreducible existence. Since minority rights is a species of group rights, there cannot, it follows, be irreducible minority rights and no separate right to personal laws either. The second objection is grounded in normative considerations. Whatever the truth or falsity of ontological individualism, groups have no moral worth (value) independent of the individuals who compose them. Since only entities with moral worth have rights, group and therefore minorities have no rights. Proponents of (B), working with the same framework, affirm the two assumptions. So, despite sharing, at some level, the same framework, (A) and (B), the radical individualist and the conservative communitarian positions, conflict because (A) denies these assumptions and (B) affirms them. I believe that by challenging the very framework embodying these assumptions, we can reject both (A) and (B). It can then be shown that a proper understanding of some of the basic feature of groups, ignored by both the positions, enables us to arrive at an alternative *reformist* position, (C), that reconciles (A) and (B) and seeks reform, not abolition of these laws. In the following section, I try to demonstrate why (A) and (B) are mistaken, and in particular, try to show how some crucial issues elude both positions, and how they misunderstand the precise character of threats to the survival of individuals and groups. I support one version of (C) in the later part.

Ontological and Normative Assumptions

Ontological individualism is the view that only human individuals exist and that groups are mere aggregation of individuals. This view is false, first, because it gets the specific ontology of groups all wrong. Human groups are neither sets nor aggregates but distinct wholes with individuals as their parts. Unlike aggregates, wholes are extremely sensitive to the relationships between their parts, and unlike sets, they tolerate changes without affecting their identity. A human collectivity is individuated by the relations among individual members. When these relations are destroyed, we are still left with an aggregate of individuals but the group has ceased to exist. Likewise, the identity of a human group, say a university, is not changed when the current lot of students, teachers, and fellow workers leave and are replaced by different individuals. It would, if the university was merely a set of these individuals. It is also mistaken because at least some attributes of individuals already presuppose the presence of group-constituting social relations and, in particular, the existence of groups to which individuals belong. This does not mean that all attributes of human individuals depend on groups and certainly not that they depend exclusively on specific groups. For example, human beings have sentient life without groups; many of their bodily needs, their felt pains and pleasures inhere in them without membership in groups.

Value individualism is the view that: (i) only lives of individuals have ultimate value; and (ii) (all) collective entities derive their value from their contribution to the lives of individual human beings.[6] First, an unhelpful vagueness that plagues it must be removed. Point (i) is ambiguous between lives of individuals understood (a) aggregatively (taken by one by one) or (b) holistically (taken together) and between lives understood (c) purely materially or (d) also, socially. If value individualism is the claim that only lives of individuals aggregatively understood have ultimate value and that all collective entities derive their value from the contribution they make to the material life of each individual taken separately, then it is false. The value of many dimensions of our lives is irreducibly holistic (group-related/collectivist): either their

    [6] M. Hartney, 'Some Confusion Concerning Collective Rights', *Canadian Journal of Law and Jurisprudence*, vol. IV, no. 2, July 1991, p. 297.

value is a value for all relevant individuals taken together (solidarity, a way of life) or, when enjoyed singly, it makes ineliminable reference to what can only be valued together (speaking a language, appreciating art, praying), and many collective entities (the family, nation, the university, institutions of a free press) derive their value from the contribution they make not to lives understood purely materially (biological needs, absence of physical pain) but also socially (collective meaning).

This claim defending group-related values does not deny a partial truth in value individualism appropriately understood, namely, the material lives of individuals understood aggregatively have basic value and (some) collective entities also derive value from their contribution to such lives. Indeed, some very powerful moral claims emerge from this recognition: many of our absolute prohibitions such as do not kill, do not maim, or do not cause suffering to others as well as positive moral claims derived from the basic needs of others, such as help the destitute, have this individualist basis. The presence or fulfilment of certain kinds of pleasures—primitive comforts and basic needs (of food, drink, sleep, sex, warmth, and ease)—and the absence of certain kinds of pains—of injury, sickness, hunger, thirst, excessive cold or heat, and exhaustion—have not only agent-neutral but group-neutral value. All these values can be a reason grounding the value of collective entities (for example, hospitals or welfare states). If the value of collective entities is partly derived from these basic individualist values, then it follows that such collective values never constitute a sufficient reason for overriding basic individualist values.

Nor must a defence of collective values be conflated with what I call the 'subsumption thesis'. According to the subsumption thesis, everything of value in the life of an individual is derived from his membership in any one group. That I do not subscribe to this view is evident from my claim that the value of the material life of individuals is independent of membership in any group. Additionally, the value of the social life of an individual is unlikely to be exhausted by his membership in any one group. Individuals interact with different individuals, and at any given point of time, are members of different groups and, therefore, the overall value of their social life is conditional upon their membership in many groups.

Threatened Groups and the Division of Moral Labour

I hope to have becalmed some fears of individualists. But there still exist issues between us that need examining. Simply put, the issue between value individualists and non-individualists is ancient, that is, the individualist must ask of everything: what is in it for me? And asks the same of his membership in a group because ultimately all he wants is his own protection and preservation. The non-individualist claims that at least sometimes we must ask: what am I required to do for the group, for the sake of collective values, because under some conditions it is worthwhile to desire and value the protection or preservation of groups.

But what do groups need protection from? What threatens group values? Now, I believe, group values can be threatened in at least three different ways that may lead to demands for their protection.

1. When the structural conditions in a society favour the values of one group but are inimical to the growth and survival of values of the other, or when the values of one group are sought to be destroyed by another more dominant group. Here a real, external threat exists.

2. When members of the group, out of *akrasia* (weakness of will), wilful or unwitting neglect (self-interest or laziness), ignorance, confusion, or delusion cease to care for group values. This might be called an internal threat.[7]

3. When members deliberating over these values realize their inadequacy or limitation and find better formulations thereof (as when a poor conception of freedom is replaced by a richer one) or discover still better values (as when hierarchy is replaced by equality) and seek to realize this change with or without the help of relatively independent agencies such as the state.

Notice that (3) threatens existing formulation of values but rarely the values themselves. Even when some values are genuinely threatened, the purported threat comes from new values that sublate (cancel and preserve) older ones. So, (3) never entails an insensitive rejection of group values and therefore need not be counted as a real threat to the existence of the group. This is not to say that it not *perceived* or *imagined* as one. But threats that are merely perceived or imagined do not legitimate special protection to groups. Some collectivists mistakenly or deliberately subsume (3) under (1) or (2). On the other hand, individualists quite rightly emphasize the importance of (3), but generally tend to think of all changes in value as instantiating it. And, although

---

[7] Tocqueville comes immediately to mind as one who warned us of internal threats. A retreat from the public good consequent upon over-privatization was viewed by him as a serious threat to liberty. See Charles Taylor, *Philosophical Papers*, Vol. 2, Cambridge: Cambridge University Press, 1985, p. 310.

less optimistic among them have begun to see the danger of external threats, they hardly ever recognize internal threats. Anyone pointing these dangers out is instantly suspected of harbouring authoritarian intentions, willing to sacrifice an individual for the sake of the group, an enemy of (3); in short, of advocating the subsumption thesis.

So, one contentious issue on which individualists and non-individualists stand divided is internal threats to group values. Generally, four possibilities exist in the face of internal threats. The first is to let group values die. Second, to coerce or manipulate some individuals into protecting them. Third, to rely on the heroism of individuals. Finally, to ensure that no one free rides, that each one sacrifices some of his desires and does his fair bit in sustaining them. Individualists rightly oppose the exercise of the second option. They grudgingly accept the third option, heroism, as voluntary but, because they do not see the full force of group values, are unable to grant validity to the fourth option. Nor do conservative communitarians who also meet internal threats by cementing what can be called an unfair division of moral labour.[8] Thus, most societies live by the second and third options: group values are preserved by the moral hard work of some (who sacrifice much more of their desires for the sake of groups), while others free-ride.

A basic feature of the ontology of groups allows this. A group can survive without all its members working for it all the time. This enables its members, first of all, to lead their material lives (they can sleep, eat, etc.); second, to be members of other groups, both over time and at any given point; third, to leave one group and join another. Groups can frequently bear costs of departure of some of its members, a feature that adds to the richness of human existence. (All these show why a commitment to irreducible groups does not entail the subsumption thesis). But the same attribute of groups that yields positive benefits also secretes a disadvantage. It encourages moral inequalities. Generally, groups become internally asymmetric such that some persons or types of persons bear unfair costs of nurturing goods that benefit all its

---

[8] The division of moral labour means different things to different people. For example, Nagel uses it to refer to the division within us between the personal and the impersonal standpoints. For others, it is linked to role-morality and to how society divides moral labour into different institutions and roles. I mean something related but the core idea is dependent upon how the protection of group values requires that its members set aside self-interest or claims of autonomy and how the costs of setting them aside are distributed amongst its members.

members. Let me give an obvious example. Most of us value family life for the enduring relations that it makes possible. Both men and women equally share the joys of family but the burdens generally are unfairly distributed. Women selflessly sacrifice their desires by indirect strategies such as the internalization of their role as glorified mothers or wives. The fact that such asymmetries exist within the family makes it a repressive group. This is the truth in individualist claims. But, it does not follow from this that the institution of family has no independent value, and therefore that the non-individualist claim is false.

To sum up: it is a truism that groups in all societies perpetually face internal threats. It is equally true that enough individuals within the group are engaged in critical examination and revision of its values. Thus, a subterranean tension exists between free riders in the group and its committed reformers. It is also a fact that reform is often read by many members of a group, particularly those who benefit from firmly entrenched power relations within it, as a threat to its very survival. In this very complex situation, the mere presence of the dominant majority may have the following negative consequence. The tension between the ultra-individualist tendencies to free ride, the critical collectivist tendency to reform one's own group, and the conservative communitarian tendency to preserve the status quo may be circumvented by: (i) public proclamations that even the slightest challenge to an existing interpretation of values jeopardizes their very survival, emboldens the majority, and thereby magnifies external threat; (ii) the curtailment of internal debate and the forging of a united front against outsiders. The striking consequence of a failure to reform is the active preservation of unfairness in the division of moral labour. Some members of the group continue to be oppressively burdened with the task of sustaining the group by upholding all its values, including ones that are palpably disintegrating or crying for ethical sublation.

Reform of Muslim Personal Law

If what I have said is reasonable, then position (A), which denies for one reason or another the value of groups or that they need protection and, therefore, collective labour for sustenance, is indefensible. Both ontological and value individualism are implausible or false. But (B) is not justifiable either; it also misunderstands the nature of groups and their relations to individuals. Groups do not hover over and above individuals and although they have irreducible value, it does not follow that the value of some properties of individuals is any less and can be overridden. In short, (A) does not recognize any group rights. However, (B) recognizes them but in the wrong way, endorsing the subsumption thesis that has no place for needs and desires of the individual; (B) rejects the necessity or desirability of justice-based reforms.

The implication of this abstract philosophical discussion is this. Muslims as a group have rights, and given the importance of law within Islam and the contextual significance in India of the domain of the private, they may even have a right to their personal laws. It does not follow, however, that Muslims have a right to the protection of existing interpretations of laws grossly unjust to women. The social majority–minority framework has a justifiable place in India but not in its present form. For a start, my account rules out, in an unabashedly individualist vein, the violation of basic individual rights in the name of group value. Freedom from domestic violence, a right to share in inheritance, and the right to maintenance for divorced and destitute women (flowing from the agent and group-neutral reason of fulfilment of basic needs) must be legally enforceable, irrespective of the group to which women belong. The state has simply to enforce the exercise of such rights, no matter how incompatible this is with the personal laws or customary practices of any group. Any custom or law of Muslim orthodoxy that violates these basic rights must be set aside.[9] Thus, a section of a Muslim personal law which decrees that a husband is liable to provide maintenance to his divorced wife only during the period of iddat and not thereafter must be brushed aside so that Section 125 of the Indian Criminal Procedure Code, which provides for the maintenance by the husband of his divorced wife till she remarries, is applicable to all women, irrespective of their religious affiliation (this was precisely the issue at the heart of the famous Shah Bano case).[10]

Other reforms in personal laws can be introduced without violating community identity. For example, marriages can be legally registered, the permissible age of marriage for women can be raised, women can be given the unconditional right to reside in their matrimonial homes, a married woman need not be treated as the property of her husband, and cruelty or the irretrievable breakdown of marriage can be made

[9] My use of the term 'basic' does not imply that, relative to other rights, they matter more to all individuals. It does mean though that other rights supervene on them.

[10] For a brief discussion of the case see Lawyers' Collective, 'Conflict of Penal and Personal Law', in I. Jaising (ed.), *Justice for Women*, Goa: The Other India Press, 1996, pp. 37–8.

a legitimate ground of divorce. No Muslim can reasonably argue that these reforms constitute an internal threat to his culture. More controversially perhaps, the 'offence of adultery' by women can be dropped as a ground for divorce, and the mother can be recognized as one of the guardians of the child.

But, and this is the crux of the problem, a prima facie incompatibility exists between Muslim personal laws and the best available standards of equality and autonomy. These standards dictate that polygamy be abolished, that women have a right to *equal* share in inheritance, and that divorce be effected by mutual consent rather than by the punitive exercise of an exclusive male prerogative. Does this straight away lead to a uniform civil code? There is need for caution here. In the absence of a clear perspective on where Islam stands on the values of gender equality and autonomy, without proper discussion at all levels on these issues, and under conditions where there anyway exists an external threat, it is not entirely unreasonable to claim that any such tampering with Muslim personal laws might be viewed as a threat to the culture of Muslims, and if a section of Muslims is behind such moves, which it is, even as an internal threat. I believe there is something to be said in favour of this view and therefore, we might support a reconciliatory position, (C), for which reform, not outright rejection, of personal laws is needed.

However, this position, as it stands, is, morally speaking, still too simple. To be sensitive to the complex moral dimensions of this issue, we need a better specification of how this reform is to come about. So, (C), the reformist position, bifurcates further. Therefore, (C1), which I shall awkwardly call *direct* paternalist reformism, argues that reforms for the good of the community can be imposed on it from above, with the exclusive initiative of the state. The other view claims that such reforms must come from within the community. The latter view is subject to further division. The first, anti-paternalist reformism or (C2), argues that the argument of reform from within entails that the state adopt a strict policy of non-interference in the personal matters of Muslim community. The second, (C3), which I call *indirect* paternalist reformism, argues for a distinction between paternalistic coercion and parentalistic interference, and claims further that the rejection of paternalistic coercion is compatible with an obligation on the part of the state to provide conditions which facilitate reform within the community. A combination of (C) with (A), in a contrasting system of priorities, completes the picture.

In India, citizens have the option of complying with the uniform civil code rather than with the personal laws of the community into which they are born. Before independence, this option was conditional upon the complete renunciation of one's religion and therefore, of one's cultural identity. This precondition virtually blocked the right of individuals to exit from their respective personal laws. Since independence, it is possible to both keep one's religious identity and opt for the common civil code. This means (D), a policy of optional civil code: combining (B) or (C) with (A). Finally, (E), there may exist an automatic compliance with a common civil code but citizens may have the option to be governed by personal laws (A is more basic but an option exists for B or C).[11] The two policies differ in the relative weight they place on secular–individual and religious-group identity. The one optional in the policy is also relatively less important for the relevant agents.

I root for the solution that advocates a version of (D), that is, which combines (C3) with (A).[12] A commitment to (C3) entails a rejection of (B), (C1), and (C2) and is consistent with what, in my view, is the best interpretation of liberal, secular and democratic principles (this version of (D), I less adventurously call the secular–democratic option). I believe reforms within Muslim personal law must come from within, but that a secular and democratic state is committed to the provision of conditions that facilitate a full and free deliberation over the entire issue, a precondition of any reform. I also believe that Muslim women must be given the right to exit the system of personal laws. Since there are no advocates for the removal of the option to be regulated by a common code (a sign, surely, that the Muslim orthodoxy does not view it as threatening and sign, too, that Muslim women do not see it as a reasonable option), on the question of deciding which of the two, a uniform civil code or separate personal laws, is paramount, I currently place more importance on separate personal laws, not on the ground that they are sacred but on the more general ground that Muslims have a right to a separate cultural identity. Since it is this more general reason that grounds the right and entails duties on individuals, groups, and the state, it would be wholly consistent with my position if, on the more specific grounds of justice, personal laws are eventually overhauled and replaced by something

[11] Position (E) is proposed by the Shetkari Sanghatan. See Gail Omvedt, 'Towards A Non-Sexist "Civil Code"', in I. Jaising (ed.), *Justice for Women*, pp. 9–13.

[12] Other versions of position (D) could combine (A) with (B), (C1), or (C2).

else that better protects their separate identity. My point, however, is that whatever it is that replaces personal law is not likely to and perhaps should not entail an entirely culture-insensitive, homogenizing civil code.

Let me try and put this point differently. Suppose egalitarians were to overhaul the personal laws of all cultural communities, with full consideration given to concerns of gender justice, I can bet that a residual cultural difference will abide in the new, reformed set of laws. Let me take an example: all religious codes include some legal criteria that make a marriage valid. For example, the Hindu marriage is solemnized according to *saptapadi*, which by all accounts is a male chauvinist tradition. Its removal does not mean, however, that all Hindu marriages be solemnized in the civil court; other progressive traditions exists within the religion which are not male chauvinist. Similarly, in the Hindu personal law, men, not women, have unequivocal rights to coparcenary property at birth. Such rights presuppose an undivided joint family governed by *Mitakshara* law. Now it is not clear why giving equal rights to coparcenary property to women must entail that dissolution of the joint family. Muslims too have multiple traditions of solemnizing marriages, even different legal traditions which do not accord the same status to women. It is not clear why more progressive legal traditions within Islam cannot be relied upon to improve the status of women. Cultural differences may remain even when all personal laws are made egalitarian.

What is my defence of this position? Everything hinges on how Muslim women view their own situation. Do most of them view themselves as under a bell jar, as surely must be assumed by those who advocate a swift imposition of uniform civil code on liberal-emancipatory grounds? Is this purely a gender issue, nothing to do with cultural identity? Or is it rather that Muslim women entirely accept their current role within Muslim culture as dictated by the *shariat*? Is the division of moral labour seen as legitimate or as unfair by Muslim women? Rather than forcing the situation of women into one or the other pigeonhole, surely it is better—certainly more in keeping with their status as full moral agents—to view their situation as riven with an internal conflict. Despite all the inequalities of their condition, Muslim women can see the importance of their cultural identity just as well as Muslim men do. They realize the value of their group. (Position A denies this and position E does not give it enough importance, at least not in the current context.) But, they can also view themselves

independent of their current status within the group, as bearers of interests that grant them greater moral worth than they currently enjoy qua group members. Such interests are foregrounded when they view themselves either qua equal interlocutors deliberating over the values of their group or as potential members of other groups. It's better to see Muslim women, and to some extent, Muslim men, as playing out this internal struggle. A Muslim cultural identity matters to (the relevant) women. But, unlike Muslim orthodoxy that wants it be so, it is not the *only* thing that matters to them. This clearly is an internal struggle within Muslims, between statusquoists and pro-change Muslims.

In the Shah Bano case, an elderly Muslim woman sought maintenance from her husband after he divorced her and obtained a favourable judgement from all Indian courts, but it earned the wrath of Muslim orthodoxy and brought India's secular laws in conflict with Muslim personal law. We can surely read the case in this manner. Recall my discussion of sources of value change.[13] Muslims in India can be seen to undergo all three processes at once (i, ii, and iii). Muslims face an external threat (the structural conditions favour the Hindu majority, surely the reason that grounds minority rights). There is also some evidence of an internal threat (the reason why Muslim orthodoxy plays a hegemonic role among Muslims today). But, there also exist persistent attempts among Muslims to reinterpret their tradition (as examples, see the valiant attempts of both modernist and traditional Muslims).[14] True, that it is always in the interest of Muslim orthodoxy to blur the line between (ii) and (iii), but the pervasive presence of (i) nevertheless creates a perpetual dilemma, above all for Muslim women like Shah Bano who reason probably in the following way: all Muslims value their group identity. They also face internal and external threats. In such a context, the line between real and perceived threats is blurred. Though the division of moral labour is grossly unjust to

[13] Given earlier, in the section, 'Threatened groups and the division of moral labour'.

[14] This struggle is waged not only by a large number of liberal–secular women and men but also by a section of Muslim theologians; organizations such as the Muslim Satyashodak Mandal, Anjuman Taraqqi Pasand, Muslimeen, and the Kerala Islamic Shariat Board; and exemplary Muslim intellectuals such as Asghar Ali Engineer. For details, see Kirti Singh, 'The Constitution and Muslim Personal Law', in Zoya Hasan (ed.), *Forging Identities, Gender, Communities and the State in India*, Boulder: Westview Press, 1994, p. 102; and Sanober Keshwaar, 'The Triple Talaq—Unjust, Untenable, Un-Islamic', in I. Jaising (ed.), *Justice for Women*, pp. 88–94.

us, Muslim women, the burden carried largely by us helps sustain our group in the face of continuing external threat. Therefore, no matter how costly it is to us, we should not press now for justice.

Now, I believe it is futile to deny that this impasse exists. I see (D) as a solution precisely because it points to a way out. Positions (A), (B), (C1), (C2), and (E) do not properly see this impasse: (B), (C1), and (C2) deny claims of gender justice, while (A) and (E) refuse to give importance to the value of groups. (D) not only takes serious note of the dilemma mentioned but also takes it by the horns: it seeks reforms of existing personal laws of Muslims, sympathetically understands the tremendous costs of exercising the right to exit but gives Muslim women the right to opt for the common civil code, and enjoins the state to create conditions for deliberation on the reforms of all personal laws, for the free exercise of the right to opt for the common civil code, for full protection to those who make this choice, and in addition, to create more opportunities for minority groups to reinterpret their identities.

No proponent of group rights committed also to gender justice would dare propose setting up a deliberative body of Muslims were he convinced that reform from *within* was in principle impossible. The proposal of a deliberative body is predicated on at least some grounds for hope of change. Is this hope justified? I believe a partial reform of Muslim personal laws is possible. This brings me to a discussion of substantive policy issues. Let me begin with polygamy. Two points need mentioning at the outset. First, the incidence of polygamous relations among Muslims is very small, smaller than in many other groups in India. Second, the Quran neither enjoins nor prohibits polygamy. I think it is pretty futile to bring in the Quran in support of such matters, because, generally speaking, for every verse or statement you enlist in support, you can almost find another that takes it away. However, widespread prejudice against Islam compels me to quote the relevant verse, 'Marry of the women, who seem good to you, two or three or four, and if ye fear that ye cannot do justice then one only.'[15] This rules polygamy out for all practical purposes, for I cannot see how patterns of perfect reciprocity within emotionally charged relations, surely required by justice, can be maintained under conditions of polygamy.[16]

[15] The Quran, IV: 3, quoted in T. Mahmood (ed.), *Family Law and Social Change*, Bombay: N.M. Tripathi Ltd, 1975, p. 36.

[16] It was roughly this interpretation of the Quran that legitimated the decision of the Tunisian president to ban polygamy.

As for justice within interpersonal and sexual relations, no society has yet properly devised standards of fairness in this domain. The Muslims are not uniquely responsible for what must surely be a deep rooted but common human failing.

Strictly speaking then, justice requires not a ban on polygamy but the availability of this option for women too! I am not being frivolous here, though it is obvious that this is an even more hopeless demand. Under the circumstances therefore, the best thing would be to build financial disincentives to polygamy into the law.[17] The main concern, remember, is the maltreatment of women, not sexual promiscuity. The emotional suffering another relationship causes cannot be handled legally but financial hardships that polygamous marriages usually bring with them can be controlled by law. In short, polygamy can be regulated.

On Talaq, the prospects are even better! First of all, the very fact that divorce is acceptable within Islam speaks of its partial liberal premises:[18] marriage, though a repository of a semi-sacred relation, is also a contract. It is a dissoluble union. Moreover, the identity of a Muslim woman is not wholly exhausted by her marital status. She continues to have an identity outside of her marriage. Her consent to marriage and to its continuance is necessary, unlike the case in other traditional systems of marriage. Second, in addition to her share of inheritance from her own parents, a woman has a right to *mehr*, that is, to her proper share in matrimonial property. Gender equality is more prevalent in Islam than in many other traditional systems. The Muslim wife can legally retain her name, her property, and independent legal status, even the school of law which is part of her faith.

This provides the general context within which the Islamic understanding of divorce must be understood. Excessive attention has been bestowed on the notion of triple Talaq. But other parts of Islamic law are hardly ever mentioned. For example, Islam also recognizes *Khul*, divorce purely at the behest of the woman. In other words, no man can force his wife to cohabit with him, if she refuses to. Khul within Islamic law is as important as Talaq. Besides, Talaq and Khul, there also exists *Mubaraat*—a process under which a couple can jointly, on mutual agreement, dissolve the marriage. It appears that if the position

[17] I have the impression that the noted scholar of jurisprudence, Upendra Baxi, makes a similar point somewhere.

[18] It is often said that Islam is inegalitarian, but it must also be said that it is curiously liberal for its time, especially when compared with laws on offer in most Hindu or Christian scriptures.

of Muslim women within their community is deplorable, it is not on account of Islamic law but of extra-legal malpractices.

I mention this not because I believe traditional Islam has all this and much more to offer for the emancipation of women. I do not believe that traditional systems are fully equipped with such resources. But stereotypes, far as usual from truth, have it that the deplorable condition of Muslim women is incomparable and is sanctioned by Islamic law. This is not true. At any rate, the point in favour of the partial reform of Islamic law is that some resources within traditional Islamic law can be deployed for bringing about gender-just laws. Surely, this is demonstrated by what has been mentioned.

THE MAJORITY–MINORITY SYNDROME IN INDIA:
HISTORY AND RESOLUTION?

Alas, conditions in India are not propitious for even the realization of position (D). Why cannot a policy be implemented that is based on a contextually reasonable and reconciliatory stand such as the one I defend? Why is reform not possible? Because a propensity to stall reforms is built into the majority–minority syndrome which continues to infect Indian politics. To understand this point, the dilemmas and paradoxes, the frustrating impasse in Indian politics and society, and the acute vulnerability this creates for Indian Muslims, a brief excursus into recent Indian history is unavoidable.

There was much in common between Hindus and Muslims in pre-independent India.[19] A majority of Muslims belong to the same ethnic group as Hindus. Urdu, widely thought to be a language of Muslims, was actually spoken by only about 30 per cent of total Muslims and by a large number of Hindus in the north. Certain social customs were

---

[19] For example, in Karla, till at least 1865, Muslim peasants were worshipping old village deities. In Altar and Bharatpur, the Meos continued to have Hindu names and celebrated—not just joined in—festivals such as Janamashtami, and the Parihar Minar forbade the consumption of beef. Muslim cultivators near Ratlam followed Hindu customs in marriage. The sect of Mehadawis near Ahmedabad, steeped in Muslin orthodoxy in appearance, were known for concealing their real, un-Islamic beliefs. In Sind, among Sunni Memans, ancient cults of the worship of trees and rivers were freely practised and both living and dead saints were revered. The list of sects and communities who, despite the formal adoption of Islam, retained their pre-Islamic beliefs and practices, is endless. For a good account of this, see M. Mujeeb, *Indian Muslims*, Delhi: Munshiram Manoharlal, 1985.

common to both communities. Many Muslims retained Hindu names. Hindu rites were sufficient in many parts of the country to solemnize Muslim marriages. Indeed, many Muslims continued to follow Hindu law in matters of marriage, guardianship, and inheritance. Muslim *pirs* had Hindu disciples and Hindu yogis had Muslim *chelas*. The caste system remained integral to both communities. Apart from Bengal, Hindus and Muslims were not divided along class lines or along the rural–urban continuum. There is then strong evidence to support the contention of several historians that 'objectively speaking', differences between Muslims and Hindus were not large enough to justify separation.[20]

Yet, a successful separatist movement occurred in India. Briefly, this movement for separation that partitioned India underwent four stages. First, the heightened use of religion as an identity marker in public spaces and the consolidation of community identities based on religion. By the end of the nineteenth century, powerful revivalist movements had sprung among Hindus, along with a sense of the need to be unified and recognized as one homogenous group. This growing self-awareness was often accompanied by the feeling that Hindus had been a subject group, subordinated first to Muslims and later to the British. Revivalist movements, therefore, frequently assumed a strident anti-Muslim character. This was to cause great consternation among Muslim elites who were thereby forced to device new strategies to create a social and political space for hardened religious identity.

Second was the development of majority–minority self-identifications and the demand for a social and political majority–minority framework. The introduction of modern census and representative institutions into India, in particular the scheme of separate representation for Muslims, ushered in this second phase. This opened up space to use religion for political mobilization, publicly launch a majority–minority discourse, form a communal party such as the Muslim League, and sow seeds that would transform a community into a nation.

Third, the public proclamation that religious communities are nations. Henceforth, a qualitatively different kind of majority–minority

[20] Muslims anyway began to feel insecure by the pressure of change put on them by the 'rise of monied men and resurgence of Hindu landholding communities and by some colonial government policies such as making it mandatory on Indian officials to be able to read both the Devanagri and the Persian script.' See Mushirul Hasan, *India's Partition, Process, Strategy and Mobilization*, New Delhi: Oxford University Press, 1993, p. 36.

framework with a demand for self-government rights was put forward by elites for statutory majority in both previously existing and newly carved provinces where Muslims were in majority. Once Muslims elites began to believe that Muslims too were a nation, they also began to dream of complete economic and political power for themselves, and entered the fourth stage, where they demanded that these self-government rights be exercised only within an independent, politically sovereign nation-state.[21]

However—and this has much relevance to what I shall claim next—these demands were laced with a long list of imaginary grievances conjured up by them. Muslim elites were really not backward but they feared being left behind in a predominantly Hindu regime, so they created the myth of the backward Muslim. They were not really oppressed but feared political domination in a Hindu-majority India, so they spun tales of Hindu tyranny. They were neither historically disadvantaged nor unable to voice their demands but still manufactured the fiction of marginalization. Perhaps the term 'imaginary' should not be identified with 'unreal'. As the historian Beni Prasad, writing in the thick of the demand for partition, said, 'in politics there is a profound significance in Adler's thesis that complexes are due not to the past but to the fear of the future'.[22] But, by the 1940s, this fear turned into paranoia and greatly contributed to the development of the majority–minority syndrome.

Nor was fear of the future the only ingredient in the syndrome. A deeply divided memory of the past also played a key role in its development. Against the dominant current of anti-colonial ideology,

---

[21] The installation of a Congress government in UP started this phase. While keen to have a large Muslim representation within the government, the Congress, believing itself to be the party of all Indians, refused to induct the largest group of Muslims in the legislature, members of the Muslim League, into the ministry, unless the League was disbanded as a party. This was unacceptable to the League. As a result, Muslim elites were deprived of a share in power. Soon they lost some of their privileges. Even more important was the realization that for any more political favours, they would now have to lean not on the British but on the Congress, a political organization that also relied on Hindu support. This generated in them a propensity to be receptive to the mobilizing strategy of the Muslim League and eventually to espouse separatism. See Hasan, *India's Partition, Process, Strategy and Mobilization*, pp. 1–43. For Hindu communalism in Bengal, see Joya Chatterjee, *Bengal Divided, Hindu Communalism and Partition 1932–1947*, New Delhi: Cambridge University Press, 1995.

[22] Beni Prasad, *India's Hindu–Muslim Questions*, p. 59.

Ambedkar made this point with cold-blooded clarity. He accepted that large sections of Hindus and Muslims have shared a common way of life but insisted that this commonness should now not be exaggerated.[23] Using Renan's arguments that to qualify as a nation, a people must share a common heritage and cherish a common memory and noting that Hindus and Muslims had divided memories, he concluded that Hindus and Muslims were two nations. Even when both referred to the same events, one remembered it with shame and sorrow and the other with great pride. Thus, there was no common cycle of participation for a common achievement. Their political and religious past was one of mutual destruction and mutual animosities. It is, Ambedkar claimed, 'embedded in their religion, and for each to give up its past is to give up its religion. To hope for this is to hope in vain'.[24]

According to Ambedkar, political and religious antagonisms divided them more deeply than the so-called common things that bound them. On the period in which Gandhi was tirelessly advocating Hindu–Muslim unity, Ambedkar claimed that it is:

no exaggeration to say that it is a record of 20 years of civil war between Hindus and Muslims…The acts of barbarism against women, committed without remorse…show the depth of antagonism between two communities…The tempers on both sides are like tempers of two warring nations…What is astonishing is that these cold and deliberate acts of rank cruelty were not regarded as atrocities to be condemned but were treated as legitimate acts of warfare for which no apology was necessary.[25]

Even though he does not use the term, Ambedkar is alluding here to what I have called the majority–minority syndrome, a diseased network of neurotic relations, so completely poisoned and accompanied by a such a vertiginous assortment of negative emotions (envy, malice, jealousy, spite, and hatred) that collective delirium and cold-blooded acts of revenge—sending groups on a downward path of deeper and still deeper estrangement—are mindlessly, alternately, cyclically generated.

[23] Many of these common features were a result not of choice, of 'conscious attempt' but due to 'mechanical causes' such as incomplete conversions, the mere fact of living on common land and under a common climate, and vestiges of a brief period during Akbar's rule when religious amalgamation did genuinely take place. B.R. Ambedkar, *Writings and Speeches, Vol. 8: Pakistan or the Partition of India*, Government of Maharashtra: Education Department, 1990, pp. 33–7.

[24] Ibid., p. 27.

[25] Ibid., pp. 184–6.

It is a feature of this syndrome that groups make demands on one other that can rarely be fulfilled; conjure up imaginary grievances; insist precisely on that which hurts the other most; at one time obsessively desire the very same thing that the other wants; at another time the exact opposite, always with the sole purpose of negating the claims of the other. Ambedkar provides several examples: 'Hindus and Muslims make preparations against each other,' he tells us, 'without abatement,' reminding one of a

race in armaments between two hostile nations. If the Hindus have the Banaras University, the Musalmans must have the Aligarh University. If the Hindu start *Shuddhi* movement, the Muslims must launch the *Tablig* movement. If the Hindus start sangathan, the Muslims must have the *Tanjim*. If the Hindus have the R.S.S. [Rashtriya Swayamsevak Sangh], the Muslims must reply by organising the *Khaksars*.[26]

Again, the Muslims (read extremist Muslims) agitated fiercely to introduce representative government in Kashmir but elsewhere they opposed it. Why? Because in all matters, Ambedkar claimed, their determining attitude is how will it affect the Muslims vis à vis the Hindus. In Kashmir, it would have meant transfer of power from a Hindu king to Muslim masses; elsewhere, where the ruler is Muslim and subjects Hindus, it means Hindu masses will be victorious.

He adds, 'The determining and dominating consideration is not democracy but how democracy with majority rule will affect the Muslims in their struggle against the Hindus'.[27] Ambedkar was wrong about Kashmiri Muslims but he had grasped the mindset of extremists more generally. As he himself recognized, extremist Hindu politics was similarly perverted. In different circumstances, a political majority–minority framework for Muslims within a united India should have been a satisfactory solution to all sides. But given the majority–minority syndrome, 'in which a hostile majority is forever pitted against a hostile minority,' Ambedkar concluded, only a separate state seemed viable.

The development of the majority–minority syndrome prevented a reasonable and accommodating solution to the Muslim question in India. It also had a debilitating impact on the possibility of reforms, particularly for Indian Muslims. This is so because anti-reformist tendencies within a group are severely intensified if a society is in the grip of a majority–minority syndrome. Ambedkar was quick to grasp this

[26] Ibid., p. 246.
[27] Ibid., p. 236.

point. When groups regard each other as a menace, he argued, all their energies are spent on preparing to meet 'the menace'. The exigencies of a common front of the majority against a powerful minority and the minority against the majority generates a 'conspiracy of silence over social evils'.[28] Neither attend to them,

even though they are running sores and requiring immediate attention, for the simple reason that they view every measure of social reform as bound to create dissension and division and thereby weaken the ranks when they ought to be closed to meet the menace of the other community.[29]

This ensures that there is social stagnation and the spirit of conservatism continues to dominate the thoughts and actions of both.

In a passage that anticipates the dilemma faced many decades later over the Shah Bano case, he laments the passing of the Dissolution of Muslim Marriage Act VIII of 1939. This act annulled the previous law for which the apostasy of a male or a female married under the Muslim law ipso facto dissolved the marriage with the result that if a married Muslim woman changed her religion, she was free to marry a person professing her new religion. The effect of the new retrograde law was to bind a married Muslim woman to her husband even if his religious faith was repugnant to her. A conversion of a woman and her subsequent marriage were seen to be undertaken solely with a view to change the relative numerical strength of communities and therefore, as a depredation by one community against the other. Thus, the real motive, Ambedkar claimed, was to prevent the illicit conversion of women to alien faiths in order to ensure that the numerical balance between the two communities remains undisturbed. Ambedkar concluded that the law was changed and the rights of women sacrificed purely in order to maintain a certain numerical balance between the two communities. Such reasoning, which turned a social issue requiring urgent reform into a contentious matter between warring communities, epitomizes a majority–minority syndrome.

David Hume says somewhere that enmity between hostile groups endures even though the original cause of animosity has disappeared and even when it goes against their current interests.[30] Resentments, hatred, and grudges are sometimes bequeathed from generation to

[28] Ibid., p. 247.
[29] Ibid.
[30] See Stephen Holmes, *Passion and Constraint*, Chicago and London: The University of Chicago Press, 1995, pp. 50–1.

generation. In India, Hindu extremists and Muslim orthodoxy and, by default, large sections of ordinary Hindus and Muslims appear to have inherited features of the majority–minority syndrome, with particularly disastrous consequences for the smaller group. The original situation of conflict may have disappeared but extremists from the majority Hindu community and, foolishly, sections of Muslim orthodoxy talk and behave in a manner that resuscitates the syndrome.

In the Shah Bano case, a slight error on the part of the Supreme Court—the judge took it upon himself to interpret the Quran—was sufficient for Muslim orthodoxy to press panic buttons about Hindu majoritarianism, to paint alarmist scenarios of great danger to Islam, and for manufacturing, a la the pre-independence Muslim League, an unending list of imaginary grievances. Internal debate was stifled, the government of the day succumbed to pressure and passed a new law favouring the status quo on Muslim personal law and poor Shah Bano was forced to retract. The slogan of Islam in danger soon turned into a self-fulfilling prophecy, as Hindu chauvinists first began to harangue Muslims on how they should shed backwardness, then charged successive Congress governments of Muslim appeasement, and eventually began to consolidate a fiercely anti-Muslim, political Hindu identity. Old Hindu grievances, mostly imaginary, were re-invented: the destruction of Hindu temples by Mughals, the temerity of supporters of partition to even ask for a framework respecting minority rights, the disloyalty induced by pan-Islamicism, the alleged Muslim propensity to flout family planning norms with the sole purpose of increasing their numerical strength, and the alleged role that polygamy and therefore, Muslim personal law plays in their march to outpopulate Hindus. Unwittingly, thanks largely to its orthodox leadership, a much weakened Muslim community had helped trigger off the majority–minority syndrome. With the syndrome in full swing (the recent events in Gujarat where the ghastly killing of fifty-eight Hindus by a provoked Muslim crowd led to a state-abetted pogrom of over 2,000 innocent Muslims by organized Hindu mobs—the closest post-independent India has come to localized ethnic cleansing—is ample testimony), anti-reformist tendencies are likely to congeal and the already unjust division of moral labour bound to be further aggravated. Now that the external threat is real, chronic, and pervasive, the Shah Banos within Muslim community are even more likely to tell themselves that despite all the unfairness, they must, in these difficult times, shoulder the burden of community values entirely on their own. The majority–minority syndrome makes reform within Muslim personal law virtually impossible.

The deadlock over reforms within Muslim personal law aggravates the quite unreasonable misgivings among otherwise reasonable Hindus about the very framework of minority rights in India. The offensive discourse of Hindu militants and the violence that frequently accompanies it leaves Indian Muslims wondering whether their citizenship in India is based on the sufferance of the majority. What then is the future of the Indian nation-state? The durability of the nation-state depends on the dissolution of the majority–minority syndrome. The syndrome can be cured, first of all, when those who exacerbate it are legally curtailed and made politically powerless. In the current context, this largely means curbing the power of Hindu extremists who, ironically, perpetuate the syndrome in trying to implement their own radical solution of resolving it. In the long run, however, it can be eliminated only when: (i) large sections of Hindus begin to really value the idea of equal citizenship and to uncouple equality from sameness; and (ii) Muslim leaders and those who blindly follow them, having fatefully embraced conservative communitarianism, begin to value individual rights and adopt a somewhat less instrumentalist attitude to liberal and democratic institutions. None of this is possible, however, unless the syndrome is treated and cast off. Alas, here, as in many other places, things move in vicious circles. Tragically, no one in India appears to have the vision or the skill to break the conundrum.

7

On the Persistent Political Under-representation of Muslims in India*

In several chapters in this book, I have given an account of, and sometimes defended, why religiously grounded political rights were rejected in the constituent assembly, why the political majority–minority framework was unacceptable to many who drafted the constitution. In this chapter, I re-examine this issue in the light of the conditions of Muslims in India today. This essay has three sections. In the first section, I provide a brief historical overview of Hindu–Muslim relations in India and of the condition of Indian Muslims today. I conclude by claiming that Indian Muslims are a marginalized minority who have been persistently under-represented in political institutions, particularly in the Indian Parliament. In the second section, I examine the case for political representation for Muslims. This was a much debated issue in pre-independent India. It was debated with subtlety and in considerable detail in the constituent assembly debates on the Indian constitution. However, with the partition of the country and the formation of the separate state of Pakistan, all debate on the political representation of Muslims ceased. I examine the merits and demerits of the case for the political representation of Indian Muslims. I also attempt a brief

* This paper was presented at a workshop on Multiculturalism and the Anti-discrimination Principle at the Ramat Gan Law School, Tel Aviv in December 2005. It was subsequently published as 'On the Persistent Political Under-representation of Muslims in India', *Journal of Law and Ethics of Human Rights*, vol. 1, Ramat Gan Law School, Tel Aviv, 2007, pp. 77–133.

explanation of why this issue has virtually disappeared from the public arena in India. I conclude in the section that although political representation of Muslims qua Muslims is desirable, it is still unfeasible in the prevailing situation in India. In other words, I would support the recommendation to the Indian state that political rights not be granted to any religious community.

If political theory was to remain a handmaiden of state policy, then the matter ends right here. However, since I believe that political theory must think for the long run and design just institutions and policies for the future, and since there is, I claim, no principled objection to the political representation of Muslims, in the third and final section, I briefly outline which of the several electoral mechanisms are best suited to ensure fair political representation for Muslims in the future. In my view, the principle of fair political representation for Indian Muslims is best fulfilled by a complex mechanism consisting of preferential voting in multi-member constituencies with intra-party quotas in proportion to the overall population of Muslims in the country.

The partition of the sub-continent left a smaller, beleaguered Muslim minority in India. They felt guilty that they may have had or would be seen to have a hand in partition, were confused about their status, and fearful and uncertain about their future in a newly born Hindu-dominated nation-state. Clearly, unlike those who successfully made it across the border, Muslims who chose to stay back or were left behind had become extremely vulnerable.

Yet political choices before Indian Muslims were not as limited after independence as it is sometimes made out to be. Nor were they dictated in the 1950s by a uniform ideological trend. Different groups vied with each other to take the mantle of Muslim leadership in India.[1] These groups were broadly divided into two. The first was represented by organizations like the 'apolitical' Tablighi Jamaat,[2] the revivalist Jamaat-I-Islami, the pro-Congress Jamiyat-al-Uleme-e-Hind, and sections among Muslims that tried to revive the dissolved Muslim League once again. These groups reflected a trend that had become strong in the

[1] On this point, my account relies on the work of Mushirul Hasan. See his *India's Muslims since Independence: Legacy of a Divided Nation*, New Delhi: Oxford University Press, 1997, chapter 6.

[2] It is a movement started in 1926 by Maulana Mohammad Ilyas in the form of an organization called Tablighi Jamaat. Its stated aim is to bring spiritual awakening in the Muslims. Its intention was to 'transform' into 'pure Muslims' converts from Hinduism who still followed their Hindu cultural traditions.

three or four decades prior to the independence of India, namely, an exaggerated emphasis on cultural and identity issues such as the maintenance of the Sharia-based Muslim personal law at the expense of issues of material well-being and development common to all Indians. The second group underplayed issues of identity. It opted for an expression of loyalty and demonstration of goodwill expressed through measures such as the observation of anti-Pakistan day, or the imposition of a voluntary ban on cow slaughter, and the formal acceptance of Hindi as official language. These people emphasized not separation but assimilation. Thus, Muslim legislators from the Congress generally avoided raising issues which were considered to be exclusively 'Muslim'. This was so for a number of reasons. First, the electoral process usually favoured those who were reluctant to raise contentious issues for fear of being denied nomination at the next election. Second, many elected representatives had a constituency other than Muslims and were not obliged to redress only the grievances of the Muslim segment of the electorate. Had they done so, they would have alienated their non-Muslim constituency. Third, fearing that they would be branded communal, they did not want to appear to work exclusively among or for Muslims. These assimilationist Muslims within the Indian National Congress (INC), also termed as 'Muslim Nationalists', tried to project themselves as the real representatives of the Indian Muslims.[3]

This claim was not entirely unfounded. Since there was no perceived schism between elite and ordinary Muslims, the virtual co-option of elite Muslims within the fold of the Congress meant that ordinary Muslims voted for the Congress as well. This happened consistently in the first three general elections: 1952, 1957, and 1962.[4] When I write that Congress Muslims were assimilationists, I did not use this term entirely negatively, because a significant reason for their preference for the Congress was the faith of the ordinary Muslim in Nehru's leadership and in his ability to provide them adequate constitutional safeguards. However, this was so also because the average Muslim voter was concerned less about the fate of the Sharia and more worried about his own survival. He wanted an ordinary life with dignity, for which he realized there was a need to build an enduring relationship with fellow citizens and with established political parties. Consequently, there was marginal improvement in the economic condition of some Muslims.

[3] See Hasan, *India's Muslims since Independence*, pp. 188–9.
[4] Ibid., p. 216.

For instance, the weaving community in UP and Bihar began to do well. Though there was a reduction in their number due to migration and riots, urban artisans in and around Delhi remained reasonably well off. The small Muslim bourgeoisie in western parts of the country expanded its business without any hindrance. The same trend was observed in the southern part of the country where Muslims did relatively well in their traditional professional fields.[5] These factors continued to propel Muslims to vote for the Congress.

All this changed, however, after the death of Nehru. For a start, a schism between the elites and the rest gradually unfolded. The Congress failed to address issues of literacy, education, employment, and improvement in the conditions of women.[6] Nor did it fully address the major issue of security which remained a concern for the ordinary Muslim: one communal riot after another left behind a disproportionately large number of Muslim victims. The incidence of violence against minorities which had showed a steady decline all through the Nehruvian period and had reached its lowest in 1963, showed a marked increase throughout the country. After Nehru, the law and order machinery was greatly 'communalized'.[7] The slow and steady rise of Jana Sangh[8] and later the BJP[9] was another important reason. In a new identity-charged

[5] Ibid., p. 216–17.

[6] Half the Muslim population is illiterate compared to the Indian average of 35.5 per cent. See Hasan, *India's Muslims since Independence.*

[7] For a fuller explication of this point, see Christophe Jaffrelot, *The Hindu Nationalist Movement and Indian Politics: 1925 to the 1990s*, New Delhi: Viking, 1996, pp. 330–7.

[8] A political party, the predecessor of the present BJP, which existed from 1951 to 1980 and subscribed to right-wing Hindu nationalist ideology. This party merged in 1977 with the Bharatiya Lok Dal, the Congress (O), and the Socialist Party, to form the Janata Party (People's Party) and fought against the Indira Gandhi-led Congress party which had declared emergency in India. The Janata Party formed the first non-Congress government in India and included former Jana Sangh leaders such as A.B. Vajpayee and L.K. Advani.

[9] It is the acronym for Bharatiya Janata Party, one of the major political parties in India, formed in 1980, after the disbandment of the Jana Sangh. It subscribes to the same ideology. It became the single-largest political party in Parliament in 1996 but could not muster enough support to form a government. After the 1998 general elections, it managed to form a coalition government in alliance with other parties called the National Democratic Alliance (NDA). But the coalition ruptured in May 1999, and fresh elections were again called with the NDA coming to power with full majority. However, the NDA lost the next general elections held in 2004.

and -dominated political context, secularism was also reduced to a mere identity-constituting ideology that offered Muslims an alternative identity of a citizen without the political or socio-economic rights that frequently go with it. This rather thin secularism was no match to a well entrenched, much thicker identity offered by Islam. Drawn from the erstwhile landlord class, most of the Muslim elite was interested in self-perpetuation, was easily satisfied with Nehru's patronage, and did little to ameliorate the condition of their co-believers. Therefore, cracks between Muslim elites and ordinary Muslims were bound to grow. Ordinary Muslims began to lose faith in their leaders and in the Congress party and gradually moved towards organizations that focused on issues of cultural identity. For example, there was a revival of the Jamaat-I-Islami in north India, the Muslim League in Kerala, and the Ittehadul-Muslimeen in Hyderabad.[10] These organizations exploited the real and imaginary grievances of the Muslims in specific regional and local settings and legitimized themselves.

MUSLIMS: A MARGINALIZED GROUP IN INDIA

Meanwhile, the condition of the average Muslim worsened in much of India. One commentator, A.G. Noorani, described the condition of Indian Muslims as 'sad'.[11] When using this term, he had in mind the unequal treatment of Muslims in employment,[12] the plight of Urdu, and the threat to the physical security of ordinary Muslims.[13]

It is important here to note the precise nature of marginalization and exclusion of Muslims in India. To say that Muslims are a marginalized community is not to claim that every single Muslim is marginalized, nor

[10] Hasan, *India's Muslims since Independence*, p. 253.

[11] Quoted in ibid., p. 280.

[12] In the Indian Administrative Service (IAS), for example, Muslims were a mere 2.99 per cent in 1981. In central government offices in thirteen states, Muslims had 4.41 per cent representation. The Muslim share of private sector employment is not any better. For detailed figures, see 'Muslim India', June 1983, pp. 261–3 and 'Muslim India', January 1984, p. 17, from *Minorities Commission Report*.

[13] On the total number of communal incidents and persons killed or injured between 1954–79, see the *Sixth Report of the National Police Commission*, Appendix 2, Government of India, March 1981, p. 60. On the disproportionality between the number of Hindus and Muslims killed between 1968–79, see Vibhuti Narain Rai, *Combating Communal Conflicts*, Allahabad: Manas Publications, 1998, p. 59. To take just one year, 1969, 558 Muslims were killed as opposed to sixty-six Hindus.

that there is pervasive and unmitigated discrimination of all Muslims. As a matter of fact, the life of religious minorities in India is comparatively better than the life of minorities in many other countries. This is not surprising because constitutionally, India is a secular state and aspires to the dissolution of inter-religious domination.[14] Parity between communities is something that is valued by the Indian constitution.[15] For example, as a distinct cultural and religious group, Muslims have a right to the survival and renewal of their own cultural resources. There are two distinct aspects of their right. The first has to do with the content of their culture, the second with the manner in which this content is generated and nourished. If Muslims have a right, then it is a right to be the guardians of the content of their culture, as well as the right to make decisions on how best this content is to be preserved.

In India, this cultural right can be divided, I believe, into four parts: first, the right to their language, or rather languages. The mother tongue of Muslims varies from region to region in India (Kashmiri, Malayali, Tamil Muslims) and this right, the right to the protection of their mother tongue, must be shared with people of others faiths. There is then the language of their religious instruction, Arabic, and finally, the language of their literati, Urdu, a unique hybrid of Farsi and local dialects of Hindi, spoken in north India, even by non-Muslims. Thus, Muslims also have a distinct right to the protection of Urdu and of the language of religious instruction. Second, they have a right to their cultural heritage, to ensuring that it is passed on from one generation to another. Though separate educational institutions are not necessary for this purpose, necessities of institutional design dictate that they have their own educational institutions. Third, the right to the protection of their places of worship. This should be taken care of in India by the fundamental right they have as individual citizens.

[14] For a detailed discussion on India's secular constitution, see Rajeev Bhargava, 'India's Secular Constitution', in Zoya Hasan, E. Sridharan, and R. Sudarshan (eds), *India's Living Constitution: Ideas, Practices, Controversies*, Delhi: Permanent Black, 2002, pp. 105–33. See also Rajeev Bhargava, 'Political Secularism', in J. Dryzek, B. Honnig, and A. Phillips (eds), *A Handbook of Political Theory*, Oxford: Oxford University Press, 2006, pp. 636–55.

[15] For an overview of India's constitutional vision, see Rajeev Bhargava, 'Democratic Vision of a New Republic: India, 1950', in Francine Frankel, Zoya Hasan, Rajeev Bhargava, and Balveer Arora (eds), *Transforming India: Social and Political Dynamics of Democracy*, New Delhi: Oxford University Press, 2000, pp. 26–59. Also, see Hasan et al. (eds), *India's Living Constitution*.

But, in view of destruction of the Babri Masjid,[16] this may be deemed a separate right. Finally, a right to their own personal laws, that is, laws pertaining to family, marriage, divorce, maintenance, inheritance, child custody, and adoption. Thus, by granting different forms of cultural rights, the constitution tries to ensure cultural justice to Muslims. This is also evident from a cursory glance of the list of public holidays in India. Of the seventeen holidays approved by the Government of India as national holidays, only three are non-religious: the Republic Day, the Independence Day, and Mahatma Gandhi's Birthday. Five relate to Hinduism, four to Islam, two to Christianity, and one each to Sikhism, Jainism, and Buddhism.

Other achievements of India's multi-cultural experiment are also worth noting. There have been three Muslim Presidents of India. The previous President of India, A.P.J. Abdul Kalam, is a Muslim from the southern state of Tamil Nadu. A Muslim rose to become the Chief of the Indian Air Force (I.H. Latif, 1978–81). Over the course of India's history, three Muslims have occupied the position of the Chief Justice of India: M. Hidayatullah, 1968–70; M. Hameedullah Beg, 1977–8; and A.H. Ahamadi, 1995–7. One of the major Indian industrial houses, Wipro, is headed by Azim Premji—a Muslim. Indians are crazy about their films and cricket. For what it is worth, the most popular film stars happen to be Muslims. The Indian cricket team has been twice led by a Muslim and the current Indian squad has several Muslims. Sania Mirza, the latest sensation on world tennis circuit, is an Indian Muslim and a role model for many young Indians. The market and the wider public do not always discriminate when it comes to their heroes and heroines. Yet, despite all this, the data on Indian Muslims makes a depressing reading.[17]

1. A majority of Muslims, nearly 71 per cent of the total Muslim population, live in rural areas and are mostly landless labourers, small and marginal farmers, artisans, craftsmen, and shopkeepers. The condition of Muslims in rural areas has deteriorated since the

---

[16] A mosque believed by militant Hindus to be the precise place where Lord Rama was born and also believed to have been constructed in the sixteenth century by order of the first Mughal emperor in India, Babar. Long under dispute, it was destroyed by Hindutva activists on 6 December 1992.

[17] See Hasan et al. (eds), India's Living Constitution, pp. 281–4 and Abusaleh Sharif and Azra Razzack, 'Communal Relations and Social Integration', India: Social Development Report, 2006. Also see C. Rammanohar Reddy, 'The Gap Widened During the 1990s', The Hindu, 13 September 2002.

1980s. In 1987–8, 40 per cent of rural Muslim households cultivated little or no land. By 1999–2000, the figure had risen to 51 per cent.

2. More than half of urban Muslim population lives below the poverty line. Indeed, there has been a rise in the number of poor among Muslims. In 1993–4, 30 per cent of Muslims were in the bottom 20 per cent in urban areas. This increased to 40 per cent in 1999–2000. Likewise, the proportion of the poor in rural areas increased over the same period from 20 per cent to 29 per cent.

3. Many Muslims continue to be poor and self-employed. Their share in regular wage work is lower than members of other religious groups.

4. The relative position of members of the two main religious groups in employment has changed over the years. In 1987–8, urban Muslims in the workforce experienced lower unemployment rates (4 per cent) than the Hindus (5.5 per cent). By 1999–2000, Muslims had a slightly higher rate of unemployment (5 per cent) as compared to Hindus (4.7 per cent).

5. The Muslim share in public and private employment is dismal.

6. In general, Muslim access to government sponsored welfare projects is limited.

7. In general, Muslims are less educated than the national average. For example, the illiteracy rate among urban Muslims was 11 per cent points higher than urban Hindus in 1999–2000.

8. Even in Kerala where their literacy level is comparatively higher, their share in public employment is much lower than others.

9. Muslim population is a little over 12 per cent of the total (over 120 million). However, their presence in the legislature is disproportionately low. Barring 1980 (9.2 per cent) and 1984 (8.3 per cent), it has hovered between 4.6 per cent and 6.2 per cent (see Tables 7.1–7.11).

I have assumed throughout that Muslims form an ascriptive group, a community rather than a voluntary association, more or less a permanent minority in India. This is a correct assumption and requires no defence. The brief historical narrative and the data provided earlier show that there has been discrimination towards Muslims in India. Some of this discrimination is intentional. Negative stereotypes of Muslims abound in at least urban India, not least because of the day-to-day effort of anti-Muslim cultural and political organizations. Although the socio-economic condition of groups such as Adivasis and Dalits is worse, there is no doubt that the socio-economic condition of Muslims is extremely bad and constitutes a denial of many of their basic rights

TABLE 7.1: Lok Sabha, 1952

Religion	No. of Legislatures	Percentage
Hinduism	433	86.9
Islam	25	5.0
Christianity	17	3.4
Jainism	3	0.6
Other	1	0.2
Sikhism	12	2.4
NA	7	1.4
Total	498	100 really 99.9

TABLE 7.2: Lok Sabha, 1957

Religion	No. of Legislatures	Percentage
Hinduism	433	86.9
Islam	23	4.6
Christianity	12	2.4
Zoroastrianism	3	0.6
Buddhism	1	0.2
Jainism	4	0.8
Sikhism	12	2.4
NA	10	2.0
Total	498	100 really 99.9

TABLE 7.3: Lok Sabha, 1962

Religion	No. of Legislatures	Percentage
Hinduism	451	88.6
Islam	26	5.1
Christianity	14	2.8
Zoroastrianism	1	0.2
Jainism	3	0.6
Other	1	0.2
Sikhism	12	2.4
NA	1	0.2
Total	509	100 really 100.1

TABLE 7.4: Lok Sabha, 1967

Religion	No. of Legislatures	Percentage
Hinduism	462	88.5
Islam	28	5.4
Christianity	15	2.9
Zoroastrianism	2	0.4
Buddhism	1	0.2
Jainism	4	0.8
Sikhism	10	1.9
Total	522	100 really 100.1

TABLE 7.5: Lok Sabha, 1971

Religion	No. of Legislatures	Percentage
Hinduism	465	89.3
Islam	28	5.4
Christianity	13	2.5
Zoroastrianism	1	0.2
Buddhism	1	0.2
Jainism	1	0.2
Sikhism	10	1.9
NA	2	0.4
Total	521	100 really 100.1

TABLE 7.6: Lok Sabha, 1977

Religion	No. of Legislatures	Percentage
Hinduism	473	87.3
Islam	32	5.9
Christianity	16	3.0
Zoroastrianism	1	0.2
Jainism	5	0.9
Other	1	0.2
Sikhism	7	1.3
NA	7	1.3
Total	542	100 really 100.1

TABLE 7.7: Lok Sabha, 1980

Religion	No. of Legislatures	Percentage
Hinduism	438	82.5
Islam	49	9.2
Christianity	19	3.6
Jainism	2	0.4
Other	1	0.2
Sikhism	10	1.9
NA	12	2.3
Total	531	100 really 100.1

TABLE 7.8: Lok Sabha, 1984

Religion	No. of Legislatures	Percentage
Hinduism	482	88.6
Islam	45	8.3
Christianity	12	2.2
Jainism	3	0.6
Sikhism	1	0.2
NA	1	0.2
Total	544	100 really 100.1

TABLE 7.9: Lok Sabha, 1989

Religion	No. of Legislatures	Percentage
Hinduism	477	89.8
Islam	33	6.2
Christianity	12	2.3
Zoroastrianism	1	0.2
Buddhism	1	0.2
Jainism	1	0.2
Sikhism	6	1.1
Total	531	100

TABLE 7.10: Lok Sabha, 1991

Religion	No. of Legislatures	Percentage
Hinduism	481	88.9
Islam	29	5.4
Christianity	19	3.5
Sikhism	12	2.2
Total	541	100

TABLE 7.11: Lok Sabha, 1996

Religion	No. of Legislatures	Percentage
Hinduism	492	89.3
Islam	27	4.9
Christianity	19	3.4
Jainism	1	0.2
Sikhism	12	2.2
Total	551	100

Source: (of Tables 7.1 to 7.11): Centre for the Study of Developing Societies (CSDS) Data Unit.

as citizens. They have a muted presence in the public sphere and their representation in legislatures is nowhere near what political justice dictates. Since there is an unambiguous connection between community identity and socio-economic and political inequality, it is entirely reasonable to conclude that Muslims constitute a marginalized group in India. They are not, of course, a historically marginalized group. They were not an oppressed group in colonial India. Indeed, in pre-colonial India, the most pre-eminent rulers and emperors all happened to be Muslims. Yet, there is a substantial number of Muslims who are either converts from the outcastes or from other backward castes and the character of their oppression did not alter after their conversion. In this sense, these particular segments among Muslims have been historically marginalized. I return to this point later in the next section.

DO MUSLIMS NEED SPECIAL
SELF-REPRESENTATION RIGHTS?

I have claimed that Muslims are a marginalized group and that they face sustained disadvantage because of structural properties of Indian society. Although they have the same legal and political rights that are available to the rest of the population, they are unable to exercise them fully. Whatever subsidiary benefits are gained by the exercise of these rights also remain unavailable to them. This should be a matter of grave concern. The state must take some remedial measures to ensure fairness to them. For example, it can initiate special welfare schemes meant exclusively for Muslims. Yet, an explicit demand for these measures and for group-specific social and economic rights more generally, does not appear to have a strong backing. A demand for Muslim affirmative action in the civil service and education did surface during the assembly by-elections in 1994 in five states of India. This demand also had some support from government led by the Congress.[18] However, nothing much came of it. More recently, in Andhra Pradesh, where more than 65 per cent Muslims live below poverty line, the newly ensconced Congress government introduced a programme allotting a 5 per cent reservation for Muslims in educational institutions. However, the High Court struck this decision down and the matter is currently pending in the Supreme Court.

Muslims are under-represented in political decision-making bodies, most notably in the Indian Parliament. However, the demand for political representation in the Parliament is even more muted. Such a demand was conspicuously missing when, in 1994, the question of instituting a programme favouring Muslim representation arose after nearly fifty years of silence on this issue.[19] To be sure, some fringe groups have expressed these demands.[20] For example, in a convention of Indian Muslims held in 1989, a group of Muslims protested against their under-representation and demanded the introduction of the system of proportional representation in elections at all levels. Likewise, the National Convention for the Empowerment of Muslims in India urged the government to take necessary steps to ensure a proportionate

[18] See Theodore P. Wright Jr, 'A New Demand for Muslim Reservation in India', *Asian Survey*, vol. 37, no. 9, September 1997, p. 853.

[19] Ibid.

[20] See, for example, Iqbal A. Ansari, 'Minority Representation'; available at http://www.india-seminar.com/2001/506 (last accessed 16 October 2006).

share of seats for Muslims in legislative bodies. But support for these has not widened.

At any rate, the rest of India gives little attention even to these fringe demands. Surprisingly, even secularists, who are generally sympathetic to the plight of the Muslims, openly refuse to support any community-specific rights for representation in legislative bodies. The most vociferous champions of the continuation of group representation for scheduled castes[21] and scheduled tribes[22] do not wish to extend this right to Muslims. Even the Indian Left did not support this measure. The Indian state does not even conceive launching an affirmative action programme to enhance the representation of Muslims in the legislatures.

Why is there so little support for community-specific affirmative action? Let me clarify that I shall not deal here with community-specific socio-economic affirmative action programmes such as reservations for Muslims in education and government employment. My concern in this essay is the political under-representation of Muslims in the central legislature. Such political representation is valuable not only in itself—it gives a legitimate voice to Muslims in the political arena, something with intrinsic expressive value—but also has instrumental value because it helps them to influence decisions that might overcome or decrease their marginalization and exclusion from socio-economic benefits. Thus, my question is: Why does such scant support exist for a fair political representation for Muslims? Some of the fears against special representative rights for Muslims can be traced to the bitter experience of separate electorates before the independence of India. Some explanation for this lack of support can therefore be gleaned by examining the history of this issue.

The Debate Over Separate Electorates

It is widely accepted that the Government of India Act of 1909 was a calculated masterstroke by imperial Britain to create divisions between

[21] Communities or castes at the bottom of the hierarchical caste system of India. Treated as outcastes or untouchables by members of the 'higher castes' and listed in a schedule prepared by Government of India. These castes are now granted special status by the Constitution of India. Fifteen per cent of seats in legislatures and government employment are reserved for them.

[22] Tribal communities who are listed in a schedule prepared by the Government of India and are accorded special status by the constitution. Seven-and-a-half per cent of seats in legislature and government jobs are reserved for them.

Hindus and Muslims and to defuse the Congress' demand for greater share in political decision making. The Act of 1909 was intended to pacify the growing discontent among the elites: it expanded the legislative councils at both the central and the provincial levels and enlarged their functions. It included nominated as well as elected members. However, it also introduced separate electorates for Muslims.[23] Separate electorates not only created a space for reinforcing religious identities but also homogenized and fixed them. A strong anti-colonial movement with a larger social base and a wider political appeal needed to be grounded in a more inclusive conception of the nation. A community organized along religion carried with it seeds of an incipient religious nationalism that would have dissipated the collective energy of a people in the making. The INC was never comfortable with the idea of separate electorates and repeatedly recommended their abolition. Instead, they demanded reservation of seats in the legislative bodies strictly in accordance with the proportion of the minorities in the overall population.

It is one thing to say that the Congress never accepted separate electorates and quite another to say that they had good reasons for it. To explore this issue, it is important to look into the debate over separate electorates in the constituent assembly, which is quite illuminating. Pocker Sahib Bahadur, an advocate of separate electorate, began his argument with the premise that human beings are bound to identify themselves with particular communities on an ascriptive basis and since such communities cannot be numerically equal, there are bound to be minorities in every land.[24] Since minorities cannot be 'erased out of existence', we need to come to terms with them, which in turn entails reconciling with the fact that total harmony between communities, the complete eradication of differences among them, is impossible. On the

---

[23] Separate electorates are best understood, at least in the Indian context, by contrasting them with joint electorates. In a system of joint electorates, the boundaries of a constituency do not coincide with the boundaries of a caste or religious community. A constituency may be reserved for members of a particular caste or community but the constituency itself is not defined along caste or community lines. Thus, a constituency reserved for Scheduled Castes will elect a Scheduled Caste Member of Parliament but the electorate which chooses him/her consists of members of every caste. In separate electorates, the constituencies are already defined by caste or religious community. Thus, not only do parties field Muslim candidates but votes are cast only by Muslims. Likewise, Hindu candidates are elected only by Hindus and so on.

[24] *Constituent Assembly Debates, Vol. 1*, 27 August 1947, Delhi: Lok Sabha Secretariat Publication, 1999, p. 211.

other hand, a minimization of differences between them is achievable, but only if minorities are satisfied with the overall political framework in which they live. A condition of such satisfaction, Bahadur argued, was that their views and grievances be given an effective voice in the deliberations of the legislature. Since all members of the minority community cannot bring their own voices in the deliberative assembly, attempts must be made to find and induct their authentic representatives, 'to lay down a procedure by which the best man who can represent that community and voice forth the feelings of that community is elected to the legislature.'[25]

Many of the premises of this argument were acceptable to opponents of separate electorates. For example, Govind Ballabh Pant accepted that in a free and democratic state, citizens would like to satisfy not only their material wants but also 'a spiritual sense of self-respect'. This self-respect, he assumed, was linked to their community-based identity. It was linked, significantly for him, also with their recognition as equals by members of other communities. More significantly, this equal recognition must be available within the political arena. Pant appeared to have understood the active dimension of citizenship. For him, citizens are hardly treated as equals in the public domain if, despite a formal right to vote, they are excluded from public deliberations by informal mechanisms. They then begin to have the lingering feeling that they are inadequately heard, that their view are not properly taken into deliberations, that they have no real say in public matters, including in those which vitally concern them. Such people then begin to have a 'shrill and discordant voice'. Pant argued that rather then be shrill and discordant, Muslim voice in the legislatures must be 'powerful'.[26]

Bahadur conceded that these premises were shared by some of the best Congressmen. Differences arose over the best procedure by which this could be effected and adequate representation for Muslims achieved. For the Congress, initially, the best procedure for this was a system of community-based reservations of a certain number of seats based on joint electorate. For Bahadur, this procedure was defective because it may elect a person favoured solely by the majority, one who fails to represent the real views and interests of Muslims. Bahadur insisted that it is extremely difficult for non-Muslims to realize the actual needs and requirements of the Muslim community. True interests of Muslims can be understood only by Muslims. However, even the fact of

[25] Ibid., p. 212.
[26] Ibid.

belonging to a community was not sufficient for proper representation. (This demand was compatible with reservations on the basis of joint electorates.) The elected person must be the right sort of man from the community and this, he argued, could be ensured only by separate electorates.[27] To elect the best man, only Muslims must choose their Muslim representative. For this requirement to be met, separate electorates were essential.

Though Pant accepted most of Bahadur's premises, he fiercely disagreed with his conclusion. To oppose separate electorates, he put forward a persuasive argument from democratic accountability. For Pant, a system of separate electorates entails that both majority and minority representatives are chosen separately by their respective communities. When that happens, representatives of the majority are not accountable to the minority community and, despite the formal presence of minority representatives, could well take decisions that went against the interests of the minority. If that happens, the chosen representatives of the minority are reduced to being mere advocates in the legislature without possessing a corresponding share in power in the decision-making process. The price of guaranteed representation in the legislature may be reduced representation in the cabinet and that, Pant argued, was heavy price indeed. Pant concluded that it was unjust for minorities to be segregated from the rest of the community, to be kept aloof in an air-tight compartment, 'where they would have to rely on others even for the air they breathed'.[28] To have a powerful, rather than a shrill and discordant voice, the Muslims must, he pleaded, reject separate electorates. In short, Pant agreed that if people are excluded from or discriminated against within the deliberative assembly solely on the ground that they belong to a particular religion, then the principle of equal citizenship and therefore, one of the core values of secularism is violated. But he argued that it is separate not joint electorates that force this exclusion and by implication breach the principles of secularism.

---

[27] The casteist overtones of Bahadur's demand could hardly go unnoticed. He was anxious that from hegemonic considerations, members of the majority may strategically vote for a lower caste Muslim candidate, 'some illiterate sweeper or scavenger', who may not be capable of understanding the real needs of the community and whose selection, therefore, could be detrimental to its long-term interests.

[28] *Constituent Assembly Debates, Vol. 5*, 27 August 1947, New Delhi: Lok Sabha Secretariat, 1999, pp. 222–4.

It is clear from this discussion that it was not community-based difference as such which was unacceptable to the best of the Congress-men. Nor, based on their initial acceptance of reservations for Muslims based on joint electorates, did they entirely reject what is frequently called, 'mirror representation', namely, the view that a legislature is representative only if it mirrors the ethnic, religious, or gender char-acteristics of the public. What the Congressmen rejected was the idea that this mirror representation should be generalized. For most of them, separate electorates embodied generalized mirror representation. Muslims could represent members of their own community but they need not, by law, have monopoly over such representation.[29] Separate electorates were rejected not because they fostered communal differ-ence as such or because they endangered a simple idea of national unity, but because they were believed to have exacerbated communal divi-sions and threatened coexistence.

The reader may recall my discussion in the first chapter where I drew attention to Liah Greenfeld's account of how the meaning (refer-ence) of the term 'nation' changed from a group of social elites to the entire population of a country and became synonymous with the word 'people'. Henceforth, every member of the population could partake of this superior, elite quality. This transformation presupposes a pro-found change in the imagination of societies, that is, from hierarchical communities to networks consisting of free and equal individuals.

This effected yet another change; in the collective self-understanding of the people, the nation exists prior to and independent of the political organization of society and therefore, possesses the power to give itself a constitution. This is linked to the idea of popular sovereignty as well as to political equality: this sovereignty is located within a people/nation whose constituent members are fundamentally equal to one another. As Greenfeld puts it, 'nationalism was the form in which democracy appeared in the world, contained in the idea of the nation as a butterfly in a cocoon.'[30] I had argued in that chapter that the unity emphasized

[29] Farzana Sheikh who claims that the Congress categorically assumed that the unit of representation simply had to be the individual is mistaken, for the Congress did not completely rule out community-based political representation. See Farzana Sheikh, 'Muslims and Political Representation in Colonial India: The Making of Pakistan', in Mushirul Hasan (ed.), *India's Partition: Process, Strategy and Mobilization*, New Delhi: Oxford University Press, 1993, pp. 81–101.

[30] Ibid., p. 10.

by several members of the constituent assembly and the tirade against sharp communal divisions had much to do with the need to create and sustain, what one assembly member called, 'the unadulterated identity of people, a democracy'.[31] This is of a piece with a point made by the political philosopher, Charles Taylor, that unlike other political systems, democratic states need cohesion, a common identity, a common personality, and a common agency.[32] Democracy, I concluded, is not just a procedural issue but also a matter of identity. It allows for differences but it cannot stomach divisions which are 'sharpened to a dangerous extent'. It was precisely for this reason that a suffrage grounded in religious classification was believed to be an outrageous suggestion and why, therefore, religion in India had to be separated from a democratic state. This is also why eventually no political rights were granted to religious communities. This, of course, is entirely a contextual issue. Rejection of political rights for Muslims was believed to be a necessity in India because religion-based divisions had become too dangerous here. The rejection of community-based political rights was entirely consistent with the acceptance of community-based socio-cultural rights. The rights granted under Article 30[33] were as necessary for a democratic state as the rejection of separate electorates under Article 325.[34]

[31] *Constituent Assembly Debates*, 27 August 1947, p. 219.

[32] See Charles Taylor, 'Modes of Secularism', in Rajeev Bhargava (ed.), *Secularism and Its Critics*, New Delhi: Oxford University Press, 1998, pp. 31–53.

[33] Right of minorities to establish and administer educational institutions. 1. All minorities, whether based on religion or language, shall have the right to establish and administer educational institutions of their choice. (1A) In making any law providing for the compulsory acquisition of any property of an educational institution established and administered by a minority, referred to in clause (1), the State shall ensure that the amount fixed by or determined under such law for the acquisition of such property is such as would not restrict or abrogate the right guaranteed under that clause. 2. The State shall not, in granting aid to educational institutions, discriminate against any educational institution on the ground that it is under the management of a minority, whether based on religion or language.

[34] Article 325 of the Indian constitution says, 'There shall be one general electoral roll for every territorial constituency for election to either House of Parliament or to the House or either House of the Legislature of a State and no person shall be ineligible for inclusion in any such roll or claim to be included in any special electoral roll for any such constituency on grounds only of religion, race, caste, sex, or any of them.'

Allow me to sum up the salient points of this debate. First, there are ascriptive communities in any society and some of these have the status of more or less permanent minorities. Second, the interests of these minorities must be safeguarded. Third, these interests must be articulated in a political forum and therefore, they must have an effective voice in the deliberations of the legislature. Fourth, in a representative democracy, this can be done by representatives of the community. Thus, some form of descriptive representation, one designed to constitute an assembly that mirrors the relevant ascriptive features of the community in question, is required for meaningful political inclusion to overcome the possible tyranny of the majority and the consequent alienation and marginalization of minority communities. Inclusion in the political process is important for the legitimacy of decisions arrived through the process. Even if a decision goes against the interests of the minority, the chances are that they would be gracefully accepted if the process through which they were made had included them in a meaningful way and given them an effective voice.

The Congress rejected generalized descriptive representation, not restricted descriptive representation. There were arguments against the specific mechanism for descriptive representation. First, they objected to the idea that Muslims alone can represent members of their community. Second, they were worried about democratic accountability. Third, that descriptive representation does not guarantee substantive representation. In other words, it is entirely possible that a Muslim represents Muslims not just inadequately but badly. Fourth, they were worried that they would sharpen communal difference to a dangerous extent and prevent the development of a healthy national life. Eventually, in the aftermath of the violence during the partition of India, this fourth reason was decisive and became the basis for the rejection not only of separate electorates but for any kind of political self-representation of Muslims.

Objections to Group-based Political Representation in India Today

Do these arguments still hold in India, today? Separate electorates were rejected because of the fear of balkanization. Is this fear still strong in India? More importantly, is it reasonable to have this fear? Before coming to this issue, I address seven possible arguments against group-representation for Muslims that still might be doing the rounds in India. I say this with some uncertainty because there is virtual silence over this issue in the public sphere. The benefits of group representation that would accrue to Muslims and the costs they continue to bear for remaining under-represented are hardly ever discussed. The arguments presented here are reconstructed then from fragments of statements that are expressed largely privately and only occasionally, in public.

The first is the standard liberal–individualist argument against group representation more generally. This argument comes in two versions. The first version is motivated by a genuine concern that any community-specific representation undermines the freedom and autonomy of individual citizens. The second is motivated by purely instrumental reasons and is deployed, ironically, by right-wing, communal Hindu forces which claim that any such right is a privilege granted to one group and therefore, undermines inter-group equality and anyway violates the basis of modern citizenship grounded as it is in individual subjectivity.

A second objection is that community-specific political represen-tation is valid in the case of historically oppressed groups, that is, groups which have faced systematic discrimination inter-generationally, over a long period of time. It is not valid in the case of marginalized groups. Proponents of this argument accept that some remedial measures should be undertaken to rectify this injustice but then go on to argue that group representation is not the appropriate mechanism to do so. This objection runs into a third one offered by secularists. For most Indian secularists, any group representation is permissible as long as religion is not the principal criterion of individuating groups. Any segmentation or classification of society along religious lines, it is claimed, contravenes the secular fabric of society. Political recognition to religion-based communities grossly violates the principles of political secularism. Since 'Muslim' falls into a religious category, any political right given to Muslims qua Muslims contravenes secularism and is therefore unacceptable. Yet a fourth objection is that the demand for community-specific political representation is pressed only by a fringe group with a nostalgia for the pre-partition political system of India. It is not preferred by a majority of Muslims who seek an alliance, if not merger, with the subaltern classes. A good system of political representation must respect the preferences of its members. Therefore, community-specific political representation is redundant for Muslims in post-independent India.

A fifth objection claims that group representation for minority communities makes the majority unaccountable to the minorities. This

202 India's Secular Democracy

argument was made in the constituent assembly most forcefully by Govind Ballabh Pant,[35] and continues to inhabit the political landscape of India even today. Some opponents of group representation believe that all arguments which were valid and sound against separate electorates hold equally well for any kind of group representation. Thus, they argue that once Muslims begin to represent themselves, non-Muslims will feel that they are no longer accountable to the Muslims. They may even take decisions that adversely affect Muslims. Thus, a measure that looks good on paper may lead to another form of majoritarianism and to the ghettoization of the minorities. Far from including Muslims in the political process, Muslims self-representation might lead to their exclusion.

The sixth argument is grounded in the value of national unity. Political recognition to religious communities is reminiscent of the demand for separate electorates which, so the argument goes, was a major contributory factor to the partition of India. Similar demands today will only bolster fissiparous forces and lead not only to the polarization of Indian society but also possibly to its balkanization.

Finally, a seventh related argument focuses less on national unity and more on the adverse impact of religion-based political representation. On this view, such a measure is self-defeating for Muslims. It is self-defeating because it is bound to generate a 'communal backlash' and revive a majority–minority syndrome. Such a syndrome, in the present context in which Muslims lack the capacity to fight back, is bound to lead to a vicious majoritarianism that would be perceived to be legitimate by a majority of Hindus. Any demand for group representation of Muslims, no matter how correct in principle, is imprudent and should be abandoned.

Responses to Objections

Given the paucity of space, I will not deal with every argument in detail. For example, I do not discuss the second version of the liberal–individualist argument. The right-wing Hindu objection instrumentally deploys the liberal argument and is therefore insincere. I discuss in this article arguments on the assumption that they are made sincerely. Any argument that is widely recognized as insincere requires an explanation, not a systematic, rational rebuttal. The objection that community-

---

[35] See the section 'The Debate over Separate Electorates', given earlier in this chapter.

specific political representation is inappropriate for Muslims because they do not constitute a historically oppressed group has already been answered earlier in the chapter[36] and need not be addressed any further. This leaves me to respond to six objections: (i) the liberal–individualist objection; (ii) the secularist objection; (iii) the objection that we need to respect the current wishes of the Muslim community; (iv) the democratic accountability objection; (v) the argument for national unity; and (vi) the pragmatic objection.

The Liberal–individualist Objection

I turn to the first objection that group representation undermines individual freedom and autonomy. It must be conceded straightaway that any theory of group representation that permits the state to ascribe political beliefs and preferences to individuals solely on the ground of their group membership and creates a system in which individuals are not allowed to express their own distinctive beliefs and preferences is deeply troublesome.[37] If a system is such that the beliefs and preferences of individuals are inferred or read off directly from their membership in groups, then such a system shows utter disregard for individual freedom and autonomy and, from a liberal point of view, is unacceptable. Thus, it is important that groups are not granted a moral status that easily overrides the moral status of individuals. Yet, sometimes there are hidden atomistic assumptions underlying the moral claims of individuals that are as troublesome as claims made on behalf of groups. All individuals are necessarily situated within social contexts, which have a deep impact on the formation of their beliefs and preferences. They also shape their sense of self-respect and self-esteem. Such social contexts include not only diffused and thin network of social relationships that we associate with modern urban life but also modern ascriptive communities. Such groups can either relate to one another as equals or be in a relation of domination and subordination. If the relationship is one of domination, then a member of the subordinate group is likely to have a diminished sense of self-respect and a low self-esteem. Her beliefs and preferences will also be affected by this experience of domination. A person who is persistently stereotyped because of his membership in a

[36] See the section 'Muslims: A Marginalized Group in India', given earlier in this chapter.

[37] Melissa S. Williams, *Voice, Trust, and Memory*, Princeton, NJ: Princeton University Press, 1998, p. 81.

group is bound to be affected adversely.[38] In short, inter-group equality is an important condition for individual freedom and autonomy. Members of a subordinate group are less likely to be free and autonomous. It follows that neither groups nor relations between them can be ignored in any discussion of individual freedom and equality that lie at the core of liberal theories. It also follows that fair representation is not just a matter of the principle of one person one vote or the equal opportunity principle in the political sphere but involves additional mechanisms to ensure fair representation of groups in the deliberative process.[39]

The institutional implication of these points is this: fair representation can be achieved by electoral mechanisms that attend to the demands of both group representation and individual autonomy. Neither a mechanism that ensures only group representation nor one that ignores it is likely to generate structures of fair representation.

The Secularist Objection

The secularist objection goes something like this: since secularism means the separation of religion and politics and further, since separation means exclusion, any inclusion of religion in the democratic process is violative of secularism. What does it mean to include or exclude religion from politics? In western political theory, it is frequently taken to mean that neither actual decision making nor its justification in the public domain should be grounded in religious rationales. In non-western societies, however, this issue is usually framed differently. The principal question to be addressed here is: is a reference to community-based religious identity permissible or not in the electoral processes? Should religious groups be included or excluded from the democratic and electoral processes? In short, inclusion of religion within the democratic or electoral process also means giving or refusing political recognition to religious communities. The exclusion of religion means refusing to grant political rights to religious communities. A commitment to secularism then entails that neither self-government rights nor special representation rights are to be granted to religious communities.

[38] Hence, in India, there is an equal concern for intra-group and inter-group equality, against inter-religious domination as much as intra-religious domination. On these points, see Bhargava, 'Democratic Vision of a New Republic', in Frankel *et al.* (eds), *Transforming India*, p. 38 and his, 'The Distinctiveness of Indian Secularism', in T.N. Srinivasan (ed.), *The Future of Secularism*, Oxford: Oxford University Press, 2000, pp. 20–53.

[39] On this see, Williams, *Voice, Trust, and Memory*, pp. 75–82.

This is consistent with the standard liberal answer to the same question. In the standard liberal view, religious identity is irrelevant to the issue of fair representation. The fair representation of religious communities does not depend, in this view, on their legislative presence but is rather bestowed by the more general principle of one person one vote and by the satisfaction of the equal opportunity principle. As long as all citizens have an equal opportunity to influence the voting process, the outcome of the process is fair, no matter what it is. For example, if they have equal opportunity to coalesce with others, to express their interest in conjunction with other citizens through interest groups, pressure groups, or political parties, then they have an equal chance to influence voting in the legislative process too.[40] In other words, fair representation is defined through an individualist understanding of procedural fairness. Legislative decisions are fair if every citizen has had an equal opportunity to mobilize politically around interests she considers most important to her. Fair representation does not dictate a 'threshold level' of group presence in legislative bodies.[41] If groups demand guaranteed proportional representation of their members in legislative bodies, then they are asking for special entitlements, that is, privileges that are not granted to other citizens. But, what if groups are absent from legislative bodies? What if their interests remain uncrystallized? What if they do not enter the political arena? If that happens, political effort must be enhanced and mobilization increased. The standard secular view that refuses special representation rights to religious communities is entirely consistent with this liberal proceduralism.

Now, I wish to argue that secularism and liberal proceduralism need not be strongly connected. More importantly, conceptions of secularism exist which are delinked from liberal individualism. To the question, should religion be included or excluded from the democratic process and should special representation rights be given or not to religious communities, secularism can give an answer other than a bland no. So, what is the secularists' alternative answer to this question? And, on what conception of secularism is it based? Elsewhere, I have argued that there is no a priori, antecedently determined general principle that excludes religion from state/politics and that is dictated

[40] Ibid., p. 10.
[41] On this point, see Anne Phillips, 'Dealing with Difference: A Politics of Ideas or a Politics of Presence?', *Constellations*, vol. 1, no. 1, 1994, pp. 74–91 and Will Kymlicka, *Multicultural Citizenship*, Oxford: Oxford University Press, 1995, p. 147.

by secularism. The separation of religion from politics may mean not exclusion but principled distance.[42] Crudely put, principled distance means that religion may be included or excluded depending on whether this inclusion or exclusion promotes or undermines the values and principles that are integral to secularism. These values and principles comprise peace and toleration between communities, and liberty and equality construed both individualistically and non-individualistically. For example, if by granting political rights to religious communities, the value of civic friendship is enhanced and alienation among citizens is diminished, then such rights must be granted. On the other hand, if by granting these rights, we increase alienation and adversely affect civic friendship, then such rights must be refused. Likewise, if by granting these rights, the voice and participation of citizens is improved in the deliberative process, then such rights must be granted. If on the other hand, giving such rights diminishes the prospects of their participation or the participation of others in the decision-making process, then such rights must not be granted.

On this view of secularism, a failure to grant political rights to groups, when such rights would enhance the participation of citizens, reproduces the political under-presentation of these religious communities. A secularism based on principled distance may be able to check this under-representation. Mainstream secularism that insists on the exclusion of religion, that refuses to grant rights to religious groups, does the opposite. In other words, the right to self-representation to Muslims violates only one version of secularism. The other version, which is enshrined in the Indian constitution, may, in certain contexts, require that religious communities be given self-representation rights.

The Objection that Muslims Prefer Not to Have Self-Representation Rights

In his recent book, *Who Wants Democracy*, Javeed Alam claimed that almost on every dimension of democracy, the proportion of Muslims responding positively is greater than the overall national average.[43] Democracy itself is affirmed overwhelmingly by Indian Muslims. In a recent survey of the CSDS, 72 per cent of Muslims agreed that

[42] On the idea of principled distance, see Chapter 3 of this volume. Also see Rajeev Bhargava, 'What is Secularism for?', in Rajeev Bhargava (ed.), *Secularism and Its Critics*, p. 515 and Bhargava, 'India's Secular Constitution', in Hasan *et al.* (eds), pp. 115–17.

[43] Javeed Alam, *Who Wants Democracy*, New Delhi: Orient Longman, 2004, pp. 61–74.

democracy is a better system of government than any other. More Muslims than one would expect believe in the efficacy of their votes. It is about 1½ per cent above the national average.

These are amazing statistics. For it is widely accepted and confirmed by the data presented in the tables that poverty among Muslims is high, their share in public jobs is low, there is more unemployment among them, they have high propensity in urban areas to be in the disorganized sector and therefore, to be criminalized, they face persistent discrimination, and have been frequent victims of communal riots and massacres. One would expect such a group to be deeply alienated from the political order, including from the democratic process. How come they still manage to have public confidence in the process? Alam has a general argument about why democracy in India enjoys legitimacy. He argues that unlike western societies, where capitalism played an important role in dismantling the feudal order and democratic institutions were installed much later in response to the demands from the vulnerable sections to negate the adverse impact of capitalism, democracy, in India, by empowering people with the right to vote, by giving them equal citizenship, has helped to break the shackles of a semi-feudal social order. In particular, it helped destroy a status-ridden, hierarchically downgrading caste system which possessed self-validating authority and which worked with the help of mechanisms that enforced conformity. Democracy has loosened these inherited social structures. As I have mentioned, it did so by giving ordinary people the identity of an equal citizen and with it, a new status, dignity, and self-respect. Moreover, it has opened up spaces for them to struggle for relief, material well-being, and dignity. Thus, democracy has also provided an arena in which vulnerable sections of society can fight for full citizenship rights.

Alam argues that this insight about the positive impact and appraisal of democracy on and by vulnerable sections has not escaped or bypassed Muslims. As they begin to identify with the rest of the vulnerable population, Muslims too feel that they have a stake in the process of democracy, that their fight for jobs, relief, dignity, and material well-being is not so very distinct from the more general struggle of other vulnerable sections. How has this happened? Was it always the case? Alam claims that this is increasingly becoming so. It has happened, first, because of a chasm that now exists between Muslim elites and all other Muslims. This has made it impossible for a meagre Muslim elite to affect the larger Muslim populace to follow their lead in politics. Ordinary Muslims no longer vote as their elites wish them to. In the Nehruvian period, the Congress took the Muslim vote for granted because the Muslim elites were loyal to Nehru. This is no longer the case, in part because of the general disillusionment with the more manipulative and opportunistic policies of the Congress towards Muslims but also because the abovementioned chasm means that Muslims no longer vote en bloc in favour of any one party. Even when Muslim elites vote Congress, ordinary Muslims might not. A second reason is that although the persistent discrimination faced by Muslims virtually everywhere in India has given them a sense of unification, in post-independent India this does not translate into their identification as a national or sub-national group. While they feel that they are vulnerable community, this sense of vulnerability is something they feel, they share with other vulnerable communities such as the Scheduled Castes, the other Backward Castes, and women. This, along with the fact that they lack both an exclusivist ideology and organizational unity, means that there is a much better chance that they would act as secularized vulnerable minority rather than as a religious community that is defined negatively by its relationship to the majority community.

This is a promising thesis. However, it underplays the deeper alienation felt by Muslims and the greater sense of separateness that they have not just because of the legacy of the partition of India but by virtue of the persistent threat they feel from vicious, Hindu majoritarian forces. Alam expresses one strand among Muslims or rather the aspiration of some secular-minded Muslims concerning this strand among the larger Muslim populace. However, I doubt if this gives us an accurate picture of what is really happening on ground. I am not denying that they cannot align with other vulnerable communities or that they feel no solidarity with them, but it is hard not to accept that most of them believe that they are specially underprivileged or targeted. This vulnerability is different from the vulnerabilities felt by other weaker groups in Indian society. Moreover, for Alam, the Muslims share the same sense of vulnerability as the Scheduled Castes (SC) and Scheduled Tribes (ST). This may be so, but two other conclusions follow from this claim than the one derived by Alam. First, that neither Muslims nor SCs/STs should be given community-specific political rights. Second, that Muslims must also be granted the same rights as SCs/STs.

The Democratic Objection

Against the argument that group representation for minority communities makes the majority unaccountable to the minorities, I reply: it is true that some forms of political representation of groups create this problem. If political representation of groups is grounded entirely on the idea of mirror representation, or if it has the effect of generating mirror representation, then this objection is sound. However, if one has a political mechanism which grants restricted mirror representation or if it reflects a strategy that mixes mirror representation with non-descriptive representation, then this problem of non-accountability is unlikely to be generated. Such a mixed strategy would include some representation of a group by members of the same group but would allow for the possibility that the same group can also be represented by persons who do not share the same religious or ethnic characteristics. It also allows for shared experience, possibly across cultures and ethnicities, to be the basis of adequate representation. Mechanisms such as this do not face the problem of non-accountability.

The Argument from National Unity

Provided certain conditions are adequately met, the argument for national unity is not convincing. Conversely, if these conditions do not hold, the argument is persuasive. It is not persuasive if national unity is founded on the idea of homogenization and assimilation. A nation does not become one if all differences are suppressed or if they are erased by the imposition of the culture of the majority. Unity is more likely to be maintained if some significant differences are freely expressed, socially recognized, and publicly affirmed so that people who come from different cultural or religious backgrounds feel that despite differences they are respected in the polity.

However, the expression of difference is not always peaceful and harmonious. Frequently, it leads to conflict, sometimes to violent conflicts. When such conflicts are persistent, pervasive, and run deep, then no society is likely to tolerate them and some suppression of these differences might be contextually appropriate—as was the case in the aftermath of the partition of India. In such times, the claim that the political recognition of difference is dangerous and detrimental to the unity of the nation cannot easily be brushed aside.

The Pragmatic Objection of the Likelihood of a Majoritarian Backlash

A final argument comes from those who claim that such a demand is self-defeating for Muslims because it is likely to lead to a crushing majoritarianism. Now, there is nothing inevitable about this. The political self-representation of groups does not lead necessarily to a backlash from the majority. True though this may be, this is a sensitive matter which can be understood only with better appreciation of India's socio-historical context. Thus, the pertinent question here is: given the current socio-historical context of India, will such a demand by Muslims lead to a communal backlash? In answering this question, a number of points need to be kept in mind. First, although in the decade following the violence during India's partition, the official policy of forgive and forget appeared successful, in more recent times, this policy does not appear to have worked. The partition of the country is still living in the memory of at least some people in north India and bitterness and rancor hasn't simply disappeared. It is true, of course, that ordinary Muslims in India had virtually nothing to do with the partition of the country. The creation of Pakistan was a product of elitist imagination. Yet, ordinary Hindus, prone to stereotyping, make no such distinction between ordinary Muslims and Muslim elites. For them, the partition was a product of a generalized Muslim self-assertion. Second, even if this memory fades, as it frequently does, there are two factors that tend to keep it alive. One is the unresolved problem of Kashmir and second, the continuing tension between India and Pakistan. Even these two issues are not sufficient to recreate the bitter memory of partition and its violence. For this to happen, there must be active political agents in society whose primary agenda is to keep the pot boiling. Crucial therefore to the generation of majority backlash is the active presence in the political arena of political agents and political parties whose sole objective, indeed the very raison d'etre of their existence, is to grab power on the basis of the alleged historic division between Hindus and Muslims. Majoritarian communal backlash is a very real possibility in India because of the presence of the right-wing, ultra-nationalist, Hindu political parties. Unless such political forces are weakened, the prospect of a communal backlash can never be ruled out. If so, it is imprudent to introduce political self-representation for Muslims in India.

I have argued that though the political self-representation of Muslims does not necessarily violate liberal, democratic, or secular principles, it is not prudent to have it in the present context in India. The political self-representation of Muslims is desirable because it ensures maximum political inclusion and a fairer system of representation, yet, it is not feasible in India today.

A PROPOSAL FOR THE FUTURE

If political theory remained a prisoner of the current context, was exclusively policy-oriented, or worse, was a mere tool in the service of the state, then this conclusion would be the end of the matter. However, political theory works for the long run. It must embody a vision of the future. It should probably not recommend anything that goes against the grain of a plausible moral psychology of the society in question nor, if there are morally objectionable features in a society, should it leave things entirely as they are, particularly when social situations are replete with injustice.

I, therefore, indulge in a thought experiment and imagine that the Kashmir problem is solved, tensions between India and Pakistan are virtually non-existent, the bitter memory of partition has almost disappeared (this has possibly happened anyway), and the ultra-nationalist Hindu party is considerably weakened or has transformed beyond recognition into just another right-wing party within a broadly liberal democratic framework. In short, I envisage a situation in which conditions are ripe for the introduction of special representation rights for Muslims. The only crucial and pertinent question then is what precise form this must take.

In India, for reasons already outlined earlier, separate electorates do not enjoy popular legitimacy. The most familiar strategy for enhancing political representation of any group is to reserve seats in the Parliament. Such reserved seats, based on joint electorates, are provided for the former 'untouchables' (SC) and for the indigenous people (ST). Should there be similar reservation for Muslims? It is important to keep in mind that reservations have several problems (and even then provisions for such reservation for SC's and ST's exist in India despite these problems).[44] First, they essentialize. They presuppose the worst understanding of mirror representation, namely, that only people who are identical in significant respects can represent one another and that only people with the same ascriptive features can understand and share each other's interests. If so, only Muslims must represent their community. Second, they ignore the possible fluidity in a person's identity, entirely

---

[44] See also the discussion of this issue in Jane Mansbridge, 'Should Blacks Represent Blacks and Women Represent Women? A Contingent "Yes"', *Journal of Politics*, vol. 61, no. 3, August 1999, pp. 652–3 and Williams, *Voice, Trust, and Memory*, p. 12.

disregarding the possibility that individuals may attach little significance to their ethnic features or may, in important ways, change their culture or their religion. Third, reservations employ the power of the law to impose a particular group identity on individuals. This too undermines individual freedom and autonomy. Fourth, in societies where past differences have turned into bitter conflicts, a policy of reservation which freezes differences has a propensity to encourage the growth of further cleavages and to permanently entrench inter-community conflict. This would be extremely damaging in India where Hindu–Muslim relations in the past have been marred by bitterness and rancour. What holds true for reservations is also true for gerrymandering, that is, community-conscious districting. Gerrymandering also generates statis and essentializes identities, both damaging for inter-communal relations. At any rate, Muslims in India are mostly dispersed so that any attempt at gerrymandering is unlikely to generate Muslim majority constituencies. Finally, they do not prevent a situation where a Muslim representative has been elected for the wrong reason, not because he best represents the interests of the community but because he serves the interests of powerful sections within his own party.

What then is the most appropriate mechanism for Muslim self-representation in the legislatures? Recall that any mechanism must remain faithful to the following four values: (i) it must fulfil the legitimate political demands of groups to have fair representation, to have a powerful voice in the deliberative process; (ii) as much as possible, it should not violate individual autonomy; (iii) part of what we mean by respecting individual autonomy is that Muslims retain their choice to be represented by non-Muslims; (iv) although there is a presumption that Muslims share the same life conditions and life prospects and therefore, the same interests, this cannot be an immutable assumption. There must therefore be some space for the idea that shared experience and participation in the same practices gives a practical knowledge to people of each others' interests, regardless of their ascriptive characteristics. If all these conditions are to be met, the following recommendation may be most appropriate in the Indian context:[45]

---

[45] On a discussion of institutions of fair representation, I have relied on Williams, *Voice, Trust, and Memory*, chapter 7; Anne Phillips, *The Politics of Presence*, Oxford: Oxford University Press, 1995, pp. 140–60; and Mansbridge, 'Should Blacks Represent Blacks and Women Represent Women?', pp. 628–57.

1. multi-member constituencies;[46]
2. proportional representation (PR) in the form of preference voting;[47]
3. intra-party quotas in proportion to population; and
4. the identification by the election commission of the constituencies where intra-party quotas are to be allotted.

My reason for the abovementioned recommendation is to balance the value of fair representation of Muslims with individual autonomy and to prevent the possibility of freezing Muslim identity and ghettoizing Muslims. My view is that the proportion of Muslims in the legislature should reflect their proportion in the population but only if Muslims choose to do so. It would be obviously unfair to guarantee disproportionate representation of Muslims in the legislature. No procedure should be put in place that enables Muslims to necessarily have more than say 12 per cent of seats in the legislature. Equally, it would be fair, if despite the opportunity of using procedures of fair group representation, Muslims qua Muslims remain under-represented because they choose this outcome. What is grossly unfair is their under-representation by virtue of the circumstances created in the absence of procedures of fair group representation.

With the assistance of intra-party quotas proportional to the population, we ensure that parties field at least some candidates from among Muslims. Intra-party quotas guarantee that Muslims have at least the

---

[46] What is a multi-member constituency? To understand it, we might contrast it with a single-member constituency. In single-member constituencies, each constituency is represented in the legislative body by one elected representative. It follows that each party fields only one candidate in any one constituency. In multi-member constituencies, several members may be elected from a single constituency and therefore, every political party may field a number of candidates within the same constituency.

[47] A system of PR tries to deliver a close correspondence between the percentage of votes obtained in elections by groups of candidates and the percentage of seats secured by them, say, in the Parliament. Through PR, a political body seeks to secure representation for citizens roughly proportionate to their share of the voting population. Moreover, PR allows individuals to form self-defined constituencies rather than be accidentally bound to specific territories. Thus, in the PR system, one selects not only one's representative but also other citizens with whom one wishes to form a representable constituency. Preference voting is one particular version of PR. It is also known as single transferable vote. In preferential voting, though only one vote is allotted to each citizen, he or she is allowed to have a preference order of candidates. See Williams, *Voice, Trust, and Memory*, p. 215.

opportunity to select someone from their own community, one that they might use or forgo. But, what if parties fill this quota by fielding Muslims in those constituencies where there is every likelihood of their losing? This possibility is prevented by multi-member constituency (1) and the identification by the election commission of constituency for intra-party quotas (4). (4) is necessary to ensure that parties do not field Muslim candidates where they are bound to lose. An impartial body such as the election commission must determine those constituencies where parties are required to field Muslim candidates. The provision of (1), that is, multi-member constituencies encourages every party to field at least one Muslim candidate, even in constituencies where there is every likelihood of winning. Multi-member constituencies eliminate any temptation that parties might have not to field Muslim candidates in non-Muslim majority constituencies out of the fear that they would not be elected. In multi-member constituencies, the majoritarian bias, if any, of a political party would be easily caught out.[48] Multi-member constituencies create an incentive for parties to run Muslim candidates. Through preference voting (2), the system ensures that Muslims can choose between a Muslim or a non-Muslim candidate. So, this proposal rejects the idea that Muslims must select a fixed number of legislators from their own community, strictly in accordance with their proportion in the population. It allows for the possibility that Muslims choose non-Muslims as their preferred candidate. In short, with the assistance of (1) and (3), intra-party quotas in proportion to population, we try to ensure fair group representation. We do this by giving adequate opportunity to Muslims to choose Muslim candidates. This is different from reservations or affirmative action programmes that guarantee proportional Muslim representation. Furthermore, (2) and (3) together give individual Muslims the choice to select a non-Muslim candidate or to choose from among several Muslim candidates. (4) prevents the possibility of system being abused by parties who are 'hell bent' on ignoring the interests of minorities. All four together helps us combine values of fair group representation and individual autonomy.

It has been argued that intra-party quotas do not ensure proper accountability of the candidates to their own constituencies. Once elected, Muslim candidates may owe their primary allegiance to the parties that provided them this opportunity, and thus may fulfil the

[48] Ibid., p. 208.

interests of their own community only if these interests coincide with the larger agenda of the party.[49] There is some validity to this objection and in defence of the recommended strategy, I suggest three points. First, this assessment assumes a parliamentary system. Second, it is a part of a package which includes preferential voting and multi-member constituency. Finally, the principal reason underlying it is to give an opportunity to Muslims to select someone of their own community, one that they might use or even forgo. In short, the value guiding intra-party quotas is individual autonomy and prevention of the hardening of community identities. It is an attempt to reconcile individual autonomy with community identity and, at the same time, to prevent the communalization of identities. Intra-party quotas are consistent with the critique of a generalized mirror representation, that is, the view that the legislative assembly must accurately mirror the voting population and the assumption that a community is a homogenous entity with all its members necessarily possessing identical socio-economic, political, and cultural interests. If Muslims have a reasonable chance of choosing a non-Muslim candidate, then even Muslim candidates become more accountable. They cannot take members of their own community for granted.

A further objection might be raised against (4) on the ground that it unduly restricts the autonomy of parties to select candidates for the constituencies of their choice. No doubt this is true, but (4) only ensures a more effective exercise of (3) which is antecedently accepted as necessary to ensure fair representation. If (3) is to be properly realized, (4) is also required. Without (4), (3) is toothless and since (3) exists to facilitate fairer representation, representation remains unfair without (4). It might still be objected that even (3) together with (4) inhibits political parties from pursuing the most effective strategy of winning. But, this morally legitimate curtailment of the freedom of the party is found in the Indian constitution. For example, the constitution forbids political parties to seek vote on ground of religion alone. If a candidate wins by pursuing this strategy, he can be lawfully unseated. This happened in India in the case of the election of R.K. Prabhoo, an independent candidate supported by the extreme Hindu right-wing party, Shiv Sena, which was declared void by the Bombay High Court on the ground that he and his agent, Bal Thackeray, had appealed for votes on the basis of the returned candidate's religion and also that

[49] Ibid., p. 212.

Thackeray's election speeches promoted feelings of enmity and hatred among citizens of India. Thus, some moral limits already exist on the kind of means adopted by party candidates in their pursuit of winning an election. The identification by the election commission of the constituencies where intra-party quotas are to be allotted—our much discussed (4)—is not a novel suggestion but part of a set of remedies to ensure the fair political representation of Muslims.

8

Inclusion and Exclusion in India, Pakistan, and Bangladesh

*The Role of Religion**

Three values guide this chapter as, indeed, they must inspire the very idea of human development: peace, freedom, and equality. These values are also presupposed by the idea of an inclusive society. Surely, part of what is meant by the term 'inclusive society' in the contemporary context is that it be a community of free and equal persons. In our discussions, it is not inclusion per se that is an issue but voluntary inclusion on fair and equal terms. Indeed, we might even say that inclusion here is a term of art of which freedom and equality are constitutive features and peace its necessary precondition. Thus, contemporary emancipatory movements do not aim to include people only in order to rank them in political, social, or cultural hierarchy. Nor is their objective to bring people into an oppressive order. They are propelled by the belief that freedom and equality for all can only be enhanced by inclusion.

Inclusion on fair and equal terms can be approached in two different ways, however. The narrow approach conceives equality in purely distributional terms and takes material resources as the unit of distributive

* This is a version of the background paper prepared for the UNDP Report on Cultural Liberty and was meant to be presented at a conference organized by UNDP in Istanbul, 3–5 November 2003. It was subsequently published as 'Inclusion and Exclusion in India, Pakistan, and Bangladesh: The Role of Religion', *Indian Journal of Human Development*, Inaugural issue, vol. I, no. 1, January 2007, pp. 67–98.

equality. Freedom is conceived here as the absence of constraints on equal access to these resources or as the ability of individuals to use these resources to achieve their very own preferred projects. Without denying this, the broader, more sophisticated approach avoids the goods-fetishism which mars the narrow view. For the sophisticated approach, moral equality, the treatment of people as equals is an important human concern and is not reducible to economic equality. Each of us wishes to be equally respected for the ability to conceive or freely endorse meaningful projects and to live a life that we have reason to value.[1] People may possess identical material resources and yet be treated as unequal because of social stigma or due to the denigration of the world view that informs their way of life and frames their identity. Our self-respect, self-worth, and self-esteem is bound up with more than the sum total of goods in our possession or with what we are able to do with them. It is also linked to the recognition of the cultural and ethical framework(s) that help us orient to the world and enable us to gain self-understanding.

These frameworks may be religious or non-religious, thinly or thickly communitarian, with or without universalist aspirations, but they all have a constitutive link with culture and ethics. An important assumption of this book is that a cultural/ethical framework plays an indispensable and extremely significant role in the lives of human beings. Its second assumption is that no single framework gives overall meaning to the life of all human beings. If it is neither possible nor desirable to eliminate cultural and ethical pluralism, then, on the sophisticated view, there is an urgent need to articulate notions of freedom and equality that take into account or are compatible with a plurality of cultural identities and ethical orientations.

This chapter consists of two sections. The first, theoretical section, introduces the key terms and principal distinctions that frame the discussion of the essay and allows me to make my important evaluative claim. Here, I outline different forms of religion-related exclusions and then try to establish that a certain kind of secular state is best able to remove all these exclusions. In the second, more empirically oriented section, I give a brief account of laws pertaining to religion and religion-related practices in India, Pakistan, and Bangladesh, and the ground reality in these societies concerning religion-related exclusions. In the process, I hope also to substantiate the main claim of the first section:

[1] The phrase is Amartya Sen's.

a South-Asian society with a secular state is more likely to be inclusive or to have potential for inclusion. Conversely, a society without a secular state has much greater potential for exclusion.

RELIGION-RELATED EXCLUSIONS

Exclusion from Religion and Religion-based Exclusion

Will Kymlicka has drawn attention to a distinction between cultural and political/economic exclusion.[2] For him, cultural exclusion occurs when the culture of a group, including its language, religion, or traditional customs, are denigrated or suppressed by the state. Conversely, cultural inclusion refers to the public recognition, accommodation, and support to the culture, language, religion, customs, and lifestyles of a group. Distinct from cultural exclusion is the phenomenon of political exclusion, that is, the denial of access to citizenship rights and economic exclusion, that is, the denial of access to certain kinds of employment or professions. I agree that cultural exclusion is irreducible to economic and political exclusions. However, I do not restrict my understanding of inclusion and exclusion to practices of the state. For me, cultural exclusion also occurs either when one group in society persistently misrecognizes, denigrates, humiliates, or suppresses another cultural group or when some members of a cultural group suppress, denigrate, or misrecognize members of a subculture of their own group. In particular, my own concern, in much of my work, is with religion-related inclusion and exclusion.[3] By religion-related exclusion, I mean to broadly cover two forms of exclusions. First, the exclusion of people from the domain of religious liberty and equality. I shall call this exclusion from religion or more simply religious exclusion. Second, the exclusion of people from the wider, non-religious domain of liberty and equality (citizenship rights). I call this a religion-based exclusion and it occurs when a person's religion or religious identity is seen to be sufficient

[2] The distinction is drawn in the background paper for the UNDP Report on Cultural Liberty, 2004.

[3] It is difficult, particularly in South Asia, to make a distinction between religion and culture. If religion is seen as part of culture, then all religion-related exclusions are a form of cultural exclusion. Obviously, if the two are indistinguishable, then all religion-related and cultural exclusions are identical. I shall use the term 'religion' to cover both phenomena: the plainly religious and aspects of culture that are enmeshed in or have a strong bearing on religion.

ground for excluding him/her from the legal, economic, and political benefits/rights available more generally.

Internal and External Exclusion

More distinctions are in order before I proceed further. Religious exclusion can be of two kinds. First, when a religious group excludes its own members from the domain of religious liberty and equality. A religious group may exclude its own members from many of its important practices. In medieval Christendom, ordinary lay persons had access to god only via the clergy. Even potentially, salvation was not, therefore, available to everyone by his own effort. For centuries, in India, a religious sanction has been granted to the horrendous practice of untouchability that excludes dalits from, say, entry into Hindu temples. I call these instances of internal religious exclusion. The suppression of internal religious differences or dissent is also a form of internal religious exclusion. This phenomenon is distinct from what I call external religious exclusion. Here, the religion of a group is misrecognized, denigrated, deliberately falsified, marginalized, or suppressed by the state or by the dominant group in society. Any denial of religious liberty and equality by members of one religious group to another religious group is external religious exclusion. So, the practice of external religious exclusion is rampant wherever there is persecution of religious minorities. Historically, Jews have been victims of religious external exclusion in most Christian societies. For my purpose, a non-religious state that persecutes people of religious faith practises external religious exclusion. So does a religious state that denigrates or suppresses people who profess no religion but live life by principles flowing from non-religious ethical frameworks.

Direct and Indirect Exclusion

The mentioned forms of religion-related exclusions—religious or religion-based, internal or external—may either be directly sanctioned by religion or be a consequence of religiously sanctioned exclusions. I shall call the first direct religion-related exclusion and the second indirect religion-related exclusion. The practice of untouchabiliy is a direct internal, religious exclusion. But, other kinds of exclusions exist not directly sanctioned by religion and these would not occur if the religiously sanctioned exclusion did not exist in the first place. This is precisely where the distinction between custom and religiously sanctioned practice begins to break down. Groups such as dalits and women suffer from waves of exclusion once they suffer from the first major exclusion.[4] The practice of female infanticide is an indirect, internal religion-based exclusion. Strictly speaking, female genital mutilation is not a religiously sanctioned practice, nor is scavenging which is the lot of many dalits in India. Yet, both presuppose direct religious exclusions in the sense that neither would exist without the demeaning conditions brought upon the victims by direct exclusions. The criminalization of sections of minorities in both India and Pakistan is surely an indirect religion-based external exclusion. The distinctions I have made help us to recognize both the internal differences and the close relations between all forms of religion-related exclusionary practices. They help identify exclusions and their specificities that might otherwise go undetected.

A society ridden with so many different forms of religion-related exclusions but keen on becoming inclusive must imagine and device multiple policies of inclusion. For example, making temples accessible to all members of a religious group is an important policy to fight direct internal religious exclusion. Granting every religious group a right to establish or maintain its own educational institutions also exemplifies a policy of religious inclusion. But, in a society that has religion-based denigration of women, so is a government policy sensitive to the needs of pregnant women an example of religious inclusion.

Given the framework outlined, I make an important evaluative claim of this essay: under contemporary conditions, certain kinds of secular states are best able to enhance freedom and equality and maintain just peace. Societies with inclusion as their objective and keen to avoid all forms of religion-related exclusions must have secular states of the appropriate type. In Chapter 3 on secularism, I have provided some sort of an argument to support this claim. Here, I briefly summarize its main points. A maximally inclusive society is one where all citizens identify with the state and enjoy the maximum possible religious liberties consistent with the liberties of others and equal passive and active citizenship rights regardless of their religious affiliations. Theocracies and states with strong and substantive singular establishments are least inclusive. They allow both internal and external religious exclusion as well as religiously grounded political and economic exclusion. To a large extent, states with substantive multiple establishment may have external religious inclusion but they allow internal religious exclusion as

[4] For a sensitive portrait of women's issues from a universalist rights-based perspective, see Martha C. Nussbaum, *Sex and Social Justice*, Oxford: Oxford University Press, 1999.

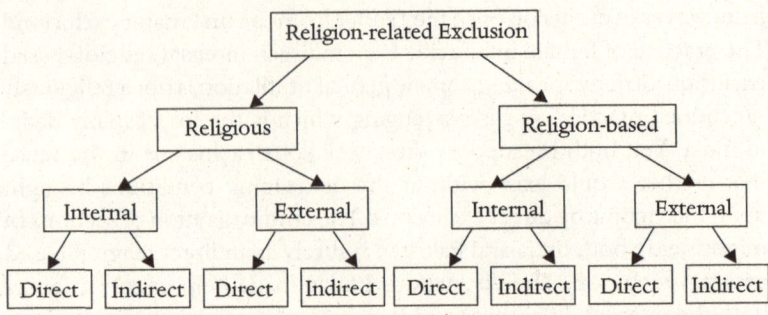

FIGURE 8.1: Religion-related Exclusion

well as religiously grounded exclusions. By and large, states with formal singular or multiple establishments have religious inclusion as well as religiously grounded inclusion. But, they may lack the fullest possible citizen identification and therefore, possibly have citizens who may occasionally feel alienated from them. They may also have remnants of laws, conventions, and practices that are potentially exclusionary. An intrinsically anti-religious secular state, in its form, is virtually like a theocracy or like a state with substantive singular establishment. It is likely to score low on the index of freedom and equality and is bound to be exclusionary. Only a contextually sensitive, liberal, democratic state, that keeps a principled distance from religion, is maximally inclusive.

RELIGION AND THE STATE: LEGAL REALITY AND SOCIAL PRACTICE IN INDIA, PAKISTAN, AND BANGLADESH

At the time of independence, South Asian states inherited a perverted majority–minority syndrome—a diseased network of neurotic relations between at least some members of two communities that takes them to an ever deepening path of mutual estrangement—that exaggerated religious and communal differences and stalled internal religious reform, features that inspire exclusion, not inclusion.[5] Despite partition and a fairly strong movement of religious nationalism that ultimately took Gandhi's life, India managed to install a secular constitution with a set of fundamental rights, including religious and cultural rights for minorities. Even Jinnah, who had led a movement of ethno-religious nationalism, said in the first Constituent Assembly of Pakistan that: 'You are free to go to your temples or your mosques. You may belong to any religion…that has nothing to do with the business of the state'

---

[5] I have discussed in detail the majority–minority syndrome in Chapters 1 and 6.

and 'We are starting with this fundamental principle: that we are all citizens and equal citizens of one state.'[6] Jinnah also hoped that in due course of time, Hindus and Muslims would cease to be Hindus and Muslims, 'not so in the religious sense because that is the personal faith of the each individual, but in the political sense as citizens of the state.'[7] Bangladesh, which attained independence from Pakistan in 1971, also had its genesis in cultural and linguistic nationalism of the Bengali people who began their existence by rejecting the proposal of West Pakistan that Urdu be imposed as the official language of the entire state. In the new constitution, Article 8 adopted the principle of secularism and all religious parties were banned. Over time, however, both Pakistan and Bangladesh have virtually abandoned their commitment to secularism, and the secular state, at least in parts of India, is periodically in crisis and in states such as Gujarat is virtually non-existent.

Self-designation of States and its Consequences for Inclusion

In the last chapter, I discussed the model of secularism adopted in the Indian constitution. What is the formal relationship between religion and the states of Bangladesh and Pakistan? What is the primary self-identification of these states? Are they theocratic? Do they establish religions? Are they secular? If secular, what kind of secularism do they embody?[8] Formally, neither Pakistan nor Bangladesh are secular states. Bangladesh dropped Articles 8 and 12, replacing the principle of secularism with a clause that stated, 'Absolute trust and faith in the Almighty Allah to be the basis of all actions.' 'Bismillah ar Rahman ar Rahim' were inserted before the preamble. Gradually, the ruling elite has tried to Islamize the polity and to build an exclusionary 'mosque-centred society'.[9] General Irshad began the process of Islamization in

[6] Quoted in Iftikhar H. Malik, Religious Minorities in Pakistan, UK: Minorities Rights Group International, 2002, p. 6.

[7] Ibid.

[8] Whatever they may formally say, in reality, most states are impure. States that establish religion do possess theocratic or secular features. Even theocratic states, in reality, contain secular features. It is an assumption of this essay that all states are imperfect and impure, whatever it is they claim to be.

[9] Amena Mohsin, 'National Security and the Minorities: The Bangladesh Case', in D.L. Sheth and Gurpreet Mahajan (eds), Minority Identities and the Nation-State, New Delhi: Oxford University Press, 1999, pp. 316. Also see, Rafiuddin Ahmed (ed.), Religion, Nationalism and Politics in Bangladesh, New Delhi: South Asian Publishers, 1990; and Anisuzzaman, 'Religion, Politics and the State in Bangladesh', in N.N. Vohra and J.N. Dixit (eds), Religion, Politics and Society in South and Southeast Asia, Delhi: Konark Publishers, pp. 60–70.

earnest. In 1982, he declared that the Martyrs Day, commemorating the sacrifices of the martyrs of the language movement of 1952, would henceforth be observed in the proper Islamic manner at the Shahid Minar through prayers and recitations from the Holy Quran and not by drawing *alpana* (act of painting the floor with the liquefied pigment of rice powder), which had been a long-standing practice and which was considered to be a Hindu custom.[10] In 1988, through the eighth amendment, Islam was declared as the state religion of Bangladesh. Other religions are formally allowed, however, to be practised in peace and harmony in the republic. At best, then, Bangladesh professes to be a tolerant Islamic state. It would be suicidal now for any political party to attempt to secularize the constitution. As Khalida Zia put it, 'any attempt to remove Islam as the state religion would hurt the sentiments of the Muslims who constitute 95 per cent of the total population of the state.'[11] The amendments to the constitution have resulted in the destruction of the ideals of the Bangladesh liberation war and taken away from the religious minorities their deep sense of belonging to the country. Citizen identification of the minorities is, therefore, extremely weak. The introduction of state religion has not, however, touched the laws of the land. No attempt has been made to bring civil or criminal laws in line with Islamic laws. As one commentator puts it, 'the once secular state of Bangladesh is still a far cry from the Islamic policy of Iran or even Pakistan'.[12] Yet, the overall consequence of blending religion and politics has not only been to divide Muslims from non-Muslims but also one Muslim group from another.

Pakistan is an overwhelmingly Muslim country with more than 90 per cent of its 142 million inhabitants adhering to Islam. In 1990, the minorities were 3.1 per cent of the total population. There were 1.76 million Christians in Pakistan, 1.72 million Hindus, 9,462 Parsis, 3,500 Buddhists, and about 3,000 Sikhs. By 1998, the minorities were anywhere near 11 and 13 million with Ahmedis, Christian, and Hindus each claiming to have a population of 4 million. Pakistan has had four constitutions since its independence. The first, 1956 constitution, declared Pakistan to be an Islamic republic. Though it granted equal citizenship rights to all men, it refused to offer the same treatment to women—a religion-based internal exclusion by a religious group of a section of its

[10] Ishtiaq Ahmed, *State, Nation and Ethnicity in Contemporary South Asia*, London and New York: Pinter, 1996, p. 126.

[11] Ahmed (ed.), *Religion, Nationalism and Politics in Bangladesh*, p. 68.

[12] Ahmed, *State, Nation and Ethnicity in Contemporary South Asia*, p. 150.

own members. By and large, however, the document did not formally commit itself to religion-related exclusions of minorities. Indeed, in 1962, General Ayub Khan, who introduced his own constitution, dropped the word 'Islamic' from the country's title and sought to make it more liberal in character. For example, progressive Islamic laws in the sphere of marriage and divorce were adopted in the constitution. Ayub attacked theocratically inclined Islamic parties and institutions. To challenge the hegemony of Islam, his government nationalized religious endowments and assumed guardianship of religious shrines. He also sought to regulate religious education.

This phase was short-lived, however, as in 1973, paradoxically, precisely when Pakistan had a constitution ratified for the first time by elected representatives, the Muslim character of the state was reiterated. The 1973 constitution defines Pakistan as an Islamic state. Article 2 of the constitution states that Islam shall be the state religion of Pakistan. Article 2(A) stipulates that principles of democracy, freedom, equality, tolerance, and justice shall be fully observed but only as enunciated by Islam. Article 31 calls on the government to promote an Islamic way of life. Article 228 gives the council of Islamic ideology an institutionalized role in overseeing legislation. Under Article 203(D), the Sharia Court, also established by an amendment to the constitution, can declare any law defunct if it finds it against Islamic injunctions. Indeed, now the Sharia is the supreme law of Pakistan, making it formally resemble theocratic states. So, the Pakistan state has a formally, and as we shall see, substantively, established state religion—Islam—with theocratic overtones. The consequences of such a state are that Pakistan has been unable so far to build an inclusive society.

The unamended Indian constitution of 1950 did not use the word 'secular' but all the features of a secular state are present in the formal structure of the state enunciated by the document. India has no state religion. No religious instruction is to be provided in any educational institution wholly maintained out of state funds. The constitution does not formally give religion any right to oversee the law of the land. All criminal laws are secular. There is only one major anomaly, a part of the civil law dealing with family, marriage, and inheritance falls within the domain of religion. Religious liberty is guaranteed and so is the freedom to exit from religion. No person is compelled to pay any taxes, the proceeds of which are specifically appropriated in payment of expenses for the promotion or maintenance of any particular religion or religious denomination. No person attending any educational institution is required to take part in any religious instruction or to attend any religious worship that may be conducted in such institution. The state is not supposed to discriminate against any citizen on grounds only of religion, race, caste, sex, place of birth, or any of them. In 1975, the term 'secular' was formally introduced in the constitution and India was declared a secular republic

However, as I argued earlier, a secular state in India does not mean that religion will be entirely excluded from the state or the state from religion. Although no specific religion is mentioned in the constitution, religious communities are explicitly recognized and schools run by them are eligible for state funding. Moreover, the state is not powerless in religious matters. Under certain conditions, it can intervene to not only promote but to also undermine specific practices of different religions. I have tried to capture this complex relationship between state and religion by the term 'principled distance'. In the interests of succinctness, a somewhat forced, formulaic articulation of Indian secularism could go something like this: the state must keep a principled distance from all public or private, individual-oriented or community-oriented religious institutions for the sake of the equally significant (and sometimes conflicting) values of peace, this-worldly prosperity, dignity, liberty, and equality (in all their complicated individualistic and communitarian versions).

The legal reality of secularism in India must not be confused with its reality on the ground, however. Whatever the formal position, evidence from the ground has always been mixed. Indeed, trends in the past decade or so are particularly disturbing, with a sustained attempt by right-wing Hindu forces to install, in effect, a homogenized, newly invented Hinduism as the established religion and Hindus as the religious group favoured by the state. This threatens de facto not only the freedom of minorities and inter-religion equality but also tries to change the plural character of Hinduism. Yet, a secular constitution constraints the activities of these forces and continues to be the basis for including minorities in Indian society.

Religious Exclusion: The Denial of Religious Liberty and Equality

We must address several issues in this section. Do individuals have freedom of conscience, the freedom to interpret beliefs and practices in their own way, to dissent from their religion, even to exit the religion into which they are born? Do they live without fear and dignity or are they terrorized by leaders of their own group, by other religious groups, or by the state? Are their places of worship protected by law or from majoritarian forces? Do religious groups have a right to maintain their beliefs and practices, aspects of their culture that are presupposed or entailed by their religion? Do they have a right to maintain their educational institutions? Is there discrimination within a religious community against some of its own members—internal minorities, women, or lower castes? What is the overall status of women within religious communities? How reflective are personal laws of particular religions and how discriminatory are they with respect to women? What role does the state play in removing obstacle to religious freedoms? These are large issues, all of which cannot be covered by this essay. Even issues that are dealt here can be given only a very cursory treatment. My attempt here is only to give a general impression of the status of these issues in India, Pakistan, and Bangladesh.

External Exclusion

Legally, Hindus, Christians, and Sikhs have religious liberty and enjoy the right to maintain their own educational institutions in Pakistan. The Pakistani constitution assures to every citizen the right to freedom of religion and to manage religious institutions. Article 22(1) assures every citizen that no one shall receive religious instruction or take part in religious ceremony other than his/her own. Article 33 makes the state responsible for safeguarding the legitimate rights and interests of minorities. Yet, ground reality in Pakistan is different. The accent on Islam has accentuated the marginalization of all minorities. The Sikhs are very small in number and became smaller after the ascendancy of the Taliban as several Afghani–Sikh families migrated out of fear. After the Babri Masjid destruction, angry mobs destroyed Hindu temples in both Pakistan and Bangladesh. In 2001, a church was attacked by grenades in Islamabad, Murree, and Taksila. One of the worst incidents against Christians took place in 1997, when the twin towns of Shanti Nagar and Tibba Colony were demolished over a supposed case of blasphemy. Thirteen churches and 700 households were razed to the ground by a strong mob of 10,000 people. The tiny community of some 4,000 of the Kalash Kafirs of the Chitral valley were victims of an aggressive conversion campaign during the Zia regime.

Several new articles in the constitution have introduced an institutionalized system of external religious exclusion. For example, the anti-blasphemy law in Pakistan has been used against both Muslims and non-Muslims. Under the Blasphemy Ordnance of 1986, Gul Masih, a Christian, was sentenced to death by a Pakistani lower court in October 1992 for allegedly making abusive remarks about Prophet Mohammad.

Despite General Musharraf's attempts to check it and the massive effort on the part of some non-governmental organizations (NGOs), Pakistan's Islamization continues to be worrisome. For example, the government is enjoined to make serious efforts to teach Islamic studies and the Sharia. Any activity deemed against the teachings of the Sharia is to be harshly dealt with. The states project of Islamizing the national educational system still appears to be in place. Teaching in schools is often tantamount to Islamization of pupils. For example, twenty extra marks are given to any candidate for admission into schools and higher institutions for memorizing the Koran. The educational system does not take Pakistan's plural traditions into account. In the Federal Ministry of Religions and Minorities Affairs, an inscription in the main hall says, 'Of course, Islam is the best religion in the eyes of God'.[13] Radio and television offer programmes on Islam but make no effort to raise awareness of other religions.

In Bangladesh, the Adibashis who live in the Chittagong Hill Tracts (CHT) are mostly Buddhists, Hindus, Christians, and Animists, and according to the 1991 census, have a total population of about half a million people.[14] Bengali nationalism, even under Mujibur Rahman, entirely excluded the Adibashis. The Adibashis have no separate cultural rights, no self-government rights, and not even special rights in representative institutions. The Garos, 90 per cent of whom are Christians and who are the fifth largest ethnic group in Bangladesh numbering about 64,000 in 1991, have no religious or cultural rights

In India, a vigorous campaign of external religious exclusion of Christians and Muslims was a feature, particularly since the late 1980s. In the 1990s, a concerted campaign was carried out against Christians.[15] On 8 July 1998, the body of Samuel Christian was exhumed from a cemetery in Gujarat and thrown outside the Methodist church. In Dang, between 25 December and 3 January 1998, twenty-four churches, three schools, and six houses or shops were burnt or damaged and nine Christian tribals suffered serious injuries. Such incidents were not

[13] Malik, *Religious Minorities in Pakistan*, p. 22.

[14] Amena Mohsin, *The Chittagong Hill Tracts, Bangladesh*, USA: Lynne Rienner Publishers, 2003, p. 16.

[15] Sumit Sarkar, 'Hindutva and the question of Conversions', in K.N. Panikkar (ed.), *Every Man's Guide to Secularism and Communalism*, New Delhi: Viking, 1999, pp. 73–7.

restricted to Gujarat. In January 1999, the Australian missionary doctor, Graham Stains, and two of his children were burnt alive amidst slogans of 'Jai Shri Ram'. Most such incidents are preceded by a systematic campaign of lies and distortions concerning Christians, disseminated through leaflets and brochures. Most of these attacks are justified by the claim that this is legitimate anger against conversion of Hindus to Christianity by anti-national Christian missionaries.

Oppression also takes more subtle forms. The chief of the RSS persists in advising Catholics to reject the Pope, and severe their association with the Vatican. Christians are frequently stigmatized as aliens. Christians and Muslims are told that if they do not acknowledge their Hinduness, for instance, if they do not accept Ram as a national hero, then they must live in subordination to the Hindu majority. Even the Sikhs are not spared. Much to the consternation of a majority of Sikhs, the RSS insists that though distinct, Sikhs are not separate from Hindus. It even tried to have the Sikh holy book, the Guru Granth Sahib, read in the *mandirs* in Punjab. For these ethno-majoritarian forces, therefore, inclusion can only be possible on terms set by them. If these terms are not accepted, then the lot of the minorities can only be severe exclusion. As one commentator put it, 'The only way the Sangh Parivar can deal with Christians and Muslims is either as hostile aliens or converts of Hindu stock awaiting purification.'[16]

Since 1984, the Vishwa Hindu Partishad (VHP) has engineered the revival of a movement to liberate 'sacred' Hindu sites believed to have been usurped by Muslims—an issue that has persistently excited and invigorated Hindu nationalists. In 1992, a well-armed mob, led by VHP activists, reduced the mosque in Ayodhya to rubble as senior BJP leaders looked on. The Ram Janma Bhoomi Movement was less about God Ram and more about Hindu consolidation, less about building a temple and more about the denigration and humiliation of Muslims, about showing Muslims their place in a Hindu country.

In most societies with majoritarian states, the minority group was at least economically powerful in the near past. This is not the case in India, where Muslim minority in much of India is among the poorest and socially 'backward'. By all measures of development—income, wealth, education, employment, ownership, health—the Muslims are among the least well off of all Indians. This is why ethno-majoritarian forces reinvent old, mostly imaginary Hindu grievances: the destruction

[16] Mukul Kesavan, *Secular Common Sense*, New Delhi: Penguin Books, 2001, p. 94.

of Hindu temples by Mughals, the temerity of supporters of partition to even ask for a framework respecting minority rights, the disloyalty induced by pan-Islamicism, and the alleged role that polygamy and therefore, Muslim personal law plays in their march to outpopulate Hindus. Hindu nationalists make instrumental use of memory, emotion, prejudice, religious difference, and generalized deprivation to advance their extremist agenda of external religious exclusion.[17]

Hindu–Muslim riots have an old pedigree. The partition of India was accompanied by violence that killed over half a million people. Even after independence, communal riots have not abated. Indeed, their incidents increased over the last four decades.[18] While no one can deny the economic and political reasons underlying communal violence, a direct exclusionary motive is always present. This was no where more evident than in the pogram in Gujarat in which over 2,000 Muslims were brutally killed after a Muslim mob allegedly burnt down a train compartment containing thirty-nine Hindus.[19] But this exclusionary motive was also present in the past. For example, on 13 August 1980, the Provincial Armed Constabulary (PAC) opened fire on several thousand Muslims at their Id prayers at Moradabad. In 1984, following the assassination of Mrs Indira Gandhi by a Sikh, her personal bodyguard, several thousand Sikhs were killed in northern India. After the demolition of Babri Masjid in 1992–3, about 600 Muslims were killed and over a thousand injured in the Bombay riots.[20]

Internal Exclusion

Internal exclusion is a problem in all South Asian societies. I shall take two examples: one of dissenting religious groups in Pakistan and the other of women and dalits, particularly in India. A turning point in the

[17] Ibid.

[18] M.J. Akbar, *Riot After Riot*, New Delhi: Roli Books, 1988; Ashis Nandy, Shikha Trivedy, Shail Mayaram, and Achyut Yagnik, *Creating a Nationality*, New Delhi: Oxford University Press, 1997; B.N. Srikrishna Report, *Crime against Humanity; Damning Verdict*, Bombay; Siddharth Varadarajan, *Gujarat: The Making of a Tragedy*, New Delhi: Penguin Books, 2002; and Ashutosh Varshney, *Ethnic Conflict and Civic Life*, New Delhi: Oxford University Press, 2002.

[19] Events in Gujarat could hardly qualify as a 'riot'. For a detailed account, see Varadarajan, *Gujarat*, p. 229.

[20] The final tally of casualty figures for December 1992 and January 1993 are: Dead—900 (575 Muslims, 275 Hindus, 45 unknown, and 5 others) and Injured—2,036 (Muslims, 1,105; Hindus, 893; others, 38). See Justice B.N. Srikrishna Report, *Crime against Humanity*.

history of inclusion and exclusion in Pakistan was Bhutto's anti-Ahmedi legislation.[21] Zia consolidated this move by declaring, under Article 260, Ahmedis to be a non-Muslim minority. Ahmedis were forbidden from using Islamic nomenclature in their religious and social lives. A whole community of people were formally excluded, both symbolically and materially, from the dominant religion of Pakistan. Ahmedis have since been tried and convicted under the law for calling themselves Muslims or using the word 'mosque' as their place of worship. They have also been physically attacked. The example of Ahmedis show that there is little freedom of dissent from the dominant religion and that religious freedom is not available to every citizen.

Under Zia's regime, the state acquired fundamentalist Sunni overtones. This resulted in the intensification of Shia–Sunni conflict and the persecution of the minority Shia community. In 2000, there were 150 sectarian killings. In 2001, between January and September, 120 professionals and scholars, mostly Shia, were killed in sectarian murders. In February 2002, Sunni militants attacked a Shia mosque in Rawalpindi and killed twelve worshippers. In February 2002, five members of Shia family were murdered by Sunni militants in Multan. Extremists, even as they go unheeded, continue to demand that Pakistan be made into a Sunni state and that Shias be declared non-Muslims.

An accent on majority Sunni Islam also threatens the small group of Zikris. The Zikris, who live in Baloch, also fear the minority status and therefore, stay away from the public domain. The Zikris believe in the idea of the revealed Imam (*Mahdi*) and consider Syed Mohammad Jaunpuri, a contemporary of Akbar, to be their Mahdi. They believe that the Imam appeared on a hilltop in Baluchistan where he performed religious and spiritual rites. Zikris who remember and constantly recite the name of god, assemble on this hilltop every year to commemorate this occasion. The opponents of Zikris allege that they do not pray regularly. They also allege that they do not go for pilgrimage to Mecca but visit the hilltop instead and that their Zikrakhanas do not have pulpits pointing towards Mecca. The Zikris too are a persecuted internal minority in Pakistan whose religious freedom is constantly threatened.

Anyone found to be denigrating the name of Prophet Mohammed is punished by virtue of an amendment to Pakistan's penal code. The law against blasphemy enables any male Muslim to initiate litigation against an individual, and if found guilty, the individual is to be given the death

[21] The Ahmedi sect owes its origin to Mirza Gulab Ahmed and after he claimed to be a prophet and formed the Ahmedi mission, it was declared a separate sect.

penalty. In August 2002, a woman, Ruksana Bunayad, became the first-ever Muslim woman to be charged with blasphemy against the Quran. There is no major religion in the world where women are given the same status as men. Women are generally excluded from several practices of their own religion. For example, Islam does not permit women to offer prayers in mosques. There are no known women archbishops, Imams, or *pujaris*. In Hinduism, there are restrictions on their participation in religious rituals at the time of menstruation. Entry to temples is similarly restricted during this period. The Ayyapa temple in Kerala forbids the entry of women between ages 15–65, entirely because their very capacity to menstruate makes their bodies impure for this entire period. But, dalits have suffered the severest from of internal religious exclusion in the sub-continent. The Indian constitution tries to remove this disability. Article 17 has legally abolished untouchability. Under Article 25(2)b, Hindu religious institutions of a public character are thrown open to all sections of Hindu society. The (Central) Untouchability (Offences) Act of 1955 provides penalties for enforcing any religious disability. Any person, who, on grounds of untouchability, prevents any other person from worshipping, offering prayer, performing religious service, bathing, using the water of a sacred tank, well, spring, or watercourse is punishable with imprisonment. Despite the constitution and other legal provisions, however, the National Commission for Scheduled Castes and Scheduled Tribes report of 1990 states that in Uttar Pradesh (UP), Tamil Nadu, Kerala, Rajasthan, and Karnataka, dalits still do not have access to temples and other places of worship.[22] This is also true of an important study conducted earlier on rural Gujarat.[23] The Andhra Committee too found that as many as eighty temples in the 249 villages it visited explicitly forbade entry of dalits into the temples.[24]

Religion-based Legal, Social, and Economic Exclusion: The Denial of Passive Citizenship Rights

Is a person's religion the basis for his/her exclusion from the social, political, and economic domain of liberty and equality? What is the legal status of women, internal minorities, and religious minorities

[22] Harsh Mander, 'Status of Dalits and Agenda for State Intervention', in Ghanshyam Shah (ed.), *Dalits and the State*, New Delhi: Concept Publishing Company, 2002, pp. 149–52.

[23] I.P. Desai, *Untouchability in Rural Gujarat*, Bombay: Popular Prakashan, 1976.

[24] Mander, 'Status of Dalits and Agenda for State Interlution', in Shah (ed.), *Dalits and the State*, pp. 149–52.

in Pakistan, India, and Bangladesh? Does the legal machinery work impartially? Does it provide equal protection to everyone? Indeed, is the state impartial? What role does the police play in inter-communal violence? Are the perpetrators of communal violence ever punished? Does the state discriminate in the distribution or provision of benefits? In civil society, is there religion-related discrimination, for example, in housing, jobs, school and college admission? What role does the state play to prevent or remove it? Do members of minority groups migrate to neighbouring countries to escape severe economic or political marginalization? How does religion-based discrimination work against women and other oppressed internal groups? What is the status of personal laws? How do they discriminate against women?

External Exclusion

Apart from Muslims, there are two main ethno-religious groups in Bangladesh: the Hindus and the Adibashis who are Buddhists, Hindus, Animists, or Christians. The Hindus are socially and economically marginalized. The economic marginalization of the Hindu community is caused by the Vested Property Act, according to which the government has power to acquire any land it considers necessary for administration. This act has been widely used against Hindus.[25] This continues a practice started as long ago as 1951, when the East Bengal Evacuees Act was passed, whereby the government could acquire the property of an evacuee. Hindu zamindars allege that their property was requisitioned even though they chose to live in East Pakistan.[26]

Similarly, when a war broke out in 1965 between Pakistan and India, India was declared an enemy country. A new act was passed, according to which all interests of the enemy situated in Pakistan were confiscated by the Custodian of Enemy Property in Pakistan. When the war ended, this act, with its overt communal bias, was continued. Worst still, despite the declaration that it was a secular state, independent Bangladesh retained this act. This 'black law' continues to cause insecurity and out-migration among Hindus. It is estimated that out-migration during 1964–91 was 5.3 million, or 538 persons each day.[27] (In 1947, Hindus

[25] See Abul Barkat et al., Political Economy of the Vested Property Act in Rural Bangladesh, Dhaka: Association for Land Reform and Development (ALRD), 1997, p. 27.

[26] Mohsin, 'National Security and the Minorities', in Sheth and Mahajan (eds), Minority Identities and the Nation–State, pp. 312–33.

[27] Ibid., p. 326. Also see, Ranabir Samaddar, The Marginal Nation, New Delhi: Sage Publications, 1999.

were 23 per cent of the population in East Pakistan. This declined to 22 per cent in 1951; 18.3 per cent in 1961; 13.5 per cent in 1974; and 12.1 per cent in 1981.[28] This decline is attributed to migration.) The act also discourages the minority community from acquiring new land. According to an estimate, out of a total arable land of 21 million in the country, one million acres of land belonging to the minority community has been transferred to the dominant sections of society.[29] According to Sultana Nahar, Hindus face persistent discrimination in business, employment, and education.[30]

The Adibashis of the CHT consider land to be communal property but, with the introduction of private property, and because of commercial exploitation and government sponsored projects of development, they have gradually lost it. For example, the construction of the dam of the Karnafuli river in Rangamati resulted in 40 per cent of the total acreage of the district getting submerged by dam waters. The Adibashis were not fully compensated for the land they lost. A 1,00,000 people were uprooted, of which approximately 40,000 became refugees in India. Is this negative outcome a result of religion-related discrimination? It is difficult to answer this question, though it is pertinent to ask whether the same fate would have befallen Muslim citizens had they been in the shoes of the Adibashis.

The Garos too are largely excluded from the economic mainstream. Garos consider the forest not just an economic asset but as the core of their socio-cultural life. They see themselves as children of the forest. To evict them from the forest is to cut their lifeline. However, several government policies have caused their displacement from the forest. The settlement of Bengalis in north Mymensingh resulted in the outbreak of riots and the migration of Garos to India. For the Garos, the liberation of Bangladesh was the 'second riot'. The contributions of the non-Muslim population who were recruited into the freedom movement have never been recognized, a fact that underlines their alienation from their society.

The legal, social, and economic position of religious minorities in Pakistan is hardly any better. Minorities continue to be excluded from socio-economic life and from high positions in civil and military sectors.

[28] Persecution is not the only reason for migration. Many people also cross the border in the hope of a better life.

[29] Mohsin, 'National Security and the Minorities', in Sheth and Mahajan (eds), *Minority Identities and the Nation–State*, p. 326.

[30] See Sultana Nahar, *A Comparative Study of Communalism in Bangladesh and India*, Dhaka: Dhaka Prokashon, 1994.

Changes in the economy have not helped the position of Christians, low caste converts from Hinduism, who were rendered landless and forced to take up stigmatized jobs such as sweeping the streets. When minorities are confined to menial, low-paid work, their self-esteem diminishes and as a result, ethno-religious stereotypes are reinforced. The nationalization of educational institutions run by Christians blocked assured access to jobs and education and further alienated the Christians. Rural Hindus remain vulnerable in Pakistan to feudal and state oppression. What is worse, there are no clear state policies to reduce the marginalization of minorities.

Despite its secular constitution, the partisan character of the state is most blatant in incidents of communal violence in India. I have already mentioned the calculated, cold-blooded massacre by a communalized police force in Moradabad that tried to cover this up by making it out to be a Hindu–Muslim riot.[31] But the communal role of the PAC can also be seen in Meerut, where custodial deaths of Muslims became a regular feature in 1987. Riots are bad enough, but much worse is the arbitrary murder committed by the guardians of law.[32]

Direct violence is not the only expression of police brutality towards religious minorities. Deliberate indifference to the plight of the needy manifests the same exclusionary intention. For example, there was delay in setting up relief camps in Gujarat. Outrageously, the Gujarat government did not set up a single relief camp for Muslim victims. It was left to Muslim-dominated panchayats or Muslim religious trusts to provide protection, and to feed and house the victims. Shortage of ration was characteristic of these camps.[33] Evidence also exists for discrimination in compensation paid to victims.[34] Damage to property

[31] Akbar, *Riot after Riot*, pp. 33–4.

[32] Ibid., pp. 151–8.

[33] The People's Union for Democratic Rights (PUDR) report notes that a camp for 700 people in Anand town was functioning from 3 March when displaced persons started arriving. With over 700 people in the camp, a week's ration arrived only on 6 March. Nothing after that happened, even after numbers rose to 1,155. The next ration, on 2 April, was sanctioned only for 247 people. Pleas for more supplies fell on deaf ears.

[34] The 28 February resolution fixed an ex-gratia payment of Rs 5,000–Rs 50,000 for permanent disability and Rs 1,000–Rs 5,000 for temporary disabilities. For the predominantly Muslim victims of the subsequent genocide, a 2 March resolution provides no payment for temporary disabilities at all. Even for permanent disabilities, the amount was substantially scaled down: Rs 2,000 for disability up to 10 per cent; Rs 3,000 for disability between 10 per cent and

owned by Muslims was rarely recompensed. Persons who lost property worth lakhs were given a mere few thousands.

Internal Exclusion: Direct

Customary practices with at least some association with local religious belief directly stipulate death for women. The whole issue of *sati*—the immolation of a widow following her husband's death—is a complicated one but there is no denying its link with local religious beliefs. Despite a law against sati, Roop Kanwar, an eighteen-year-old student was burnt alive in Rajasthan in India on the funeral pyre of her husband. Soon after the event, she began to be revered and glorified as a goddess. Public outrage followed in India, not least thanks to powerful women's movements. A stringent new law was passed in the Parliament prohibiting the glorification or justification of sati. This has had some effect but the practice continues.

In many countries with Islamic laws, women require some form of male guardianship to enter into contracts. A conflict between religious legal systems and the constitutional provision of equality is common in India. For example, in 1983, Mary Roy, a Syrian Christian challenged the Travancore Christian Act that governed them in Kerala on the ground that it violated the equality provision guaranteed by the constitution. When the Supreme Court overturned the act to be replaced by the Indian Succession Act of 1925 that grants daughters and sons equal rights, several members of the Christian community protested against the judgement and were supported by the Synod of Christian churches.

Similarly, in a landmark judgement in 1985, the Indian Supreme Court granted a small maintenance allowance to Shah Bano, a seventy-three-year-old divorcee, to be paid by her husband under the provisions of the CPC. The husband had appealed to the court that since he had fulfilled his obligations under Muslim personal law by paying her an allowance for three months during the *iddat* period, he was not bound to maintain her any further. The court ruled that Indian criminal law overrode all personal laws and therefore, rejected the appeal. For reasons still not entirely clear, the then Congress government enacted a legislation that 'literally adopted the provisions of the Shariat into

---

30 per cent; Rs 5,000 between 30 per cent and 40 per cent; and Rs 50,000 for above 40 per cent disability.

the secular law'[35] and excluded Muslim women from secular legal provisions.[36]

In India, although secular marriage is available as an option, secular divorce is not. For divorce, a couple must appeal to the religion of their birth. There is no right of exit from one's religion when it comes to important issues such as marriage or death. This is a direct infringement of one's freedom. In most systems of Islamic law, a woman is the guardian of a male child only until he is seven years old. Till very recently, the Hindu law regarded only the father as the natural guardian of the child, except for children under the age of five.[37] The mother could have custody only of an illegitimate child. The right to adopt a child is also directly affected by religion. For many years, the Hindu Adoptions and Maintenance Act, passed in 1956, was the only law of adoptions in India and applied only to Hindus. This meant that for all these years, only Hindus could adopt a child and only a Hindu child could be adopted.[38] All attempts to enact a new law covering all religions was resisted by conservative Muslim leaders on the ground that adoption is forbidden by the Quran. In 1980, a new bill was passed and adoption rights were granted to Jews, Christians, and Parsis but Muslims were exempted. The orthodoxy denied members of its own religion an important human freedom.

More on Direct, Internal Religion-based Exclusion: Dalits in India
Gopal Guru writes poignantly about the exclusion of dalits.[39] He argues that historically dalits have been denied the freedom to control their own time and space. For example, in south and western India, dalits

[35] Paul Brass, *The Politics of India since Independence* (2nd edition), Cambridge: Cambridge University Press, 1994.

[36] See Zoya Hasan, 'Uniform Civil Code and Gender Justice in India', in P.R. deSouza (ed.), *Contemporary India: Transitions*, New Delhi: Sage Publications, 2000, pp. 282–301. For a philosophically informed reflection on the same issue, see Rajeev Bhargava, 'Do Muslims have a Right to their Personal Laws?', in P.R. deSouza (ed.), *Contemporary India*, pp. 182–202.

[37] See Kirti Singh, 'The Constitution and Muslim Personal Law', in Zoya Hasan (ed.), *Forging Identities: Gender, Communities and the State in India*. Boulder: Westview Press, 1994, pp. 96–107.

[38] See Nussbaum, *Sex and Social Justice*, p. 99.

[39] Gopal Guru, 'Dalits: Reflections on the Search for Inclusion', in P.R. deSouza (ed.), *Contemporary India*, pp. 59–72. Also see Shah (ed.), *Dalits and the State*, New Delhi: Concept Publishing Company, 2002, especially the articles by Harsh Mander, M. Thangaraj, Ramesh Kamble, Susan Chaplin, and

238 India's Secular Democracy

were confined to prescribed areas and without the permission of the upper castes, who policed these boundaries with both physical force and an ideology of purity and pollution, were not allowed outside internment camps. Dalits had no freedom to walk on the main streets of the villages. When they did walk these streets, it was only to serve the upper caste feudal lords and always with brooms tied to their waist so as to erase polluting footprints, and with earthen pots around their necks to protect the earth from their impure sputum. Guru argues that the religious core found in the Hindu text, *Manusmriti*, sanctions restrictions on freedom of space or mobility for dalits.

Dalit life was also marked by a complete lack of control over their time. They worked round the clock for their feudal lords, except when their appearance was dangerously polluting. Under the Peshwa rule in Maharashtra, dalits could enter public streets that went past upper caste homes only around noon because during this hour, the shadow of the dalits was shortest and therefore, least likely to pollute the upper caste. As Guru puts it, 'the beautiful mornings and cool evenings were denied to dalits';[40] in their lot fell only the scorching afternoon. Thus, even their time was policed by upper castes.

Much of this has changed for many dalits. The arrival of colonialism itself was a blessing of sorts. Emancipatory ideas came with colonial modernity and sections of dalits were quick to use them. Some control over space and time was now possible, as was the opportunity to enter educational institutions or the legal domain. After independence, dalits benefited from constitutional provisions that initiated political inclusion at several levels. Yet, it has been an uneven, partial success, at least partly because the force of specific cultural memory is not diminished by colonialism, capitalism, or the law.[41] Religiously sanctioned structures of exclusion and marginalization still remain intact. Institutionalized ideas of impurity and pollution lurk in the hearts, minds, and actions of large number of people in rural India and even, urban India.

Several empirical studies indicate that untouchablity—the practice of avoiding physical contact with persons and things believed to

---

S.R. Shankaran; and S.M. Michael (ed.), *Dalits in Modern India*, New Delhi: Vistaar Publications, 1999.

[40] Guru, 'Dalits', in P.R. deSouza (ed.), *Contemporary India*, p. 61.

[41] Peter Robb, *Dalit Movements and Meanings of Labour*, New Delhi: Oxford University Press, 1993, p. 66.

be polluting—is an integral part of the experience of dalithood. The findings of both the National Commission for Scheduled Castes and Scheduled Tribes and the Ambedkar Centenary Committee in Andhra Pradesh, in 1990, concluded that untouchability was still prevalent in many areas. For example, the Andhra Committee found that of 249 villages, in 122 tea shops, tea was still served in separate glasses for dalits who had to wash the tumblers themselves. In many parts of Tamil Nadu, UP, Rajasthan, and Kerala, dalits were denied access to the village well, even barbers and washermen, because none would serve them. Participation in social ceremonies was difficult and discrimination existed in the use of even cremation grounds. Dalits are still excluded from most occupations considered dignified and worthy. They are forced to work in jobs considered demeaning such as the tanning of leather and scavenging. In sixteen of the 249 villages studied by the Andhra Committee, it was revealed that dalits had never walked through the streets with any type of footwear.

Internal Exclusion: Indirect

Amendments to the penal code made by the Zia regime in Pakistan deepened socio-legal discrimination against minorities as well as against Muslim women.[42] The law of evidence holds on par the evidence of two women or two non-Muslims with that of a single male Muslim.[43] Qanoon-e-Shahadat establishes the intrinsic superiority of Muslim men over women and minorities, and contravenes the fundamental principles of equality. Perhaps the most outrageous instance of indirect internal exclusion is the Hudood ordinance, an anti-women measure that punishes women unable to establish that they have been raped. Under the Hudood ordinance, rape convictions require four male witnesses. A failure to produce such witnesses results in the prosecution of the complainant who is liable for punishment for fornication (zina). Women's groups have been struggling to remove this ordinance but so far have not been successful. The 1973 Pakistani constitution forbids

[42] For a good and succinct account of the impact of Islamization on the exclusion of women, see Shahla Zia, 'Women, Ismalisation and Justice', in Kamla Bhasin, Ritu Menon, and Nighat Said Khan (eds), Against All Odds: Essays on Women, Religion and Development from India and Pakistan, New Delhi: Kali for Women, 1997, pp. 70–81.

[43] For a detailed treatment of this issue, see I. Ahmed, The Concept of an Islamic State: An Analysis of the Ideological Controversy in Pakistan, London: Frances Pinter, 1987.

discrimination on the basis of sex alone. How then can these exclusions occur? Women are excluded because of other contradictory provisions in the constitution and even more due to the constitutional stipulation that no law be passed if it is against the injunctions of the Quran and the Sunnah.

Violence against women is not uncommon in South Asia. Women are easily subjected to violence not only because direct sanction by religion is available but because of the subordination that flows from religious world views. When such sanction is not available, it is invented. For example, Noorjahan, a young Bangladeshi from the Sylhet district was charged with adultery on the ground that she married a second time without securing a divorce from her first husband.[44] The village maulvi issued the *fatwa* against her, and together with the village elite pronounced that she be punished. She was buried waist down and stoned 101 times. This public humiliation drove her to suicide. But the case against her was largely fabricated because she was legitimately divorced from her husband, the real culprit, who failed to provide maintenance for her in accordance with the law of the land and the Sharia. Noorjahan's family sought legal redressal for her death. They were supported by women's organizations and the media. Their pressure succeeded in punishing the maulvi and the village elite who were convicted for seven years rigorous imprisonment for the murder of Noorjahan. Dowry killings, only indirectly related to religion, are also not uncommon.[45] In many parts of India, Hindu widows undergo a social death, excluded from virtually every aspect of social and domestic life.

Women are most severely affected in communal riots, due both to the death of loved ones and to the brutal injury and humiliation to which they are subjected, sometimes minutes before they are killed. Disturbingly, inquiry commissions are 'unable' to determine the exact or approximate numbers of rapes and murders of women. In filing the first information reports (FIRs), charges of rapes are collapsed with that of general looting or robbery, thus obfuscating heinous crime.

---

[44] Roushan Jahan and Mahmuda Islam (eds), *Violence Against Women in Bangladesh: Analyses and Action*, Dhaka: Women for Women and South Asia Association for Women Studies, 1997.

[45] Pakistan is known to have 'honour killings'. A Human Rights Report claimed that in 2000, there were 315 killings in Punjab alone. Most persons so killed are women.

A formal and legal equality granted to women in the Indian constitution does not always change their status or alter their living conditions. For example, the female child in India always suffers more from hunger and malnutrition as well as from unequal access to basic health care than the male child. Several Human Development reports give us much data on health care among girls and women. According to the 1999 UNDP report, the female to male ratio in India had recently fallen to 938—from 945 females per 1,000 males in 1991 and 1,010 females per 1,000 male children in 1941.[46] The unfavourable ratio is due to higher levels of mortality among girls and women in their child-bearing years. This is due to discriminatory practices which treat women as an economic burden. The past two decades have seen a resurgence in India of the practice of female infanticide. According to the *Human Development in South Asia 2000 Report*, there were 40,000 known cases of female foeticide in a single year in Bombay alone and 10,000 in Ahmedabad. About 72 per cent of pregnant women in South Asia are anaemic, and 9.2 per cent of maternal deaths in India are directly caused by this anaemic condition. Several studies conducted in Punjab showed the low nutritional status of female children. This lower status was irrespective of the economic group into which they were born, confirming that it is not caused by poverty alone.

Legally, women have equal access to education but female literacy rates in India tell a different tale. They are much lower for women compared to men. In 1997, it was 39 per cent compared to 67 per cent in males.[47] The percentage of women working outside their home continues to be much smaller than men. The earned income share in 1995 for women compared to men was 34 per cent, and the economic activity rate in 1997 for women was 50 per cent of the economic activity rate of men.[48] The most elementary (passive) citizenship rights are therefore denied to large sections of women in India because they

[46] On the missing women in Asia, see Amartya Sen, 'More than 100 Million Women are Missing', *New York Review of Books*, 20 December 1990. The female/male ratio in Bangladesh is 954 and in Pakistan 937.

[47] However, it is worth noting that the percentage of increase from 1970 to 1997 is marginally better for women than it is for men. Male literacy rate has increased from 47 per cent to 67 per cent and female literacy rate from 19 per cent to 39 per cent.

[48] *Human Development in South Asia 2000*, Oxford: Oxford University Press, 2000. In Bangladesh, female illiteracy is 74 per cent compared to 51 per cent in males. In Pakistan, it is 76 per cent compared to 46 per cent in males.

are not seen to possess the same worth as men, an attitude indirectly encouraged by most religions.

More on Indirect, Internal Religion-based Exclusion: Dalits

In urban India, greater anonymity and occupational mobility blurs caste identities and has diminished the practice of untouchability. This is particularly true in the public and the political sphere. But it has not disappeared altogether. Inclusion is uncommon in marriage, inter-dining, and other forms of social intercourse. This 'new' inclusion is infused with newer forms of hierarchy and inequality, however. Instead of becoming equal participants in the mainstream, dalits are jostled to the margins and perpetually remain on the verge of exclusion. For example, they are still unable to get decent jobs and continue to perform work that no one else wants to. In a soap factory, they are forced to handle tallow. In textile mills, they are excluded from weaving on the ground that they would pollute the entire fabric. Dalits are often kept out of hotel industry and would certainly not work in the kitchen. In educational institutions, they are frequently ghettoized in one part of the hostel, generally acknowledged to be the filthiest. Paradoxically, what is bestowed as a special privilege soon begins to perpetuate exclusion. This is certainly the case with backward class hostels, Ambedkar Foundations, and schools run by the Social Welfare Departments. Guru rightly points out that the dominant framework of these provisions is a demeaning form of charity rather than an uplifting vision of equal concern and respect.

In many parts of rural India, dalits continue to suffer from all kinds of exclusions. Several invisible castes remain in independent India that are not included in the list of SC communities, beneficiaries of the provisions of affirmative action enshrined in the constitution. One such community is the Kahars in Bihar. Their social exclusion is so extreme that even other dalits do not deign to interact with them. 'We are not allowed into the vicinity of the others houses. And they won't even let us catch fish in the river or in regular ponds.'[49] So, the Kahars fish by draining ditches and catching them with bare hands. They are paid a wage far below the official minimum wage and remain outside the public distribution system. Most of them are landless and without the requisite skills necessary for raising a standard of living. Their

---

[49] P. Sainath, *Everybody Loves a Good Drought*, New Delhi: Penguin Books, 1996, pp. 175–8.

houses, if they can be called houses at all, are never lit. 'The average kahar home is really a hovel'.[50] A vanishing group, the main demand of the Kahars is to be included in the SC list. Apart from this, they want education and land. 'If these demands are not met, there may be no kahars to count some years from now.'[51]

Dalits present the most heart-rending example of indirect religious and religiously grounded exclusion of communities and individuals. What is worse, this form of exclusion is also found in the professedly more egalitarian religions such as Christianity. The Pulaya Christians of Kerala, who were formerly untouchable Hindus, are still treated as untouchables by the Syrian Christians. Similarly, conversion to Islam has helped dalits to read the namaz in the mosques along with co-believers. But this religious inclusion has not curbed indirect religious exclusion. The social stigma attached to them has not evaporated and non-dalit Muslims avoid dining or having marital relations with them.

Religion-based Political Exclusion: The Denial of Active Citizenship Rights

Do religious minorities have a right to vote? Are votes cast on the basis of joint or separate electorates and what is the effect of these on actual empowerment? Do religious minorities have a right to stand for public office? Is there religion-related discrimination in the public sector or in the state machinery? How do public officials take oath? Do all religious groups have a right to participate in collective deliberations on the future course of society? Do minority religious groups or individuals have an effective presence in the media and the wider public sphere? Answering these questions in detail requires a whole book. I can take only a cursory glance at the status of active citizenship rights in these countries.

External Exclusion

The minorities in Bangladesh are virtually absent in the political process. The Bangladeshi Parliament has no seats for ethno-religious minorities. The three seats reserved for the CHT can all be appropriated by Bengalis. The Garos do not have the wherewithal to fight elections, which is why they are not represented in the Parliament. The invisibility of the hill people is such that the government can confidently say that there

[50] Ibid.
[51] Ibid., p. 178.

are no Adibashis in Bangladesh. If this is the official position, how can special representation or self-government rights be even conceived? In Bangladesh, the entire electoral system reproduces ethno-religious majoritarianism.

In Pakistan, too, Islamization, the basis of exclusionary ethno-nationalism, is inscribed in the institutions and practices of its political society. For over three decades, citizenship in Pakistan is defined with reference to majoritarian and exclusionary Islamic parameters. Therefore, political exclusion is built into the basic law of the land. By making adherence to Islam mandatory for anyone aspiring to the two highest offices in the country, that of the president and the prime minister [Article 41(2) and 91(3)], the constitution ensures the exclusion of religious minorities from high political office. There is no political equality in Pakistan. The very formulation of oaths is designed to exclude non-Muslims.[52]

The secular state in India depoliticized religion with the result that there is neither a separate electorate nor reservation of seats for Muslims. Given the ghettoization implicit in the institution of separate electorate and the separationist legacy it still carries in post-independent India, the rejection of separate electorates appears justified. However, in view of the severe under-representation of Muslims in the Indian Parliament, indeed its steady decline over the years, one wonders if justice does not require some form of representation-enhancing policy for them. The Muslim share in public employment hovers around 3 per cent.[53] Muslim representation in the police is also inadequate. For example, in Delhi, it is only 2.3 per cent; in UP, 4.9 per cent; and in Maharashtra, 4.2 per cent.[54] The Indian Armed Forces do not mirror the social diversity of the Indian population. In the paramilitary forces, the percentage ranges between 1.81 per cent and 6.9 per cent.[55]

Internal Exclusion

Despite a vague consensus that representation of women must increase in the Parliament, there has been no real effort in India by political parties to push through the women's representation bill that guarantees 33 per cent of seats to women. Therefore, in reality, women's

[52] Malik, *Religious Minorities in Pakistan*.

[53] Mushirul Hasan, *Legacy of a Divided Nation*, New Delhi: Oxford University Press, 2001, p. 282.

[54] Ibid., p. 294.

[55] Omar Khalidi, *Khaki and the Ethnic Violence in India*, New Delhi: Three Essays Collective, 2003, pp. 62–3.

representation in the Parliament is a hotly contested issue. In 1999, women occupied an abysmal 8.7 per cent of seats in the Parliament. After the 73rd amendment and the introduction of the Panchayati Raj Bill, women's representation in village panchayats has increased but the entire institution is still suffused with patriarchal values. Under the constitution, the SC/STs have 22 per cent reservation in the Parliament and in the government. Thus, both the SCs and the STs are adequately represented in the Parliament. But real empowerment is still a long way away. In rural India, their political marginalization continues. The National Commission for SC/STs found that in Tamil Nadu and UP, and to some extent, in Rajasthan, discrimination in panchayats, village *chaupals* (an informally designated place at a centrally located public place where views are aired and news is exchanged by village elders), and Ram sabhas continue to exist.[56]

* * *

I have argued that in order to build inclusive societies, we need a particular form of secular states. All other forms of states are exclusionary. Theocracies and states that formally and substantively establish single religions are the most exclusionary. They curtail religious liberty in all its forms and undermine equality within and between religious groups. Thus, they perpetrate internal as well as external religious exclusions. They fail to grant passive or active citizenship rights or else actively undermine them. Hence, they introduce and perpetuate both direct and indirect, internal and external religion-based exclusions. States with multiple establishments tend to be more inclusive but are compatible with strong exclusionary practices because they exclude non-believers and tend to exclude internal minorities, dissenters, and women.

I have also argued that the structure of an authoritarian, anti-religious secular state is identical to a theocracy or a state with established religions. The kind of secular states that, in my view, are necessary for building inclusive societies are not of the strict wall of separation or the strictly neutral variety. I suggested that principled distance is the best interpretation of 'separation'. To make their societies more inclusive, South Asia must have secular states of the principled distance variety.

A theocracy or a state with established religion(s) is structurally incapable of inclusion. If societies with such states develop inclusive features, they do so despite and not because of them. Their overall impact is to inhibit forces of inclusion. On the other hand, most secular

[56] Shah (ed.), *Dalits and the State*, pp. 149–53.

states are structurally inclined towards inclusion, and when a society with a secular state develops exclusionary properties, it does so despite it, rather than because of it. Secular states constrain forces of exclusion.

All South Asian societies inherited a legacy of the majority–minority syndrome and have a propensity to thwart the internal reform of religion. All of them have majoritarian forces bent upon imposing their own will on minorities. Fortunately, all of them also have possibilities within their societies to generate secular political practice. In this, they are helped not only by elements within their respective religio-cultural traditions but also by alert citizens in their civil societies. Equally noteworthy is the fact that states in all these societies began with the intention of being inclusive. However, only the Indian state has managed to contain ethno-religious exclusionary forces, at least for some time, and at the moment it appears that it alone has the capacity to resist and perhaps even tame them. This is not because of some innate propensity of Hindus or Indian Muslims but largely due to the presence of certain institutional structures.

Let me briefly mention the inclusive potential of the secular state in India. Gujarat's genocide, by the then Prime Minister of India, Atal Behari Vajpayee's own admission, is a blot on the country. I have already spoken about the state-sponsored violence there. Yet, the entire political machinery of the country did not collapse. The Chief Election Commissioner (CEC), Lyngdoh, played an exemplary role. He came down heavily on the Gujarat government for its purported claim of readiness to face the next state elections. He used the state's own report that '151 towns and 993 villages covering 154 out of 182 assembly constituencies in the state and 284 police stations out of 464 police stations were affected by the riots', to falsify the Gujarat chief minister's claim that the riots were localized only in certain pockets of the state.[57] The structural impartiality of the office of the CEC and its autonomy from the government of the day was demonstrated when Lyngdoh recommended that, in view of the vitiated atmosphere in the state, elections be held at a future date. He successfully resisted the pressure of the ruling party bent upon exploiting Hindu communalism in Gujarat for its electoral benefits. The National Human Rights Commission (NHRC) and the National Minorities Commission demonstrated their integrity and their autonomy by bringing to the notice of the Supreme Court the threats faced by witnesses of the pogrom in Gujarat. When,

[57] Varadarajan, *Gujarat*, p. 329.

in June 2003, the fast track court of H.V. Mahida at Vadodara, set up to speed up trials involving serious offences, acquitted, for lack of evidence, all twenty-one persons accused of killing fourteen Muslims in the Best Bakery case, the Supreme Court granted permission to the NHRC to file a special leave petition seeking the quashing of the trial court's judgement and the retrial of the case. The Supreme Court also issued notices to the central and Gujarat governments for their sloppiness in handling such cases. It asked the chief minister of Gujarat to quit if he was unable to ensure justice to the victims.[58] The secular Constitution of India continues to inhibit the exclusionary designs of ethno-religious forces.

It would be entirely mistaken to conclude from this that secular states are sufficient for building inclusive societies. Secular states are part of a wider institutional matrix and a larger public and political culture. They work well only in appropriate public, political, social, and institutional settings. For example, no secular state can work without a properly functioning regime of rights. More generally, they work only with an appropriate legal culture, one that is free from impunity. They also require a democratic culture with space for dialogue, discussion, criticism, as well as accommodation. Without these background conditions, a secular state cannot work well. Yet, a secular state, no matter how imperfect in form, can itself contribute to the creation of these wider cultures. The struggle for a secular state is related to and dependent on a struggle for an appropriate legal, rights-endowed, and democratic culture. But so is the struggle for a rights-endowed, democratic culture dependent on an appropriate way of relating religion and the state. These cultures and institutions must work in tandem with one another. One plain conclusion from this is that it is not enough to have a single short-term public policy to solve the problem of religion-related exclusion. Rather, it is important to have a package of policies, some that are to be floated together right away and others that must follow today's policies at an appropriate time. In short, every single policy must be complimented with a vision of other succeeding policies.

[58] The Gujarat High Court Chief Justice, V.N. Khare admonished Additional Solicitor-General who appeared for the Gujarat government: 'I have no faith left in the prosecution and the Gujarat government. I am not saying Article 356. You have to protect people and punish the guilty. What else is raj dharma? You quit if you cannot prosecute the guilty. It is not your personal property. If you cannot protect the property of the people, you cannot continue.' See *Frontline*, 27 September–10 October 2003, pp. 37–8.

It does not follow from what I have said that Pakistan and Bangladesh should follow the Indian model of secularism or that they should have the same set of institutional structures. This is neither likely nor desirable. No two societies can have a uniform set of institutions to prevent religious-based exclusion or to promote religion-related inclusion. All I have tried to establish is that they need to be broadly secular. I take it for granted that they will work out an institutional design suited to their own socio-cultural context, that they will be secular in their own distinctive way.

III
SPECULATIVE AND CONCEPTUAL EXPLANATIONS

9

Liberal, Secular Democracy, and Explanations of Hindu Nationalism*

The last few years have seen the growth of an enormously varied and rich scholarship on the rise of militant Hindu nationalism (Jaffrelot, Hansen, Corbridge, and Harriss, to name a few). My objective in this chapter is to fill an important lacuna in the intellectually astute and engaging explanations of this phenomenon available to us. Without building a coherent causal narrative, the first section lists some of these explanations for the resurgence of Hindu nationalism. The second section identifies an important feature absent in these explanations, namely, the normative vocabulary of liberal democracy embedded in the Indian constitution. In the next section, I argue against the view that its presence in the Indian public domain is anyway weak and wholly superficial. The fourth section, the meat of the chapter, delineates why and how it shapes the motivational structure of Hindu nationalists and how in turn they shape it. I argue that though constrained by this framework, Hindu nationalists negotiate it by stretching the criteria of the application of key normative terms such as democracy and secularism. In doing so, they seek to transform not merely the meaning of words but an entire political culture. This crucial step has

* This paper was first presented at the University of Bristol in May 2001. It was subsequently published as 'Liberal, Secular Democracy and Explanations of Hindu Nationalism', *Commonwealth and Comparative Politics*, vol. 40, no. 3, November 2002, pp. 72–96; published by Taylor and Francis.

to be undertaken by them if they are to advance any further.[1] Since a complete explanation of a phenomenon must answer not only why-questions but also how-questions, the story of this ideological battle is a crucial ingredient in a fully adequate explanation of the resurgence of Hindu nationalism and the form it assumes. At the end, I hint towards a possible discourse-related, concept-sensitive explanation of the current crisis of secularism.

EXPLAINING RESURGENCE OF HINDU NATIONALISM

What made the reemergence of a vigorous anti-secular politics possible? What has put the saffron wave on the boil? What explains its 'move from the margins to the centre'? Before I proceed further, allow me to list a set of factors, neither exhaustive nor arranged in causal hierarchy, that explain the resurgence of Hindu nationalism. My sole purpose here is to draw the attention of the reader to the missing link in the explanatory chain.

Long-term Standing Enabling Conditions

1. The availability of certain forms of identities generated by specific religious regimes in India and the presence of certain strands of Hindu nationalism within most varieties of Indian nationalisms.[2]
2. Colonial classification and enumeration that reified/essentialized communities and made their legal codification into discrete and incompatible groups possible.[3]

---

[1] This statement assumes the presence of peaceful conditions. Everything can change if militancy creates a condition of virtual civil war or, what I have elsewhere called, symmetric barbarism. See Rajeev Bhargava, 'Restoring Decency to Barbaric Society', in Robert Rotberg and Dennis Thompson (eds), *Truth Vs. Justice: The Morality of Truth Commissions*, Princeton and Oxford: Princeton University Press, 2000, pp. 45–67.

[2] Peter van der Veer, *Religious Nationalism: Hindus and Muslims in India*, New Delhi: Oxford University Press, 1996, p. 40.

[3] B. Cohn, *Colonialism and its Forms of Knowledge: The British in India*, New Jersey: Princeton University Press, 1996; S. Kaviraj, 'The Imaginary Institution in India', in Partha Chatterjee and Gyanendra Pandey (eds), *Subaltern Studies VII*, New Delhi: Oxford University Press, 1992; Thomas Hansen, *The Saffron Wave: Democracy and Hindu Nationalism in Modern India*, New Delhi: Oxford University Press, 2001; S. Corbridge and J. Harriss, *Reinventing India*, Cambridge: Polity Press, 2000.

3. The presence of an irreversible process of social egalitarianism that persistently challenges traditional hierarchies and forever throws up new interests and identity claims.
4. The institutionalization of representative democracy and its propensity to encourage ethno-religious political mobilization.

Short-term Standing Enabling Conditions
1. The presence of majoritarian democracy since the 1980s.
2. A communalized state machinery causally linked to gradual erosion of the state's commitment to secularism.[4]
3. The availability of new bargaining strategies and the opportunities to directly undermine political opponents and to brazenly manipulate symbols in the political field.[5]
4. Pervasive consumerism and an unconstrained disposition to pursue brutal self-interest (greed), fostered by the deployment of neo-liberal economic strategies.

Long-term Actions by Primary Political Actors
(Proponents of Hindutva)
1. The relentless ideological and organizational work of militant Hindu nationalists day after day, every morning, against the 'Gandhi–Nehru vision of India' and to build politically useful 'welfarist' networks in civil society.[6]
2. The sustained political manipulation of symbols of group identity to bolster the centralizing and homogenizing tendency within Hinduism and, by the simultaneous stigmatization and emulation of others, to seek not only a massive comparative advantage for a modern, centralized, semitized Hindu community but to also replace liberal, secular democracy by the Hindu *Rashtra*.[7]

Short-term Actions by Primary Political Actors
1. Ideological and political campaigns such as the Ekmatayajna and around issues such as the Meenakshipuram conversion, Babri Masjid, Shah Bano, and the missionary work of Christian organizations.

---

[4] Christophe Jaffrelot, *The Hindu Nationalist Movement and Indian Politics, 1925 to the 1990s*, New Delhi: Viking, 1996, pp. 330–7.
[5] Hansen, *The Saffron Wave*.
[6] See Jaffrelot, *The Hindu Nationalist Movement and Indian Politics*, pp. 330–7.
[7] Ibid.

2. The attractive packaging, at the right time, of historically produced notions of Hinduness.[8]

Long-term and Short-term Actions by Social Actors

1. The strategy of the Congress to alternately abet majority and minority communalism.
2. The role of the Congress in fostering Hindu majoritarianism.
3. The politicization of institutions, for short-term political gain, by the Congress party.
4. The instrumentalist attitude of Left parties to liberal–democratic institutions.

Long-term and Short-term Actions of Social Actors

1. The support given to Hindu nationalists by upper castes/middle classes to curb the rising assertiveness of hitherto marginalized classes, castes and to tackle the political uncertainty generated by it.[9]
2. Sections of Indian people support Hindu nationalism because it appears to rectify the apparently disastrous consequences of modernization and to provide solution to the atomization, anomie, fragmentation, and alienation seen to be necessary features of modernity.[10]

WHAT'S MISSING?

I have here merely mentioned these factors. It is not part of my objective to construct a story out of this list, to assign causal weights to factors, or to assess their relative significance. On my part, I find each of these plausible. However, I believe something important to be

---

[8] On this, see Hansen, *The Saffron Wave*, p. 19.

[9] Ibid. For Hansen, Hindutva is a way of imposing order on a disorderly world of democratic politics so that people can learn to live with the 'undecidable character of the social worlds they live in'.

[10] See Hansen, *The Saffron Wave*, p. 19. Because it connects meaningfully with everyday world, Hindu nationalism enables people to make sense of, and cope with, their everyday anxieties of security, a sense of disorder, and, more generally, the ambivalence of modern life. See also Harold Gould, 'Religion and Politics in a UP Constituency', in D.E. Smith (ed.), *South Asian Politics and Religion*, New Jersey: Princeton University Press, 1966, pp. 51–73, particularly p. 73, where Gould points to the support for the Jana Sangh provided by those wedded to tradition and disgruntled by modernity.

missing in these accounts. The missing feature is this: the discourse of liberal democracy that compels even Hindu nationalists to legitimate their actions in terms of its normative vocabulary.

Readers may have noticed that explanations offered thus far focus on actions and their enabling conditions. As a first step towards identifying the missing pieces in a more comprehensive explanation, we must notice the structural constraints at work. The social and political fields that disenable human beings from acting in certain ways also direct them to seek alternative ways of acting and therefore, contribute to the explanation of what they do and how they realize their objectives. For instance, Jaffrelot claims that the success of Hindu nationalists has varied with the character and performance of the Indian state. The Nehruvian state, determinedly secular, kept Hindu nationalism firmly in check till the 1960s.[11] However, over time, with the communalization of the legal machinery and of the wider public domain, a resurgent Hindu nationalism was witnessed. Going further, Hansen claims that wider constraints moulding Hindu nationalism are still at work today. For him, no matter how strongly they rely on hate speech or on violence against minorities, Hindu nationalists have had to advance, by and large, by following the procedures of parliamentary democracy and by respecting 'the judiciary, the electoral process and the rules of the game'.[12]

Indeed, both Jaffrelot and Hansen are sensitive to constraints on political actors imposed not only by institutions but by the availability of discursive genres and strategies. For Hansen, political action is conditioned by the 'structured archive of possible connotation and reconstruction available in the production of political legitimacy'.[13] Jaffrelot, even more explicitly, draws upon the work of Bourdieu and Bailey, and refers to the 'legitimating problematic of politics', to 'normative rules' by which particular actions are judged right or wrong and publicly justified or condemned.[14] I join hands with this discourse-sensitive analysis of political action because I believe, as its proponents do, that the resurgence of Hindu nationalism cannot be explained only by material interests, by the will to power or even by ideals of nationalists themselves. A sound explanation must refer to public values and norms

[11] See Jaffrelot, *The Hindu Nationalist Movement and Indian Politics*, pp. 102, 106, 165, 330–2.

[12] Hansen, *The Saffron Wave*, p. 6.

[13] Ibid., p. 27.

[14] Jaffrelot, *The Hindu Nationalist Movement and Indian Politics*, p. 106.

of justification that are constitutive of the conditions that inhibit or enable certain kinds of political acts.

Hansen clearly believes in the efficacy of certain kinds of discourses in shaping and perhaps even restricting the resurgence of Hindu nationalism. However, given his belief that liberal democracy never quite took root in India, it is not entirely clear whether, in his view, the discourse of liberal democracy is part of the legitimating problematic of politics that constrains Hindu nationalism. On the other hand, Jaffrelot's reference to the constraining power of the secular state on the activities of Hindu nationalists explicitly includes secularism as a legitimating norm. In the Nehruvian era, certain kinds of political actions were rendered impossible by the prevailing legitimating problematic. For example, the normative vocabulary of secularism frequently inhibited ethno-religious mobilization and therefore, curbed the rise of Hindu nationalism. However, over time, as secularism lost its legitimacy, the very same acts, once inconceivable, became publicly acceptable. Quite clearly, Jaffrelot has a good sense of how values and principles enable or constrain political action. By and large, only those acts which can be publicly legitimated are realizable. If an action currently inhibited by available norms of public justification is to be performed, the content of these norms must first be altered. This indeed has been done. Over time, the discourse of public justification has in fact changed, a point amply demonstrated by the erosion of secularism. Hence, the proliferation of Hindu nationalism.

I agree on the explanatory significance of public norms and values with both Hansen and Jaffrelot, but differ on an important detail. For Hansen, the constitutional discourse of liberal–democratic norms and values has never been salient in India (this is different from a more broadly conceived democratic discourse to which he does give overwhelming importance). For Jaffrelot, this discourse was once salient, but, with the gradual erosion of Nehruvianism, is now completely eclipsed. Indeed, its absence explains the rise of Hindu nationalism. For me, the discursive field set out by liberal democracy continues to shape, enable, and constrain the political strategies and discursive performance of Hindu nationalists. I believe, liberal democracy is part of the standing discursive conditions in Indian society and that, therefore, Hindu nationalists frequently possess a motive to legitimate their actions in terms of its normative vocabulary. The central objective of my chapter is to show how this is so, and to identify the actual mechanism by which this happens. Modestly stated, I wish to carry forward and fine-tune Jaffrelot's analysis and in the process, hope to bring to light the micro-level mechanisms by which Hindu nationalists are able or are disenabled from implementing and advancing their agenda. Hardly anyone disagrees about the erosion of secularism. But surely, differences can arise over the extent and outcome of this erosion and its precise mechanism. No doubt, the legitimating norms that govern Indian politics have changed but perhaps, not quite in the manner suggested by Jaffrelot. The story of their erosion is more complicated. Conversely, the sedimentation of liberal–democratic norms, both its dispersion and the depth it has reached in Indian society and polity is more than is currently believed by many academics.

DOES A LIBERAL–DEMOCRATIC DISCOURSE REALLY EXIST?

I have assumed the existence of a liberal–democratic discourse so far. But does it exist at all? Many critics believe it does not. Predictably, there are two versions of this critique, one strong, the other weak. The stronger version, that I have earlier called the cultural inadaptability thesis, and which I associate with Ashis Nandy and T.N. Madan, makes a claim that modernity, western by origin and character, is entirely alien to home-grown outlooks and can exist in India only superficially, by more or less coercive, external imposition.[15] For example, Madan argues that secularism is impossible in South Asia if viewed as a shared credo of life, impracticable as a basis for state action, and impotent as a blueprint for the foreseeable future. For Madan, secularism is impossible because it depends both on the distinction between the sacred and the profane and on the availability of a relation of equality between the two domains they inhabit. However, either South Asian religions make no such distinction or when they do, it is invariably encompassed within the sacred giving the religious a distinct priority over the secular. This makes it impossible to give equal validity to the domains of the sacred and the profane. Under such cultural conditions, secularism, born out of a dialectic between protestant Christianity and the enlightenment, cannot take root in India.

I agree with the view that modernity originated in the West and migrated elsewhere, and also with the claim that in some spheres and to

[15] On the cultural inadaptability thesis and its critique, see my review of T.N. Madan's *Modern Myths, Locked Minds* in *The Book Review*, vol. XXI, no. 8, August 1997, pp. 11–13 and Rajeev Bhargava, 'What is Secularism For?', in Rajeev Bhargava (ed.), *Secularism and Its Critics*, New Delhi: Oxford University Press, 1998, pp. 486–542.

varying degrees, it failed on its arrival to take root because non-modern cultural systems by which ordinary people lived their lives were deeply entrenched, resilient to change, and not easily displaceable.[16] However, this view fails to notice two other processes also at work in India. First, western modernity found a safe niche in these societies quite easily. To take just one example, westernization was adopted for purely instrumental reasons. Something akin to this process had begun as early as the late seventeenth century, when a section of the commercial middle class was seen to be 'clad in a more stylish garb, with a head-dress of calico-coiled turban, light vest, and loose trousers. They all spoke English, offered their services for small wages, and waited on the passengers to execute their business.'[17] A rational choice to be western was also not entirely uncommon in the early eighteenth century. Calcuttan youth, shocked by the murky excesses of traditions,

openly adopted an aggressive attitude to everything Hindu and openly defied the cannons of their inherited religion...while some of them offended public opinion by their youthful exuberance, such as drinking to excess, flinging beef-bones into the houses of the orthodox and parading the streets shouting, 'we have eaten Musalman bread'.[18]

In short, hyper-westernization became a form of protest against the filth in one's own traditions, something started by Ram Mohan Roy and continued to this day by dalits (the bespectacled statue of Ambedkar in a blue suit, and polished shoes, with the constitution in hand is an apt reminder). Quite possibly, changes in society necessitated certain functions to be performed and, in the absence of functional analogues within existing cultural systems, this role could be fulfilled only by elements within western modernity. This explains the painless, rather smooth acceptance in India of modern educational and legal systems. As early as 1841, 'it was noticed that the Chamars, despised untouchables of northern India were not afraid to bring suits against their landlords'.[19] This quick absorption of western modernity had another reason. Perhaps it contained many elements that correspond to deep mythical

[16] For a detailed argument to this effect, see Rajeev Bhargava, 'Are there Alternative Modernities?', in N.N. Vohra (ed.), *Culture, Democracy and Development in South Asia*, New Delhi: Shipra, 2001, pp. 9–26.

[17] B.B. Misra quoted in Yogendra Singh, *Modernization of Indian Tradition*, Delhi: Rawat Publications, 1988, p. 89.

[18] Charles Heimsath quoted in Singh, *Modernization of Indian Tradition*, pp. 91–2.

[19] O' Malley quoted in Singh, *Modernization of Indian Tradition*, p. 100.

structures within non-western civilizations. Despite differences on the surface, if any feature of western modernity had a deeper universal structure, its absorption was a mere formality. Something along these lines is suggested by Ashis Nandy in his explanation of why cricket, an early modern English game, gained huge popularity in the entire sub-continent.[20]

However, a second equally important process also requires attention. When western modernity began to interact with local cultural systems, something like a hybrid culture began to emerge, possibly by creative adaptation, for which an analogue can be found neither in western modernity nor in indigenous tradition. These new phenomena resemble western modern and traditional entities and can be mistaken one for the other, but they escape the interpretative grid and discourse relating to both. This cluster of newly developed phenomenon forged from western modern and indigenous traditional cultural systems begets a different, alternative modernity. In non-western societies, different modernities emerged as non-western peoples broke loose from not only past practices but also from the shackles of a particular version of western modernity imposed on them.[21]

Weaker versions do not defend the impossibility of the entry of modernity into India but claim that despite the efforts of early social reformers, the discourse of liberal democracy could not be easily transplanted or flourish on Indian soil for specific historical reasons. This point has already been well illustrated by my discussion in the first chapter, where I argued that the claim that the entire discourse of rights was detached from its individualist framework and plugged into a collectivist world view is over-simplistic. Such a view is mistaken for two reasons. First, it radically misunderstands Indian intellectual history. It buys the orientalist view that people of India conceived themselves wholly in terms of communities and that individualist self-conceptions reached India only with colonial modernity. A strong shadow of a deeply ahistorical understanding of an immutable caste structure falls patently on this perspective. It might be argued that I caricature the orientalist view. After all, does it not accept that an other-worldly

[20] Ashis Nandy, *The Tao of Cricket: On Games of Destiny and the Destiny of Games*, New York: Viking, 1989.

[21] This explains the general ambivalence of non-western intellectuals such as Gandhi and Tagore to modernity. On the relationship between modernity and tradition in India, also see, L.I. Rudolph and S.H. Rudolph, *The Modernity of Tradition*, Chicago and London: University of Chicago Press, 1967.

individualism has always been integral to the world view of Hindus and Buddhists? But this misses my point. My critique is more subtle. I believe that the orientalist does not see a non-western but this-worldly self-orientation in Indian history.

To support my claim, I provide two examples. The first comes from Vir Shaivite movement that condemned child marriage and arranged marriage, opposed caste distinctions, and opposed the intermediary role of brahmins in the performance of rites and ceremonies. Although one cannot transpose modern individualist ideas on to the twelfth century, it is hard not to conclude that some form of this worldly individualism is presupposed by this radical agenda.[22] My second example is from late nineteenth century. Henry Clark, an Evangelist, was perplexed to find that the palanquin-bearers in parts of Punjab were using tobacco even though they were Sikhs. When asked, they told him that their hard labour demanded that they refresh themselves with the *hukkas*, so when they left their homes for the town they gave up Sikhism and had their hair cut. On their return home for the winter, they paid a few annas and were reinitiated. Quite clearly, this movement in and out of religious identities is not possible without some individualist self-understanding.[23] This is why I claimed that something akin to what we now call liberalism existed in India well before the advent of colonial modernity. Anyhow, and this is my second reason, many western liberal ideas could make a considerable impact on an aspiring middle stratum of Indian society because it genuinely articulated and responded to their needs. How else does one explain the substantive liberal content in the Indian opposition to the infamous Rowlett Act that proposed the extension of emergency powers and arbitrary detention after the end of the First World War? Western individualist liberalism did not arrive in India only through the spoken or the written word but as a structural need of a modern polity. A claim such as Khilnani's that the discourse of liberal democracy could not take root in India is overstated.

A different, perhaps more subtle view is found in Hansen which notes that 'early intellectuals strove to retrieve the conceptual grammar of liberal democratic discourse from the connotative domain it had developed in the west and to implant it in the colonial context as a critique of colonial incompatibility with true universalism' and

[22] See Kenneth W. Jones, *Socio Religious Reform Movements in British India*, Cambridge: Cambridge University Press, 1994, p. 11.

[23] Quoted in Harjot Oberoi, *The Construction of Religious Boundaries*, New Delhi: Oxford University Press, 1997, p. 3.

recognizes the existence of 'a language of negative rights defined in opposition to colonial power', but finds that liberalism did not take deep roots in India as 'the discourse of rights and equality was applied almost entirely to collectivities' and therefore, the language of negative rights 'was subordinated through out colonial struggle to rights of communities to representation, separate legislation, recognition and national self-determination.'[24] But, Hansen merely asserts this claim without citing any evidence in its support. True, the language of collective rights had a visible, sometimes overwhelming presence in India but it hardly follows from this that it automatically subsumed the language of individual rights. In fact, Hansen's claim begs the question: were the two languages always mutually exclusive? Did one have to subordinate the other? Could not one complement the other, occupying and responding to different spheres of equally valuable human aspirations? Indeed, Hansen's claim sits uncomfortably with his view that the agrarian movements of the 1970s reveal that as commercialization and democratization transform class and status, the language of rights and entitlements—the right to protest, assert oneself, to be heard by the government—has become naturalized in rural India.[25] This language of political assertion and protest is part precisely of the discourse of 'negative rights defined in opposition to colonial power'.

This is not to deny that liberal–democratic discourse is in crisis in India today. Liberal institutions in India appear to be prematurely fatigued. Given the western origins of liberal democracy and its apparent distance from traditional Indian cultural ethos, and because of the increasing delegitimation of liberal–democratic institutions in contemporary India, it is tempting to believe that whatever else it might be, Indian democracy never was and never can be liberal. However, this view is not convincing. On the contrary, I believe the present crisis of liberal democracy is due in large part to its own success. The introduction of civil liberties gave voice to the mute, and the stage for action was set by the democratic process for those hitherto debarred from the public domain. They entered it with new modes of speech and action to which the initiators of liberal democracy were unaccustomed, and in numbers that greatly exceeded the tiny upper crust that led the national movement. It is no doubt true that those empowered by institutions of liberal democracy do not come from a cultural background with an obviously liberal or democratic character. However, from this it would

[24] Hansen, *The Saffron Wave*, p. 40.
[25] Ibid., p. 141.

be mistaken to conclude that this newly empowered class is wholly maladjusted to these institutions. I am more tempted to believe that a more vibrant presence of dalits and Other Backward Classes (OBCs) will change the form of liberal democracy in India, not negate it. To sum up, I stand by my claim that assertions about the absence of liberal democracy in India are grossly exaggerated, that an Indian version of liberal–democratic discourse has been and continues to be part of the standing discursive conditions, and that it provides a valuable normative resource, and therefore, in different and often unacknowledged ways, shapes the motivational structure of almost every social and political agent in India.

LIBERAL–DEMOCRATIC DISCOURSE AS A STANDING CONDITION, AS A LEGITIMATING MOTIVE

It is time to return to the explanatory narrative. So, how does the real story go, especially in conditions that have become more propitious for the consolidation of Hindu nationalism? Every society has an ethical identity or a range thereof. By the ethical identity of a society, I mean a certain kind of awareness of ourselves, constituted partly by the values and principles in terms of which we aspire to judge our collective practices and institutions. I believe the professed and projected ethical identity of Indian society, no matter how fiercely contested, is still shaped, at least partly and in some significant ways, by the normative vocabulary of liberal democracy embedded in the constitution—by the language of freedom and equality, of rights, justice, secularism, and democracy. Furthermore, I believe that the discursive field created by the constitution continues to hem in ultra-Hindu nationalists in the sense that they are continually compelled to justify their unseemly acts in terms of the normative vocabulary of the constitution.

This means that Hindu nationalists must remain constantly alert to any inimical assessment of their acts by defenders of the constitution, to meet the challenge posed by such critics and to hope to overcome it. They must convince their critics that the key evaluative terms that constitute the core of the normative content of the constitution can be used in reasonably suitable re-descriptions of actions that are mistakenly believed to be constitutionally illegitimate. They are frequently forced to point out to their critics that the standard criteria of the application of terms by which their ideological foes evaluate the constitutionality of their own actions also render constitutional the seemingly improper acts of the BJP.

Suppose then that Hindu nationalists act in a way that, on the standard interpretation of legitimating norms of the constitution, is condemned as improper, say that it violates norms of democracy, or secularism, or rights. Hindu nationalists can respond to this objection in at least two ways: either to say, so what, and who cares?[26] Or else, say that the act under consideration does not violate rights, or democracy, or secularism because these terms are not what they are standardly taken to mean but connote something different, that which had hitherto never been brought to light. They can then go on to claim that, when understood properly, by their lights, which is the only relevant way to understand them, their acts are perfectly consistent with what rights, or secularism, or democracy really mean. So they can now say, 'Look here, contrary to your claim, I really am a rights-supporter, or a supporter of secularism, or a supporter of democracy'. The pertinent question to ask is: Do they or do they not have a motive to take this second option? In short, do or do they not possess a motive to legitimate their acts in terms of the normative vocabulary of the constitution?

I believe they do, for three reasons. First, what might be called the residual normative power of the constitution; no matter how mauled, abused, or neglected, the constitution still retains instrumental value, even for Hindutva forces. Despite all its alleged shortcomings, it has after all given some space to these forces to carry forward their agenda. Second, visibly ascendant social forces such as the dalits, which even Hindu nationalists can not afford to ignore, support the constitution. For them, its language—with its grammar of rights and democracy—remains a living force because in their own distinctive yet amorphous way, they recognize it to be an integral part of the conditions that improve their material well-being. In a small but important way, the constitution really does empower ordinary people. Because it promises emancipation to a large majority of people, and captures the aspiration of those left behind or out of the processes of 'development', the constitutional discourse is a major, though not hegemonic, discursive resource.

Perhaps a comparison between the moral language of the constitution and the English language can be instructive here. English no longer enjoys the status that it once enjoyed in post-colonial India, no longer bestows privilege on its speakers as it once did, but it is clear enough to everyone that it still brings enormous material benefits. Much the same may be true of our constitutional discourse. It may

---

[26] This is exactly what many do. The point is that others of the same ilk are forced to distance themselves from such expressions of defiance.

no longer—perhaps never did—have the halo around it which the makers of the constitution thought it would or should enjoy, but, designed to give opportunity, entitlements, and a life of dignity to everyone, it has immense practical utility. People may not care much about the high theory that surrounds or informs the constitution but they can nevertheless straightaway understand how it helps improve their day-to-day existence. The political party of Hindu nationalists, the BJP, is an electorally driven, culture-sensitive party, in search of moral hegemony and looking to extend, by all possible means, its moral legitimacy across diverse groups. Therefore, wherever possible, it hopes to co-opt the language of the constitution. Since the BJP lacks complete legitimacy in the moral climate in which it finds itself, it cannibalizes other values in order to legitimate its behaviour.

A third reason is to do with the nature of the Indian middle class, the main support base of the BJP. This middle class does not act in defiance of the western world but rather in the hope of being recognized properly by western eyes. In this sense, the progamme and strategy of a party supported by this middle class is bound to be different from the behaviour of a party led, say, by Khomeni. Since the language of rights and democracy continues to be an important constituent of international norms of public justification, and a part of the legitimating problematic of the politics of western countries, it is not easily shrugged off. Those who seek recognition by the West must take care to legitimize their actions in terms of this discourse. So, in my view, the BJP does possess a motive to legitimize its practices in terms of the normative vocabulary of the Indian constitution.

To say that Hindu nationalists have a motive to legitimate their actions in terms of the normative vocabulary of the constitution is not to suggest they take the normativity of this vocabulary seriously, that they really believe in these values or principles. I am not committed even to the view that they act out of mixed motives, combining their own paramount, sectional interests with a half-hearted belief in a smattering of constitutional principles. The situation under discussion is one where acts are guided neither wholly nor partly by professed constitutional principles. Everyone, all relevant parties, the subjects of these acts themselves, the co-inhabitants of the same political field, as well as observers, share the view that political actors do not hold or follow the principles they profess. On the contrary, all evidence, including the one provided by subjects themselves, suggests the assessment of the critic to be right—their acts blatantly violate liberal–democratic principles and are frequently meant to. Yet, a need is also felt by at least some members of the BJP that an appeal to others must be made in a language wholly alien to their own ideological ancestry and that their actions be legitimated in terms of this normative resource. It is of course true that straightforward manipulation may be involved here. The real aim of Hindu nationalists is to alter the ethical identity and character of Indian politics and society. This real motive is camouflaged by putting on a mask, with as much sham sincerity as can be mustered, to publicly claim that actions condemned by ideological opponents can be easily re-described so that any disapproving judgement must be withheld. Despite these very real motives, and because agents are interested in the public legitimation of their actions, they are forced to adopt a rhetorical device, compelled to use the language of the constitution, to talk and sometimes even behave as if the professed norm, value, or principle was in fact part of their motivational set. They must pretend that their acts are in conformity with the principles and values in the normative tradition made available by the constitution.

Undoubtedly, this is a cynical and unscrupulous move, ideological in the worst sense of the term, but it recoils on Hindu nationalists in that by adopting this rhetorical device, they limit themselves only to those acts which can be so legitimated.[27] It is extremely difficult, if not impossible, for them to continue to perform acts which, despite all the manoeuvre, can never get this legitimacy. Some acts are so blatantly beyond the pale of constitutional legitimacy, possessing an unethical character so obvious and plain, that it is impossible for political agents to simultaneously adopt the rhetoric, feign sincerity, and perform them. The need for legitimation, and the hold of the rhetoric of rights, democracy, even secularism, is so strong that the performance of some acts must be forsaken. If Hindu nationalists continue to possess a motive to legitimate their actions in terms of the public, normative vocabulary made available by the constitution, then, in a sense, the conditions that prohibited certain kinds of acts in the past continue to operate even today.

[27] See Q. Skinner, 'Some Problems in the Analysis of Political Thought and Action', in J. Tully (ed.), *Meaning and Context: Quentin Skinner and his Critics*, Cambridge: Polity Press, 1988, pp. 97–118. My own analysis is directly inspired by Skinner's approach. Skinner develops his methodology primarily for the study of the history of political thought. My focus, on the other hand, is collective political action. I try to apply some of his insights to the study of political action.

However, they do not operate in the same way and their hold has certainly loosened. This has happened because an ascendant Hindu nationalism, though constrained by this discourse, has also had an impact on it. It has had to confront it, but it has no reason to follow it in spirit. It has a motive to legitimate its actions in its terms, but no motive to comply with it. Thus, many of its acts which would be inhibited in the past, can now be performed provided they can *appear* to be constitutional. If so, the same constitutional language both constrains some type of acts and is part of the enabling condition of others.[28] How has this happened or how can this be done? How do Hindu nationalists manage to perform acts which they could not possibly have performed in the heyday of Nehruvian secularism? They do this by further muddying an already muddled discourse, by generating enough confusion and ambivalence to befuddle the observer. They do this, as Skinner puts it, in an entirely different context, 'by the performance of a linguistic sleight of hand.'[29] The actors now perform an ideological trick, confounding the critic by dropping some criteria that apply in ordinary, standard cases of the use of an evaluative term but retaining others. They either try to stretch the meaning of constitutional terms or extend the range of cases to which they apply. If the strategy is to succeed, the manoeuvre has to be played delicately, with a considerable degree of deftness. Hindu nationalists must drop neither too many nor too few of the relevant criteria. If they do not drop enough, it will be obvious that the term does not apply to their acts. If they drop too many, it is again obvious that an entirely different meaning is invested in the old term, that it has been thoroughly distorted and abused.[30] Either way, it leaves the critic unconvinced.

In order to make my point, let me take as examples two key constitutional terms, democracy, which I discuss briefly, and secularism, of which I speak in some detail.

Democracy

In the constitution, the term 'democracy' refers to a complex, five-feature system in which: (i) decisions are reached by a peaceful procedure wherein (ii) the widest possible range of individual as well as group

[28] Ibid., p. 117. Skinner convincingly argues that 'any principle which helps to legitimate a course of action must be amongst the enabling conditions of its occurrence.'

[29] Ibid., p. 115.

[30] Ibid.

interests are represented (iii) by persons, elected through a system of universal franchise, (iv) who discuss and accommodate the enduring needs and current preferences of each others' constituencies, and who (v) are inhibited from arriving at decisions that may adversely affect the common interests and rights of all citizens.[31] The constitution particularly emphasizes our identity as citizens in as much that it presupposes political community and political equality, regardless of caste, religion, gender, or race, and identifies democracy with the alternating rule of temporary political majorities which must never infringe the legitimate rights of individuals or of religion-based minorities. Equality of citizenship, rule by temporary political majority, and the protection of individual and group rights are central to this conception of democracy.

Gradually, the political practice of very nearly every major political party and the sustained ideological work of Hindu nationalists has transformed the constitutional meaning of 'democracy'. The final assault has come by a deft, though not entirely planned, strategy of subtracting some criteria of using the constitutional sense of the term. Features (i) and (iii) are retained: democracy remains a system where decisions are taken by a peaceful procedure by representatives elected by all adults. But, from both features (ii) and (iv), elements crucial to the earlier view are dropped. The widest range of interests may no longer be adequately represented in the decision-making arena, and the enduring needs of individuals and particularly minority communities need not be discussed or accommodated. Dropping these features opens up the strong possibility that feature (v) is violated. If so, an entire series of outcomes are rendered possible: the exclusion of certain communities from the system, the violation of community-specific or individual rights, the infringement of the principle of equality of citizenship. The critical distinction between the temporary rule of a political majority and the more or less permanent rule by an ethno-religious majority is fudged. Democracy is identified now with majority rule. For many, it has begun to *mean* rule by a permanent majority, a system of peaceful rule by a political/ethno-religious group legitimately elected under a system of universal suffrage. It is crucial that the meaning of 'democracy' not be mutated beyond recognition. Only if some of the older criterion

---

[31] A proper analysis of the concept of democracy in the Indian constitution is still awaited. However, for a broader and insightful understanding of this issue, see Granville Austin, *The Indian Constitution: Cornerstone of a Nation*, New Delhi: Oxford University Press, 1966.

continue to apply do enough people remain convinced that the actions of political groups and the system generated by them are democratic. So, democracy remains an important ingredient of the legitimating problematic; only it now means something very, very, different.

Secularism

Secularism provides my other example. In the third chapter, I outlined the distinctive conception of secularism to be found in the Indian constitution and in the best practices of the Indian state. I argued that the Indian state is anti-theocratic and against the establishment of any religion. In this sense, it upholds the separation of the state both from the ultimate goals of different religions and from organized religious institutions. The state in India is set up to establish peace between communities, to uphold religious liberty of individuals, the autonomy of religious practices of religious communities, and the same bundle of political rights of all citizens regardless of their religion. At the same time, it rejects the idea that separation must be understood as mutual or one-sided exclusion. It also eschews strict equidistance. Instead, it adopts a sophisticated stance of principled distance. It might help to summarize the main features of Indian secularism (Table 9.1).

TABLE 9.1: Main Features of Indian Secularism

Feature A	Anti-theocratic
Feature B	Disestablishment of religion
Feature B1	No legal recognition to religion
Feature B2	The separation of state institutions and religious institutions
Feature B3	The separation of state personnel and religious personnel
Feature C	Principled distance of the state from all religions
Feature D	Peace and prevention of barbarism
Feature E1	Religious liberty of individuals to criticize and challenge their own religion
Feature E2	The liberty of an individual to reject the religion into which he is born and to embrace an another religion
Feature E3	Equality of religious liberty
Feature E4	The autonomy of religious groups to maintain or change their religious practices as they deem fit
Feature F1	Equality of passive citizenship: to physical security, minimum material well-being, to ordinary life with dignity
Feature F2	Equality of active citizenship: to vote and to hold public office
Feature F3	Equality of active citizenship: to deliberate freely in the public domain

The state in India is not merely anti-theocratic but opposed, in principle, to the establishment of religion. Furthermore, it keeps a principled distance from religious institutions for the sake of peace between communities, the religious liberty of individuals, and where relevant, the religious autonomy of communities (rights of religious minorities). It eschews establishment also to uphold equality of citizenship—to maintain the ordinary and dignified life of *all* citizens and to protect the political rights of every citizen to vote and to deliberate on the common good, irrespective of their religious affiliation.

However, over the years, and particularly due to the sustained work by BJP ideologues, the term 'secular' has become unrecognizable. Secularism now connotes a political strategy underpinning the practices of a non-theocratic state by which it: (i) maintains peace between communities (Feature D); and under certain conditions, within specified limits, (ii) protects the religious liberty of individuals (part of Feature E). The BJP frequently cites the absence of communal rioting during their tenure as evidence of the secular character of states governed by it.[32] However, by persistently attacking the social and cultural rights of religious minorities, Hindu nationalists have snapped the link between secularism and minority rights. Furthermore, thanks to the change in the meaning of democracy, the connection with (F) is almost completely broken. If secularism is just (D) and part of (E), then it is fully compatible with the privatization and depoliticization of non-Hindu religions and the deprivatization and re-politicization of Hinduism. Full citizenship rights now depend on ethno-religious allegiance and need not be distributed equally. Principled distance (Feature C), too, can now be reinterpreted to mean the distance of the state from religious institutions for the sake of communal peace and religious liberty of individuals and is compatible with the public–political presence of the majority religious community. In short, secularism is now indistinguishable from the ideology of established states (Feature B is virtually cancelled). Much of the spade work for this complete distortion of secularism was effected by the gradual fudging of the difference between secularism and multiple-establishment (a confusion also generated by publicizing secularism as equal respect of all religions) and then, due to a further distortion of the meaning of multiple-establishment. The complicity and practice of most

[32] It is another matter that violence in the public domain ceases precisely when its cynical, manipulative perpetrators manage to achieve what in the first place they had used it for, namely, radical communal polarization.

political parties ensured that multiple-establishment became a system that pampers the self-appointed, wholly non-accountable leadership of the fanatical fringe of almost every religious group. Secularism was now identified with the alternating appeasement of extremist religious groups. Once the connection of secularism with norms of equality and justice was obliterated and secularism identified with this peculiar form of multiple-establishment, not much conceptual work was required to force the term to mean simply (A), (D), and a narrowly interpreted (E 1), that is, a non-theocratic state with an overwhelming allegiance to the dominant religious group that, under conditions of inequality, still manages to maintain a modicum of peace.

Unlike the meaning of the term 'democracy', this piecemeal chopping of the criteria for the use of the term 'secular' has defiled the term beyond recognition, so much so that it is hard for even the most gullible to believe that its current connotation could be one of its possible meanings. It blatantly, in every conceivable way, infringes the idea of equality—of equal respect for religions or equality of citizenship—that lies at the heart of secularism. No matter how hard one tries, it is rather hard for anyone (for both who defend and oppose it) to stomach the view that secularism *means* a formal alliance of the state with the religion of the majority. This irretrievably abuses the term. Hindu nationalists first tried to bolster and popularize this bizarre meaning, retain the positive, evaluative tone of the term 'secular', and coined the negative term 'pseudo-secular' to designate other more pertinent meanings. But when this strategy did not work, they abandoned this irreparably damaged term or altered its 'speech-act potential'; instead of expressing approval, it is now frequently used to condemn certain morally defensible views and actions (for instance, respect for the rights of minorities and justice for all).

Once secularism and democracy were conceptually complementary, now they are presented as mutually exclusive of which we must choose only one. If democracy means the rule of an ethno-religious majority, a view that is part of middle class/upper caste common sense, and further, if the conceptual link cannot after all be snapped between secularism and equality (and therefore, equality of citizenship/minority rights), a conceptual association also part of their common sense, then, given the current conjuncture of meanings, a choice between democracy and secularism is inescapable. And herein lies the crisis of secularism. Paradoxically, the very resilience of the original meaning of secularism plunges it into a deep crisis.

I have argued that because of the presence in India of a liberal–democratic discourse, Hindu nationalists have a motive to legitimate their acts in terms of its normative vocabulary. However, they possess an even stronger motive not to comply with its principles. This gives them an equally strong motive to change the criteria of their application. Without dropping the use of these terms, and much to the horror of committed constitutionalists who immediately see through the trick, they seek to appropriate this discourse and stretch, indeed over-stretch, the meaning of key terms. In altering the meaning of terms, they transform a whole political culture. I believe this change in political culture is a necessary condition of their takeover of the political arena and the state. The story of the relationships between this discourse, the major political actors in India, and the broader political arena which they inhabit is an irreducible part of a comprehensive explanatory narrative of the resurgence of Hindu nationalists. Without it, we may possess a loose, passable grasp of why they do what they do but not a tight enough grip over how they do it. Without it, the mechanism at the micro-level will continue to elude us.

One final word: a subterranean cultural rebellion has been underway for a long time. Ultra-Hindu nationalists have been painstakingly chipping away at the discourse they oppose. But, it is intellectually lazy and politically foolish to literally write off the discourse of liberal democracy. Because it is there, it can be retrieved, refashioned, reinvigorated.

10

The Ethical Insufficiency of Egoism and Altruism

*India in Transition**[1]

There is much that troubles me about the India I personally know and occasionally read and hear about (I mean the middle and upper class, middle and upper caste, predominantly though not entirely urban

* A version of this paper was first presented at a Seminar on Egoism and Altruism organized by Professor Surendra Munshi in Calcutta in 1999 and soon after at a conference organized by Rajendra Vora and Suhas Palshikar on behalf of the Department of Politics and Public Administration, University of Pune in January 2000. It was subsequently published as 'The Ethical Insufficiency of Egoism and Altruism: India in Transition', in R. Vora and S. Palshikar (eds), *Indian Democracy: Meanings and Practices*, New Delhi: Sage Publications, 2003, pp. 215–31.

[1] This chapter attempts an understanding of contemporary India, normally achieved by empirical and interpretative skills only available to social scientists. I hope to take an alternative route of pursuing an acceptable form of philosophical practice: take an issue of interest, begin by focusing on intuitions, impressions, and personal experience related to it. Then, with familiar tools of conceptual analysis and philosophical argument, arrive at a considered judgement. I concede that an understanding arrived at in this manner may be lopsided but I cannot dispel my impression that some facets of the issue cannot be illuminated by conventional social science alone. I apologize to those readers who may find the discussion excessively personal or even philosophical. It is in part a personal and in part a formal essay, combining a conversational, first-person voice with a detached, general third-person account. I thank Tani Sandhu and Valerian Rodrigues for helpful discussion on the chapter and Anthony Stephen for helping me cope with the excesses of an idiosyncratic computer.

India). To articulate this unease, I will begin with an example. A few years ago en route to university, driving on the then wide and spacious Ring road, I was nearly hit by a Maruti car that dashed out from a side lane. I brought my car to a screaming halt, sprang agitatedly towards the offender and asked him if he knew that the driver on the main road has the right of way. Completely unruffled, he replied without much ado, 'jo jis road par chalta hai, wahi road uske liye main road hoti hai'. At that time I used it as an example to teach my students the meaning of relativism. But, it can as easily be used as an example of the reigning moral insensitivity and egoism that characterizes Indian society today. The movement of traffic in the city of Delhi is only a symptom of a much wider social malaise. The growing insensitivity of the middle class to the poor, the sick, and the aged is another example. On an entirely different plane, consider the demands for reservations by sections of the jats in Rajasthan, the more aggressive form of nationalism and the overall rise of communalism. What all these examples share is an excessive concern for the individual or communal self, together with complete disregard to the sensitivities and interests of others.

A very worrying aspect then about this particular India is that it is ravaged by egoism; it is rare to find for its own sake a concern for others, at least in the public domain. There is a pervasive belief that something must be *wrong* with people who are not motivated by self-interest because they *should* be guided only by it. It is as if an active concern for others is blacked out from their ethical conceptions. So, this impression of a rampaging egoism is my initial claim and the starting point of the chapter. The first section explains how this claim is to be understood. In the next section, I try to answer why India is in a vice-like grip of generalized egoism. My brief answer, which I attempt to substantiate through the agrument of this essay, is that such unabashed egoism is likely in societies transiting from a hierarchical to an egalitarian social order. The third section asks what could be done about this. It seems obvious that among other things, egoism can be checked by the rehabilitation of inter-personal morality. This can be achieved by transforming current practice and by designing appropriate institutions. Equally imperative is the articulation of an alternative vision of non-egoistic practices and institutions. The normative political theorist has a job cut out for him. I argue that if a non-egoistic ethical vision is to motivate real flesh and blood people in India then it must abstain from being excessively other-regarding. Moreover, it must specify the proper form of the other-regarding domain. Clearly, any attempt in an egoistic society to formulate a moral vision shuns hard-nosed realism. My point is that it must also eschew utopian thinking.[2] Let me sum up these claims.

1. India is ravaged by a full-blooded egoism.
2. This is always highly likely in societies transiting from hierarchy towards an egalitarian order.
3. In my view, altruism, which is insufficiently ethical to the same degree and gravity as egoism, cannot check this egoism. Rather, egoism can be checked by the rehabilitation of the other-regarding (moral) domain, so long as it does not take an improper form or make excessive demands.

ETHICS AND ITS DIMENSIONS

I must clarify some key terms and draw a few distinctions before I proceed any further. Always and everywhere, human beings relate to each other and the world around them and, howsoever minimal, diffused, and inarticulate, they relate to themselves. In short, their attitudes and actions can be divided into three kinds: those which are self-oriented (intra-personal), those oriented towards other persons (inter-personal), and finally, those oriented to the non-personal world (impersonal). Invariably, some relations are seen as possessing greater importance than others. This judgement is made with the help of what may be called a framework of strong evaluation.[3] This framework tells us whether or not something is to be valued; if valued, what its value consists in and why it is valued. Consider first the intra-personal domain. Here the framework illuminates the kind of life or activity that is worth pursuing, what the ultimate ends of life are, which character and virtues command respect of those around us and are worth nurturing and therefore, what our dignity consists in. Typically, in the inter-personal domain, we ask what obligations we have towards others, how diverse social purposes are to be harmonized, what mechanisms of conflict resolution are to be deployed. I use the term *ethics* to refer to this framework of strong evaluation and, irrespective of the domain to which they belong, to all the entities evaluated by it (the intra-personal,

[2] I am using the term 'utopian' in the sense given to it by Thomas Nagel. For Nagel, an ideal is utopian if reasonable individuals cannot be motivated to live by it. See T. Nagel, *Equality and Partiality*, New York: Oxford University Press, 1991, p. 21.

[3] Charles Taylor, *Sources of the Self*, Cambridge, Massachusetts: Harvard University Press, 1989, p. 4.

inter-personal, and impersonal domains when brought within the framework of strong evaluation become part of what I understand by ethics). The strongly evaluated inter-personal domain, I shall refer to as the *moral* dimension of ethics.

An ethic specifies what we value and what we don't in ourselves, in others, and more generally, in the world. Ethical conceptions have this positive and negative dimension. However, there can be a purely negative ethic, call it nihilism, for which nothing is valuable—the world itself has no intrinsic value. At the other extreme, lies a truly universal ethic wherein every fundamental type of entity in this universe has intrinsic value. Ethical conceptions may be inclusive as well as exclusive. A universal ethic is entirely inclusive. By definition, an exclusive ethic excludes some types of entity from what it conceives as having intrinsic value. For example, nihilism is a purely exclusive ethic. Between a purely negative ethic such as nihilism and a universal ethic lies a continuum of ethical conceptions that are inclusive or exclusive in varying degrees. A humanitarian ethic, true to its name, must hold that the entire human species has intrinsic value, but it excludes from its domain of value, other living species as well as inanimate matter. Conversely, a positive, non-nihilist ethic that is misanthropic can be imagined. For such an ethic, every other thing in the world is intrinsically valuable, but not human beings.

Self-interest

In this essay, I take self-interest to be the key category in the intra-personal domain. Interest refers both to the awakened attention with which we attend to something, as in the phrase 'taking an interest in', as well as to the good of the subject whose attention has been awakened towards it. Self-interest then is the awakened attention of the self towards its own good, howsoever this good is defined. This awakened attention to one's own good may lead one to desire it when it is absent, to actively pursue it in order to attain it, and to have positive feelings towards it when in fact it is achieved.[4]

It is possible for there to exist interests of the self in which the self takes no interest. Likewise, there can be interests of the self in which others take an active interest. To attend to the good of another person, without regard to self-interest, one's own good, or advantage, is what I

⁴ Thomas Hurka, 'Self-interest, Altruism and Virtue', *Social Philosophy and Policy*, vol. 14, no. 1, 1997, pp. 286–307.

276 India's Secular Democracy

take to be the key category of the inter-personal domain. This awakened attention to the good of another person may lead one to desire it when it is absent, actively pursue it so that it is attained, and to have positive feelings towards it when the other has attained it.

It is important that self-interest, in the sense outlined earlier, is distinguished from a primitive, positive relationship that one must have with oneself and which I believe is a condition of achieving minimal agency and personhood. Let me explain. In order to undergo a coherent experience, to hold on to beliefs and desires that propel me to act and to move my body in alignment with any of these beliefs and desires, I must have a positive relationship to myself, a positive self-orientation.[5] I do not think it helps to conflate this positive self-relation with self-interest. Indeed, this positive self-relation should be seen as an essential background condition of psychological self-preservation. Without it, other higher goods conditional upon it can never be realized. Each one of us must give greater weight to this good of ourselves than to any other good, whether of one's self or of the other. This natural partiality to ourselves is a condition for securing self-interest as well as the interest of others.

Poor and Rich Conceptions of Self-interest

Hitherto, I have hardly said anything about the real content of self-interest. Self-interest, I said, is interest in one's own good. But how is this good to be understood? I suggest that there are two basic ways of understanding the good of the self that I call the poor and the rich conceptions of self-interest. By a poor conception of self-interest, I mean one outside the framework of strong evaluation. On the poor conception of self-interest, there is nothing to differentiate between what is good for me and what I happen to desire. Values, in this view, are nothing but contingent desires that human beings just happen to have. When the interests of human beings are reducible to these given, unevaluated desires, then we have a poor conception of self-interest. A person who is compelled to switch on the television every time it is within reach and who indiscriminately watches whatever is televised has a poor conception of self-interest. Since to be ethical, an entity must

[5] Although even these minimal conditions of agency and personhood depend, at one level, upon other agents and persons, the primary responsibility for accomplishing this minimal agency and personhood remains with the subject in question.

be strongly evaluated, a poor conception of self-interest is unethical or at least non-ethical.

In contrast, a rich conception of self-interest depends upon and is informed by the language of strong evaluation incorporating qualitative distinctions between worthwhile things and those that merely are desired or valued weakly. A person with a rich conception of self-interest pursues worthwhile projects. A person habituated to indiscriminately watching every serial on television can hardly be said to be engaged in a worthwhile project. Likewise, the life of a socialite who party hops day after day can hardly be said to be worthwhile. The same cannot be said to be true of a person who is actively engaged in the lives of a small circle of what Aristotle called virtuous friends. Since such friends add worth to a person's life, and make it meaningful, only someone with a rich conception of self-interest can have virtuous friends. A rich conception of self-interest includes the interest of a person in being accorded dignity and self-respect, in having a secure environment for the protection of one's language, culture, or religion, in developing the fullest possible capacity for practical deliberation, and in realizing one's life plans or ground projects.

It is clear that the possession of a rich conception of self-interest is not purely a subjective phenomenon, not something merely felt or desired intensely. Meaning and worth are generated or discovered by strong evaluation that necessarily involves a distinction between something that is merely felt, intensely desired, or weakly valued and anything else that has worth independent of either or all of these.

Egoism

It is now time to elucidate the basic structure of egoism and altruism. Egoism is a non-nihilistic, largely exclusive, predominantly negative ethical conception for which only persons have possible value and within this sphere of persons, only one person has value, namely, the self.[6] All other persons are without value, have significantly lesser value than one's own self, or possess only instrumental value. It is an ethical conception because it deploys a framework of strong evaluation. It is non-nihilist because it does, after all, find something valuable! It is

[6] Jean Hampton, 'The Wisdom of the Egoist: The Moral and Political Implications of Valuing the Self', *Social Philosophy and Policy*, vol. 14, no. 1, 1997, pp. 21–51.

largely exclusive because there is only one entity it finds valuable, and largely negative because it finds all other entities worthless.

A number of things follow from what is stated. First, the absence of a strongly evaluated inter-personal domain makes egoism immoral or at least outside the moral domain. Egoism altogether lacks a moral dimension. Second, depending upon his conception of self-interest, an egoist may be rich or poor. When a person leaves behind a poor conception and develops a rich conception of self-interest, he does not necessarily acquire a moral dimension. Rich egoists may be as immoral as poor egoists. Some people argue that if we enrich our interests and acquire ground-level fundamental commitments, then we are justifiably exempted from morality. I take the opposite view that a properly worked out morality legitimately excludes the pursuit of certain rich interests. Third, we must note that the structure of egoism may be found at each of the three levels generated by what are called the boundaries of the self. The boundary of the self may be circumscribed by a particular biological organism with a specified spacio-temporal location that has its own psychological states. This generates individual egoism. It may extend further to encompass several such biological organisms and their psycho-social states. This generates what might be called communitarian egoism or what is called communalism in India. Such communitarian egoism may be focussed on the family, the caste, the religious community, or the nation. For communitarian egoism, only particular communitarian selves and individuals who partake in it have value. Finally, we have what we might call species egoism, for which while the whole of humanity is valuable, other living or non-living things are worthless. I hardly need to add that each of these three forms of egoism have their rich and poor varieties. Besides, any given society may combine one or the other of these, say, poor individual egoism with rich communal egoism.

This is an opportune moment to remove possible misunderstandings. An agent does not become an egoist if his internal motivations include positive self-relation. Far from being so, this, I claim, is a necessary condition of personhood. Egoism, in the sense relevant here, is anyhow an ethical conception about the value of motivations, dispositions, and character, and not a view about what human nature, agency, or personality *is*. Furthermore, a person who positively evaluates or pursues self-interest is not necessarily an egoist. To love one's good for its own sake rather than instrumentally for its consequences is not egoism. Nor, finally—and this is not always properly recognized—to act out of disregard for others a sufficient condition for egoism. Egoism prevails only when an act disregarding others is propelled by the deeper belief that others have no intrinsic value. A world without ethical egoism is not a world that has banished every act opposing the interests of others nor is it a world where self-interest is not pursued.

Let me offer some examples to illustrate my point. Suppose that before two persons, X and Y, lies an apple (an apple stands for any scarce resource). While X already possesses six apples, Y has none. Both X, who is greedy, and Y want the apple. Y, disregarding the current interests of X, takes it. Though X has pursued his self-interest at the expense of Y's interests, she is not an egoist. Take another example. X and Y are travelling in a compartment of a fast moving train. Neither can leave the compartment. X smokes but Y does not because he suffers from asthma. Y requests X not to smoke but is disregarded. Y snatches the cigarette from X and throws it out of the window. She has acted, protecting her interests and disregarding the interests of X but she is not an egoist. These are not fanciful examples of philosophers. The poor who suffered in the Orissa cyclone and looted food reserves of local *baniyas* because of the complete breakdown or corrupt functioning of the public distribution system can hardly be called egoists.

Altruism

Unconditional altruism, or altruism for short, is a non-nihilistic, largely inclusive, and predominantly positive ethical conception which recognizes the value of all persons but one, namely, one's own self. For altruism, the self may have an instrumental but no intrinsic value. While the interest of the other matters in itself, self-interest is entirely insignificant. This view of altruism and egoism appears to confirm common sense evaluations that tell us that egoism is bad but altruism is good. Closer examination reveals this to be untrue. Let me explain. I argue that any workable ethic must have an intra-personal and an inter-personal dimension.[7] Moreover, it must attempt to strike a proper balance between the two. However, it does not follow that it achieves this balance automatically. Not finding the proper balance between the two, some conceptions emphasize one dimension over the other. Thus, we might say of a conception purporting to be ethical that it is insufficient because it under-emphasizes one or the other of its dimensions. We might say that an ethical conception is *gravely* insufficient if it is entirely

[7] For this discussion, I shall ignore the world-related impersonal dimension.

blind to one of its dimensions. Egoism is gravely insufficient because it is immoral. The insufficiency of altruism is equally grave because it is entirely self-effacing.

I view altruism as somewhat symmetrical in structure to egoism but in content it is very opposite. Its structural symmetry lies in the fact that, like egoism, it is an ethical conception that places exclusive value on persons. It is the exact opposite of egoism in that it values precisely what egoism devalues, namely, other persons, and undervalues what egoism overvalues, that is, the self. Here, too, some clarifications are in order. Altruism is not just the name for a set of other-regarding motivations. An act motivated by a concern for others is not altruistic, not even one motivated entirely for the sake of the other. When, without regard for our own interest, we act for the aged, the sick, the physically challenged, and for children, we are being profoundly moral and not altruistic in the sense outlined earlier. To keep the formal symmetry with egoism intact, altruism exists only when an act for the sake of others is also moved by a deeper disregard of self-interest. Altruism is an ethical conception that necessarily involves selflessness to an extreme. It must be self-effacing, self-denying, and self-abnegating. For me, altruism is best typified by Nita, the central character in Ritwik Ghatak's *Megha Dhaka Tara*.

WHY GENERALIZED EGOISM?

I have hitherto spoken as a philosopher. Perhaps it is time now to wear the cap of the social scientist. This is so, quite simply, because motivations and conceptions are held by people within distinct social structures. A particular cluster of social relations reshapes these motivations and alters their precise import. By this, I mean two things. First, our conceptions may be distinct but still be mutually interdependent. We may be moved by different motivations but the reason why I am moved by *my* motivation may depend entirely on the kind of motivation that underlies *your* action. More concisely, I may be an egoist only because you are an altruist. There may exist a causal/constitutive nexus between altruism and egoism. Second, this nexus between my egoism and your altruism may exist entirely because of our distinct positions within the social order. In some types of social orders, my altruism may be a reason for you to be altruistic too, but this may not be so in other social orders. I believe precisely this in the case of hierarchical societies.

Let me explain. Consider a society with a small number of egoists. Will not the life plan of egoists be boosted if a great many people neglect their own interests and devote time and energy to to serve the egoist?

This makes, of course, for a remarkably unethical society in which a few egoists are served by an army of slaves and saints. The few live by egoism, the many by altruism. The 'herd' must live by morality, but 'men of distinction' are exempt from it. No doubt both the egoist and the altruist live by their distinctive ethical conceptions, but in realizing his distinctive life plan, the altruist simultaneously realizes the life plan of the egoist. This is the nexus between altruism and egoism.

What is the character of social relations that sustain this nexus? I suggest that such a nexus frequently presupposes a profoundly hierarchical order. A large number of people can be entirely self-abnegating only when they genuinely believe that their worth as persons is significantly lower than that of others. Likewise, people can be excessively self-regarding when they come to believe that their value is significantly higher than others and these others believe this too. Unconditional altruism is a plausible world view for people without a sense of self-worth, who believe their desires to be unworthy. In a hierarchical order, where it is widely believed that people are born or are intrinsically superior or inferior, this precisely is the case. In such societies, egoism is the natural ideology of the 'superior', and equally naturally, altruism is the ideology of the 'inferior'. A society with caste or gender hierarchy is an obvious example.

What happens when such a hierarchical order begins to collapse, when ideas of natural superiority and inferiority are delegitimized? In the first phase of such a transition, those with a belief in their natural superiority over others can hardly be expected to give up egoism. However, I believe, individuals and groups who hitherto believed in their natural inferiority but are on the verge of acquiring self-worth will cease to be altruistic. They will start to think in terms of self-interest and are likely to model their own conception of self-interest after the only conception of it available in their society, that is, the egoist one. On any reckoning, therefore, the collapse of a hierarchical order tends to usher in a period of generalized egoism. This point can be reformulated. Hierarchical societies are arenas of massively repressed desires over a long, long period that have not even been expressed, leave alone been fulfilled. When such inegalitarian societies disintegrate, as indeed is happening in India today, there is a glut of desires and any constraint, legitimate or otherwise, is likely to be brutally set aside. Since each person's desire has begun to count for as much as anybody else's and must therefore be satisfied, there are simply no holds barred on the means deployed to satisfying them. Anything will do and indeed does.

In such a social environment, generalized egoism and moral vacuity is not surprising or unexpected.

In the context of societies moving away from hierarchy, an attack on altruism, viewed as the legitimizing ideology of the other-regarding actions of lower classes, women, or lower castes becomes an important constituent of a nascent egalitarianism. Not surprisingly, to break the altruist–egoist nexus, the early liberals put forward the idea of universal self-interest, even though it was rather poorly conceived.[8] For them, the egalitarian idea of reasonable self-interest lay between the unrestrained egoism of a few superior beings and the unlimited altruism of the greater number of so-called inferior beings. Liberals argued that it was wrong for a great many people to persistently forsake the fulfilment of their own desires to indiscriminately satisfy the whims of a few people. The interests of the self are as valuable as the interests of others. It is entirely legitimate and morally permissible to be motivated by a concern for one's own self. For people accustomed to the denial of their own desires and moved only to benefit others, shame and guilt must accompany the first stirring of self-interest. This is why early liberals openly declared that it was not shameful to pursue personal advantage and that self-interested action is not ethically degrading.

However, it is not desire alone (the poor conception of self-interest) that is liberated from the crushing burden of altruism. Recall that altruism generates a loss of self-respect, self-worth; indeed, the very sense of self within the 'inferior'. Frequently, it threatens the most fundamental and primitive relation with oneself, the natural partiality of the self mentioned earlier. An anti-altruistic assertion of even poorly conceived self-interest frequently accompanies the re-discovery of self-worth and an affirmation of self-respect. However, the art of valuing oneself is accomplished generations after a people have formally ceased to be subordinate. Lack of self-confidence and ambition bears negatively not only on the ability to perform well or achieve objectives ordinarily realized in society but also adversely affects the manner in which the altruist relates to other people. Persistent altruism turns people into willing doormats. The pursuit of self-interest can stop at the drop of a hat and the altruist can slip into the 'normal business' of attending to others. The birth of an egalitarian society does not abruptly end subordination but is just the beginning of self-retrieval.

[8] Albert O. Hirschman, *The Passions and the Interests*, Princeton, New Jersey: Princeton University Press, 1977 and Stephen Holmes, *Passions and Constraint*, Chicago and London: The University of Chicago Press, 1995, p. 42.

I have claimed that underlying a poorly conceived egoism there already exists, even at the individual level, a rich conception of self-interest. At the level of local communities, the content of egoism is richer still. Why is this so? Altruism is the general ideology of subalterns in hierarchical societies but not the only ideology by which they live. Subaltern groups live also by local norms that regulate their internal lives. The collapse of altruism is likely to be replaced by generalized egoism at the individual level and to propel local norms to the status of potentially generalizable ethical conceptions. Henceforth, every group tries unabashedly to openly realize its own conception of the good conceived in exclusive, communal terms.

Indeed, by a deeper mechanism, individual and collective egoism is pushed even further. The French sociologist, Tocqueville, drew attention to this mechanism linked to the process of equalization. Tocqueville argued that when people hitherto debarred from the public arena, enter it for the first time, they bring along not only their poorly conceived self-interest but also their norms. A diverse people naturally bring diverse sets of norms. Two features accompany this proliferation of norms. First, a greater dogma in adherence to a particular set of norms. In the face of different, potentially conflicting norms, people wear their own norms on their sleeve flamboyantly. This fosters collective egoism. My norms are the best, so says everybody, but this ostensible confidence is matched by a second feature. A deep-rooted uncertainty grows around them. If they are not the *only* valid norms, perhaps they lack any validity altogether. So, it is an interesting psycho-cultural fact about humans that when they are face-to-face with innumerable principles, all which are uncertain, they tend to fasten on to material interest and prejudice because amidst everything evanescent and effervescent, at least these provide an anchor of bedrock support. So, both poor individual egoism (the pursuit of pure material interests) and rich collective egoism (sustained by prejudice) proliferate. It is not surprising, therefore, that a core morality with an impartial content is disregarded.

HOW TO CHECK EGOISM AND ALTRUISM?

All right, something akin to an epidemic of egoism, a poor egoism at the level of the individual and a rich egoism at the level of community exists. What can be done about this? Hard-nosed realists would abandon political theory and seek a modus vivendi; a workable, merely pragmatic arrangement among egoists. But egoism has to be fought because of its grave ethical insufficiency and moral vacuity. This requires a change in attitudes and a desire to develop institutions that sustain non-egoistic motivations. In short, a non-egoistic ethic needs to be worked out. Plainly, one job cut out for the political theorist is to identify the political and moral ideals of such an ethic. However, it is crucial that these ideals be such that creatures for whom they are meant can be persuaded to accept them. The problem of egoism needs a solution with an identifiable ideological content and a list of possible institutions to sustain it. This is the big task ahead of political theory, particularly in India. But the smaller task, possibly within immediate reach, is to provide a form of such a solution.[9] In what follows, I try this out.

Allow me to briefly mention three possible solutions to the problem of egoism, all of which I reject. The first, the solution adopted by the hard-nosed realist, has already been mentioned earlier. For the hard-nosed realist, the pre-theoretical, commonsensical reactions and intuitions of the addressees places irredeemable constraints on the very possibility of a normative solution. If egoism has already become the common sense of society, then it is unreasonable to expect any change in the motivational structure of such a people. To ask them to be different is to expect a complete and impossible transformation in their character. Thus, for the hard-nosed realist, it is useless to expect people to leave behind their egoism, concern themselves with the interest of others, or attain any degree of impartiality. Not even to a slight degree is abstraction from identity or alienation from ground projects possible for the collective egoist. Since ethical conceptions with moral content require some or all of these, such a conception is ruled out in a society of egoists. If so, the hard-nosed realists say, a solution must depend on the fears and vulnerabilities of egoists. No matter how unfair the outcome, one cannot expect more. In my view, this solution takes an overly pessimistic view of our society, confuses egoism with the legitimate pursuit of self-interest and paradoxically, has a profoundly unrealistic estimate of the growing demand and need for justice in our society.

The second solution conflates egoism with the legitimate pursuit of self-interest and altruism with the pursuit of the interest of others, though it recognizes their respective importance as well as potential conflict. It seeks to resolve this conflict by enlarging the conception of the self. By making the interests of different selves causally as well as

---

[9] Readers are likely to detect here a strong influence of Thomas Nagel. I am deeply indebted to his writings for the rest of the essay.

metaphysically interdependent, this solution argues that self-interested action advances the interests of others. Likewise, acting out of altruistic motives is a way to advancing self-interest. On this view, which Brink calls metaphysical egoism, similar to what I call communitarian and species egoism, loving someone else is a special case of self-love.[10] I grant that this eudaemonic conception is true for 'significant others' and provides a necessary corrective to views that see a permanent, irreconcilable conflict between self-interest and the interest of others. However, its scope is far too narrow. No matter how enlarged the self is, some separation and therefore, conception of the other is bound to reemerge and with it, the irreducible distinction between self-interest and the interest of others. When this happens, metaphysical egoism, that relies on self-extension, is bound to fail.

A third solution admits the irreducibility of the interests of other persons, exaggerates its significance, and ends up by altogether swallowing self-interest. It recognizes the need for impartiality but has an entirely awry form. For example, objective reason may discover the right solution to the problem of egoism but fails to meet baseline constraints set up by what Flanagan calls the principle of minimal psychological realism—a principle which requires that when constructing a moral theory or projecting a moral ideal, we must ensure that the character, decision processing, and behaviours prescribed are possible, or are perceived to be possible for creatures like us.[11]

It is important not to mistake the principle of minimal psychological realism for hard-nosed realism. For the latter, we must always take people *exactly* as they are, as if permanently locked in the state they happen to be in. On the other hand, for minimal psychological realism, 'what is right must be possible, even if our understanding of what is possible can be partly transformed by arguments about what is right'.[12] Thus, the third solution, which ignores this principle, is the diametric opposite of hard-nosed realism. If strong realism will not budge from people as they are, utopianism will not take any cognizance whatsoever of the motivational structures of people and the possibilities of change or resistance within them. Familiar examples of such utopian thinking

[10] David O. Brink, 'Self-love and Altruism', *Social Philosophy and Policy*, vol. 14, 1997, pp. 122–57.

[11] Owen Flanagan, *Varieties of Moral Personality*, Cambridge: Harvard University Press, 1991.

[12] Nagel, *Equality and Partiality*, p. 26.

come from utilitarianism that confuses impartiality with impersonality and detaches desires and preferences from 'what they are in fact attached to',[13] certain versions of Kantianism for which agents ought to set aside their personal interest in every conceivable ethical situation or Marxism that seeks to create new persons by an impersonal transformation of social individuals as if they were creatures without personal motives. A similar utopian solution is to be found in what Charles Larmore calls political expressivism, for which ideals valid in public life must be valid in personal life as well.[14] For example, for some utopian views, neutrality is not a political but a more general moral ideal.[15]

In opposition to the hard-nosed realist and the metaphysical egoist, I claim that we need an irreducible domain of the interest of others for their own sake. In short, the moral dimension of ethics needs to be rehabilitated without feeling squeamish about it. This moral dimension must be freed from unconditional altruism and must not be allowed to assume a utopian character. What then is the proper form of morality in an egalitarian society which would save us from the ethical failures of both egoism and altruism?

I reckon that in order to fight individual and collective egoism, a morality must satisfy two conditions. First, it must not set up an irredeemable conflict between self-interest and the interest of the other. To succeed in this endeavour, it must become an integral part of a larger ethic rather than become a self-contained 'institution of morality'.[16] Such an ethic must be impartial and from this impartial standpoint, must give due weight to both self-interest and the interests of others. In short, it must necessarily be egalitarian. An egalitarian ethic, in turn, implies the following: (i) it must treat all individuals as equals; and (ii) in

[13] Flanagan, *Varities of Moral Personality*, pp. 32–8.

[14] Charles E. Larmore, *Patterns of Moral Complexity*, Cambridge: Cambridge University Press, 1992, pp. 73–6.

[15] One must note here that it is not mere abstraction from individual self-interest or community identity that distinguishes utopian thinking from non-utopian thinking. Some abstraction from one's own interest and identity is crucial for a proper recognition of the legitimate interest of others. What distinguishes utopianism from non-utopian thinking is that it over-abstracts or abstracts the wrong kinds of things, in the wrong kind of way. Quite clearly, all varieties of utopian thoughts mentioned factor out things which should be factored in, for example, self-interest, or else assign a disproportionate weight to things factored in, for example, the interest of others.

[16] Bernard Williams, *Ethics and the Limits of Philosophy*, London: Fontana Press, 1985, p. 6. Also, chapter 10.

relevant respects, it must treat all groups as equals. Treating individuals as equals implies the granting of equal rights to basic liberties, to fair and equal opportunity so that those with the same abilities have the same chance in life and, more controversially, the implementation of what Rawls has called the 'difference principle'.[17] It certainly means guaranteeing a dignified life to all and therefore, a commitment to meet the basic material needs of every person in society. It also requires immediately addressing the most urgent needs of the poorest. I cannot see this happening without a relatively impartial state that implements a progressive system of taxation. Some qualities of affirmative action are required to realize even a limited egalitarianism.

Treating groups as equals requires that there be a state not merely negatively or passively tolerant but one that proactively encourages equal respect. In India, this means working out a variant of secularism finely tuned to the rights of religious and cultural groups. It follows that secularism in India cannot endorse a simple model of individual citizenship that implies too strong an abstraction from one's collective identity. Checkmating collective egoism is possible in India more by a reform of communities rather than by their neglect or elimination.[18]

The second condition flows from some remarks made earlier. If morality with an impartial, other-oriented content can work only when it is an integral part of ethics, and if, further, a large number of distinct ethical conceptions exist in society, then it follows that the idea of universal justifiability must be rejected.[19] Such a rejection is implicit in Rawls' notion of an overlapping consensus.[20] A common moral content can be agreed upon, provided it does not come from a single source or is reached by a single route. This gives the freedom to explore distinctive ethical traditions to reach an overlapping moral content. In a country like India with its legendary diversity, something like this is crucial.

[17] John Rawls, *A Theory of Justice*, USA: Oxford University Press, 1971. The difference principle is this: social and economic inequalities are to be arranged so that they are both: (i) to the greatest benefit of the least advantaged, consistent with the just savings principle; and (ii) attached to offices and positions open to all under conditions of fair equality of opportunity.

[18] See my 'What is Secularism For?', in *Secularism and Its Critics*, New Delhi: Oxford University Press, 1998, pp. 486–542.

[19] Larmore, *Patterns of Moral Complexity*, pp. 73–6.

[20] John Rawls, *The Idea of an Overlapping Consensus in Political Liberalism*, New York: Columbia University Press, 1993.

IV

FEAR AND HOPE

11

The Right to Culture*

Cultural rights are the latest addition to the type of rights available to humans. It is not uncommon to claim that apart from civil, political, and socio-economic rights, humans also have a right to culture. But this claim is fraught with difficulties. First, the bearers of these rights are widely seen to be groups not individuals. Second, the right to culture appears to be a right to all kinds of practices that are in deep conflict with other, often more basic, individual rights. The right to culture is controversial, to say the least, and needs to be asserted with caution, subtlety, and some unavoidable qualifications. I need hardly add that the controversy around cultural rights is not just an academic dispute but one that many societies, particularly India, face acutely, literally on a day-to-day basis. In India, we need to urgently address if people, especially groups, have a right to culture, under what conditions, and why. Above all, I hope to tackle this question because of its crushing political urgency.

A few clarifications are in order before I come to the main substance of this piece. First, this chapter does not purport to explain social and political events; rather, with the help of some conceptual clarification and by tidying up an already existing argument, it proffers some prescriptions on what, in some crisis situations, can be expected from ourselves and from the state. In other words, this is part conceptual and part normative exercise. Second, it is only addressed to those who are

* This paper was first presented at a seminar on communalism organized by Social Scientists in New Delhi between 29 and 31 March 1990. It was subsequently published as 'The Right to Culture', in K.N. Panikkar (ed.), *Communalism in India*, Delhi: Manohar Publishers, 1989.

willing to be co-opted into a discourse of rights. It is directed primarily at left–liberals, including those Marxists with a toehold in the framework of rights. Perhaps, all those committed to our constitution form the audience of this essay. Any one who espouses the language of force and violence rather than speak with reason and argument may well quit reading any further. Why persist in appealing to those who have casually sidestepped parameters set by the constitution or those who refuse to listen to argument? At best, the essay is in the conditional mood with an argument that hopes to work in the following way: if you adopt the framework of rights, then you must also accept some of its presuppositions and implications. Moreover, the argument relies on the idea that even our ordinary modes of thinking and speaking secrete deeper anthropological and ethical commitments of which we may not always be aware. It also accepts that a relation exists between words and the social world. Social things are what they are, at least partly, by virtue of the descriptions they possess. Therefore, it matters what we call them. Descriptions of things in part determine our orientation towards them and even our evaluations. These are very many largish things to keep in mind but necessary to specify if only to render defensible the charge that the essay does not address itself to real issues or to people who matter most.

Let me begin by again drawing attention to three situations that must persistently trouble any reasonable person: the ban on *Satanic Verses*; the immolation of Roop Kanwar; and the Shah Bano case. I wish to raise a specific question in relation to these issues: how is a leftist, who also takes his liberalism seriously to respond to these situations? How is he to react to a setting in which: (i) the majority in a community seeks a ban on a work of fiction on the ground that it offends their religious sensibility; (ii) a teenage girl is said to perform sati on the alleged plea that she is intentionally enacting an age-old, much revered custom; and (iii) women of a particular religious group are denied alimony because this is impermissible under the Islamic law. An initial, intuitive reaction of the left–liberal is to dismiss these actions as medieval, primitive, and obscurantist. His enlightened sensibility treats all religious practices as humbug and some of these, including those under discussion, particularly offensive. Since his liberalism permits the use of the language of rights, he might claim that such practices violate individual rights, particularly those of women. Since a liberal state is committed to the defence of such rights, he would seek state intervention on such matters.

Another set of intellectuals argue, however, that such leftist response is radically mistaken, it mindlessly follows mainstream western thinking on these issues, and therefore, it is Eurocentric. In short, it simply fails to understand what is going on here. The term 'understand' is to be taken in all its philosophical seriousness. To not understand these situations is to bypass the internal descriptions of the participants of a culture, to fail to grasp the way religious people conceive their own specific situation. It is to overlook the self-perceptions of the agents, their own complex intentions, motivations, and orientations. In brief, here is an implicit attempt to finesse the self-understanding and interpretation of participants by forcing upon them an external framework that is completely out of tune with their beliefs and value judgements. This total failure of understanding shows the bankruptcy of the leftists, so the argument goes, who cannot see that, given their conceptual world, what the agents do is just the right thing to do. Furthermore, if what they do is right in the context, then within that context, they have a right to perform that action. After all, a group of people possess a right to follow their own customs and practices, live in accordance with their idea of how lives ought to be led. Taking recourse to the same liberal discourse on rights, these intellectuals, enraged by what they take to be the blind rationalism of the left, go on to claim that a people have a right to their own culture. If they take their liberalism seriously, so the argument goes, leftists should recognize this right. Indeed, if they do not hold their liberalism in bad faith, they should leave these people alone. Rather than seek state intervention, they should demand that the state must let these people decide what is good for themselves. Is it not true that what is wrong for some is right for others. After all, in matters of ethics, no indisputable facts of the case exist. If so, the state should be neutral in these matters. Liberalism, correctly understood, recognizes cultural rights and demands that they not be violated. Some such reasoning that has wide academic respectability can be marshalled in support of the statements made by some Congress ministers in favour of the Muslim Women's bill.

So the leftist is vulnerable to the charge of having misunderstood a radically different standpoint, of misconstruing another culture, and therefore, of not being liberal enough. Charged with failing to give due recognition to the cultural rights of a group and faced with this attack, the leftist who also takes seriously the discourse of rights must begin afresh his search for arguments that adequately defend his position or conclude that his socialist commitments are at odds with his liberalism, that it really is impossible to have your cake and eat it too.

But, one must first ask if an implicative relationship exists between understanding a culture and granting its members a right to their culture. The aforementioned argument trades on an ambiguity in the notion of right to which many political theorists have drawn attention but which is insufficiently noted in political arguments.[1] To begin with, an improper use of the word 'right' must be immediately disposed of. A person blandly asserting that he has a right to X is taken merely to mean that he is bent upon making some good, benefit, or opportunity his own, or that come what may, he will act in a certain way. This use is wholly inappropriate because rights are claims which must be buttressed by some argument, reinforced by reasons. A person must in principle be able to offer a reason (other than that he just wants to) supporting his claim that he has a right to have, do, or be something. But here no reason is given at all. A demand that is not backed by reason is outside the framework of rights.

Second, and more relevantly, it might be said that a person has a right to do something because it is the right thing to do in the circumstances. This is precisely the sense which is relevant in cases cited earlier. It is even an acceptable sense of the term because here at least some reasons are on offer. Even so, these reasons are subjective and strongly contextual. They implicate no more than a subjective plea to be left alone; a far cry from a rationally grounded assent from others. The political and philosophical sense of the term, on the other hand, is much stronger. When an individual claims to possess rights with respect to something in this stronger sense, he must be able to advance reasons against interference in any matter concerning that thing, even if the costs of such non-interference are greater than the benefits to be had from interference. For example, when an individual asserts that he has a right to read pornographic literature, he must be able to muster enough reasonable backing for his claim that he be free to do so, as well as enlist in support strong justification against any interference with this indulgence, even if there exists reasonable certainty that generally people will be much better off if pornography were banned. Likewise, a group must be able to offer reasons against interference with its

[1] See, for example, Ronald Dworkin, *Taking Rights Seriously*, London: Duckworth, 1977, p. 188.

practices that offset the social costs involved. They must obtain rational consent from others that interference is unjustified despite problems caused by these actions.

In this conceptual framework, rights threaten consequentialist reasoning, challenging its legitimacy by recruiting the help of even better reasons. And these reasons are better, at least partly, because their force is accepted even by others. In other words, rights are always buttressed by arguments and reasons that can be intersubjectively validated. It follows that an enormous abyss lies between the claim that for Y, x is the right thing to do in the context and the one that it is Y's right in the strong sense to do x. Furthermore, a leap across this chasm, from one claim to another, is not licensed by logic. The second one simply does not follow from the first. For example, when we say that it was right for a poor man to have stolen bread, we do not necessarily endorse (although we may) the claim that he has a right to steal bread. Similarly, we might, under some circumstances, think that it is right for a person to take the law in his own hands but from this it does not follow that we approve that he has a right to do so. Understanding has an implicative relationship only with the weaker sense of right, not with the stronger, politically more relevant sense. If this is true, then understanding another culture by no means binds us to granting members of that culture a right in the stronger sense. Clearly, the critic possesses a successful case against the original left position only by equivocating on the term right, by working with its weaker sense. Left–liberals can therefore claim to understand a culture without granting its members a right to many of its practices.

This answers one set of critics but the left–liberal may face yet another quandary. The critic might now concede that understanding a culture has no necessary bearing on the issue of cultural rights, but still argue that left–liberals must grant any community a right to culture. This time the leftist who takes his liberalism seriously gets into a bind not because of his liberalism but on account of his leftism. That it is not due to his liberalism can be easily seen by acknowledging that for traditional liberalism, no such thing as a right to culture exists. This is so for at least two closely related reasons. One, a right to culture is believed to be a collective entity but for liberals, collective rights cannot exist. This flows from the liberal commitment to individualism, to the view that only the individual defined in abstraction from other individuals is the final source of moral and cognitive authority and therefore, he

296 India's Secular Democracy

alone is the ultimate unit of moral worth. A commitment to individualism leaves no room within the liberal framework for the notion of collective rights because collective rights flow from what Hegel called *Sittlichkeit* or ethical life, from the ongoing customs, practices, and mores of a community, all of which an individual rather than invent, merely discovers. Since the community has no life of its own and lives solely through individual members who constitute it, it cannot, by definition, come into conflict with the claims of particular individuals.

A second argument also stems from the liberal tie to atomism with the difference that it accepts the possible existence of collective rights but not their autonomy from the more basic individual rights. It contends that if freed from their bondage to individual rights, collective rights can always be used to abridge individual ones and that is a distinctly illiberal thing to do. For example, each individual has an equal right to citizenship. But this basic right can be violated when cultural or minority rights are secured. Consider as an example the policy of restricting property ownership in Kashmir only to Kashmiris. Such restrictions are imposed also on the plea that Kashmiris possess a collective right to maintain their distinct cultural identity and this would be disturbed if people with different cultures are free to settle in what has traditionally been their homeland. Liberals might argue that, constitutional propriety apart, this violates the individual right to property. This particular use of the argument might appear pernicious but any pretence that there is something intrinsically invidious about it can be unmasked by pointing out that the white South African regime also uses the argument from minority rights to support Apartheid. Rights of culture, so the argument goes, are always used to restrict or violate individual rights. Therefore, they cannot be accommodated within a liberal framework.

Should a leftist with liberal leanings fight his critics by denying, like the traditional liberal, the right to culture? I believe that a left–liberal has no conceptual resource for denying such rights. Not only that, I also believe that he *must* accept the existence of such rights. While the traditional liberal position is just what suits the proclivities of right-wing individuals who make a fetish of abstract individualism, leftists must uphold the thesis that an individual is what he is only by virtue of his socio-cultural context, that the distinctively human capacities of moral agency and rationality are shaped by and therefore depend upon culture, that complex beliefs and second-order desires are individuated by social context, and that beliefs and purposes exist not simply as states of minds in the heads of individuals but are embedded directly in social practices and institutions.[2] Now, one might ask what all this has got to do with the issue of rights. The answer to this query is simple. To grant rights to creatures is to accord them respect, to view them as agents who deserve respect and this is so only on account of certain capacities possessed by them.[3] But if this is so, people must not only have the right to do this or that thing but also the right to develop those capacities that enable them to do or be anything at all. Since capacities require a socio-cultural context, can only be sustained collectively by a group—as the thesis about the social nature of beliefs, purposes, and skills shows—people must have the right to develop and bolster the culture on which these capacities and therefore, their distinctly human identity depends. Only in a rich and stable cultural context can we be aware of who we are, identify the precise nature of the situation surrounding us, and assess the availability of options. The meaningful exercise of human choices depends crucially upon a cultural context.[4] In brief, the right to culture flows from a position, which takes both its leftist and its liberal credentials seriously.

It appears now that the critic of the left–liberal position has succeeded in demonstrating a blatant inconsistency in the initial position of the left–liberal. The left–liberal denies that certain groups have a right to their culture but his own principles commit him to the existence of precisely such a right. The left–liberal may well find strange and foolish the cultural practices of a different group but he must leave them as they are, must not strive to change them. This for the reason that the concerned group has a right to follow its own customs and practices and leftists who take their liberalism seriously must not interfere with them. Liberalism, it appears, restrains the leftist from intervening in

---

[2] See Charles Taylor, *Philosophical Papers, Vol. 2*, Cambridge: Cambridge University Press, pp. 187–210.

[3] Ibid.

[4] As I read these two sentences, I felt that this language is precisely what Will Kymlicka uses in his justly famous book, *Liberalism, Community and Culture*, Oxford: Oxford University Press, 1989. As far as I know or remember, I had not read Kymlicka's book when I wrote this article, in India, in the same year. My argument about culture is derived from Charles Taylor's work as well as from my own thesis on methodological individualism. Yet, the resemblance of the idea expressed here with Kymlicka's formulation is so striking that I must have picked it up in Oxford possibly from Yael Tamir who was working on her thesis on liberal nationalism at the same time as I was labouring on a critique of methodological individualism. [Footnote added in this volume]

these situations. It is interesting that it is only the left–liberal who is caught in this jam. Intervention is open to an insensitive colonizer, to the dictator, or to the right–liberal, either on the ground that rights do not exist or on the plea that at least the right to culture does not. Since he takes his liberalism seriously, the left–liberal recognizes the existence and desirability of rights. And because of his rugged commitment to a leftist view of the 'social', he recognizes the existence and desirability of the right to culture. It is only the left–liberal, therefore, who appears to be trapped in this dilemma. But is he?

I think not. Stating why this is so needs further examination of the notion of rights. As I have already pointed out, rights involve rational claims advanced by groups or individuals for something against other competing, rationally justified contentions for the same or any other thing by other individuals or groups. It follows that rights function only in a context of rationally defensible arguments in situations of overt and covert difference. Moreover, they presuppose a specific conception of man, one in which rationality and autonomy are his most significant capacities. We might say then that the discourse of rights presupposes a specific culture of rights that encourages the desirability of some rather than other capacities and bolsters some ways of living in opposition to others. One might ask just what this culture of rights is? This question needs a very long answer but a shorter one can at least be this: a culture of right presupposes the existence of differences. Also, a commitment to settle these differences peacefully and through reason. It also accepts that all circumstances are not equally propitious for resolving these differences by reason. However, it insists that the cost of an enforced settlement is greater, at least in the long run, than the cost of accepting unresolved differences. The notion of rights is, therefore, culture-laden. To accept the language of rights is to proclaim, in the same breath, an obligation to sustaining this culture. A left–liberal who takes his liberalism seriously is no doubt committed to the right to culture but only as long as it is compatible with this culture of rights. Surely, people have a *right* to their culture but only on condition that they abjure doing anything that threatens the very presuppositions that sustain that right.

We are now beginning to have an answer to our initial query. The left–liberal response to hysteria over the publication of the *Satanic Verses*, to the Shah Bano case, and to sati must begin with careful understanding of the motives and intentions embedded in relevant cultural practices. But, it cannot end by legitimizing them. Even if, given the beliefs and practices of the relevant communities, the hysteria is perceived to be inevitable, alimony seen to be impermissible, and self-immolation judged to be fully in accordance with norms, even if it is right for people to behave and react the way they do, the left–liberal cannot grant them a right to behave or react in that way unless intersubjectively valid reasons are offered for those actions. Furthermore, he must be convinced that they operate within a culture of rights. There must be some evidence that a framework of rights is present in their culture or that it has been adopted. If no such evidence exists, then, no matter what they say, they do not grasp the concept of right. And, people who do not grasp the concept of right cannot have a *right* to their own culture and to whatever practices are sanctioned by that culture.

Much the same applies to a political group that denies the presence of differences which do in fact exist, or that insists on a resolution of these differences by threats, force, or violence, or that is too impatient to live with differences and therefore, opts for obliteration rather than concessive settlement. Members of such a group may use the word 'right' but know nothing of its sense. Racists, fascists, and die-hard communalists often induct the term 'right' into their discourse but either use it in bad faith or with total, deliberate dishonesty. At best, they do not understand the full import of the discourse of rights. If racists and fascists were ever serious about rights, they would not seek violent solutions to settle differences. Similarly, if communalists were really committed to the framework of rights, they would neither propagate an ideology of enforced homogenization nor seek violent methods of resolving conflict of interests. In general, all these political groups often refuse to acknowledge differences, which others believe to be crucial for their identity. When they do recognize the existence of differences, they find it difficult to amicably settle or live with them. They claim to be fully rational and autonomous themselves but do not grant these capacities to others outside their group. In brief, they have no culture of rights.

Groups that have a legitimate claim to the culture of rights are deeply at odds with those without that legitimacy. It follows that left–liberal discourse competes for the same political space with a discourse based on the ideology of force and violence or with any framework that denies individuals and groups their preferences for no manifest and reasonable consideration. Indeed, left–liberals and, say, fascists and communalists are not fighting for the same political space as much as battling for the very assumptions of that space. For example, they are not competing within the framework of the Indian constitution as much as fighting over the very nature of that constitution. If that indeed is so, then a host of consequences follow. A left–liberal must earnestly fight anyone—an individual, group, the majority community, or even the state—who has abandoned the discourse of rights, and in this battle, enlist the support of all those who have some commitment to it. Furthermore, a liberal state cannot afford to be neutral between two groups, one of which accepts and the other denies this discourse. For example, in a multi-religious society, a state, if it has any serious liberal intentions, cannot be neutral between two groups, one of which works within the framework of the constitution and the other that subverts it.

Now, it might be objected that all this is no great news. But, recall what was stated very early in the essay: it matters what we call something, what descriptions things have. There is an enormous difference between the bland assertion that I must follow my way of life and the claim that I have a right to lead a life that I deem fit. Those who use the language of rights, must, if they are at all serious, go whole hog and accept the cultural presuppositions of rights. If their ideologies do not permit this, then a serious conflict is bound to emerge that can only be resolved if one or the other is abandoned. If they forsake the framework of rights, then they must also admit to have entered an arena that is bound by different rules.

12

Secular States and
Religious Education

*The Indian Debate**

This chapter addresses the following question: should religious education be available in schools funded by the state? More specifically, I am concerned with the vexed question of the relationship between religious education and secular states. It is obvious that in theocracies and in states that establish religion, all schools must impart religious education and get state funding. The issue of whether or not this should be done will never arise in such states. But in secular states, this question is important and urgent. Therefore, I raise it here, though I deal with it contextually, as it presents itself in India, as well as from a particular angle, the perspective of normative political theory.

Before exploring this issue, I must specify what I mean by religious education and then ask if, in modern societies, religious education should be available in any kind of school. And before addressing this question and even more hastily, I must specify what I mean by religious education. Religious education means a deeper, more thorough understanding of the cumulative tradition of a particular religion and by cumulative tradition I mean, the historic deposit of the past religious life of the community in question: temples, scriptures, theological and philosophical systems, dance patterns, legal and social institutions, moral codes, myths, and so on, anything that can be transmitted from one person or generation to another and that even a scholar (an outsider) can

* This paper was first presented at the East West Center, Hawaii in June 2005.

grasp more or less objectively.[1] Education *in* the cumulative tradition of a particular religion is different from education about it. Education in religion is part of the larger process of religious instruction, the whole purpose of which is to initiate the child into a faith or to strengthen it if she already has it. Education about the cumulative tradition may be possessed even by the outsider. Hence, the phrase 'religious education' is ambiguous between education in (religious instruction) and education of the cumulative tradition of a religion.

With this clarified, let me return to the question: should religious education be available in any kind of school? For those who hold the mainstream enlightenment view of religion (or at least to one version of it), all religious education is religious instruction and religion, quite simply, is a storehouse of superstition and obscurantism, inculcates blind acceptance of authority, and undermines any capacity for independent thought. The true function of education, in this view, is to impart a sense of individual autonomy (critical thinking, independence of thought) and the core value of citizenship (openness, capacity to deliberate and to listen to others, reasonableness, respect for difference, solidarity, a sense of justice, inclusiveness, and accommodation), features believed to be central to a secular vision. Religious education, it is claimed, undermines both. Thus, subscribers to this view, the hard secularists, argue that religious education must not be part of the curriculum of any school, public or private. Rather, there must be *one* common school which provides only secular education to believers and non-believers.

That this view is unrealistic, over-simple, and one-sided is hardly worth stating because it is undeniable that humans have an interest in relating to something beyond themselves, that for many this means relating to god or some god-like entity, that they do so in different ways, and that this manifests itself as individual belief and feeling as well as social practice in the public domain. Furthermore, religions constitute cumulative traditions[2] and are a source of the identity of many people. Yet, to accept all of this does not endorse the view held by dogmatic believers who wish all children to be sent to one common school that provides only or predominantly religious education (religious education here is, once again, equated with religious instruction). This view is found in theocracies and in states with established religions and is

[1] Wilfred Cantwell Smith, *The Meaning and End of Religion*, Minneapolis: Fortress Press, 1991, pp. 156–7.

[2] Ibid., pp. 154–69.

generally forgetful or neglectful of the oppressiveness, injustice, and violence of these traditions. Here, in this chapter, I try to steer a middle course. No doubt citizenship and individual autonomy are important, but it does not follow that all parents in any society would want schools to build only good citizens for the future. Parents might have a strong commitment to their identity as citizens and may wish to transmit this commitment to their children, but they may also have other equally strong, if not stronger commitments and, given the significance of religion to the lives of many persons, they may even have strong religious convictions. Parents may wish to transform their children into believers as much as they might wish that they became citizens. Therefore, they would be keen to pass on these convictions to their children.

But why cannot this transmission take place at home? Why must we depend for this on institutions of civil society? One reason is that parents may wish this transmission to be enduring which is not possible without formal and systematic training and may not themselves have the time and qualities required for such training. Second, even when they have time and inclination, they may additionally require the help of formal teaching and curriculum to supplement instruction at home. Thus, they may wish religious education to take place in schools. Third, the tradition may be so rich that it can be taught only by institutions much larger than the family. Once the value of limited religious education in schools is accepted, we are still left with the question: which type of school? Is it to be conducted in common schools, as part of or in addition to secular education or in separate schools run by religious communities on their own? And, should these separate schools be, nor merely run, but also funded by religious communities?

The argument for separate schools has been furnished by both religious believers and secularists. There are important reasons why believers might want separate religiously affiliated schools for their children.[3] First, parents might want that languages, history, art, and politics be taught from a religious perspective. Second, they might want to send children to religious schools to give them a deeper sense of their community identity. In the context of a larger, non-community oriented world in which the pressure to de-link oneself from one's community is ineluctable, this need may be felt by members of any religious community. But, it is felt particularly by members of minority

[3] Jeff Spinner-Halev, *Surviving Diversity*, Baltimore: The Johns Hopkins University Press, 2000.

religious community who may wish to establish their own schools in order to protect the identities of their members. Protection of minority cultures and religions may be possible only when children are taught within their community. For example, a religious community is marked by rituals and celebrations of faith. Public schools, where religious communities mix with one another, may be insensitive to the special religious needs of one community and may make it difficult for children of that community to participate in its common religious life. If Muslim students are educated in schools run by Muslims, then they may not feel out of place when participating in their own practices, rituals, and festivals, as they might had they studied in a common school (for example, Friday is of special importance to Muslims as it is not for, say, Christians and Hindus). Third, religion and morality are often intertwined. To be a believer is not just to have certain kinds of beliefs but to possess certain kinds of moral qualities or virtues, to develop a certain kind of moral character. This, it may be felt, can only be done in separate schools.

However, arguments in favour of separate religiously affiliated schools rather than religious education in common schools may also come from an entirely opposite angle, from those who are suspicious of religious education or at least are less positively inclined towards it. Suppose then that secularists and religious believers equally accept the importance of religion, of even the importance of religious education in schools, it might still provoke the question: why should not parents interested in religious education send their children to religiously-affiliated private schools of their choice? Why should religious teaching/instruction be permitted in schools run and funded by the state?

This and other related issues were debated in the Constituent Assembly of India. In the assembly, the case against religious instruction in state schools was made on four grounds. First, the financial cost of providing such education is borne by citizens who do not benefit from it. In an egalitarian and democratic society, public funds raised by taxes must not be utilized for the benefit of any particular religious community. Thus, consider a school established by a district board that gives religious instruction in Hinduism on the ground that a majority of students in the area are Hindus. This violates the given principle because it requires that children of Muslims and other religious communities not attending religious instruction in Hinduism would nonetheless pay for this instruction. But why should they carry this unfair burden? The cost of religious instruction must be borne by the religious community itself. As K.T. Shah put it, all the funds for the provision of religious education must be supplied by the community that desires it, not by everyone.[4] Since state schools are publicly funded, religious education must remain a wholly private affair.

But, what if the state provides education not in one but in all religions? Several arguments were put forward in the assembly against this proposal. First, as Shah argued, in a liberal, pluralist, and democratic society, secular education frequently conflicted with specialized religious instructions. Though Shah did not elaborate his reasons for this view, they were not hard to discern. In the first place, religious instruction usually teaches students obedience but not the art of questioning. Second, it frequently inculcates insulation from the rest of the political community. The boundaries of religious and political communities do not always coincide. Loyalty to one may conflict with loyalty to another. These limitations obstruct the growth of students into good citizens of a free, democratic society. It is the function of the state to educate children to become good citizens and discourage anything that undermines this process. A state may allow the presence of schools that are detrimental to the value of citizenship, but surely it cannot permit this to occur in educational sites that belong to it! Second, a point made by Ambedkar: given that many religions claim that their teachings are the only right path for salvation, social peace, and harmony are bound to be disturbed when doctrinal controversies are brought into the public domain.[5] Social peace is possible only if all religions publicly declare that they do not have monopoly over ultimate truth or are publicly silent on this matter. Since religions that believe that they have monopoly over ultimate truth cannot publicly deny it, the most that can be expected from them is that they do not publicly assert this belief, but remain silent instead. This means that the doctrines of such religions must not be brought into the public domain. It follows that instruction in these religion should not be permitted in publicly funded institutions. Given, further, a commitment to egalitarianism, it follows that no religious community should be given the right to religious instruction in state aided institutions.

A third related objection came from those who feared that religious instruction exacerbates communalism. K.T. Shah wanted the article concerning religious instruction to be framed keeping in mind not sects

[4] *The Constituent Assembly Debates, Vol. VII,* 8 December 1948, Lok Sabha Secretariat, New Delhi, 1999, pp. 877–8.

[5] Ibid., pp. 883–4.

and denominations as they might exist in some ideal world but as they really are. Really existing sects and denominations frequently forget the basic truth of all religion, he argued, and 'exalt their own particular brand as any advertiser in the market lauds his own wares'.[6] Renuka Ray, argued that religion 'had been exploited and prostituted [sic] in the country and has lead to the worst horrors that could be perpetrated in the name of religion'.[7] Similarly, R.K. Sidhwa, a Parsi member, argued that

the religious books of the various communities are translated by various authors in a manner that has really brought disgrace to religion. The authors have translated the beautiful original phrases to suit their own political ends with the result that today on religious grounds, the country has broken into various pieces.' Therefore, 'under existing circumstances, there should be no religious education provided in any educational institution which receive state aid.[8]

Sidhwa, pointing out several instances of the preachings of communal hatred in the name of religion, argued that unless the meaning of religious education is specified in the constitution, the same hateful religious education may be taught. The constitution cannot give people 'the freedom to teach religion in any manner they like'.[9] A fourth practical difficulty was raised by several people. In a multi-religious society, it is physically impossible for the state to make provisions for the teaching of all the religions. Under these circumstances, the only solution is to avoid religious instruction in state-aided schools. Finally, there was an argument propelled simply by anti-majoritarian impulse. For instance, most Sikh members supported a total ban on religious instruction in educational institutions maintained wholly out of state funds because they feared that this inevitably favours the religion of larger communities. Indeed, some wanted the ban to be extended to the media.[10]

It appears then that in a pluralist and democratic society, only common schools should be supported by the taxpayer's money. All right, it might be said, religious teaching should neither be altogether banned from all schools nor be permitted in state schools, but can we allow some public funding for privately run schools with religious affiliation? At first sight, it appears, the correct answer is to reply in

[6] Ibid., p. 877.
[7] Ibid., p. 878.
[8] Ibid., p. 906.
[9] Ibid.
[10] Ibid.

the negative. After all, arguments against public funding of religiously-affiliated schools are similar to arguments against religious education in state-run schools. If it is impermissible for state-run schools to provide religious education, how can it be proper for states to give financial support for religious education in private schools? Would an affirmative answer here not imply an exaggerated sense of the power of states and a correspondingly lower estimate of the power of private institutions to do so? If the object of our concern is the threat to liberal and democratic values, then we must attend to the source of this threat, whatever that might be. If religiously affiliated private schools undermine liberal and democratic values, then ways must be found to discourage them to the same degree, in much the same manner as we might wish to prevent states that pose a similar threat. If so, should a secular state not intervene in these institutions? Should it not discourage them by refusing to publicly fund them? This kind of argument proves at best that religiously-affiliated schools and state schools do not deserve public support to the same degree, not that they do not deserve any support whatsoever. To arrive at this conclusion, we must show these arguments to be so strong or invincible that they rule out even a disproportionately small public funding of private, religiously affiliated schools. For instance, it must also be shown that religiously affiliated schools always violate liberal and democratic values. Only then will even partial funding of religiously affiliated separate schools be unjustified.

So, does no justification exist for even the partial funding of separate, religiously affiliated schools? The answer to this question depends, as I said, on the assessment of arguments against religious education. Consider first the argument of unfair burden. This argument is sound if funding is provided to schools run by only one religious community but loses at least some of its force if funding is given to schools run by all religious communities. Moreover, this argument assumes that separate schools impart only religious education. This is almost always not the case. Most educational institutions run by a religious community teach much more than religion, which remains only a fraction of the overall curricula and, in many schools, is not its dominant feature. Should financial support not be given to the secular part of education in such schools? If religious communities had originally set up schools to teach their respective religions, and if secular education is publicly funded, would it not place an unfair burden on religious communities if they were to also support secular education in their schools? Why, for instance, should a school lose public funding for science just because it holds a few classes for the purpose of teaching religion? It is not illegitimate for taxpayers to pay for good quality secular education in all schools. In any case, others are unfairly burdened only when denied entry to such institutions. If admitted, and if they can partake equally of its non-religious curricula, then, they more or less pay for something from which they clearly benefit. The unfairness of the burden is also considerably lessened if those who study in such schools or colleges are exempt from instruction in the dominant religion of these institutions. Perhaps an element of unfairness continues to persist if public grants are given to some but not to other religious communities, but if available on a non-preferential basis to all religious communities, then nothing much remains of the argument that partial funding of educational institutions run by religious communities imposes unfair burden on other citizens of a society.

What about the argument that majoritarianism may be fuelled when educational institutions that impart religious instruction get funding from the state? Given its dominance in civil society, is it unlikely that the majority religious community will hog large chunks of state funds for its own educational institutions? If so, will state funding not help the majority community? However, there is an equally good argument that without partial funding of educational institutions of minority communities, the majority will benefit at the expense of minorities. If a particular religious community dominates a society, then it does not need public funds or especially created religion-centred schools to ensure community boundaries. When the majority of students and teachers come from the same religion, then the ethos of most public schools will be that of the majority. In such situations where the dominant ethos is permeated by the culture or religion of the majority, the minorities may feel estranged, and feel as misfits. To avoid having this feeling of alienation, they may wish to assimilate. On the other hand, if there are state-supported, religiously affiliated schools, they may be able to more easily maintain their community identity. If so, state funding is likely to benefit the minority community. A majority religious community may successfully run its educational institutions without support from the state but, given its relative marginalization in civil society, a minority religious community may, on its own, not be able to sustain its schools and colleges. In India, Article 26 may be empty without Article 30(2). Thus, the argument from majoritarianism against partial funding of educational institutions of religious communities is not compelling.

A second argument for religious education is grounded in a peculiar feature of Hinduism. The very distinction between religion, philosophy, and culture makes no sense in Hinduism. Therefore, taking religion out of public education would mean virtually excluding Indian culture and civilization. In this context, Ambedkar made an interesting distinction between religious instruction and religious education and argued in favour of religious education. When asked if institutions where the Vedas, the Smrithis, the Gita, the Upanishads are taught and which are maintained wholly out of state funds will be shut down once the constitution comes into force, Dr Ambedkar replied that there is a distinction between religious instruction and religious study. Religious instruction means the teaching of dogma. Religious study or religious education is different (religious study must imply that we also question dogma because all education implies possible critique, that is, critical questioning of anything under scrutiny).[11] The implication was clear. The critical study of religious texts is not only permissible but must be positively encouraged.

It appears then that, given some important qualifications, partial funding to separate, religiously affliliated schools must be granted. This still leaves us with one problem, however. State schools, on our model, do not teach religions. Private schools, on the other hand, must teach religion and teach it in the right way, for example, without deriding other religions, but they do not teach *other* religions. If so, we are in a situation where no school imparts proper inter-religious education, necessary for inter-religious understanding and eventually, civic friendship. Is this a justifiable state of affairs? It is pertinent here to mention that not much validity resides in the claim that teaching religions in schools invariably leads to violent communal conflicts. Ismail's point in the constituent assembly that communalism is exacerbated only because people misunderstand each other's religion overshoots its aim but is not entirely mistaken.[12] Though some religious conflicts could arise only because we properly understand the religion of other, others are intensified instead by false propaganda, stereotyping, and caricature. Proper teaching of different religions assists in dispelling these and also, diffuses tension between religious groups. It should do so as much by minimizing prejudice as by helping us see the futility of trite answers such as all religions are essentially the same.

[11] Ibid., p. 885.
[12] Ibid., p. 875.

Second, inter-religious education is crucial because just and peaceful societies cannot be built either without persons of faith or when people of different faiths clash with one another. Nor can they be built any longer by foolishly persevering with the belief that all religions other than one's own are wrong, by the domination of one's own faith. They can be built only when diverse groups of believers and non-believers can come to effective mutual understanding, accommodation, and acceptance. Third, what is needed today is not just that Muslims, or Hindus, or Christians be good Muslims, Hindus, and Christians only in their respective religious communities but rather that they be good Muslims, Hindus, or Christians in a world where other intelligent and sensitive people are not Hindus, or Muslims, or Christians.[13] This is possible only with sensible multi-religious education.

It might, here, be argued that this problem can be overcome if children from different religious backgrounds meet one another, as they do in state-run schools, and learn that ways of thinking and being exist other than the one taught by their parents. They may even learn to respect other ways of life and thought. Besides, this diversity need not be restricted to public schools. It may be encouraged in religiously affiliated schools if these schools are also thrown open to children from other religions, as they are in India. Though less than in schools run wholly by the state, this diversity may still be good enough to encourage inter-religious toleration and this may, in turn, help civic friendship and values of citizenship. Even religiously affiliated schools may encourage people to listen to one another, to negotiate, and compromise with one another. Yet, thus far, a school only incidentally provides an arena for inter-religious toleration. It does not address the issue of inter-religious education, of properly learning about other religions.

So, we need multi-religious education. This still leaves us with the question: what is the proper site of inter-religious education? Should state-run schools provide inter-religious education or should they keep off all types of religious education but make it a condition of public funding that private, religiously affiliated schools give education not only in their own religion but also in other religions. I do not think it is fair to expect separate, private schools to do this job. The whole point of keeping them separate is to give them the opportunity to initiate children into beliefs and practices associated with a particular

[13] Wilfred Cantwell Smith, *Modernization of a Traditional Society*, Bombay, Calcutta: Asia Publishing House, 1965.

faith. To expect them to do otherwise, is to expect them to make a paradigm shift, a rather impossible expectation. So, my own view is the following:

1. To procure public funding, separate, religiously affiliated schools must meet minimum conditions of
   (i)   general standards of national curricula;
   (ii) not discriminate on grounds of religion in their policy of admission;
   (iii) not compel children to attend instruction in the religion of the community that runs the school; and
   (vi) not foster negative stereotypes of other religions.
2. The state should itself undertake the important task of providing inter-religious education.

At this stage, another objection might be raised. Should a secular state commit itself to multi-religious education? Does a state remain secular when it undertakes religious education in any form? Is there a significant difference between education in one religion and education in many? This is yet another issue that dominated the assembly debates. Several members worried that a state that provides multi-religious education may compromise on its secular character. However, this worry is unfounded. It stems from wrongly equating the secular character of states with one particular manifestation of it. This point needs elaboration.[14]

It is commonplace that political secularism means the separation of state and religion. But, to unpack the metaphor of separation and to grasp what is really at issue here, we must see separation in terms of possible disconnection at three distinct levels. A state may be disconnected from religion at the level of ends (first level), at the level of institutions (second level), and the level of law and public policy (third level). A secular state is distinguished from theocracies and states with established religions by a primary, first-level disconnection. A secular state has free-standing ends, either substantially, if not always completely, disconnected from the ends of religion or conceivable without a connection with them. States with established religions have something in common with secular states—at least a partial institutional disconnection. But, secular states go further in the direction of disconnection; they break away completely. They

---

[14] For a detailed explication, see Rajeev Bhargava, 'Political Secularism: Why it is Needed and What can be Learnt from its Indian Version', in Geoffrey Brahm Levey and Tariq Modood (eds), *Secularism, Religion and Multicultural Citizenship*, Cambridge: Cambridge University Press, 2009, pp. 82–109.

withdraw favours or privileges that established churches had earlier taken for granted. Finally, a state may be disconnected from religion even at the level of law and public policy. When it disconnects at even this third level, it excludes religion altogether from every form of state activity. Such a state maintains a policy of strict or absolute separation. In this incarnation, it typifies a hysterical brahminical attitude: religion is untouchable, so any contact with it contaminates secularist purity. Secularism here becomes a doctrine of political taboo; it prohibits the state to come into contact with religious activities. Such a view proposes that religious and political institutions live as strangers to each other, at best with benign respectful indifference. When a state is disconnected from religion at all three levels in this particular way, then we may say that a 'wall of separation' has been erected between the two. On the wall of separation conception of secularism, religion must be outside the purview of the state, and in this sense, must be privatized. Now, this conception of a secular state in which the state is disconnected from the religion at all three levels is not the only available conception of secular state. A state can be secular if it disconnects itself from religion at the first two levels but is connected at the third level. In short, when, instead of excluding religion at the third level, it keeps a principled distance from it. The policy of principled distance entails a flexible approach on the question of inclusion/exclusion, engagement/disengagement, and intervention/abstention, dependent on the context, nature, or current state of relevant religions. It accepts a disconnection between state and religion at the level of ends and institutions but does not make a fetish of it at the third level of policy and law.

Principled distance is premised, therefore, on the idea that a state that has secular ends and that is institutionally separated from the church or some church-like entity may engage with religion at the level of law and social policy. This engagement must be governed by principles under-girding a secular state, that is, principles that flow from a commitment to the values mentioned earlier. Thus, even religion may be included, or so may equality, or any other value integral to secularism. For example, citizens may support a coercive law of the state purely grounded in a religious rationale if this law is compatible with freedom or equality. Or, a state may grant aid to religious institutions or may itself provide multi-religious education if it promotes equality or fraternity. Since a third level disconnection is not constitutive of secular states, a state does not lose its secular character if it aids religiously affiliated schools or provides multi-religious education. I have argued that under some circumstances, a secular state may directly provide multi-religious education. I am not here claiming, of course, that this is the only function of schools run by states. This would be an absurd claim and more in line with states with established religions than with secular states. Rather, my proposal is that multi- or inter-religious education can and, in some circumstances, must be an integral part of the larger project of secular education by the state.

I end this chapter with one more proposal and a hope. The proposal is that there must be some form of cooperation between state-run or -recognized common schools and separate, religiously affiliated private schools. This cooperation is essential because each type of school serves an important social or public purpose. Separate religious schools make children fluent in their own religions and enable them to sustain and renew their particular religious traditions. Common schools make children fluent in a language that helps them understand the economic, political, and social forces affecting their lives and to be articulate about them in the public sphere. A programme of inter-religious education in common schools can teach them a language to engage each other respectfully and critically across different religious traditions. But, how might this cooperation work? Two possibilities come immediately to mind, one which was discussed in and discarded by the constituent assembly. The first allows students to attend public schools in the morning and religiously affiliated schools in the afternoon. Though the split-day programme fosters ideals of inclusion and diversity, and for some, is even a better option than state funding for religiously affiliated schools, it places undue burden on students. A good alternative to it is that children who wish to get religious education attend religiously-affiliated schools at the primary and secondary levels and a common school at the senior level. This helps them to secure benefits of both, without unduly burdening them with an unbearably heavy schedule at the primary and secondary levels.

My hope is that one day we will discard the form of multi-religious education that, in the current context, I have endorsed. In the present form, multi-religious education means learning about a religion that is one's own and then, secondarily, learning about religions that are not one's own, which belong to others. However, this idea of separate religious systems to which each of us owe distinct allegiance is not a natural idea, as Wilfred Cantwell Smith, the great historian of comparative religions, so brilliantly showed. Asian faiths, the great faiths of the East, are not and can become religions only with cataclysmic distortion.

It is well known that in the recent past, a person in parts of rural India could easily be both a Hindu and a Muslim. Even today—and I must be corrected if I am mistaken here—a single Chinese may be and usually is a 'Confucian, a Buddhist, and a Taoist'. This may baffle many for it is difficult for us to imagine how a single person can belong to three different religions. But, as Smith reminds us, this perplexity arises from an inappropriate imposition of the concept of a religious system on what really are three rich and complex traditions of thought. These schools of thought have been cherished for centuries in China. Their teachings are available and everyone partakes of them but what each person does with them is entirely up to him. (Take the case of political thought and theory. As a student of political thought, I cherish the thought of Plato, Aristotle, Locke, Burke, Rousseau, Marx, Gandhi, and Ambedkar but I do not necessarily become an ideologically committed Lockean or Burkean or even Gandhian as I do so. I embrace a part of their thought, without swallowing the whole. Nor do I feel the need to build a closed community around each tradition of thinking.) One day, I hope it will be possible for each one of us to partake of the rich traditions of the Jains, the Buddhists, the several communities that fall under the umbrella of Hindus, the Muslims, the Jews, the Christians, as well of the many indigenous peoples without the compulsive need to publicly display that we belong first and foremost to only one of these.

13

Indian Democracy and Well-being
Employment as a Right*

Large projects, like big ideas, are exhilarating, generate excitement in their inventors, and thrill their conjurors but run the risk of being damp squibs when put into practice. In stark contrast, a little idea, a small initiative, and a modest goal may sometimes have a far-reaching impact.

The big 'plans' in India that figure in the imagination of its current policy makers are to do with turning the country into a mighty economic and military power. The buzzwords in the elite circles of contemporary India are globalization, liberalization, and privatization, mantras that would catapult the economy closer to the G8. But, in 2005, we saw small initiatives set in motion at the behest of a small, enlightened political group that might make some difference to the lives of ordinary people and eventually, to the way the country is governed.

In August 2005, the coalition government, led by the Congress party, passed the National Rural Employment Guarantee Act (NREGA) that guarantees employment to every household for a minimum of 100 days a year and thereby tries to ensure basic subsistence to the poorest of the rural poor in about 200 districts of India. In five years, schemes flowing from the act are expected to cover at least 400 more districts. According to the act, any adult member of the household can voluntarily apply for

* Originally published as 'Indian Democracy and Well-being: Employment as a Right', *Public Culture*, vol. 18, no. 3, 2006, pp. 445–51; published by Duke University Press.

asset-generating manual labour, that is, work that helps develop rural infrastructure. Hopefully, sanitation will get better, the conditions of roads will improve, and as more canals are dug or desilted, there might be an increase in agricultural production. More importantly, this may halt the tragic suicides of impoverished farmers, something alarmingly frequent when 'India was shining'.

Other features of this historic act are worth noting. First, if the government fails to provide employment to the applicant within fifteen days of receipt of application, he / she is entitled to a daily unemployment allowance. Second, all payments of wages, which admittedly are still abysmally low (less than 2 US dollars per day), must be made in cash and given directly to the applicant. Third, all injuries caused by an accident arising out of or in the course of employment, entitles the injured to free medical treatment. Fourth, when workers are employed outside their village, then they are entitled to transport allowance. Fifth and most important, at least a third of these jobs must go to women. To provide incentive to such women, a crèche is to be provided at the site for children below the age of six.

The act is not without problems. The economist, Jean Drèze, who helped draft the original bill was not exactly elated by the form in which it was passed by the Parliament. For a start, the fixed minimum wage makes for poor subsistence. Second, employment is guaranteed for a mere three-and-a-half months during the year. Third, its range is severely restricted; far too many rural and all urban districts fall outside its purview. Finally, it is likely to create resentment and bitterness within families and, despite its courageous attempt at gender justice, may in fact discriminate against women. Typically, large households consisting of several men and women characterize poor societies. Which adult member from this lot should get the job? Since it restricts itself to one member per household, women are most likely to lose out to men. Anyhow, Rs 60 per day is woefully inadequate to sustain such households.

Yet, like many others in India, I maintain that this act is of monumental significance. Social rights, including the right to work, have long been part of the Directive Principles of State Policy, a desirable goal of the constitution but not a justiciable matter. Occasionally, the Indian Supreme Court, on the ground that civil and political rights are meaningless without the resources necessary to exercise them, has converted basic needs such as freedom from hunger into justiciable rights. This has given social rights an instrumental significance but has failed to integrate them into the core idea of citizenship and democracy. By enacting this law, the Indian Parliament has unfolded a process that makes a significant welfare provision constitutive of the very idea of citizenship. To be a citizen of a polity is to be entitled to an opportunity to work.

It is true that manual work in extremely hot conditions, on parched terrain is more an energy-draining, back-breaking chore, sheer necessity rather than a freely chosen activity and galaxies away from work as self-realization, central to the emancipatory vision of Hegel and Marx. And yet, paid labour is equally distinct from charity. Under conditions of equality, living on charity is demeaning and lowers self-esteem. There is a sense in which *any* paid work, no matter how hard, quietly uplifts and enhances dignity. By enacting this law and making employment a legal right, the Indian Parliament has taken an important step towards connecting the idea of citizenship with human dignity.

But, how has this occurred in the current climate of hyper-antistatism? Do we not know that in this new world order, the public provision of public goods is meant to get scarce? How could a new regime of social policy, pivotal in developing societies for the resurrection of the welfare state, installed in conditions where state intervention in the economy is routinely scoffed at, the welfare state is widely subjected to a moral and economic critique, and the market reigns supreme, be expected to address even the basic subsistence needs of the people?

The New Right of the western world and powerful international organizations never tire of propounding that no alternative exists to privatization, and that the proper role of the state is to be a night watchman, an alert warden of external defence and internal order, not a custodian of peoples' welfare. But, is this roll-back-the-state recommendation really implemented in their own backyard? The welfare state in the western world has survived all the hype of the New Right and pressures of international economies. If the evidence available is carefully examined, it can safely be concluded that the rate of growth of aggregate expenditure on welfare in these countries has slowed down at best. But, this is hardly the same thing as rolling back the state. In fact, according to Francis Castles, real spending per capita and per dependent between 1980 and 1998 has increased significantly in all the Organisation for Economic Cooperation and Development (OECD) nations. As he puts it, 'crisis threats (to the welfare state) made

318 India's Secular Democracy

with increasing stridency since the mid-1970s have remained uniformly unfulfilled'.[1]

Ironical then that those with a welfare state of their own either demand that it be dismantled or prevent its establishment in countries where it is most needed. Also, quite telling is the fact that these recommendations are taken far more seriously by powerful elites in Southern states than by their counterparts in the North (the current Bush regime is perhaps the only exception to this). Spurred by greed and visions of grandeur or obsessed by a skewed conception of efficiency, and like their international counterparts, they insist that markets alone are to decide what goods must be produced, regardless of the impact on the availability of basic necessities for the poor.

How then did this act come about? What made the Indian government go against its own economic proclivity and oppose what has been touted as a global trend? Why and how did it manage to avoid international pressures? Like any important initiative, this act too has long been in the making. A severe drought more than twenty-five years ago, propelled the then Maharashtra government to put in place a somewhat restricted Employment Guarantee Act that saved, from starvation, a large population in drought-prone districts. Following this initiative, several Indian states gradually initiated Food for Work programmes and schemes of mid-day meals for school-going children of the poor. The real momentum to this act came, however, after the BJP-led coalition government, intoxicated by a seemingly galloping growth rate, seduced by the upper class glitter of its own campaign, and deluded into believing that the long era of its rule had only just begun, was forced out of power by the rural and urban poor in the general election of 2004. Thirty years ago, the Congress, the then ruling party in India, was jolted out of power by a demos that publicly expressed its preference for individual choice and political freedoms that were snatched away from them during the Emergency. Now, in 2004, another ruling party was compelled to see that the same demos not only values socio-economic rights that underpin what Charles Taylor calls 'ordinary life', that is, the life of production and reproduction but also perceives a close link between state action, a dignified ordinary life, and the commonplace political freedoms of democratic regimes.

[1] Francis G. Castles, *The Future of the Welfare State*, Oxford: Oxford University Press, 2004, p. 168.

Political theorists frequently emphasize that democracy without some measure of socio-economic equality is hollow. Some have even argued that economic equality is a precondition of effective political participation. Indian democracy shows that the causal arrows do not fly only in one direction. Just as some economic parity is necessary for a more effective exercise of political freedoms, just so democratic freedoms are crucial for enhancing socio-economic well-being.

This is not an original point. Several well-known philosophers and economists such as Amartya Sen have mooted it. But this realization comes naturally to those who value Indian democracy. A famine was averted not because a morally sensitive, pro-poor government took immediate notice of the implications of the drought in Maharashtra but because it was compelled to do so by democratic institutions and processes. Rulers in Maharashtra would have acted with impunity in the absence of opposition parties, a free press, and the threat of being thrown out of office. Democratic governments do not spontaneously provide remedies for the collective ailments of societies, nor automatically respond to even the basic needs of ordinary citizens. They react positively only when they are forced to, and they are forced to do so when crucial issues become salient in the public arena, backed by a sufficiently large public opinion, and when political parties see some electoral advantage in supporting it. Alternatively, governments listen to ordinary people only when they know that they can be penalized for failing to do so, and no penalty is more severe than being thrown out of office. The NREGA would never have seen the light of day without pressure from below. And this pressure would not be forthcoming without political freedoms, if people did not possess the right to vote. No form of accountability is more direct than elections.

I have claimed that the NREGA could not have come about without democracy. But, what are the inner springs of democracy in chronically impoverished societies? What makes it possible for the poor to imagine that their votes matter? Why do they not fall instead into depths of despair and resignation? This is because political freedoms help them to change the way they experience their present condition. Call it the reconstituting or reconditioning role of political freedoms in human life. In democracies, an issue such as the need to be employed is connected to political freedoms in an important way. Unemployed persons without political freedoms can practically do nothing about their unemployment. They can neither publicly complain nor act to change this condition. If so, they are not only unemployed now but are likely to remain so even in the future. Such persons have no hope, no alternative future. The importance of political freedoms is that it gives hope to the jobless and the hungry that they can do something about this condition. They can act on their own or get others to act on their behalf so that the issue of unemployment does not remain unheard and unaddressed. This also makes a qualitative difference to the manner in which they live with their misery now. Perspectives on the future make a profound difference to how the present is experienced. People live with the pathetic condition of the present a bit differently if they have the hope that they can overcome it someday. Political freedoms such as the right to vote help attack sources of unfreedom by changing the perspective on the current condition of unfreedom.

A careful look at how something like the NREGA emerges in a reasonably functional but poverty-stricken democracy also helps to remove wrong-headed ideas about the insignificance of political freedoms. For instance, it is widely believed that political freedoms mean nothing to those without shelter, clothing, or food. Can the emaciated, poverty-stricken beggar, dying of starvation, heat, or cold, console himself by the assurance that he has the constitutional guarantee to freely proclaim that his elementary needs remain unfulfilled? Amartya Sen refers to the honey collectors of Sundarbans who are frequently killed on the job by tigers. Clearly, dire urgency of their economic needs forces them to put their lives at such enormous risk. If the poor are ready to put their lives at risk to earn their daily bread, why would they not give up their liberties and rights to keep their lives going? Is it not plain commonsense that the fulfilment of basic economic needs trump political freedoms? Surely, a government that satisfies the basic needs of everyone successfully is better than one that respects the political rights of its citizens but leaves their basic material needs unfulfilled. If so, impoverished people may prefer a minimally welfare-oriented authoritarian government to a democratic government that fails to redress poverty.

Even a cursory glance at Indian democracy prevents this anti-democratic implication from being drawn. Consider a routine example from India, say of a person who goes through a rough, daily grind to make two ends meet. He feeds himself and his family but with Herculean effort that takes the very life out of him, day after day, month after month, year after year. Will he do something to escape this crushing state of affairs? It entirely depends on the price he must pay for transformative action. If these costs are bearable, then quite certainly he will. To begin with, he will speak up against this horrendous condition. Perhaps privately at first and then, in public. If there is someone to apportion blame, he will. But mere expression or even communication will not satisfy him. If he could, he would do more. He would wish to earn a living by less severe form of labour. If exploited, he would want to end it; not just temporary respite from exploitation but its permanent termination. Since this is unlikely to happen instantly, he might wish to join a group with similar objectives. If a political party with such promise exists already, he might vote for it. Now, give this person the choice between his daily grind and his right to speak out freely, to associate with others, and to vote. He would certainly not give up his daily grind, even if he wanted to. But, nor will he surrender his political freedoms. He would simply not accept that he has to choose between the two. He would want his political freedoms now in order to escape the daily grind in future. In short, he would want to transcend his current situation, to have both political freedoms and a life of less arduous labour. Since this altered life-context can only be had with the exercise of his political freedoms, he would put up with his back-breaking daily toil so long as he has his political freedoms. The birth of the NREGA shows that because it presents us with a false dichotomy, a perspective that accords basic needs priority over liberty is misleading, if not phony.

14

Academic Freedom in India*

Academic freedom is widely understood as the freedom of scholars to conduct enquiry, and the freedom of teachers and students to exchange and collectively deliberate on scholarly ideas without fear of sanction, censure, or illegitimate interference. It is distinct from the more general freedom of thought and expression of citizens in a democratic society because it is attached to social roles embedded in particular practices through which goods internal to these practices, such as explanation, understanding, and insight, are realized in the course of trying to meet standards of excellence constitutive of academic activity. Since academic practices are sustained within institutions, academic freedom must also be understood to imply the autonomy of institutions within which teaching and scholarly research is conducted.

In general, the freedom of scholars and autonomy of academic institutions is threatened in three distinct ways: (i) directly by state action, when the coercive apparatus of the state suppresses them; (ii) by conservative and authoritarian communities or by unbridled market forces within civil society; and finally, (iii) when distortions creep into academic institutions and motivational impediments fetter the mind of academics. Such internal threats develop when academic freedom is lost in the amorphous generality of other freedoms or when academics lose sight of goods and standards internal to academic practice.

What is the status of academic freedom in India and how is it threatened? Placing Indian universities within a quasi-historical perspective

* Originally published as 'Academic Freedom in India', *Academe*, July–August 1999.

will help to understand this issue. In India, universities have undergone three distinct phases. In the first, pre-independence phase, Indian universities developed an autonomy from society without altogether losing links with it. Since society itself was suffused with ideals of freedom, equality, and self-determination, the university became the natural site where these were articulated, tested, and perfected. The dominant threat to academic freedom came from outside, from the British colonial state.

The value of the university, to use Wendy Steiner's felicitous phrase, lies in its 'simultaneous relevance and irrelevance to society', and this requires the maintenance of a principled distance, that is, neither amalgamation and capitulation nor detachment and arrogant aloofness. Autonomy must never be confused with insulation. The consolidation of the university's autonomy and eventually its insulation from the rest of society is the feature of the second phase. By developing interests and ideals in abstraction from society, by cultivating an unacknowledged indifference to the rest of society, the campus became a world of its own. In this phase of autonomy-cum-insulation, the main threat to academic freedom was internal.

In the third phase, the university began to once again blend with society but one from which ideals typical of the first phase had vanished. Hence, in this phase, where the university is neither autonomous nor insulated from society, academic freedom is gravely endangered by external social forces.

These points need elaboration. Interestingly, barring a brief period of political emergency between 1975 and 1977, academic freedom in post-independence India has never been actively threatened by the state. I cannot remember a single instance of the monitoring of seminars, the banning of an academic book, or the imprisonment of an academic for his views. Nor has academic research been stymied by state interference.[1] However, subtle and not so-subtle pressures on academic institutions by democratically elected governments are commonplace. The Congress party had begun to interfere in institutions with the end of the one-party dominant system. As it became insecure and edgy about its power, it became more unprincipled and randomly interventionist. But, perhaps the most unabashed attempt at government interference

---

[1] However, mention must be made of the government notification that permission must be taken from the relevant ministries for international seminars on certain issues. This causes unnecessary hurdles to academic work.

occurred when the right-wing Hindu nationalist, BJP-led coalition government interfered with the prestigious Institute of Advanced Study in Shimla. The institute's governing body was packed by hand-picked supporters of the BJP, who then systematically tried to subvert every previous decision taken by the institute's director. The ratification of fellows selected prior to the constitution of the new governing body was delayed, an ideological monitoring of research proposals was set in motion, senior fellows such as the eminent writer, Krishna Sobti, were humiliated, and a politician was arbitrarily selected to deliver the Radhakrishnan memorial lecture. Plainly, non-academic considerations had short-circuited the autonomy of the institute.

The persistent, bit-by-bit pestering by illiberal communities is by far the most serious danger to academic freedom in India as it enters the third phase. A case in point is the fate of the historian, Mushirul Hasan, also the Pro-Vice Chancellor of Jamia Milia Islamia, who was victimized for a rather innocuous remark against the ban on Rushdie's *Satanic Verses*. All hell broke loose in his own university after his interview appeared in a magazine. A systematic campaign of intimidation was launched against him, which resulted in a virtual ban on his entry into the campus. When he returned several months later, he was mercilessly beaten up. I must add here that this problem is not restricted to Muslim orthodoxy. In Punjab, Sikh scholars attempting a non-conformist, contextual interpretation of the Guru Granth Sahib, the sacred scripture of the Sikhs, or an unbiased account of Sikh history have been ostracized by the Akal Takht, the principal centre of Sikh temporal authority.[2] Nor is the problem confined to the interface between the university and religious communities. The vandalization of the Bhandarkar Institute by Shiv Sainiks following the publication of a book on Shivaji is a case in point. I reckon that an academic living, say in Assam, is unlikely to be able to publish his objective views on the militant, pro-autonomy, Bodo Movement.

Despite such threats, the record of academic freedom in India is not all that bad. What is unclear, however, is whether this is due to a high level of social tolerance or simply due to a pernicious form of anti-intellectualism manifested by a plain indifference to the world

[2] I particularly have in mind the plight of the historian Harjot Oberoi, who has been a victim of intolerant sections of the Sikh community, both in India and abroad, for having given what is widely regarded as an excellent account of how a separate Sikh identity was constructed in the nineteenth and twentieth centuries.

of intellectuals. What is worse, it could be a result of the considered judgement of the wielders of social power that impinging on academic freedom is not worth the trouble because the views of the academic are irrelevant and anyhow, have little impact on public opinion.

A relatively new threat to academic freedom comes from a growing consensus within the establishment, encouraged also by statements in recent World Bank documents that subsidies to institutions of higher education must be reduced because higher education is a 'non-merit good', that is, it does not merit societal intervention in the form of financial subsidies. Since such pro-market cuts have an adverse impact on the teaching of humanities and the social sciences, the liberal character of universities is bound to suffer. This undermines a secure environment for scholarly autonomy.

A number of factors together pose an internal threat to academic freedom in India. The first is what I call the over-ideologization of the progressive mind. The progressive academic was overeager to relate instantaneously with the poor and the marginalized, precisely at the time when he had over-abstracted himself from them. The very same process that protected academics from general social intolerance also widened the chasm between their own culture and that of the rest of society. It is part of the conditions of academic freedom that the relation of academics with the 'people', with society at large is indirect and somewhat fractured. Confronted and baffled by this intellectual distance, the progressive intellectual forsook open-ended deliberation, replacing it by new dogma and prefabricated solutions—the very ingredients of over-ideologization. Instead of a dispassionate search for a solution to the many problems at hand, academics busied themselves with closing each other's minds and ultimately their own; while outside, in the real world, problems multiplied.

Other internal threats to academic freedom flow from the deficiencies of a wider societal culture in India that lie too deep to quickly dissipate. Tocqueville warned of the tendency of nascent democracy, in its passionate anti-feudal mood of general social levelling, to breed mediocrity and to catapult envy as the dominant sentiment in society. This has an obvious and particularly pernicious effect on academic practice. Envy erases qualitative distinctions and drags the qualitatively better down to the level of the mediocre. This derecognizes work of proven superiority. Indeed, the greater its worth, the stronger the campaign of its erasure from the public domain; a subterranean pretence that the work doesn't even exist grips the collective mind. Over a period of time, the persistent non-recognition of his work also induces in the author a doubt about its worth. In the end, it is a no-win situation for everyone because the very sense of internal goods and standards, vital to academic freedom, is lost.

Some problems of the academic world stem from vestiges of a pre-democratic, feudal era. For example, merit-based institutions are customarily converted into little fiefdoms, run by tin gods, doling out petty patronage to loyal supporters and creating suffocating tyrannies for others. In such contexts, ideas are applauded or condemned with a view not to their intrinsic worth but as to who articulates them. This is no doubt part of a larger malaise of a knee-jerk personalization of every issue, a deeper inability to imagine and sustain impersonal institutional structures. Comically, even factions within university departments are based on personal loyalty rather than on principle or ideology. Intra-group cooperation also depends on personal loyalty to a leader. Within impersonal situations of equality, as in large rule-governed universities, cooperation gives way quickly to intense rivalry, to atrophy, and to isolation. Therefore, projects that require sustained team effort are difficult to execute. Such habits of the mind are hardly conducive to the growth of stable traditions of scholarly work without which academic freedom is pointless.

Appendix

Multiple Incarnations of Secularism*

Not long ago, we could not stop wanting to be secular. Everybody swore by secularism. It was a visible sign of brotherhood, the luminous symbol of education, the very mark of civility.

All this seems to be changing, but perhaps only just so. The halo around secularism may be fading but it is still difficult to be openly irreverent towards it. Even those who decry it, do so uneasily and are careful not to give the impression that they have wholly discarded it. And, if and when they abandon it, even they will not do so without some show of grief. If they ever manage to force us to shed our secularism, they will never to do without also shedding some tears.

I do not believe that secularism has persisted in India merely because it has generated votes. In one way or another, we have all been helplessly driven to make it an important constituent of our cultural identity; or, if not our cultural, then at the very least, our political identity. Our political elite, our rulers have always wanted to appear to be secular. And we have always wanted them to appear to be secular. Secularism has not only been highly valued in our country but has been hugely popular.

Popularity has its own costs, however. No concept can be popular without sacrificing precision. Of course, I am not speaking here of mathematical precision. It is commonplace that rich and complex concepts are defiantly messy. They cannot help being vague. But 'secular' appears to have fallen into

---

* This piece was published in *Frontline* as 'Strands of Secularism', 27 April–10 May 1991, pp. 49–51. This is not exactly how I would distinguish different varieties of secularism. Readers might also notice that this is less a normative account of secularism in India and more a sociology of the everyday concept of secularism.

real bad times. Secularism seems to be sprouting in every other backyard. As many secularisms exist nowadays as there are people. Worse still, the word may well be trapped in fruitless ambiguity. The term 'secular' may be popular, but I fear it might already have been rendered irretrievably vacuous. It is bandied about freely, but nobody any longer knows or even bothers to know what it really means.

But, can a concept be at once popular and perilously close to being empty? Are not concepts devoid of substantive content precisely when we lose all interest in them, when they no longer have any use, when they are dead?

The short answer to this question is a resounding no. It is a common enough opinion that a concept is shared, is popular, only when all those who have it are also fully agreed on its meaning, when a consensus exists on its usage. But this view is mistaken. Often a concept is popular precisely when its meaning is disputed fiercely. Concepts are not infrequently hollowed out just when they lie at the centre of bitter struggles, and such battles would not occur if these concepts did not matter to people.

The term 'secular' and its associate 'secularism' are among the few hotly-contested concepts in our polity. A mind-boggling conceptual pot-pourri has been cooked because different groups have ceaselessly been offering their own distinctive conception of secularism, their own particular elaboration that comes into conflict at crucial junctures with other interpretations. By now, different political visions have well and truly entered this concept. It is overstretched, warped beyond recognition, precisely because of intense political rivalry. Careful examination of its variable meanings can bring us closer, therefore, to understanding one of the major political struggles of our times.

What then are these contesting versions, the many incarnations of secularism in our country? I believe there are five principal variants, each with a distinct flavour, currently doing the rounds. In what follows, I shall try to briefly delineate their features. And, I do so not from a value-neutral standpoint. Because I cannot bring myself to see them isolated from two other equally important political values, freedom and equality, I ask what bearing each has on them; in other words, the extent to which they meet the most minimal norms of freedom and equality.

In the first version, to be secular is to be anti-religious. Advocates of this version share the mainstream enlightenment view on religion as a massive source of error and falsehood, a storehouse of superstition and obscurantism, as the severest form of humanity's alienation from itself. A secular state, therefore, must be anti-religious. The state must be actively hostile to religion, play dominant, energetic role in discouraging religious practices, inhibit the growth of religious institutions, and encourage an education that is visibly inimical to religious thinking.

Not only because it seeks to curtail religious freedoms, such a state is unambiously anti-libertarian. It is also anti-egalitarian. It discriminates between the religious and the non-religious with a marked preference for the latter. Curiously, if any secularism is entitled to the prefix positive, it is this one; positive, because it seeks an active role from the state on behalf of the secular outlook, because it favours state intervention in all religious matters. But, its secularism is a trifle unsophisticated, a bit too crass. This is partly because it has a simple, undifferentiated view of religion. It sees nothing understandable or good in it.

This version has at least a partial legitimacy in certain historical contexts, especially when the more pernicious aspect of religion has overwhelmed whatever it is that is desirable in it. But, because it restricts some freedoms and violates the principle of equality, it can never have total and unambiguous legitimacy. Particular forms of this version have been associated with some variants of Marxism but it is also common to some varieties of liberalism. Contrary to the received wisdom of some intellectuals and politicians, this model has not been actively pursued in the Indian context. That it has been a wish or prejudice of some intellectuals is, however, an altogether different issue.

In the second version, the state is not anti- but merely non-religious. For exponents of this version, the secular outlook is distinct from, but not necessarily hostile to, most religious world views. For them, a common framework exists at a certain level between the secular and the religious; both, therefore, raise similar questions but offer divergent, conflicting answers. Sophisticated variants of both the secular and the religious outlook acknowledge the finitude of men and women, the bounded horizon of man's knowledge, the limits of conscious human action, the point beyond which humankind cannot control, explain, or understand both nature and human history. But, religion constructs a different subject, larger than the whole of humanity, from whose point of view everything is explicable and rendered meaningful. The secular perspective refuses to make this jump. But it understands why people are tempted to take this plunge and therefore, it is somewhat sympathetic and tolerant of religious views.

On this sophisticated view, the state is non-religious but permits religious practices outside its own sphere. Because it forbids neither religious nor non-religious practices, this version allows greater freedom within the state than the first. It is also more egalitarian, for it shows no preference for the non-religious over the religious. Furthermore, the state does not discriminate in favour of any religious community. The religion of one person is as good, or indeed as bad, as the religion of another. From the point of view of the state, all citizens are equal. Whether or not one subscribes to religion, or which of the many religions one endorses in irrelevant in matters of law, state policy, and for employment in public institution.

This probably is the only version available of negative secularism. The state is secular in the sense that it is non-religious but does not intend to encourage or discourage religion. On the sophisticated secular perspective, the state cannot be actively inimical to many of the sophisticated aspects of religion. Of course, there are limits to this indifference, just as there are limits to the exercise of any liberty. The point is that it no more restrains religion than it does any non-religious activity. All activities, religious or otherwise, are bound by the rule of law and must respect the rights of all citizens.

This version is most commonly identified with liberal democracies but with equally sound reasons, it can be associated with socialist democracies. In the Indian context, it is precisely this version of secularism that was advocated by Nehru.

The third variant of secularism identifies the secular with multi-religious. For this reason, it proposes that the state be multi-religious. This is the first of the many versions of positive secularism with a peculiar Indian flavour. Its defenders argue that in India, a land that has given birth to and nourished some of the major religions of the world, a state policy of indifference to religion is neither justified nor workable. Since most people in India are religious, the state cannot keep away from religious matters or adopt a stance of mere neutrality between the religious and the non-religious. Rather, it should actively promote religion. The state should play a positive and dynamic role in the pursuit of a religious life. But, in a land of many religions, the state cannot discriminate in favour of any one religion. It should grant equal preference to all.

Now, this version is neither fully libertarian nor egalitarian. It allows less freedom than some other forms of secularism because it does not permit the active pursuit of atheistic beliefs and practices. It violates the principle of equality because it discriminates against those who are non-religious. Nonetheless, it contains within it both libertarian and egalitarian potential that cannot be ignored. This comes out in the open, however, only upon a selective interpretation of all religions, when only the benign and sophisticated dimension of religion is culled from the rest and, more significantly, when atheism and agnosticism are viewed sympathetically, as plausible world views that take seriously the questions posed by religions but offer radically different answers. I believe that the inegalitarian and anti-libertarian interpretation of this version is often passed off as the Gandhian version of secularism but it is the second, more refined conception which is more properly Gandhian.

A fourth incarnation of secularism, also positive, is a vulgarization of the cruder Gandhian variant wherein the state should give equal preference to the fanatical fringe of all religious communities. Like the third variant, it favours the religious over the non-religious. But unlike it, the worst specimen of all religions is selected for preferential treatment. It overlooks, perhaps even deliberately glosses over, the more desirable, universalizable aspects of religions and over-emphasizes its closed, aggressive, and therefore, communal dimension. Its only saving grace is that it distributes its favours equally amongst all communal groups. Because it ignores or oppresses the sophisticated aspects of both the non-religious and the religious, it is far more anti-libertarian and inegalitar-ian than even the crude Gandhian variant of secularism. Here, we find a bizarre conception of the secular as multi-communal. To be secular is to be neither anti-religious nor non-religious. It is not even to be multi-religious. It is to be multi-communal. It follows that a secular state must be multi-communal. If there is any version of secularism that has been energetically followed in India for the past twenty years or so, surely, it has been this one.

The final variant is the only one to have embraced the nomenclature of positive secularism. It has been in the fray for decades, becoming ever more combative and dismissing rival conceptions as pseudo and perverted. For this version, the state should actively promote the religious world view and, there-fore, positively discriminate in favour of the religious over the non-religious. But, it must not equally favour all religions. In India, so the argument goes, Hinduism is the religion of the majority and the state must favour Hindu over other religious groups. Religion cannot be irrelevant to matters of state policy. What is even more significant, one religion must carry more weight than others. Positive secularism is not necessarily hostile to religious liberty but is firmly against religious equality.

It is openly inegalitarian in two distinct senses. First, it does not treat as equal the religious and non-religious. Second, with its pronounced bias in favour of one religion, it is bound to treat unequally the people of minority religions. To be positively secular, then, is to be pro-Hindu. A state that is positively secular, it turns out, is one that intervenes on behalf of Hindus. A positive secular state then is a predominantly Hindu state.

We now have in our midst a version that differentiates itself from all other incarnations of secularism. It decries the first variant for its antagonism to religion and the second, Nehruvian one, for its indifference towards it. It opposes the third and the fourth versions for showing equal respect for all religions and communal groups.

Positive secularism is flexible enough to accommodate two closely related but differing perspectives on the state. There exist two distinct ways of interpreting this secularism. Secular here can mean either mildly or strongly communal. If against all odds, it tries to emphasize the more tolerant and universalist aspect of Hinduism, then it would advocate a somewhat benign Hindu state. This positive secularism is mildly communal. The state may inhibit the beliefs and practices of the non-believer, but it grants freedom of religious groups. In this minimal sense, it is tolerant of all religions. The state is secular in the sense that it permits the beliefs and practices of all religious groups. But, if it incorporates the political vision of one aggressive section of Hindu community, with a deliberate policy of active discrimination against, even the persecution of, religious minorities, then we get a strongly communal, perhaps even a fascist state. Such a state is not merely inegalitarian but is mean with liberties, particularly with the religious liberties of the minority.

So, by a miraculous quirk of our destiny and a unique feat of the proverbial Indian rope-trick, the term secular has covered all the places along the religious/ non-religious spectrum, from being at one end virulently anti-religious to vociferously being in favour of the majority religion at the other. It has moved from a stance of active hostility to communalism to the most unabashed alliance with it. All the different avatars of secularism are born of a stupendously free play on the meaning of the term 'secular' that covers anti-religious, non-religious, multi-religious, multi-communal, and mildly or strongly in favour of the majority religious or communal group.

The story of the shifting meanings of secularism in our country is stranger, more obscure, far more bewildering than what is suggested by this ahistorical sketch. A finer understanding of these issues is essential for people who wish to join the political battle. But, much has already been lost by the failure to realize that political conflicts are at least, in part, conceptual battles in which the eventual loser is the one who has impatiently shoved conceptual distinctions aside merely because the first, few steps towards their understanding were either too neat and swift or else, too slow and faltering.

Index

Abdullah, Sheikh 51
academic freedom, in India 322–6
Adibashis, in Bangladesh 228, 233, 234, 244
Adler, 176
adult suffrage 32
agnosticism 330
Ahamadi, A.H. 188
Ahmed, Syed 125, 128
Akbar, Emperor 71, 177n23, 231
Akbar, M.J. 230n18, 235n31
Alam, Javeed 206, 207, 208
alienation 47, 205, 208
altruism 272, 279–80
    check on 283–7
Ambedkar, B.R. 42n9, 93, 159, 177, 177n23, 178, 179, 258, 305, 309, 314
Ambedkar Centenary Committee, in Andhra Pradesh 239
American War of Independence 8
amnesty 150
Andhra Pradesh, reservations in educational institutions in 193
Anglicans, in USA 77
Anjuman Taraqqi Pasand 171n14
anti-Ahmedi legislation 231
anti-secular regimes 69

Apartheid, in South Africa 20, 296
Article 370, opposition to 53, 62
Aristotle 277, 314
ascriptive communities 200
Ashoka, King 71, 120
Assam, problems in 49
    secessionist demand in 45, 47
assimilation, of minorities 21–2, 46, 156, 209
    see also minorities
atheism 150, 330
atomism 296
Aurangzeb, 35, 117, 122
autonomy, demands for, by states 44
authoritarian collectivism 11

Babri Masjid, destruction of 188, 227, 229, 230, 253
backward castes 208
Bahadur, Pocker Sahib 196, 197
Bailey 255
Bangladesh, 'black law' in 233
    Buddhist Adibashis in 228, 234
    constitutional amendments in 224
    ethno-religious groups in 233
    exclusion, of Garos in 234
        of minorities in 243–4

inclusion and exclusion in 217
Islamization in 223–4
land ownership in 234
principle of secularism in 223
state and religion relationship in
    223
Vested Property Act in 233
barbaric society 134–7
and minimally decent society
    137–42, 140
Beg, M. Hameedullah 188
Bengal, partition of 37
Bengali nationalism 228
Best Bakery case 247
Bhakti movement 122
Bhandarkar Institute, vandalization
    of 324
Bharatiya Janata Party (BJP) xix,
    185n9, 229, 262–6, 269
government's interference in
    educational institutions 324
Bharatiya Lok Dal 185n8
Bhattacharya, Mohit 56, 57n25
Bhutto, Z.A. 231
Bihar, massacre of Muslims in 114
Bodo movement 324
Bombay, riots in 230
province, division into
    Maharashtra and Gujarat 44
Bourdieu, Pierre 255
Brass, Paul 45, 46n14, 47n16, 51,
    237n35
Brink, David O. 285
British colonialism, provinces under
    35–6
British imperialism 7

Cabinet Mission Plan 37
Calcutta, violence in 131–3, 141
caste, assertion of xix
hierarchies 89
system 84, 175, 207
Castles, Francis 317, 318n1

Catholic churches 71
see also church
centralization 42, 60
Centre, and state, distribution of
    power between 61
Chandigarh, as capital of Punjab and
    Haryana 48
Chatterjee, Partha 63, 83n18, 85,
    252n3
Chattisgarh 44
Chaudhuri, Nirad C. 118, 119n19,
    128n48
child marriage, abolition of 90
Christianity, establishment of 70–1
and forgiveness 149, 150
and secularism 100–1
Chirol 120
Church, attack on 227
establishment of, and religion 70
separation of State and 67, 70,
    73–5, 89, 97, 100
citizenship 28, 78–9, 87, 98, 267
equal 27, 80, 87, 202
rights 28–9, 67, 98, 102, 219,
    232–3, 241, 243, 269
denial of active 243–5
civil liberties 9, 12
introduction of 4
collective identities 42
collective injustice, memories of 144
colonialism, injustices of 136
common civil code 172
'communal', conflicts/backlash 210,
    309
concept of 129
harmony 133
hatred 113
riots 185
communalism 14, 15, 92, 109
Communist Party of India (M) xviii
communitarian egalitarianism 15
communitarianism 14, 15, 181
community(ies), -based religious

identities 175, 204
    rights, tension between individual
        and 11–16
    -specific rights 92–3
    State's non-interference in 26
Congress (O) 185n8
Congress Party xviii, xix, 37, 38, 48,
    49, 52, 53, 60, 110, 111, 114, 123,
    126, 127, 133, 185n8, 186, 254,
    315, 323
    electoral defeat of xix
    interference in institutions 323
    and Muslim League 37n3, 123,
        125
    Muslim legislators from 184
    on Muslim's share in decision
        making 195
    and Muslim votes 208
    on political liberalism 12
    on separate electorate for
        Muslims 195
Constitution of India 7, 43, 81, 263,
    266–7
    adoption of 6
    amendments to 43
    framers of 4
    on secularism 81, 83
Constitution of India Bill of 1895
    32
constitutional democracy, in India
    6, 8, 10
constituent assembly 158
    debate on religious instructions in
        schools 304–6
    setting up of 60n30
contextual secularism 93–6
'cooperative' federation 57
coparcenary property, rights of men
    in Hinduism 170
cow slaughter, voluntary ban on 184
Crane, R.I. 119, 121
crime, perpetrators of 143, 144
criminal justice system 141

criminal procedure code of, 1898
    160n4
critical respect 91
culture(al), communities 13, 15
    and ethical framework, role of
        218
    and ethical pluralism 218
    exclusion 219
    homogeneity 54
    inclusion 219
    left-liberals on 294, 295
    right to 291
Custodian of Enemy Property in
    Pakistan 233

Dahl, Robert 28, 53n22
Dalits, in India 237–9
    constitutional provision for 238
    exclusion of 242–3
    problems faced by 230
    socio-economic condition of 189
Dar Commission 39
Das, Veena 135
democracy xxiv, 3, 199, 266–8, 315
    and citizenship rights 28–9, 102,
        219, 232–3, 241, 269
    growth of 7
    liberal 4–5, 251, 255, 256
    Muslims on 206
    and nationalism 28–33
    positive impact of 207
    secular 4, 24–8, 56, 63, 81, 102,
        206, 248, 268–71
Deshmukh, 92
Devadasi dedication, abolition of 90
Dewey, John 14
Directive Principles of State Policy,
    right to work under 316
Dissolution of Muslim Marriage Act
    VIII, of 1939, dissolution of 179
divorce, right to 90
divorced women, maintenance of
    167, 168

domestic violence, freedom from 167
Dravida Munnetra Kazhagam
    (DMK) 45
Drèze, Jean 316
drought/famine 319
Dworkin, Ronald xviii, xx, 18n21, 89,
    294n1

East Bengal Evacuees Act 233
education(al), institutions, and
    religion 71
    multi-religious 310–12
    religion in 302
    right to establish 92
egalitarianism 286, 305
    ethics 286
egoism 277–80, 283–7
    altruism and 272
    check on 283–7
    generalized 280–3
Election Commission 213, 214, 216
Elster, Jon xviii, 110n3
Emergency, of 1975–77 xix, 43
emergency powers 9, 43, 260
    and the writing of History 116
employment, as a right 315
English, as official language 46
English historians 118, 119, 120
equal respect, principle of 91n23
equal treatment, principle of 79
    and treatment as equals 89
equality xviii, 13, 61, 68, 217
    of citizenship 27, 78–81, 83, 87,
        98
    inter-group 61, 204
    right to 13
ethical identity 262, 265
ethical life 296
ethics, dimensions of 274–5
ethnic identities xx, 37
ethnic sub-nationalism 51
evil, concept of 136, 137
exclusion, direct and indirect 220–2

external 233–6
internal 236–7
religion related 218, 219–22

family life, value of 166
federalism xxv, 39, 42
    concept of 59, 61
    in India 56
    nature of 53–4
federation, functional 54
    India's asymmetry in 58–9
    in India and USA 57
    see also linguistic federalism
female infanticide 221
female literacy, in India 241
Flanagan, Owen 285
Food for Work programmes 318
forgiveness, grounds for 147–51
    and mercy 115, 151
France 8, 67, 98
    Saint Bartholomew massacre in
        144
freedom 217, 218
    academic 322
    of conscience 81
    and inclusive society 217–18
    political 318–21
    of thought and expression 322
French Revolution 8
French secularism 99
fundamental rights 12

Gandhi, Indira, Congress under 48
    imposition of Emergency by
        43n10, 185n8
    killing of 230
Gandhi, M.K. 8, 12, 36n2, 37, 49, 50,
    125, 126–7, 129, 141, 150n34, 188,
    222, 259n29, 314
    and Congress 5, 12
    fast unto death by 132
    on Hindu–Muslim unity 177
    mass politics of 8

–Nehru discourse 127
philosophy of non-violence 117
satyagraha of 8
strategy of reconciliation 151
and truth commission 131
version of secularism 330–1
Gandhian schema, of moral action
131–4, 138, 146
Garos, in Bangladesh 234
gender equality, in Islam 173
gender justice 170, 172
Ghatak, Ritwik 280
globalization 315
good, conception of 137, 151, 165,
168, 184, 275
Government of India Act, of 1909
194, 195
Government of India Act, of 1919
35, 36n1
Government of India Act, of 1935 36
'Great Calcutta killing' 131
Green, T.H. 14
'green revolution' 48
Greenfeld, Liah 31, 32, 198
group-based political representation
200–16
democratic objection to 208–9
liberal–individualist objection to
203–4
right-wing Hindu objection to
202–3
secularist objection to 201, 204–6
group-related values 163, 165
group rights 14, 95
and minority rights 23
Gujarat, atrocities on Muslims in 180
religious violence in 230, 235, 246
Gupta, Parthasarthy 117
Guru, Gopal 237, 238, 242
Guru Granth Sahib, interpretation
of 324

Habib, Irfan 120, 122–3

Hampshire, Stuart 89n21, 136, 137
Hampton, Jean 143n18, 148, 149n32,
150n35, 277n6
Hansen, Thomas 251, 252n3, 253n5,
254n8, n9 and n10, 255, 256, 260,
261
Hasan, Mushirul 175n20, 176n21,
183n1, 184 n3, 185n6, 186n10,
198n24, 244n53, 324
hatred, moral 148
Hegel, G.W.F. xvii, xviii, 10, 96, 296,
317
Hidayatullah, M. 188
hijab, controversy over, in France 67
Hindi, as official language 46
Hindu Adoptions and Maintenance
Act, 1956 237
Hindu extremists/militants 9,
180, 181
Hindu joint family, *Mitakshara* law
governing 170
Hindu law, of adoption 237
Hindu majoritarian forces 208
Hindu marriages, *saptapadi* in 170
Hindu–Muslim relations 122, 123,
125, 127–8, 130, 212, 235
Hindu nationalism 251, 266
resurgence of 252–7
Hindu nationalists, militant 54, 116
support of constitution 263
Hindu personal law 170
Hindu *Rashtra* 253
Hindu Right 83n18
Hinduism xix, 70, 84, 226
and assertive politics xix
internal plurality in 103
intervention in 25, 85
laws interfering with 90
reforms in 26, 28
and religious education 309
spirit of social justice in 12
and the state 331
women's position in rituals in 232

Hindutva xix, 253, 263
history 117–23
    critical 111, 117
    and emotion 110, 113, 118, 123
    intellectual and political 6
    monumental 116
    objectivist 111, 117
    official 117
    relativist 111, 117
historiography, Indian 109, 130
history writing, in the middle of
    twentieth century 111–13
Hobbes, Thomas xvii, 14, 144, 145
Hobhouse, L.T. 14
homogenization, of individuals 21,
    209
Hudood ordinance, in Pakistan 239
Hume, David 145n24, 179
hyper anti-statism 317

iddat period 160
identity, -constituting features in
    society 153
    -dependent majority and minority
    18
    linguistic 37n4
    religious 21, 25, 115, 169, 175,
    204–5
Ilyas, Maulana Mohammad 183n2
Imperial Legislative Council 29
inclusion, and exclusion, in India,
    Bangladesh, and Pakistan 217
    internal 230–3
inclusive society, religious liberty in
    221
India, abolition of untouchability in
    232
    academic freedom in 322–6
    Hindu–Muslim riots in 230
    inclusion and exclusion in 217
    invasion by Muslims 145
    legal equality for women in 241
    Muslim minority in 229

political representation of
    Muslims in 244
religious liberty in 225
religious violence in 228–9
secular constitution in 222, 226
Indian Criminal Procedure Code 167
Indian federalism, distinctiveness of
    53–60
    origin of 35–43
Indian National Congress 5, 7, 36, 37,
    38, 126, 184
    and freedom struggle 36
    and Muslims 128
Indian nationalism, during British
    rule 119
Indian penal code, introduction of 9
individual liberty 14
individual rights 7, 11, 13–14, 18
    and group rights 14, 95
individualism xviii, 157, 295, 296
individualist egalitarianism 14–15
inequalities 13, 103, 165
    social 29
inequities, elimination of 155
injustice 13, 17, 62, 136, 138, 144,
    155, 201
    elimination of 155
    historic 13, 142–5
inner springs, of Indian democracy
    319
inter-personal domain 274–5, 278
inter-religious domination 187
inter-religious, conflict 86
    education 313
intra-personal domain 274
intra-religious domination 85
Irshad, General 223
Islam, in Bangladesh 222–4
    conversion to 243
    in Iran 70, 224
    Kashmiri 51
    mubaraat 173
    in Pakistan 228, 230, 231, 244

proselytization by 122
recognition, of *khul* in 173
Islamic laws, on women 236
Ismail 309
Ittehadul-Muslimeen, in Hyderabad 186

Jaffrelot, Christophe 251, 253n4, n6, 255, 256, 257
Jaiswal 120
Jamaat-I-Islami 183, 186
Jamiyat-al-Ulema-e-Hind, pro-Congress 183
Jana Sangh, rise of 185
janapadas 35
Jayaprakash Narayan 43n10
Jews, persecution of 72, 101
    victims of religious exclusion 220
Jharkhand 44
Jinnah, Mohammad Ali 29, 114, 125, 222–3
joint electorate, reservation for Muslims under 198
judiciary 42
justice 12–13, 93, 139, 159
    basic procedural, 137–9
    gender justice, 170–2, 237, 316
    substantial conception 134, 137
    in transition 139–46

Kahars, in Bihar 242–3
Kalam, A.P.J. Abdul 188
Kashmir, Article 370 on 50, 53, 57
    accession to Indian Union 52, 57
    Centre's patronage to 51
    demand for autonomy 52
    importance of, in Indian politics 50
    militancy in 52
    problems in 50–3, 211
    religion and language in 51
    secessionist demands in 45, 47

Kashmiri Islam/Muslims 51
Kerala Islamic Shariat Board 171n14
Khaksars 178
Khan, Ayub 225
Khilnani, Sunil 4n2, 5, 6, 13n14, n15, 260
khul, recognition in Islam 173
Kothari, Rajni 44
Kunzru, Hridaya Nath 93
Kymlicka, Will 11n9, 14n17, 205n41, 219, 297n4

language, -based federal units 37
    reorganization of states on basis of 46, 60
Larmore, Charles 286, 287n19
Latif, I.H. 188
laws, religion and 218
legislature, Muslim representation in 192
liberal democracy 4–5, 251, 255, 256, 271
    crisis of 4
    discourse of 257–62
    as legitimating motive 262–6
    western origins of 4, 7
liberal individualism 205
liberalism xvii, xxi, 4, 8, 10, 13–16, 260–2, 292–4, 297–8, 329
    and rights 292–3
liberalization 315
liberty 68
    in a secular state 77–8
    values of xxi, xxv
linguistic identities 37
linguistic federalism 34, 43–7, 61
    and its problems 43
linguistic minorities, rights of 4
    struggle of 46
Lok Sabha, representation from states 58

Madan T.N. 63, 97n31, 257
Madras, reorganization of 46
Maharashtra, Employment
    Guarantee Act in 318
majority–minority framework 16–24,
    154, 155–6
    'political' and 'social' 156–9, 167
majority–minority syndrome 19, 20,
    23, 92, 152–5, 174–81, 222, 246
majoritarian backlash 209–10
majoritarian democracy 253
    and educational institutions 308
Majumdar, R.C. 116, 117n13, 119,
    120–6, 130
Malaviya, Madan Mohan 29
Marx, Karl xviii, xix, xxi, 112, 314, 317
Marxism 329
'Marxist' xxi
Mary, Larry 146
Mill, James 119, 120
minimal psychological realism,
    principle of 285
'minimally decent' society 139
minorities, alienation of 200
    assimilation of 21–2
    culture, protection of 304
    legal status of 232–3
    –majority framework 16–24, 154–9,
        167
    –majority syndrome 23, 92, 152–5
    persecution of 72
    political representation of 201–3
    rights of 28, 152
    see also religious minorities
Mitakshara law 170
Mizoram, formation of 49
Mizos, victimization of 49
mobilization 38, 45
modern secularism 97, 100, 102
modernity xxiv, 20, 21, 55, 118
    western 55
moral equality 218
moral values 140

Motilal Nehru Report of 1928 32
Mubaraat, in Islam 173
multi-member constituencies 183,
    213n46, 214, 215
Murphy, Jeffrie 143, 148, 149, 150
Musharraf, General 228
Muslim League 37n3, 50n21, 51,
    60, 110, 111, 132, 175, 176n21,
    180, 183
    and Congress 123, 125
    ideology of 114
    in Kerala 186
    on separate of state of Pakistan
        114
Muslim Personal Law 152, 159–60,
    180, 230, 236
    on adultery and divorce 193
    on divorce 160
    on maintenance 160
    on marriage 160
    reform of 166–74
    on women's share of parental
        property 160
Muslim Satyashodak Mandal
    171n14
Muslim Women's Bill 293
Muslimness 51
Muslim(s), assertion of xix
    cultural identity of 171, 213
    demand for separate electorates
        for 194–200
    discourse of 128
    elite 38, 176, 185, 186, 207, 208
    and Hindus, relationship between
        122, 123, 125, 127–8
    identity 160
    leadership 184
    marginalization of 182, 186–92
    'nationalists' 184
    orthodoxy 152, 169
        on Shah Bano judgement 171
    partition and, minority status of
        158

political under-representation of
    xxv, 182
poverty among 207
representation, in legislatures 192,
    212, 213
    in Uttar Pradesh government
    176
rights of 159, 167, 187–8
in rural areas 188–9
self-representation rights, need
    for 193–4
status of 152
under poverty line 189
women, condition of 174
    inequality position of 170–2
    role of, with Muslim culture
    169, 170
Mutiny of 1857 101, 117

Naga customary law 58
Naga National Council 49
Naga rebels 49
Nagaland State, formation of 49
    special status to 57–8
Nahar, Sultana 234n30
Nandy, Ashis 63, 80n17, 230n18,
    257, 259
nation, concept of 29
    -state 31, 181
National Commission for Scheduled
    Castes and Scheduled Tribes 239
    Report of 1990 232
National Democratic Alliance (NDA)
    185n9
National Humans Right Commission
    (NHRC) 246, 247
national integration 126
national identity 118
National Rural Employment
    Guarantee Act (NREGA) 315–16,
    319, 320, 321
nationalism 3, 7, 32, 109
    democracy and 28–33, 101, 102

Hindu ultra 251, 254
religious 48, 195, 222
secular 50
nationalist history 118, 121, 124
natural rights 5
Nauroji, Dadabhai 36n2
Nazi regime, horror of 136
negative rights, language of 260–1
Nehru, Jawaharlal 37n3, 38, 39, 42,
    43n10, 48, 49, 125, 126, 184–6,
    207–8, 253, 330
    address to National Convention
    of Congress Legislature 32
    law and order after 185
    politics of 51
Nehruvian state 255
Nietzche, F. 116n11
nihilism 275
Normative theory xxi–xxii, 67, 152
Noorani, A.G. 186
North-East 49, 50
    tribal people's demand in 49
Nozick, Robert xviii

ontological individualism 162
Organization for Economic
    Cooperation and Development
    (OECD) nations 317
Ottoman Empire, Millet system in 72
'overlapping good', politics of 22

Pakistan, abandoning of secularism
    in 223
    amendments to penal code in 239
    anti-blasphemy law in 227–8
    blasphemy charges in 232
    Blasphemy Ordinance of 1986
    in 228
    citizenship in 244
    conflict between India and 50
    Constitution of 225, 227
    conviction of Ahmedis in 231
    creation of 210

demand for 115
dissenting religious groups in
    230, 231
formation of 182
inclusion and exclusion in 217
as Islamic State 224, 225
Islamic teachings in 228
legal, social and economic
    position of religious minorities
    in 234–5
Muslim majority Punjab's
    incorporation into 47
nationalist historiography of 109
political exclusion in 244
position of women in 232
religious violence in 227
right to freedom of religion in 227
Sharia Courts in 225
State and religion relationship
    in 223
Panchayati Raj Bill, women's
    representation in 245
Panikkar, K.M. 12, 119
Pant, Govind Ballabh 196, 197, 202
Parliament 42
    representation of Muslims in 182
partition, of Indian sub-continent 34,
    60, 114, 123, 134, 183, 210, 222
    on religious basis 38, 158
    and violence 230
Patel, Sardar Vallabhbhai 105, 159n3
paternalist reformism 168
patronage 186
personal law, of Hindus 159, 160, 170
    of Muslims 152, 159, 160, 180
pluralism 39
political culture, of India 59
political empowerment 13
political equality 198
political freedom, and democracy
    318, 319, 320, 321
political rights 156
    of Muslims 199

politics xxiii
    liberal strand in India's 7–11
Polybius 117
polygamy 172, 173
poverty, and political freedom
    319–20
Prabhoo, R.K. 215
Prasad, Beni 124, 126, 159n3, 176
Presbyterians, in USA 77
President's rule, in states 43
press, freedom of 9
princely states, accession to Indian
    union 43, 57
procedural justice, basic 137, 139
    collapse of 140
'principled distance' 27, 64, 87–93,
    102, 206, 226, 312
proportional representation (PR)
    system 213
Protestant churches 71, 72
provinces, powers of 39
    reorganization of 39
public space, religion as identity
    marker in 175
Punjab 47–8
    incorporation of Muslim majority
        part into Pakistan 47
    militancy/secessionist demands
        in 45, 17, 48, 133
Punjabi suba 44–5, 48

Quakers, in USA 77
Qanoon-e-Shahadat, in Pakistan 239
Quebec, English conquest of 145
Queen's Proclamation, of 1858
    101
Quran, injunctions of 240
    interpretation of 180
    on polygamy 172
Qureshi, I.H. 122, 124n40, 126, 127

Rajya Sabha, states' representation
    to 58

Ram Janma Bhoomi Movement
229
Ranade, M.G. 12
Rashtriya Swayamsevak Sangh (RSS)
178, 229
Rawls, John xvii, xix, 287
Ray, Renuka 306
Ray, Satyajit 113
reconciliation 94, 95, 131, 151
reforms, rights and 158–74
religion/religious, affiliated schools
304, 306–8, 310
and the church 70
conflicts 101
depoliticization of 104
distinction between religious
education and instruction
302, 309
and educational institutions 104
establishment of multiple
70, 71
exclusion 220, 226–32, 243–8
identities 25, 73, 169, 204
inclusion 221
instruction 81
-based legal, social, and economic
exclusion 232–43
liberty 27, 72, 77–8, 79, 97, 225,
268, 269
and equality 220
persecution 72
and political institutions 88
and political mobilization 175
secular state and education in
301, 309
and the state 24, 27–8, 75, 79, 80,
83, 87 , 91, 222–45, 331
tax 72, 81
religious minorities, assimilation of
21–2
-majority framework 16–24, 154
persecution of 72
political representation to 84

rights of 4, 16, 28, 84, 85, 152, 153,
187, 199n33
see also Muslims
Renan, Ernest 110, 144, 177
representation, definition of 205
representative democracies 154
reservations 212
see also Scheduled Castes and
Scheduled Tribes
responsibility, collective 147
shared 146
revenge 131, 136, 142, 147, 148, 177
and retribution 151
and self-destruction 133
revivalist movements 175
right(s) 4, 259, 298
cultural 156, 188
discourse of xxv, 299
to dissent xviii
and duties 83
essays on xviii
framework of 156
to freedom of expression xviii
group and individual 5, 159–62
left-liberal discourse on 293, 297,
300
to life, liberty and material
welfare 78
minority xix, 19, 20, 23, 152,
153, 159, 161, 171, 181,
199, 222, 230, 269, 302–5,
309,
to progress and propagate
religion 81
to property 296
and reform 158–74
special 21, 23
to vote 13
Roman Catholic church 70
Roop Kanwar, sati by, in Rajasthan
236, 292
Roy, Mary 236
Roy, Ram Mohan 7, 9, 12, 14, 258

Rowlatt Act 9, 260
Rushdie, Salman 324

Sachar Committee Report xxv
Sangh Parivar 229
Sapru, Tej Bahadur 29
Satanic Verses, ban on 292, 298, 324
sati 236, 292, 298
satyagraha 8
Savarkar, Veer 115, 121
Scheduled Castes (SCs) 13, 208
    representation in Parliament 245
    reservations for 211
Scheduled Tribes (STs) 13
    representation in Parliament 245
    reservations for 211
    secessionist movements, in
        Punjab, North-East and
        Kashmir 45, 47
secular states 74–81, 246, 301,
    311–12, 328
    and principled distance 87–93
    values of a 77–81
secularism, in India xix, xx, xxv, 4,
    24–8, 56, 63, 81–4, 102, 206, 248,
    268–71
    American 77
    and Christianity 100–1
    colonial 76n11
    conceptual structure of 69–74
    constituents of 65–6
    critics of 24, 67–9
    distinctiveness of Indian 68, 69
    and equal respect to all religions
        103
    French 99
    Gandhian version of 330–1
    multi-religious 330–1
    negative 327
    and notion of principled distance
        99, 102
    positive 331
    principle of 223

threat to 63, 64
    values of 94–5, 99
    secularism, in South Asia 257
    and self-governance 29–30, 61
self-interest 275–7, 283, 284
    poor and rich conception of 276–7
self-representation, Muslims on
    206–9
self-respect 30, 118, 138, 144, 148,149,
    151, 155, 196, 277, 282
    and violence 138, 147
Sen, Amartya xviii, 218n1, 241n46,
    319, 320
Sen, K.C. 12
separate electorate 211
    demand by Muslims 194–200
    rejection of demand for 104–5
Shah, K.T. 305
Shah Bano case 167, 171, 179, 180,
    253, 292, 298
    judgement on 236
Sharia-based Muslim personal law
    184, 240
shariat 170
Shia community, persecution of, in
    Pakistan 231
Shiv Sena 215
shuddhi movement 178
Sidhwa, R.K. 306
Sikhs, demand for Punjabi Suba 48
    massacre of, in Delhi (1984) 135,
        139
Sikkim, accession to India 58
Skinner, Q. 66n2, 265n27, 266
Smith, Donald 24, 25, 26, 27, 83, 84,
    85, 86, 87
Smith, Vincent 120
Smith, Wilfred Cantwell 109, 110,
    111, 113, 114, 115, 122, 302n1,
    310n13, 313, 314
Sobti, Krishna 324
social exclusion 242
social rights 92

socialism, collapse of xx
Socialist Party 185n8
socio-religious groups, protection
    of 25
South Africa, Apartheid in 20, 296
    victims in 150
South African Truth Commission
    133, 151
Stains, Graham, violence against 229
state(s) xxiv, 43
    with established religion/church
        73–5
    federalization of 34
    and religion 25, 27–8, 79–81, 83,
        87, 222–45
    reorganization of 44
    as separate from religion 69–70
    with single religion 71
    unitary character of 34
States Reorganisation Committee 44
Steiner, Wendy 323
subas 35
Suhrawardy 132
Sunnah injunctions 240
Sunni Islam, in Pakistan 231

Tablig movement 178
Tablighi Jamaat 183
Talaq, importance of, for Muslim
    community 160
    notion of triple 173
Taliban, accent of 227
Taylor, Charles 30n35, 66n2, 78n14,
    94n29, 164n7, 199, 274n3, 297n2,
    n4, 318
Thackeray, Bal 215–16
Thapar, Romila 117, 118, 120, 123
theocracy 69, 70, 71, 245, 301, 311
    distinct from state with
        established church 71–5
A Theory of Justice xvii, xix, 287n17
threatened groups, and division of
    moral labour 163–6

Tilak, B.G. 32
Tocqueville, Alexis de 167n7, 283,
    325
toleration 23, 73, 77, 96–8, 103, 158,
    206, 310
tribal communities 39
    special status to 194n22
Truth and Reconciliation
    Commission, South Africa 133,
    146–51
    and Gandhi 134
    importance of 142–6
    objectives of 138
Tuker, Francis 131
two-nation theory 50n21
Tyagi, Mahavir 93

unemployment 319
uniform civil code 42, 160, 169
unitary state 53
UNDP report, of female ratio 241
United States of America (USA),
    federalism in 54, 55, 56, 57
universal franchise 4, 6, 28–33, 81
university, autonomy for 322, 323
untouchability 226, 238, 242
    abolition of 8, 84, 232
Untouchability (Offences) Act of
    1955, 232
Urdu language 46
    policy on 47
    spoken by Muslims 174
utilitarianism 7, 8, 9, 11
Uttarakhand 44

Vijayanagar kingdom, Shaivism,
    Vaishnavism and Jainsm in 71
Vajpayee, Atal Behari 185n8, 246
value individualism 162–4
violence, arbitrary xxiv
    justification of 148
    perpetrators of 149
Vir Shaivite movement 260

Vishwa Hindu Parishad (VHP) 229
Vivekananda, Swami 12

Waldron, Jeremy 143, 144
Walzer, Michael 140
welfare state 317, 318
    in western societies 317
Western modernity 7, 30, 55,
    258, 259
western secularism 25, 66–8, 75, 96,
    98–101, 105
    departure from 84–7
Wolin, Sheldon 144, 145
women, equality for 8
    justice for 160

laws unjust to Muslim 167
legal equality in India 241
legal status of 232
position of, in religious rituals
    232
representation in Parliament
    244–5
role of, subordinate 29
    as wives and mothers 166
violence against, in Pakistan 240

Zikris, in Pakistan 231
Zia, Khalida 224
Zia ul Haq 227, 231, 239